The Fallacy of Campaign
Finance Reform

The Fallacy of Campaign Finance Reform

JOHN SAMPLES

THE UNIVERSITY OF CHICAGO PRESS   CHICAGO AND LONDON

JOHN SAMPLES is the director of the Cato Institute's Center for Representative Government.

The University of Chicago Press, Chicago 60637
The University of Chicago Press, Ltd., London
© 2006 by The University of Chicago
All rights reserved. Published 2006
Printed in the United States of America
15 14 13 12 11 10 09 08 07 06   1 2 3 4 5

ISBN-13: 978-0-226-73450-7 (cloth)
ISBN-10: 0-226-73450-1 (cloth)

Library of Congress Cataloging-in-Publication Data

Samples, John Curtis, 1956–
    The fallacy of campaign finance reform / John Samples
        p. cm.
    Includes bibliographical references and index.
    ISBN-13: 978-0-226-73450-7 (cloth : alk. paper)
    ISBN-10: 0-226-73450-1 (cloth : alk. paper)
        1. Campaign funds—United States. 2. Campaign funds—Law and legislation—
    United States. I. Title.
    JK1991.S26 2006
    324.7'80973—dc22

                                                            2006017449

TO EVELYN SAMPLES

And as I speak here of mixed bodies, such as republics and religious sects, I say that those changes are beneficial that bring them back to their original principles.

Machiavelli, *Discourses on Livy,* III, 1

Contents

Preface

The struggle to restrict money's influence in politics and thereby freedom of speech grows from a story of sin and redemption. A democratic government should obey the will of the people, but wealthy and powerful special interests corrupt public officials by offering campaign contributions in exchange for policy favors. Democracy is redeemed by public-spirited reformers who selflessly and heroically battle the special interests to enact laws that restrict and eventually prohibit private financing of political activity. Being a story of sin and redemption, this dominant narrative is emotionally satisfying: it lays out heroes, villains, and a happy ending. The power of this story should not be underestimated. It has contributed to the passage of laws and advanced the presidential ambitions of a prominent senator. But the satisfactions it offers do not make it true. We still should ask whether anyone sins all that much and whether the redemption on offer is likely to improve our world or agree with American political ideals. In the pages that follow, I argue that the reformer's story contravenes both the facts as we know them and the ideals that informed the founding of our republic. Not least of those ideals is the command that Congress make no law abridging freedom of speech.

I begin also to tell a different story about money, politics, and elections. In part, my story belongs to the genre of political realism. For all the talk of sin, redemption, and democracy, I see restrictions on money in politics as ways to advance the interests of those who propose such laws and regulations. In part, the aspirations of the partisans of restrictions are ideological: they see limitation of campaign finance as a necessary step toward equalizing political influence, which itself is a means to equalizing wealth. Beyond that fantasy lies a harder reality: campaign finance laws tend to advance the interests of those who write them, namely, incumbent legislators. But I, too, am an idealist. Like Machiavelli, I believe that republics are preserved by changes that lead them back to their origins. The origins of the United States may be found in the Madisonian vision of politics, and I seek to both expound and vindicate those ideals.

The reader may conclude that my story is incomplete. Experts often note that campaign finance laws have unexpected consequences. No doubt they do in some cases. I try in this book, however, to identify the systematic factors affecting campaign finance regulation. Unexpected consequences are, by definition, random. I have assumed that informed opinion concerning these matters should be guided by predictable rather than unpredictable considerations. I have also written little about presidential decisions to veto or to sign campaign finance legislation. I assume that those decisions are specific to time and circumstances and not very amenable to systematic analysis. Finally, I have said less than I would have wished about the influence of the media in the success or failure of campaign finance restrictions. To be sure, several decades' research say the media have few effects on public attitudes and opinion. Research notwithstanding, I do not doubt that the dominant media, like incumbent public officials, have a strong interest in suppressing alternative views so that their own may be more prominent and more influential. That interest is well served by restrictions on spending on political advertising, perennially included in campaign finance laws. It is hardly surprising, therefore, that the news reporting and editorials in the *New York Times* and the *Washington Post,* among others, strongly support more restrictions on the ways everyone but the media can spend money on politics. A systematic study of the interests and activities of the media in this area, however, must await another day and, perhaps, another scholar.

Libertarians are often said to be overly individualistic and against social cooperation. Nothing could be less true. We do insist that social cooperation be a matter of consent rather than coercion. I am happy to report that many fine individuals consented to help me write this book. The donors to the Cato Institute made my research and writing possible with their money, their ideas, and their good cheer. In particular, Fred Young supported the Center for Representative Government at Cato during much of my work. Fred also emphasized the importance of First Amendment concerns at a point when I was wandering off into political analysis. Ed Crane and David Boaz also supported this project from the start. I appreciate their patience and encouragement. Ed's principled commitment to free speech in this field should be a model for heads of think tanks.

Many people contributed to this manuscript in its various stages. Peter Van Doren and Ilya Somin offered thorough and helpful reviews of the first version of the manuscript. Two anonymous readers for the University of Chicago Press examined my proposal for this book and made crucial suggestions. Later, two other anonymous readers of the draft manuscript offered a thorough, fair, and helpful set of criticisms. At about the same time, Alison Hayward, Steve Hoersting, and Bob Bauer gave me close and detailed criticisms that greatly improved the final product. Conversations with Bob also affected my thinking about Progressivism, McCain-Feingold, and much else. Similarly, my lunches with Herb Alexander, Lance Tarrance Jr., and Paul Teller clarified my thinking. My colleagues at Cato have been helpful and supportive in many ways. At the risk of overlooking someone, I would like to thank Bill Niskanen, Patrick Basham, Jagadeesh Gokhale, Brink Lindsey, Jerry Taylor, Tom Palmer, and Bob Levy for their assistance and encouragement at various times during this project. I appreciate the chance to teach the material in this book offered by Ben Ginsberg at Johns Hopkins University. Access to the Sheridan Libraries at Johns Hopkins was essential to my work on this book.

I also wish to thank my editor at the University of Chicago Press, J. Alex Schwartz. Alex and the press have supported a project that might have been considered too controversial by others. Alex and Parker Smathers have been responsive and helpful. Jane Zanichkowsky edited the manuscript with skill, aplomb, and good humor. I appreciate the many improvements she introduced to the work. Thanks are also due Leslie Keros for her skill and tact in seeing the book through to the reader.

Finally, my wife Cynthia has supported my career and interests and tried with limited success to convince me that people are not wholly rational. My son Colin has, before the age of twenty, worked as a congressional staffer and as a lobbyist. The insights from his experience have left some mark in these pages. More important, he's a good kid who holds up his end of the argument around the dinner table.

Money and Speech

On March 20, 2002, the United States Senate, by a vote of 60 to 40, passed the McCain-Feingold Act, otherwise known as the Bipartisan Campaign Reform Act of 2002.[1] Because the House of Representatives had already passed it, the bill needed only President George W. Bush's signature to become law. Despite his past promises to the contrary and urgent pleas from leaders of his political party, Bush signed the bill into law on March 27. He described the bill as "flawed," however, and refused to hold a public ceremony for the signing, a typical ritual for major legislation. The law's chief sponsor, Senator John McCain (R-AZ), learned about the signing from a White House staff member. Afterwards, Bush left for a three-state fundraising trip for Republicans. Later that same day, opponents filed suit in federal court seeking to have the new law declared unconstitutional.[2] After five years of struggle in the legislature, the fate of the new law shifted to the courts. Near the end of 2003, McCain and his allies would also win in that forum. The partisans of the law rejoiced.

In the pages that follow I argue that the victory of McCain-Feingold—indeed, the sheer existence of almost all federal campaign finance law—is reason for lamentation, not rejoicing. For more than three decades the federal government has widened its ambit over the financing of electoral struggle, making everything from small contributions to advertising for political documentaries a matter of government control and oversight. Today no one should exercise his or her First Amendment right to freedom of speech without advice from counsel, preferably one schooled in the intricacies of campaign finance regulation. In the United States, speech is no longer very free in any sense of the word.

How did we reach this point? As always with restrictions on free speech, political ambition and interests tell part of the story. "Freedom of speech for me, but not for thee" expresses an enduring truth about politics and human life. Public opinion also lends less support for First Amendment rights than we might like to think, particularly for protections related to campaign finance.[3] Money, most people seem to think, has little to do with freedom of speech or other rights enunciated in the Constitution.

Most people are wrong.

You are reading these words right now because of money. The University of Chicago Press has spent tens of thousands of dollars producing this book. If the government restricted that spending, my and their right of freedom of speech would be limited, perhaps to the point of silence. Your right to learn about and consider the ideas in this book would similarly be restricted. Those who donate to the Cato Institute supported my work on this book. If the government restricted or prohibited such contributions, this book might well have not been written. The fact that donors give to the institute to support this and other work concerning public affairs commends the value of liberty and libertarian policies to other citizens. Money talks in many ways in elections as well as in writing about public policy.[4]

Many people would rather not listen. Some Americans would have been happier if this book had never been written, and if written, not published, and if published, not read. Most people support campaign finance "reform" because they believe it will apply to people and ideas they do not like.[5] I myself have illiberal feelings from time to time about speech I find uncongenial. Apparently everyone has such feelings now and then. We have the First Amendment to constrain the consequences of those feelings, thereby lending strength to the better, or at least more liberal, angels of our nature. Unlike most of us, members of Congress can and do act on such illiberal feelings. They also have powerful interests at stake in suppressing spending on politics, a conflict of interest that also evinces the wisdom of the First Amendment. In campaign finance matters, the illiberal feelings and political interests of public officials and many citizens are expressed in the language of high ideals and noble public purposes. To be sure, those high ideals *also* express noble aspirations and genuine concerns about the integrity of our politics. Such are the complexities of life in a mature polity. But we should not be misled into thinking that restrictions on campaign finance *primarily* seek noble ideals and a pure politics. We might begin to sort out the ideals and interests at stake by exploring the purposes behind McCain-Feingold.

Purposes of the Law

Public Law 107-155 (McCain-Feingold) runs for five titles and about thirty-five pages in the statute book. Setting aside the qualifications and verbiage, the law tried to change the world in three major ways. It prohibited fundraising by the political parties (so-called soft money) that had previously been legal. Henceforth, the parties would have to raise funds strictly within the contribution limits and disclosure requirements set by federal law in 1974. McCain-Feingold also doubled those contribution limits. Finally, the law sought to expand the ambit of federal election law to include fundraising for certain kinds of broadcast advertising that had previously been exempt from the requirements and restrictions of the law. Forgetting the trees to see the forest, one can say that McCain-Feingold expanded government control over the way Americans fight federal elections.

McCain-Feingold says little about its purposes beyond providing "bipartisan campaign reform." According to the *American Heritage Dictionary,* the noun *reform* means "a change for the better; an improvement" and "correction of evils, abuses, and errors." The law does not explicitly define the "evils, abuses, and errors" it proposes to correct. Its first title does take as its goal "reduction of special interest influence," but it does not define those interests. One might infer that they are known by what they have done: giving money legally to the political parties that is not captured by the restrictions of federal election law. So defined, the special interests would be no longer once the law went into effect because they would no longer be legally able to donate soft money. But that is just a guess. McCain-Feingold itself is silent about the identity of the special interests that are the targets of its strictures.

If we look beyond the law to the speeches made in the Senate in its defense, we see that its supporters expected that the new law would accomplish many purposes.

Curbing Special Interests

Today's vote . . . is about curbing the influence of special interests. Now is the time to enact real reform and return the power to the people and restore their faith in the Government. (John McCain)[6]

It is a key purpose of the bill to stop the use of soft money as a means of buying influence and access with Federal officeholders and candidates. Thus, we have established a system of prohibitions and limitations on the ability of Federal officeholders and candidates to raise, spend, and control soft money. (John McCain)[7]

Ending the Appearance of Corruption

When the very people who have legislation before you are coming to you with greater and greater amounts of money for your political campaign, that creates a potential conflict of interest that we simply do not need. It does not look good. The American people think, the average Joe on the street thinks, that with that much money being paid to that few people, they are expecting something for it. (Fred Thompson)[8]

Reducing Some Kinds of Political Advertising

It curbs issue ads, those special interest ads that clearly target particular candidates in an attempt to influence the outcome of an election. (Thomas Daschle)[9]

This bill is about slowing the ad war. It is about calling sham issue ads what they really are. It is about slowing political advertising and making sure the flow of negative ads by outside interest groups does not continue to permeate the airwaves. (Maria Cantwell)[10]

If you cut off the soft money, you're going to see a lot less [attack advertising]. Prohibit unions and corporations [from making soft money contributions] and you will see a lot less of that. If you demand full disclosure for those that pay for those ads, you're going to see a lot less of that. (John McCain)[11]

Promoting Democracy

[It will eliminate] huge contributions that distort the democratic process. (Jean Carnahan)[12]

If we look at the rising tide of money in politics, the influence that money buys and the corrosive effect it has on people's faith in government, the answer, then, is clearly no. Ours is a government "of the people, by the people, and for the people." It is not a government of, by, and for some of the people. With this vote, we stand on the verge of putting the reigns of government back into the hands of all people. (Thomas Daschle)[13]

This bill . . . will make many needed changes to our campaign finance system and reconnect the electorate with their candidates for federal office. (James Jeffords)[14]

Working with our friends in the House, we have drafted a bill that promotes important first amendment values, promotes enhanced citizen participation in our democracy, is workable, and is carefully crafted to steer clear of asserted constitutional pitfalls. (John McCain)[15]

Increasing Political Equality

It will cleanse our politics and make it possible for the voices of ordinary Americans to be heard. (Jean Carnahan)[16]

[It is the first step to] getting big money out of politics. (Paul Wellstone)[17]

Regaining Control of Campaign Finance

We are moving to get control of a system that is out of control. (Barbara Boxer)[18]

No wonder there is a strong sense that campaigns in this country have spiraled out of control. There is a strong sense that elections are no longer in the hands of individual Americans. As the old saying goes, perception becomes nine tenths of reality. (Olympia Snowe)[19]

Realizing the Public Interest

We in the Congress who have supported this effort know we have acted not out of self-interest, and not for the special interests but for the public interest. This bill is for the American people, for our democracy, and for the future of our country. (Russell Feingold)[20]

Restoring Trust in Government

We are making headway to do something that will reduce the cynicism in this country that will help this body, that will help us individually. (Fred Thompson)[21]

With this vote, we are one giant step closer to a new era of campaign finance, a new era of voter confidence in our government, and a new era of better and stronger democracy. . . . We have to restore the system of regulated contributions. If we don't, the cynicism and distrust and lack of engagement that are already so pervasive will continue to spread. Our citizens are increasingly tuned out from our democratic process. (Charles Schumer)[22]

I have supported campaign finance reform for 18 years, and I believe that even legislation that takes only a small step forward is necessary to begin to restore the dwindling faith the average American has in our political system. (John Kerry)[23]

Increasing Electoral Competition

[It] will trade increased hard money limits for the reduction of soft money, a tradeoff that will help challengers reach a threshold credibility when they want to challenge us in these races. (Fred Thompson)[24]

Improving Political Discourse

The currency of politics should be ideas, not dollars. It is time for us to start putting the currency back into circulation. (Thomas Daschle)[25]

I am also pleased the bill includes an amendment that Senator Wyden and I offered to raise the level of discourse in campaign ads. (Susan Collins)[26]

But I would ask the proponents of this argument whether what we are seeking in our democracy is electioneering that has no more depth or substance than a snack food commercial. Despite the ever-increasing sums spent on campaigns, we have not seen an improvement in campaign discourse, issue discussion or voter education. More money does not mean more ideas, more substance or more depth. Instead, it means more of what voters complain about most. More 30-second spots, more negativity and an increasingly longer campaign period. Less money might actually improve the quality of discourse, requiring candidates to more cautiously spend their resources. (John Kerry)[27]

Reducing Spending on Elections

This bill forces all of us—candidates, parties, and groups that seek to influence the outcome of elections—to play by the same rules and raise and spend money in lower amounts. (Maria Cantwell)[28]

A more extended reading of the *Congressional Record* might reveal more purposes for McCain-Feingold.[29]

The Supreme Court has recognized preventing corruption or the appearance of corruption, providing public information, and preventing the circumvention of campaign finance law as legitimate reasons for restricting freedom of speech. We have reason to doubt that senators truly believed that the law addressed corruption: "Both Democratic and Republican members rejected any suggestion that the bill was required to address actually corrupt conduct, because they agreed that they were not responsible for any. . . . Senator Feingold advised his colleagues that they were required to cite corruption, regardless of whether it existed, to satisfy the demands of the *Buckley* Court. The diversity of views and rationales was such that, after Senator Specter introduced an amendment with a 'findings' section, in order 'to provide a factual basis to uphold the constitutionality of the statute,' he subsequently was compelled to withdraw it when agreement proved impossible."[30] Even putting aside such bad faith, almost all the goals of the law mentioned by the senators are not sufficient to justify McCain-Feingold's core restrictions on political activity.

The statements by the senators reflect a larger set of political ideals that have informed debates about money in politics for more than a century. At one time or another, however, campaign finance restrictions have been proposed as ways to achieve all of the goals noted earlier. The senators quoted here were simply stating what proponents have always said would be accomplished by reform.

Political Visions and Campaign Finance

Those who demand restrictions on money in politics—the "reform community"—have dominated (and dominate) most public debates about campaign finance. They contend that money corrupts American democracy by perverting representation, undermining democratic political culture, lowering political discourse, fostering inequality, and reducing electoral competition. Democracy must be protected, they say, from the corruption brought by money and its owners.

Do campaign contributions and spending corrupt American democracy? *Corruption* implies a failure to live up to some ideal, and determining which ideals are relevant and the proper tradeoff among them depends on "the way the world should be," a conception that in turn comes from a set of political ideals that might be called a political vision. To understand the dispute over campaign finance, we need to understand the implicit visions of politics that are at stake in that debate.

The struggle is not a case of "we the people" against "they the corrupt," the nation against its enemies. It is a conflict between two political visions that have marked the development of the United States as a nation.[31] The effort to restrict and "reform" campaign finance reflects one part of American political culture, the Progressive vision of politics and its trust in government under the control of an ethical and enlightened elite. The Progressive vision, however, did not inform the founding ideals for the United States, which can be read in the Constitution and the Declaration of Independence and make up what might be called the Madisonian vision of politics. Those ideals may be summed up as natural rights, individual liberty, and limited government. The senators who opposed McCain-Feingold did so in defense of freedom of speech. They favored, in other words, limits on the government's power to regulate political activity, limits enshrined in the First Amendment to the Constitution.[32]

Much of what follows concerns the Progressive vision, the ideals that have animated and informed the long crusade to restrict money in politics. Understanding that vision helps us understand why certain people care so much about this issue. Moreover, insofar as the unfolding logic of an ideal drives the politics of campaign finance regulation, the Progressive vision can tell us the likely future directions of such laws. But Progressivism is a negation as well as an affirmation. It began by rejecting the Madisonian vision. The Progressive critique of money in politics is thus one aspect of a more general rejection of the ideals of the American founding that began in the late nineteenth century and continues today in the editorial pages of the *New York Times* and the speeches of Senator John McCain. Perhaps that rejection is justified. Progressives have long argued that private money corrupts politics. We shall see whether their vision has much to do with empirical reality.

These visions of the way the world should be also offer answers to the problem of private interest in politics. Consider two examples of this problem. Consumers receive more for their money if international trade remains free of government control. Because most people are consumers, we can say that the nation has a general interest in free trade and the economic competition it fosters. But not everyone has an interest in free trade; the owners, managers, and workers in firms exposed to international trade would have higher incomes if the government protected them from international competition. Their particular interests run counter to the general interest of consumers in free trade. The problem of interest is not limited to economic issues. Voters have an interest in open and free competition for elected offices; it gives them more choices and ultimately more control over their representatives. Elected officials are like the firms exposed to international trade. Incumbents have an interest in retaining their office and thus in less competition for their seat. Their interests run counter to the general interest of voters.

The Madisonian and the Progressive visions frame the debate about campaign finance by identifying the general interest, the particular interests that threaten it, and what is to be done about that particularity. For the past three decades, Progressives have driven this debate. Their vision of politics says that economic elites—variously defined as "Big Money," "the rich," or "corporate America"—compose a particular interest that corrupts American government, thereby preventing a redistribution of wealth that would realize the Progressive dream of an egalitarian nation. The symbol and means of that corruption is private spending on elections and politics. For Progressives government is both the victim of these private interests and the solution to their dangerous particularity. If government heavily regulates or eliminates private interests (and thus private spending) in politics, the common interest in egalitarian economic outcomes will be vindicated. Progressives see government as a benevolent force that overcomes the threat posed by private interests fostered by the market economy. In later chapters I examine the Progressive assumption that the arrow of corruption runs from the economy to government.

Madisonians think government is the problem. They identify the general interest with liberty and hence with natural rights recognized by an empowered and limited government. The greatest threat to that general interest is a predatory majority bent on abrogating a minority's right to life, liberty, or property. The founders designed the U.S. Constitution to protect that general interest against that threat. But they did not look to government to impose a substantive notion of the general interest by suppressing particular interests. Instead, Madison and others proposed a political structure that would set interests into conflict, thereby limiting government and preserving liberty. The First Amendment reflects that strategy: particular interests have a right to be heard in the national debate. The Madisonian vision suggests another problematic particular interest: the government itself. Instead of assuming that only economic elites threaten democracy, we might also consider the danger posed by those who have political power.

Particular Interests

Campaign finance laws regulate and restrict the use of money in elections and in politics. They therefore affect the outcomes of elections. This suggests that campaign finance laws, like other regulations and government actions, provide private benefits to those who pass the law and to the coalition they represent. But campaign finance laws pose a special problem. They are enacted by members of Congress who participate in elections governed by these laws. They matter much more to members than to the rest of us. In the words of former congressman Guy Vander Jagt (R-MI), "When you are dealing with campaign [finance] reform, you're talking about one of the most precious things a Congressman deals with. You're talking about his political life or death."[33] Members of Congress thus have every reason to pass campaign finance laws that increase the likelihood that they will be reelected and that their party will hold (or continue to hold) a majority in the legislature. Such regulation is more often about politics than about principle, a truth that holds for citizens as well as political activists. Americans are far more likely to support restrictions on campaign finance for groups they do not like than for groups they favor.[34] In fact, such restrictions serve two kinds of interests.

Partisan Interests

The formal name of McCain-Feingold is the *Bipartisan* Campaign Reform Act of 2002. The term *bipartisan* is an interesting choice by the sponsors of the law. It is as if they are responding to an implicit assumption that all laws governing campaign finance seek to advance the electoral interests of one party or the other. By including the term in the title of the law, the sponsors are saying: "You might think all campaign finance laws pursue partisan interests, but this one does not." Of course, the sponsors of the legislation included two Republicans and two Democrats. Appearances notwithstanding, other evidence indicates that their assertion is not persuasive. Partisanship guided the final votes on BCRA.

About 80 percent of Republicans in the House of Representatives and in the Senate voted against McCain-Feingold. More than 90 percent of

Democrats in both chambers voted for the bill. In the Senate, two Democratic senators (of fifty) voted against it. If the vote on McCain-Feingold was not partisan, no roll call in Congress can be called partisan.

In recent history, Republicans have generally raised more money than have Democrats. Republicans have also relied more heavily on money to fight elections. In contrast, Democrats can count on unpaid labor provided by members of their coalition and favorable free coverage by a largely sympathetic national media. Neither volunteers nor the media have been seriously regulated by campaign finance laws. By reducing a Republican advantage while ignoring a Democratic strength, campaign finance law has generally biased elections toward the Democrats. As we shall see, the 1974 Federal Election Campaign Act—the foundation of campaign finance regulation—responded to certain threats to the Democratic majority that then controlled Congress.

That said, we should keep in mind that campaign finance law seeks partisan (and not simply Democratic) purposes. Because the restrictions inhibit electoral challenges to incumbents, we should expect that any party with a majority will be tempted to pass such regulations. As Bradley Smith, a former chair of the Federal Election Commission, has said, "One of the problems with campaign finance laws is that they are not nonpartisan, good government. . . . They are tools, partisan weapons to be used to attack the political power on the other side, and we should expect it to happen." [35] It is possible, perhaps even probable, that the future will see Republicans using campaign finance restrictions for their own ends.

Incumbent Interests

Amid all the paeans to democracy and the public interest in the Senate debates about McCain-Feingold, Senator Barbara Boxer offered an odd and revealing endorsement of the law while noting a shortcoming: "We will not be hit by these last-minute ads with unregulated soft money at the end, to which we will be unable to respond. . . . We still have a big problem. One thing got knocked out of the bill, which was ensuring that the lowest rates would be available to us on television." [36] What did Boxer mean in saying "we" and "us"? The people in question could not be the American people in general. They have not been hit by "these last-minute ads," nor are they eligible for the lowest advertising rates on television. Very few Americans buy broadcast advertising. Hence, it is not the American people that on March 20, 2001, still had "a big problem." The people in question—the ones who are hit by last-minute ads, buy ad time, and still have a big problem—were the senators listening to Boxer. Judging by her remark, the party of incumbent senators and, more generally, members of Congress clearly understand that campaign finance law affects their interests in reelection. If Americans can spend money freely on political ads, incumbents may get hit by last-minute attacks on their record or character. Such advertising might even cost an incumbent his or her seat in Congress. As Boxer suggests, incumbents can also control the price of the advertising they need to fight for reelection. No doubt last-minute attack ads and costly advertising are problems for incumbent members of Congress. After all, Boxer confirms the threat, and we have no reason to doubt her expertise. We might well doubt that such ads and relatively higher prices for television time are big problems for most Americans.

In other words, campaign finance laws are like a game in which one participant writes the rules and employs the referees (Congress created and oversees the Federal Election Commission). Like the official story, this alternative focuses on interests and corruption. The interests that threaten the public good, however, are those of public officials, not private actors. Elected officials, not businesses or labor unions, threaten democracy. The arrow of corruption runs from the government to civil society. Chapters 7 and 8 of this book flesh out my alternative story by recounting how the powers that be fashioned campaign finance law to serve their ends.

The conflict of visions in campaign finance struggles pits Progressives against Madisonians. The conflict of interests, on the other hand, set insiders against outsiders. From 1969 to 1994, Progressive ideals and insider interests were largely in accord; anything that helped incumbents win reelection helped preserve Democratic control of Congress, which itself advanced the Progressive cause, at least in light of the alternative. Conversely, restrictions on campaign finance harmed challenges to sitting members of Congress, thereby damaging the Republican minority's aspiration to take charge. Republicans thus might have learned the importance of limits on government control of money in politics. Since 1994, as we shall see, ideals have become detached from interests: Democrats have become outsiders, the natural targets of state control over speech. Republicans have gained power and, with it, the temptation to use government to protect their position in control of Congress. To be sure, Democrats on the outside have remained committed to "reforms" that may endanger rather than advance their partisan interests. Republicans also have in practice both affirmed and denied the free speech ideals they learned to love in opposition. In the politics of campaign finance, like most politics, interests are fundamental, but ideals shape what individuals find to be in their interest, if only for reasons of coherence and electoral credibility over time. Both parties are less sure now that their ideals accord with their interests in campaign finance struggles. Only incumbents can be sure that increased regulation serves their fundamental interest in electoral survival.

Conclusion

The pages that follow contest what is almost always taken for granted in discussions of campaign finance. Above all, I refuse to write about these issues with the loaded and biased terms that shape and perhaps decide these debates. The proponents of restrictions on campaign finance have manipulated language to advance their political agenda. *Campaign finance reform,* the most common term used in the debates, means "restricting money in politics," especially contributions to public officials. As we saw above, *reform* means "a change for the better; an improvement" and "correction of evils, abuses, and errors." By getting everyone to talk about campaign finance reform, the reformers win the debates by definition rather than by argument because restrictions on campaign finance are identified with abolishing abuses and errors. Apart from the title, I have tried to avoid the word *reform* in this book when referring to such restrictions. I believe we should assess existing or proposed restrictions on money in politics on their merits, which is to say, according to their logical coherence or empirical validity. We ought not to bias that investigation and analysis by calling such restrictions reform. In fact, I believe that what we take to be reform in ordinary language is an abuse of political power. Supporting that belief, however, requires evidence and arguments. It is not enough to simply say some magic words—reform, corruption, special interests, Big Money, corporate—to make a case about public policy. Politics, despite all evidence to the contrary, deserves to be more serious than that.

My doubts about campaign finance "reform" go beyond the corruption of language. I do not believe that campaign contributions have corrupted representation or American political culture in any significant way. I do not believe that Congress creates campaign finance laws to attain the public interest or the common good. I do not think such regulations are in the interests of most Americans. I do not believe that increased regulation of campaign finance will realize the Progressive vision of politics. I do not believe that Congress has the power to systematically restrict and regulate the funding of political activity. If it had that power, I do not believe that the laws we have governing campaign finance would be good public policy. In a world of true believers in campaign finance restrictions, count me an agnostic on the path to atheism. I do profess what used to be called the liberal faith that the freedom to speak and to struggle supports individual liberty and limited government. The chapters that follow give the reasons for my doubts and for my faith.

PART I

The Conflict of Ideals

CHAPTER ONE

The Madisonian Vision of Politics

Politics often concerns compromise, but the First Amendment to the U.S. Constitution is uncompromising. It states that "Congress shall make no law . . . abridging the freedom of speech." The founders thought freedom of speech should be free of the usual tradeoffs that mark the birth of most laws. Why did they give speech such thorough protections?

The Constitution reflects both the political philosophy and the political science of the founders, which I will call the Madisonian vision of politics.[1] This vision grew out of the political philosophy of the English political theorist John Locke, who argued that humans possessed natural rights prior to living together in political associations. Humans created government to vindicate those natural rights; at the same time, those rights constrained what government could do to the life, liberty, and property of citizens. For Locke, natural rights form a higher law that informs and constrains all law, including the Constitution.[2] Unfortunately, citizens tend to become corrupt, thereby endangering natural and constitutional rights. Political science fashions institutions that resist that corruption and preserve the republic. In the Madisonian vision, freedom of speech in the Constitution is both a natural right and an institutional antidote to the dangers posed by corruption of the republic.

Most Americans support freedom of speech, at least in the abstract. Many doubt the value of money in politics and support restrictions on campaign spending. If freedom of speech is essential to American democracy and spending money is essential to freedom of speech, Americans must choose between their support for liberty and their doubts about money in politics. Insofar as their founding ideals still inform contemporary politics, Americans will affirm liberty and its instrument, money. Those ideals, however, have an uncertain hold over the current generation of Americans. I begin by recalling the Madisonian vision that animated the founding of the United States, a political theory that offers arguments and implications for our debates about money in politics.

Natural Rights and Limited Government

Political philosophers have long looked to nature to provide standards and ideals for political life. Aristotle believed that nature was teleological; everything in it tended toward a goal. Humans also have a natural telos that exists objectively apart from the will or interests of any individual. The individual should realize the human telos that requires the exercise of reason in political deliberation and debate. For Aristotle, man was a political animal by nature.[3] Individuals neither created their government nor had rights against it. Indeed, the individual did not exist apart from collective life. Later, God, as the author of nature, became the source of political authority and obligation. Right was divine in origin and accorded to rulers, not the ruled.

Between 1500 and 1700 two enormous events called into question the traditional authority of nature. First, Galileo effectively demolished Aristotle's teleological understanding of nature and the universe. He urged scientists instead to use a method of resolution and composition that analyzed a phenomenon by breaking it into its component parts.[4] Second, religious wars tore Europe to pieces. The schism in Christianity fostered those wars and raised questions among intellectuals about the unity of truth, nature, and religion. The sheer costs of these struggles also turned minds toward setting aside religious disagreements in favor of peace, the necessary condition for life, if not liberty.

The English civil war (1648–1660) was especially ugly.[5] One participant in that struggle, Thomas Hobbes, believed that religion had caused the conflict. If so, the older accounts of political life could not be sustained; they led to war rather than peace. Hobbes set out a different foundation for politics. Instead of God and nature, Hobbes began with the individual living in a state prior to political association, in "a state of perfect freedom." He argued that the prepolitical state of nature would be violent and brutal; individuals would create the state to achieve peace and its benefits. Individuals create government by means of a social contract that transfers their natural power to look out for themselves to the state, which in turn protects all against all and against external threats. The state is neither natural nor sanctioned by a deity. It was created by the consent of individuals.[6] Humans want peace and create the state to end the state of war and provide security for individuals. Once established, the state recognizes few limits on its power to achieve that goal. The individual cannot assert rights against state power.[7] The Hobbesian social contract was not subject to revocation for nonperformance by the state.

Hobbes had taken a step forward toward limited constitutional government. Government existed for individuals; individuals did not exist for government. Hobbes's theory suggested that government should be answerable to individuals, even if that answer would be given only one time. His theory pointed toward a world where government had to justify its actions (especially abridgments of individual freedom) according to the desires of individuals. Yet Hobbes fell far short of limited government. The Leviathan created by individuals had full power to design a peaceful order. The power of the sovereign to that end included all that we might take to be the liberty of individuals, not least the content of their religious beliefs. Once the social contract was signed and sealed, the parties to the agreement had no recourse if the sovereign decided to take their life, liberty, or property. Hobbes had thrown out the baby (nature) with the bathwater (civil war), leaving individuals with a chance at peace and the certainty of a Leviathan.

Unlike Hobbes, John Locke did not trust the state. He agreed with Hobbes that individuals and their choices are the origins of legitimate political authority. Locke offered a more benign account of the state of nature. Individuals were free and able to create property by their labor. That process of creating property establishes a right to it. Consequently, Locke's natural man comes to the table to negotiate the social contract with more in mind than peace at any price. In Locke's state of nature, humans possess not only life but also liberty and property. Their ownership of these is not merely a convention of the state of nature; for Locke, life, liberty, and property are natural rights that exist prior to the state. Lockean individuals create government to vindicate their natural rights against other individuals. That vindication concerns *all* other individuals, including those who exercise political power.

Many contemporary theorists reject natural rights because they associate such rights with religion, in part because Locke (and those who drafted the Declaration of Independence) believed that a deity gave humanity such rights. Yet religious faith is not essential to the natural rights argument. In the Virginia Declaration of Rights, for example, George Mason referred to the "inherent natural rights" of individuals without mentioning a creator.[8] Natural rights theorists argued that reason could apprehend and apply natural rights through a natural law method of analysis. That method took the general form "Given that the nature of human beings and the world in which they live is X, if we want to achieve Y, then we ought to do Z."[9] Liberals such as Locke used the natural law method to justify certain natural rights that protected a sphere of liberty for individuals, a "space within which persons ought to be free to make their own choices."[10] Natural rights arguments could be controversial; humans would disagree about the nature of the human situation (the given), the goals for humanity (the if), or the means to those goals (the then). But the controversy need not be about the true will of God. Natural rights reasoning could be a secular disagreement about the conditions for successful political life, a conflict that could be mediated by reason rather than revelation. Whether a particular right should be deemed natural depended on the persuasiveness of the analysis and not on an accurate interpretation of God's will.

Having set up the state to protect their natural rights, Lockean individuals might well worry about government's failure to live up to the social contract. In that case Locke posited another right: the right to revolution. If the state violated rather than protected the rights of individuals, the social contract creating the government ceased to bind, and individuals could revert to a prepolitical situation and set about creating a political association that would protect their life, liberty, and property. Far from trusting the state, Locke saw government as contingent. A state should exist insofar as it worked for individuals and their rights.[11]

Locke's ideas influenced the founding of the United States.[12] Some state constitutions, such as Pennsylvania's, had preambles stating that "all government ought to be instituted . . . to enable the individuals who compose [the commonwealth] to enjoy their natural rights."[13] More famously, Thomas Jefferson declared that individuals have an inalienable right to life, liberty, and the pursuit of happiness, that governments are instituted to secure these rights, and that if a government fails to do so, the people have a right to create a new government that will do the job better. When introducing the Bill of Rights as amendments to the Constitution, James Madison noted that "government is instituted, and ought to be exercised for the benefit of the people; which consists in the enjoyment of life and liberty, with the right of acquiring and using property, and generally of pursuing and obtaining happiness and safety." Like Jefferson, Madison thought "the people have an indubitable, unalienable, and indefeasible right to reform or change their government" if it ran counter to these purposes.[14] A distrust of political power informed Madison's remark that "in framing a government which is to be administered by men over men, the great difficulty lies in this: You must first enable the government to controul the governed; and in the next place, oblige it to controul itself."[15]

The natural rights tradition that culminated in the political ideas of John Locke and the founders of the United States transformed Western societies. That tradition denies that government was above and beyond humanity. Instead, Locke argued, individuals created government to protect their rights, which existed prior to government. Individuals thus created a limited government that might be held accountable to their purposes. Such accountability, even if enforced by revolution, restrained government in theory and in fact. These ideas informed the writing of the Declaration of Independence and the Constitution. That tradition focused on rights to life, liberty, and property. What about freedom of speech? Was it among the natural rights protected by and against government?

Freedom of Speech as a Natural Right

John Locke believed in the freedom of conscience and the important of tolerance, especially about religious matters.[16] Although Locke did not make an explicit connection between liberty, natural rights, and freedom of speech, his followers did. The English writers John Trenchard and Thomas Gordon anonymously published 144 letters concerning political liberty and tyranny from 1720 to 1723 in two English newspapers. Trenchard and Gordon wrote under the name Cato, taking as their model the Roman politician Cato the Younger (95–46 BC), the implacable foe of Julius Caesar.[17] "Cato's Letters" followed Locke's natural rights philosophy; they reflected his concern for liberty and his distrust of government.[18] Cato's Letters deeply influenced American colonial thinking about political philosophy and the limits on government.[19]

Trenchard and Gordon devoted their fifteenth letter to freedom of speech and its relation to liberty. Freedom of speech, they write, "is the right of every man, as far as by it he does not hurt and control the right of another; and this is the only check which it ought to suffer, the only bounds which it ought to know."[20] The most careful contemporary reader of Cato's Letters concludes that for Trenchard and Gordon "freedom of speech is as much a natural right as is the right we each have to the fruits of our labour."[21] By the mid-eighteenth century, many people living in the American colonies had learned from Locke and Cato that freedom of speech was a natural right.

The Constitution as ratified did not contain an explicit protection for freedom of speech. During the ratification debate, the Federalists, who included Alexander Hamilton and James Madison, urged adoption of the Constitution without amendments. They saw the document through the lens of social contract theory: it was a delegation of powers from their original owners, the people, to the government. Powers that were not delegated were not granted the government. Because the people did not grant power over freedom of speech to the government in the Constitution, it followed that freedom of speech could not be regulated by the U.S. government.[22]

We owe the First Amendment to the libertarian instincts (and political interests) of the anti-Federalists, who opposed the Constitution and insisted on explicit protections for freedom of speech. They took from theories of the Federalists a clear implication that all rights not mentioned in the basic law could be regulated by government and relinquished by individuals.[23] In November 1787 a leading anti-Federalist writer who took the nom de plume of Cincinnatus invoked the author of Cato's Letters, among others, to explain why explicit limits were necessary: "Such men as Milton, Sidney, Locke, Montesquieu, and Trenchard, have thought it essential to the preservation of liberty against the artful and persevering encroachments of those with whom power is trusted. You will pardon me, sir, if I pay some respect to these opinions, and wish that the freedom of the press may be *previously* secured as a *constitutional* and *unalienable right,* and not left to the precarious care of popular privileges which may or may not influence our new rulers."[24] By the summer of 1789 James Madison had recognized the political and philosophical wisdom of adding a Bill of Rights to the new Constitution. On June 8, 1789, Madison rose in Congress to introduce the Bill of Rights he had fashioned to "expressly declare the great rights of mankind secured under this constitution."[25]

First of all, "the people shall not be deprived or abridged of their right to speak, to write, or to publish their sentiments, and the freedom of the press, as one of the great bulwarks of liberty, shall be inviolable."[26] The final version of the First Amendment, of course, changes the right of the people into an absolute limit on the power of government: "Congress shall make no law . . . abridging freedom of speech or of the press." Under the U.S. Constitution, the federal government had never possessed the power to control freedom of speech. On December 15, 1791, the day the Bill of Rights was ratified, this incapacity became a positive and absolute restriction on the federal government.

Those who created the U.S. Constitution regarded freedom of speech as a natural right.[27] The new government could not have the power to restrict or abridge that right, a truth recognized ultimately by the First Amendment. The endorsement of the founders counts as a reason to value freedom of speech, especially in tandem with the clear language of the First Amendment. Tradition need not be the only reason to support freedom of speech. We can discern why the founding generation might have thought of freedom of speech as a natural right. We can also determine whether that argument should carry any weight with us today.

A leading proponent of natural rights reasoning provides a contemporary formulation of the argument: "Given the pervasive social problems of knowledge, interest, and power confronting every human society, if human beings are to survive and pursue happiness, peace and prosperity while living in society with others, then their laws must not violate certain background natural rights or the rule of law."[28] Mutatis mutandis, we might say, "Given the pervasive problems of knowledge, interest, and power, if human beings are to survive and pursue happiness, peace, and prosperity while living in society with others, then their laws must not violate a background natural right to freedom of speech."

The hypothetical clause establishes purposes for politics that should elicit broad agreement: survival, the pursuit of happiness, peace, and prosperity. The natural rights argument claims that freedom of speech is more likely to realize those ends than all other realistic alternatives given the nature of the human situation. The argument may be divided into three parts. The first establishes how free speech deals with the "givens" of the human situation so as to advance the purposes of political life. The second part examines alternatives to free speech in light of the givens of the human situation and the purposes of politics. The third brings the analysis together to assess whether free speech bests the alternatives. This chapter shows how free speech deals with the problems endemic to political life and adumbrates alternatives to it. Chapter 2 sets out the second and third parts of the argument.

The hypothetical clause of the natural law method poses several core questions for politics. How might humans survive while living together? What arrangements are most conducive to the pursuit of happiness? How might we obtain and preserve peace in a polity? How may a group attain and sustain prosperity? Citizens and rulers alike do not know the answers to these core questions. If they did, politics would be surplus to requirements. But human reason is fallible and serves self-interest, vanity, and momentary passions. In a state of liberty, humans offer a plethora of answers to the core questions of political life.[29] Even absent passion, humans are inevitably ignorant of the factors affecting their wants and desires.[30] How might we proceed given the limits and shortcomings of our reason?

Freedom of speech means at least that the government does not restrict what can be said in response to the core questions of political life. With government out of the picture, individuals, alone and in groups, will propose and defend many answers to these questions. In proposing these answers, they will rely on personal knowledge, "the knowledge unique to particular persons of their personal perception, of their personal preferences, needs, and desires, of their personal abilities, and of their personal opportunities."[31] In other cases citizens will call on their local knowledge, which is both public and limited to a group smaller than the nation.[32] Personal and local knowledge are crucial to politics and governance. They provide vital information about the preferences and commitments of citizens as well as insights into the likely and real consequences of policies for individuals, groups, and the nation.

By the nature of the case, personal or local knowledge is located with other people; it is decentralized and fragmented. For such knowledge to inform politics and decision making, it must be publicly available. If the government suppresses freedom of speech, it prevents such knowledge from becoming public. In contrast, freedom of speech allows personal and local knowledge of various kinds to become more widely available and thus to inform the answers relevant to the core questions of politics. Those who would restrict freedom of speech assume either that they already have the knowledge necessary to answer those questions or that the excluded knowledge is irrelevant or contrary to any worthwhile answers to those questions. Those who have the power to restrict speech must believe they have the answers (or the set of possible answers) to the core questions of politics. That assumption must be accurate if restrictions on speech are to offer better answers than does freedom of speech.

Human beings are inclined to be self-interested. They tend to favor their own preferences and needs rather than the concerns of others. Many hard things are said about self-interest—often termed selfishness—so we might begin by noting its advantages. The pursuit of material self-interest in market economies has led to immense wealth in developed nations. But self-interest is not simply about material interests. Humans prefer the well-being of the families of their fellow citizens to the well-being of other families and of citizens of other nations. Such partiality fosters heroism as well as tragedy.

Randy Barnett has described the way in which self-interest poses a problem for political life. Each person tends to act on his partial view of the world, sometimes at the expense of others' interests. The partiality problem means that society should "allow persons to pursue their own partial interests including the interests of those to whom they are partial . . . while somehow taking into account the partial interests of others whose interests are more remote to them."[33] This problem becomes especially difficult when people are called on to make judgments that involve the interests of others as well as their own.

Consider the American framework for politics. Individuals create governments to secure their natural rights to life, liberty, and property. The self-interest of the public officials selected to enforce those rights may be perfectly compatible with securing liberty and property. They may see it as being in their interest to enforce the social contract. They also face a conflict of interest that has personal and political facets. They may be tempted to simply take the property of citizens to increase their own wealth. Of course, public officials may violate natural rights on behalf of a political coalition they represent, thereby augmenting both the power of the officials and the wealth of the members of the coalition. If officials pursue their self-interest in governing, they violate natural rights and subvert the purposes of the social contract.

James Madison was familiar with the problem of interest. In his Federalist no. 10 he identifies two dangers to a republic: the people and their leaders. Madison associates political corruption with partiality, or the tendency to be the judge in one's own case: "No man is allowed to be a judge in his own cause; because his interest would certainly bias his judgment, and, not improbably, corrupt his integrity."[34] He recognized in particular that elected officials could have personal interests that could run counter to the interests of their constituents.[35] A majority seeking to legislate a principle of distributive justice such as equal shares (or forgiveness of debts) or "any other improper or wicked project" would be corrupt because they would benefit directly from their judgment. For Madison a majority faction posed the problem of interest most acutely because a majority is the power in a popular government.[36]

How should we deal with the problem of interest in a government ruled by the people? Madison dismissed out of hand eliminating the liberty that permits factions to form because the remedy is worse than the disease.

Liberty is as essential to politics as air is to animal life; eliminating liberty would end political life in the name of saving it. Partiality must somehow be reconciled with liberty.

Before Federalist no. 10 appeared, political theorists and many knowledgeable people assumed that the problem of interest could only be overcome by fostering a sense of the common good, a commitment to the public interest possible only in small republics such as those in ancient Greece and Renaissance Italy. Many colonial Americans idealized the ancient Greek city-state of Sparta because it embraced this principle. These neo-Spartans condemned prosperity because the desire for wealth and luxury would foster self-interest and thereby erode citizens' devotion to common good.[37] For them, "any public action that was not purely and selflessly motivated by the imagined public good was proscribed as corrupt."[38] In colonial America, however, the stringent demands of the Spartan ideal provoked doubts. Americans understood that the new nation would probably become prosperous. The Spartan ideal thus offered a counsel of despair that had little appeal. Instead American political thinkers turned to the task of revising the relation between wealth and republicanism. In part, they came to believe that commercial life, especially the life of the owner of land, fostered active and independent individuals of the sort demanded by self-rule.[39] With these changes came a different ideal of politics.

That ideal, the Madisonian vision of politics, may be found largely in Federalist no. 10. Madison argued that such democracies only seemed to overcome private interest by imposing a conception of the common good. What was said to be a good common to all was in fact "a common passion or interest . . . felt by a majority of the whole," an interest inimical to the peace and rights of a minority. The older claims of a common good contravened the nature of human beings. Madison denied that citizens could have "the same opinions, the same passions, and the same interests."[40] He argued that partiality—the ultimate cause of faction—was "sown into the nature of man."[41] Reason and self-love, along with differences in talents and circumstances, lead to differences in interests that foster a tendency toward faction, which means human are far more likely to harm one another than to cooperate for their common good. To submit human diversity to a common aim was "impracticable." How, then, to deal with the problem of interest?

At first Madison appears to have seen representation as an apt means to control the effects of partiality. Those elected by the voters are more likely to attain the public good and the interest of the country than is

direct rule by the people. Yet if majorities tend toward corruption, politicians also corrupt them. Madison writes in Federalist no. 10 that "[m]en
of factious tempers, of local prejudices, or of sinister designs, may by intrigue, by corruption or by other means, first obtain the suffrages, and
then betray the interests of the people."[42] Representation in itself offered
no guarantee against majority faction and the death of a republic. To attain the public good, it must be part of a larger institutional context.

The received tradition asserted that republics must be small to preserve
their sense of commonality. A large republic such as the United States
would soon come to grief. Madison turned this argument on its head. By
encompassing a large population and territory, the new American republic would "take in a greater variety of parties and interests . . . [and] make
it less probable that a majority of the whole will have a common motive
to invade the rights of other citizens; or if such a common motive exists,
it will be more difficult for all who feel it to act in unison." Moreover, the
increase in the number of people participating in politics would make it
more difficult for demagogues to "practice with success the vicious arts"
that corrupt citizens and lead to tyranny.[43] Far from endangering liberty,
the sheer size of the new republic would be its best answer to the problem
of interest.

For Madison, partiality is an inevitable challenge to a republic; it is
not a mistake to be corrected by wise rulers. Instead of imposing a common passion or interest (and thereby ending liberty), Madison called for
expanding the public sphere to include more interests. He did not demand
that founders or political leaders make humans forget their partiality in
favor of the public interest. Instead they pursue their interests within a
broader framework of struggle, a framework that militates against the
danger posed by the self-interest of a majority. He concluded that controlling the effects of self-interest rather than removing its cause was the only
option for founders of a republic.[44]

This view implies that the freedom to speak in politics will necessarily
be a freedom to speak partly in defense of self-interest. The political arena
will comprise a variety of different positions and interests, a claim confirmed by even a causal glance at contemporary Washington. By allowing
a broad spectrum of interests to find their voice, freedom of speech fosters
political organization and struggle; such freedom fosters the struggle of
self-interest against self-interest, ambition against ambition. Freedom of
speech is the way Madison's "multiplicity of interests" engage in political
struggle, thereby making the triumph of corrupt majorities less likely.

Madison did not forsake the idea of the public good. In Federalist no. 10 he refers to the "permanent and aggregate interests of the community" as well as to the public good and private rights.[45] Madison's idea of the public good cannot mean a common interest or passion inculcated prior to political struggle because he had already rejected that idea. For him the public good is the result of the process of politics, not a substantive condition for the success of that process.[46] Citizens create the public interest via struggle among a multiplicity of partial interests within a framework of representative institutions, constraining rights, and limited government. Representatives give voice at the end of the day to a public good that has been created by such struggle. In part, Madison's idea of the public interest is negative: the struggle itself precludes the tyranny of the majority. But Madison had something more in mind. If citizens are free to organize and struggle over politics in a fragmented polity, government will often do nothing. The struggle of disparate interests within constitutional constraints will lead to stalemate that can be in the public interest, especially if the next alternative is either tyranny of the majority or predation by an organized minority. On the other hand, in a Madisonian world, doing something in politics requires expanding the coalition in order to pass a law. Given the concern for minorities embodied in the institutions of American politics and the size and fragmentation of the nation, that expansion must take into consideration minority interests. The Madisonian system leads to political competition that fosters policies that reflect the concerns of a more general set of citizens than a simple majority. For that reason, Madison could say that the voice of representatives heard at the end of this struggle is likely to be more consonant with the public good than is the voice of the people issuing directly from an untrammeled majority.[47] In this way, the liberty to pursue self-interest will attain the public interest even though no one sought that end. The public good is a spontaneous order endogenous to a large constitutional republic, suitably constrained by exogenous rights and institutions.[48]

Madison's ideas about interests suggest two other implications. The struggle of interests in a Madisonian republic implies a freedom of speech that includes a freedom to associate for political purposes. As the U.S. Supreme Court would later acknowledge, "freedom to engage in association for the advancement of beliefs and ideas is an inseparable aspect of the 'liberty' . . . which embraces freedom of speech." As Madison understood, freedom of speech "is undeniably enhanced by group association."[49] More recently, the Court noted that freedom of association was essential to protecting core First Amendment rights.[50] In these respects, at least, modern Supreme Court doctrine seems fully in line with Madison's constitutional theory.

Just as government may forbid political speech, it also may not compel people to speak in support of a political position. Such coercion would be an extreme infringement of liberty. It would also require citizens to speak on behalf of the interests of others, perhaps in the name of the common good or for the public interest. But if the common good were a consequence of the political process, it could not be used to inform that process via coercion. The end of the political process could not be the ground for coercion aimed at improving the process. Inevitably, forcing people to speak on behalf of interests favored by government would distort the political struggle that led to the public good.

Madison was not very concerned with what today are called the *special interests* or *special interest groups,* small minorities who ostensibly dominate government and public policymaking. Madison believed that a majority held power in a republic and would be more than capable of defeating the "sinister designs" of a small minority.[51] Some contemporary scholars argue the opposite: in contrast to large, diffuse groups, small groups have stronger incentives to organize and obtain benefits from government. They expect, in other words, that special interests, rather than majorities, will dominate policymaking.[52] Whether they do so by way of campaign contributions is addressed in subsequent chapters.

Finally, natural rights theorists deal with the problem of power. John Locke pointed to the dangers of centralized political power in the case of absolute monarchy, "where one Man commanding a multitude, has the Liberty to be Judge in his own Case, and may do to all his Subjects whatever he pleases, without the least liberty to any one to question or controle those who Execute his Pleasure[.] And in whatsoever he doth, whether led by Reason, Mistake or Passion, must be submitted to[.]"[53] The monarch is both partial and empowered to act on his partiality, thereby threatening a return to the state of nature. Power corrupts or at least enables the powerful to act on their self-interest without limits.

Many classical liberals focused on the threat posed by the unchecked power of kings. When Madison introduced the Bill of Rights into Congress, he reflected on the dangers posed by government. He noted that the most potent threat to individual rights came from the community itself, "the body of the people, operating by the majority against the minority." Accordingly, "prescriptions in favor of liberty" such as the Bill of Rights "ought to be leveled against that quarter where the greatest danger lies, namely, that which possesses the highest prerogative of power."[54] From the start, the Bill of Rights aimed at forestalling the corruption endemic to republics, the tyranny of one part of the community over another, the tyranny of a majority.

The founders devoted much attention to the abuse of power by one or by many. Madison urged a fragmentation of power in which the politically ambitious would struggle against one another, thereby controlling the "abuses of government."[55] Freedom of speech should be seen as an "auxiliary precaution" against the abuse of power. The liberal writers who influenced the founders appreciated the constraints freedom of speech placed on government and political power. The authors of Cato's Letters thought the citizens' use of the liberty to speak would force government officials to be open and accountable and to conduct business in the interests of the people. It was essential to free government and the security of property, and it worked against tyranny and government violations of natural rights. For that reason, Trenchard and Gordon noted, those who would subvert a free government fear and suppress freedom of speech.[56]

Madison explicitly linked freedom of speech to limited government in response to the threat to liberty posed by the Sedition Act of 1798. In a report to the Virginia House of Delegates, he affirmed that the "right of freely examining public characters and measures, and of communication is . . . the only effectual guardian of every other right." He noted that the "right of electing the members of the government constitutes more particularly the essence of a free and responsible government." This right of election, however, "depends on the knowledge of the comparative merits and demerits of the candidates for public trust, and on the equal freedom, consequently, of examining and discussing" them. The Sedition Act, in contrast, would fine or imprison anyone who "shall write, print, utter, or publish . . . any false, scandalous, and malicious writing or writings against the government of the United States." Madison pointed out that punishing malicious writings would inevitably limit the right of freely examining public characters; after all, free criticism would bring public officials into disrepute insofar as the criticism was deserved. Indeed, officials who oversaw an incompetent administration would be all the more inclined to punish free speech in order to evade responsibility for their failure.[57] If government could control and punish the expression of political views, its citizens had become subjects who could be forbidden to criticize their masters. Without freedom of speech, those who should be servants, the politicians, would become the masters.[58]

Madison recognized the malevolent motivations behind restrictions on freedom of speech. He pointed out that the Sedition Act affected candidates for office differently. The incumbents who wrote it would be free of any criticism that exposed them to "disrepute among the people," but those who challenged them would be subject to attacks and thus "the contempt and hatred of the people." Granting the power to limit freedom of speech thus gives an "undue advantage" in electoral competition to those who wrote the act, an advantage that impairs the right of election and the blessings of a free government.[59] More than two centuries before McCain-Feingold, James Madison understood that incumbents restrict freedom of speech to enhance their electoral prospects, a purpose best achieved by fashioning laws that differentially affect incumbents and challengers.

Did Madison believe that freedom of speech was the only effectual guardian of *every* other right? The skeptic might say he does not offer free speech as a solution to the threat of majority tyranny over minority rights discussed in Federalist no. 10. Madison focuses in that essay on institutional safeguards for individual rights. Yet the logic of that paper does not exclude Madison's later clear profession that free speech was the only effectual guardian of every other right. The danger posed to liberty by government might be great enough to justify both institutional safeguards and absolute protections for freedom of speech. Accordingly, we might see Madison's later profession as a supplement to the institutional argument of Federalist no. 10, an explication called forth by the exigencies of the Sedition Act.

In sum, the idea of natural rights and the concomitant notion of limited government defined the American political tradition from the start. Natural rights admit both a religious and a secular interpretation, the latter embracing a rational appeal to the necessary conditions of political life given the human condition. Freedom of speech is necessary to solve the problems of knowledge, interest, and power that complicate political life. Apart from consideration of natural rights, many Americans in the abstract would acknowledge the importance of freedom of speech. They might doubt, however, whether money has anything to do with freedom of speech. Does it?

Money and Freedom of Speech

Electioneering during the founding era did not involve large sums of money. Candidates stood for election based on their reputation among voters and thus spent little on advertising and campaigning. For example, in his first race for public office, Madison's major electioneering cost

would have been for food and drink for the electors.[60] The engaged and
partisan press of the time did spend significant sums on electoral coverage
and disputation. The politicians and thinkers did not reflect much on the
relation of money to politics. Their unsurprising oversight does not matter. The Constitution enunciates principles for politics but does not direct
every application.[61] Because the founders did profess strong support for
freedom of speech, the question must be whether money matters for that
fundamental liberty.

In campaign finance debates, money matters as either campaign spending or campaign contributions. Candidates, party leaders, and interest
groups spend money to influence the outcomes of elections. They spend
money to persuade voters to come to the polls and to select their favored
candidate (or to support a particular cause). In the contemporary United
States, much spending goes toward buying advertising time on various
media and to getting out the vote by direct contact with voters. In a few
cases, candidates fund their own electioneering. In most cases, however,
candidates, parties, and political organizations must persuade individuals
and groups to give them money to spend on electioneering. Campaign
contributions are logically and practically tied to campaign spending.
Without contributions, there can be no spending unless individuals fund
their own campaigns. Are campaign spending and contributions tied to
freedom of speech?

Spending

In 1976 the U.S. Supreme Court decided the case of *Buckley v. Valeo*.
Among other things, Congress two years earlier had imposed restrictions
on spending by a variety of candidates for federal office. The Court decided that those spending limits violated the First Amendment protection
for freedom of speech: "A restriction on the amount of money a person
or group can spend on political communication during a campaign necessarily reduces the quantity of expression by restricting the number of issues discussed, the depth of their exploration, and the size of the audience
reached. This is because virtually every means of communicating ideas in
today's mass society requires the expenditure of money."[62] Money is tied
to speech because money buys the means of communicating with voters.
By restricting spending, Congress had necessarily restricted speech. Of
course, Congress had not *directly* limited what anyone could say during
an election. The Federal Election Campaign Act of 1974 did not forbid

anyone to publicly say, "Vote for Gerald Ford for President." It did forbid everyone from spending "too much" money supporting the spread of the message "Vote for Gerald Ford for President." The difference between what citizens wished to spend on electioneering and what they could spend constituted FECA's suppression of speech.

For this reason, spending limits per se have been constitutionally forbidden. This constraint on government has not pleased those who favor restrictions. Critics of *Buckley* have often asserted that the Supreme Court said "money equals speech." But the Court did not use that phrase anywhere else in the opinion.[63] Those who interpret *Buckley* along those lines do so to make the decision seem absurd. If they succeed, then money is property and nothing more. As we shall see, if money in politics is property, it can be regulated and restricted in virtually any fashion.

The absurdity of *Buckley,* however, comes from the intentionally misleading interpretation, not from the decision itself. The Court actually said that in a modern society money is so intertwined with political speech and activity that limits on spending inevitably restrict speech, although the two are ontologically distinct. As a later justice of the Supreme Court put it, "Money is not speech, it is money. But the expenditure of money enables speech; and that expenditure is often necessary to communicate a message, particularly in a political context."[64] Consider an example from the real world. Suppose Congress decided that the *New York Times* has too much influence over public opinion and public policy. To deal with that, Congress imposed spending limits on the *Times*'s budgets for newsprint, Internet access, salaries, and marketing. Imagine that those limits were set at 50 percent of current spending on each item and that the limits did not adjust for inflation. If the advocates are to be believed, these imaginary limits on spending by the *Times* concern only property, not speech. Yet such limits would greatly reduce the ability of the owners, editorialists, and reporters to disseminate the news and to discuss politics and policy. The *Times*'s money is not speech, but it is intimately connected to its freedom of speech.

Contributions

The decision in *Buckley* defended spending by candidates and parties, but political spending by individuals and groups to support campaigns was another matter. The *Buckley* majority argued that restrictions on freedom to contribute to political campaigns served the "compelling state interest" of preventing "corruption and the appearance of corruption spawned by the real or imagined coercive influence of large financial contributions on candidates' positions and on their actions if elected to office."[65] Contribution limits thus "safeguard the integrity of the electoral process," which would be undermined "to the extent that large contributions are given to secure a political quid pro quo from current and potential office holders."[66]

The Court argued that contributions, unlike other kinds of political spending, did not implicate the First Amendment because donations were a "general expression of support" for a candidate and his views. The size of a contribution "provides a very rough index of the intensity of the contributor's support for the candidate." Contributions enter political debate by supporting speech by someone other than the contributor.[67] The freedom to contribute thus enjoyed less constitutional protection than the freedom to spend money on electioneering.

If the Court were right, and contributions did not implicate the First Amendment, restrictions on donations might be legal. But the Court was wrong. Contributions do implicate freedom of speech. Spending on elections by candidates and parties depends on spending by contributors. If candidates and parties do not raise money, they cannot spend it. If government criminalized contributing anything to campaigns, candidates and parties would have no money to spend apart from their own wealth or their share of public financing, the money government would extract from taxpayers to fund campaigns. Of course, government does not (yet) criminalize all private contributions to campaigns. But if it did, we would have much less spending on campaigns and much less speech.

Short of banning private contributions, do limits on donations reduce spending (and thus speech)? They make it more difficult and costly to raise a fixed sum of money to spend on elections. For example, imagine that an interest group needs to raise $9 million to contest an election.[68] The group might be able to raise the needed money from one donor. If the money had to be raised under federal election law, however, the $9 million would have to be raised in increments of a few thousand dollars from a much larger number of donors who would have to be found and persuaded to donate to the group. We would expect that by increasing the cost of an activity (such as fundraising), all things being equal, we would get less of it and thus smaller sums raised than we would under less regulation. Less fundraising would translate into smaller aggregate sums available for spending and thus to less speech during an election.

Contribution limits suppress electoral speech in a more subtle way. Such limits make it impossible for wealthy individuals, institutions, or groups to donate large sums of money related to electioneering. This makes it difficult for an organization to get up and running. As a result, fundraising and electioneering after 1974 have been sharply biased toward organizations (labor unions and businesses) that already exist and have independent sources of income that support the costs of fundraising. Grassroots groups, in contrast, have favored lobbying, not electioneering, because fundraising for the former is free of federal contribution limits.[69] Of course, the speech that those grassroots group might have funded and might have uttered is forever denied to the voters.[70]

We need not be content with theory on this point. Early in 2004, the staff of the Federal Election Commission issued an advisory opinion that expanded the legal definition of *expenditures* to include a "communication that promotes, supports, attacks, or opposes a clearly identified Federal candidate." Such expenditures would be governed by federal election law and its strictures, including contribution limits.[71]

Nonprofit organizations on the political left and right immediately discerned the danger posed by the advisory opinion. A lawyer representing 324 groups on the left, B. Holly Schadler, objected to the new definition of *expenditure.* Her clients, she noted, "regularly seek to educate the public and to advocate positions on progressive legislative and policy issues, including the positions taken by federal officeholders with respect to these issues." If the advisory opinion became law, those groups would no longer be able to advocate their positions unless they "raise and spend funds in accordance with the source and contribution limitations of the FECA." According to the *Buckley* decision, meeting those limits would hardly affect the speech rights of such groups. Yet Schadler thought otherwise: "For most of our organizations, raising funds under these restrictions would be impossible. . . . Therefore this opinion would entirely shut down many of the advocacy activities of our organizations."[72] If those organizations were shut down, their efforts to educate the public—surely a core example of freedom of speech—would end. According to the groups involved, that speech would be lost not because of spending limits but rather because of the "source and contribution limitations of the FECA."

The sponsors of the latest limits on campaign contributions do not deny that such restraints restrict speech. In fact, they celebrate it. Prior to passage of McCain-Feingold, interest groups could raise money as they wished and run ads commenting on issues, comments that inevitably implicated and criticized politicians. Such speech is no longer free of federal regulation. McCain-Feingold defines such speech as "electioneering" and forces those groups to raise the money for such ads within federal contribution limits. According to Senator John McCain, that imposition of contribution limits would eliminate many of the ads: "If you cut off the soft money, you're going to see a lot less of that [attack ads]. Prohibit unions and corporations [from making soft money contributions] and you will see a lot less of that. If you demand full disclosure for those that pay for those ads, you're going to see a lot less of that."[73] A year later, Senator Maria Cantwell (D-WA) said, "This bill is about slowing political advertising and making sure the flow of negative ads by outside interest groups does not continue to permeate the airwaves." She added, "This bill forces all of us—candidates, parties, and groups that seek to influence the outcome of elections—to play by the same rules and *raise and spend money in lower amounts.*"[74] In other words, Cantwell was admitting that the contribution limits—which according to *Buckley* had no effect on political speech— would in fact reduce spending on elections. Cantwell was recommending McCain-Feingold to her Senate colleagues precisely because contribution limits will restrict political speech. About the time McCain-Feingold first appeared in Congress, Senator Barbara Boxer (D-CA) celebrated the promised silencing of views: "These so-called issues ads are not regulated at all and mention candidates by name. They directly attack candidates without any accountability. It is brutal. I have seen them. I have seen them from both sides. I can tell you, it is totally unfair and totally unregulated and vicious. It is vicious. We have an opportunity in the McCain-Feingold bill to stop that and basically say, if you want to talk about an issue, that is fine, but you can't mention a candidate."[75] Thus, according to members of Congress—the institution that the Supreme Court says has the greatest expertise to judge electoral matters[76]—imposing contribution limits where none existed will reduce political speech. Perhaps we should take McCain's word for it.

Campaign spending receives constitutional protection because it is closely related to speech. If the government forbids spending on bullhorns, it reduces the scope of speech in our society. The same goes for advertising. Advertising allows candidates, political parties, and groups to speak out on issues and upcoming elections. Contributions to candidates work the same way.

Consider the case of Eugene McCarthy's 1968 presidential campaign. McCarthy was a relatively unknown senator from Minnesota who decided to challenge the incumbent president, Lyndon Johnson, largely because of the Vietnam War. McCarthy relied on a $200,000 contribution from the liberal philanthropist Stewart Mott to support his unlikely candidacy, which "gave voice to the anti-war opposition within the Democratic Party."[77] The arguments and ideas given voice by his contributors had an effect. McCarthy did well in the New Hampshire Democratic presidential primary in March. He drew 42.2 percent of the vote, compared to 49.5 for President Johnson. Shortly thereafter, Johnson stopped his reelection effort and stepped up peace talks.[78] Six years later, such donations might have landed the senator and his contributors in jail. Congress had criminalized giving "too much" money to a political cause.

Campaign contributions also speak to voters by carrying information, independent of how the money is spent. Donald Wittman notes that "voters can also look at the list of campaign contributors (who typically make their endorsements public) and infer the characteristics of the candidates' policies (pro or con). . . . Interest group endorsements are like signals in the market and provide strong cues about candidates' preferences."[79]

A prosaic example shows that voters can trust the quality of the information purveyed by campaign contributions. Recently I sought a contractor to remodel the upstairs bathroom of my house. Engaging someone to do this job involves risks similar to those inherent in voting for a public official: if I select the wrong candidate for the job, it will be difficult and costly to make things right. Imagine I have two sources of information to use to select the contractor: I know that a friend has recently made a down payment to a contractor to remodel her bathroom (though the work has not yet been done), and another friend has assessed local remodeling contractors by reading consumer magazines and the Internet. Which source of information should I follow in selecting my own contractor? I would focus on the contractor who got the down payment. Why? The friend who spent the money concretely shares the risk of my situation; her down payment conveys important and reliable information, the best advice available for my decision. The well-read friend has nothing at stake and has invested nothing. Similarly, campaign contributions suggest a serious judgment by informed individuals or groups about the likely conduct or character of a public official. Voters have good reason to listen to what contributions say.

Voters need the high-quality information offered by campaign contributions. Finding good information about bathroom contractors is costly, but accurate knowledge yields many benefits (if only by avoiding large losses). Voters have few incentives to gather information about candidates since their vote is unlikely to change the outcome of the contest; voter ignorance is rational, if not exemplary.[80] Citizens thus rationally seek shortcuts to align their policy preferences with their voting on Election Day.[81] Contributions provide quality information and thus a good shortcut for voters who need only identify groups of individuals who share their political views. For example, George Soros, the wealthy investor, contributed more than $20 million to groups formed to defeat President Bush in the 2004 election. Those contributions told like-minded partisans that Soros truly believed Bush's reelection would be a disaster for the United States. Notice that what Soros had to say came from the size of his contribution and not from the ultimate expenditures funded by the money.[82]

We commonly observe that contributions are mentioned in campaigns only as a reason to vote against a candidate. The demonization of money leads to this result. The speech value of contributions depends on citizens' believing that contributions convey neutral information about the positions of a candidate. Citizens do not believe this. Proponents of campaign finance regulations have spent large sums to convince Americans that money is the root of all evil in politics. Voters have come to see donations as efforts by special interests to gain favors and so candidates will not reveal contributions to their own campaigns (even from large groups with popular causes) mainly because the public assumes that all such gifts are "tainted." Candidates will point out contributions to their opponents from unpopular groups. Money may move an election, but only by convincing voters to vote against a candidate.

Notice the perversity of this scenario. If money taints politics, a voter is unlikely to use contributions as a way of discerning the positions of a candidate and casting his or her vote. The information provided by contributions will lead to the election of candidates because they were not their opponents, not because they represented the views of the voters. The "root of all evil" argument together with the logic of electoral competition excludes information that ties the positive agenda of voters to their elected officials. It tends toward a government composed of officials selected for who they were not rather than what they stood for.

Dhammika Dharmapala and Filip Palda have conjectured that voters take information from the dispersion (or concentration) of contributions to a candidate. What could that tell voters? They might care about whether candidates raise money from many or few donations for two reasons. Voters might assume that contributions are attempts by interest groups to gain access to make their case to elected officials. If the officials received gifts from relatively few donors, they will have less information after the election with which to make policy decisions than they would if they had received money from a broader range of groups. Voters may reasonably conclude that less information will lead elected officials to make relatively worse policy decisions. Voters would thus prefer candidates with a larger donor base as a way of predicting the quality of their policy decisions after they have won election. Of course, voters must assume that interest groups give money as a way to make arguments and provide their expertise to policymakers and that the donations lead policymakers to give favors to the interest groups. If so, voters would have good reason to prefer a candidate with many donors. After assuming office, the more donors a candidate has, "the larger the number of groups engaged in lobbying [and] the more they will tend to counteract each other's efforts," thus reducing the likelihood that any one group will obtain special treatment or subsidies.[83]

These theoretical arguments explain why voters might rationally consider the concentration of a candidate's contributions. Do we have any empirical evidence that voters punish candidates with a narrow donor base? Dharmapala and Palda have investigated whether receiving money from a broad or a narrow range of contributors affected a candidate's vote share and chances of winning. They looked at more than 650,000 PAC donations to House candidates in elections from 1980 to 1992. Their study found that if a challenger or candidate in an open seat election got support from a relatively small number of contributors, their chances of winning went down sharply, all things considered. The picture with incumbents was quite different: the number of contributors seemed to have little effect on their electoral success.[84]

Madison thought republics tended toward self-destruction via a tyranny of the majority over minorities. Affording campaign contributions the full protection of the First Amendment gives minorities a fighting chance, no less and no more. Endangered minorities, including religious minorities as well as the affluent, can use contributions to support candidates for office who will work against abuses of power by a majority, by trying to convince others of the dangers and injustice of such tyranny. If contributions are not limited, minorities may support candidates or groups that defend their rights by introducing legislation or by recalling the Constitution to the people. Through contributions and other means, minorities can play the game of politics in order to vindicate their rights under the Constitution.

Contributions, like all forms of speech, offer a chance to make your case, not a certainty of having your way. If they bought a policy, they would monopolize political debate and struggle. As we shall see, they do not buy elections or policies. Contributions are part of the mix that affect policies by influencing the beliefs and calculations of lawmakers. At the margins, and no more, contributions serve as an auxiliary precaution to restrain the tyranny of the majority. If we afford contributions the same protections we give campaign spending, we are affirming the republican principles that informed the United States Constitution.

Freedom of Association

Much of the contemporary struggle over campaign finance has turned on freedom of speech. As mentioned above, however, Madison's vision of politics implies the centrality of freedom of association. Does the regulation of money in politics pose any threat to that right? In recent years, the U.S. Congress has extensively regulated the activities of political parties, including get-out-the-vote efforts and voter registration drives, activities that inevitably involve association for political purposes, as indeed, does the act of raising money for campaigns.[85] A ban on such fundraising would end the relevant associations and speech. Mandatory disclosure of contributions also reveals a donor's association with a campaign, a party, or a political group. If the disclosure of that relation leads to adverse publicity for the donor, the right of association may be burdened or chilled.

Conclusion

The founders fashioned a constitution that recognized (but did not create) individual rights to life, liberty, and property. They were concerned about the abuses of political power throughout human history. In particular, they feared the tyranny of the majority or similar abuses that would lead to the decline and death of the new republic. The U.S. Constitution thus fragments authority and denies the government the power to restrict several liberties, including freedom of speech. The money spent on politics as direct expenditures and as contributions both realizes the natural right to freedom of speech and provides an auxiliary precaution against overweening power.

The Madisonian vision has informed most of American history and lives on today in the healthy distrust many Americans have for political power. But the Madisonian vision is not the only influence on American politics and lawmaking. Another vision, often called Progressivism, has influenced politics and government in the United States for more than a century. It differs from the former in every important way. It also serves as the intellectual foundation of the movement to restrict campaign finance. To understand that movement, we need to understand that vision.

The Progressive Vision of Politics

Beginning in the late nineteenth century, Progressives fashioned a distinctive vision of politics that has profoundly affected the United States to the present day. Progressive ideas have become commonplace and largely unquestioned, so much so that we might be inclined to see this vision of politics as a modification of the original ideas underpinning the U.S. Constitution, a reform movement affirming the values of the nation's founding. But we would be wrong. The creators of this vision completely rejected the founders' constitutional vision of politics. They fashioned a new regime in thought that eventually became in part a new regime in power.[1]

The political vision of the Progressives continues to inform contemporary politics, not least the struggle to impose ever more restrictions on campaign finance.[2] The influence of this vision is both overt and implicit. The Progressives' faith in government and their hostility to business remain staples of daily politics in the United States. Other themes receive less emphasis. For example, the original Progressives were often Puritanical zealots who subordinated politics to their religious commitments. Today they oppose such mixing of God and man, if not the whole idea of religion itself. But that does not mean partisans of campaign finance restrictions do not still seek to realize a "kingdom of righteousness" in the United States or that the religious impulse that gave birth to Progressivism has not lived on in a secular form.

This vision of politics rejected the foundations of the Madisonian vision: individualism, limited government, and representative democracy.[3] These were replaced by a reforming, regulatory state and direct democracy guided by an ethical elite. This reform aims at the common good, often understood as an egalitarian distribution of wealth. That goal requires

government control of political activity. In the end, progress runs counter to restrictions on government power over the liberty and property
of citizens.

The Progressive Critique of the Madisonian Vision

The founders argued that individuals created government (and society itself) by means of their actions and choices. For the founders, the liberty
of the individual was a negative freedom, a freedom from government
and from others. Politics and government thus played a marginal though
important part in human life. Most of life concerned the individual in civil
society, the large domain free of government control. This individualism
dominated the political culture of the United States when Progressivism—
which was profoundly antagonistic to American individualism in all its
manifestations—emerged in the late nineteenth century.

Progressives linked "rights claims to individualism and individualism
to selfishness and greed."[4] George Herron declared that "the law of self
interest is the eternal falsehood which mothers all social and private woes;
for sin is pure individualism."[5] The Progressive publicist Herbert Croly
decried "selfish appetites." For Mary Follett, the individualism of the U.S.
Constitution and the Bill of Rights "make[s] it possible for individuals to
aggrandize themselves at the expense of society."[6] Similarly, the Progressives decried political parties for many reasons, not least because they
were built on "the despotism of the selfish appetites of the unredeemed
American individualist."[7] Far from being the creator and master of government, the individual was selfish, particularistic, and solitary. By equat-
ing individualism with self-interest and selfishness, the Progressives de-
valued the foundation of the American republic. Indeed, for John Dewey,
a return to the older tradition of individualism would mean "inequity,
harshness, and retrogression to barbarism."[8] Laissez-faire individualistic
liberalism had outlived its usefulness and become little more than "regres-
sive social attitudes and institutional forms."[9]

The Progressives' doubts fostered "a persistent attack on rights and
individualism as worthy foundations for American national democracy."[10]
In particular, they rejected the idea of natural rights and a noninterven-
tionist state.[11] Rights belong to society, not the individual, which means
"there are no rights, except rights of way in the performance of social
functions."[12] If society grants a right to individuals, Dewey argued, that

grant "indicates an active acknowledgment on the part of society that the free exercise by individuals of the power in question is positively in its own interest. Thus a right, individual in residence, is social in origin and intent."[13] Mary Follett exemplified this vision when she declared that "the theory of government based on individual rights no longer has a place in modern political theory."[14] If the individual existed for the government or for society, rights against the government had no meaning. Violations of rights that had been taken for granted and civil liberties thus became "the price of progress" and for Herbert Croly, at least, a matter of indifference.[15]

This hostility to political individualism led the movement to reject the negative concept of freedom that informed the nation's founding.[16] Not surprisingly, we find Mary Follett expressing contempt for merely negative rights and liberties, not to mention "the crudities of the Declaration of Independence."[17] Progressives rejected the natural rights and negative liberty recognized in the U.S. Constitution in favor of a Hamiltonian centralization of power in the federal government.[18]

The natural rights recognized at the founding included that to private property, which implied that economic activity would be free of government control. The Progressives rejected all theories of property rights premised on the natural rights of the individual.[19] Indeed, they rejected all protection of private property against the state. Any right to property, according to them, "should be seen as granted by the community contingent on the performance of duties by the community."[20] John Dewey thus writes: "Property, likewise, is not only a possessing, but a 'right,' and thus, like all rights, involves the questions why and how far society should support the individual in his interests and claims."[21] The quotation marks around the term *right* indicate Dewey's skepticism that private property has any claims against the state. The question is not whether an individual has the right of property against the government but rather whether the government should grant a right to property to individuals (that is, "support the individual in his interests and claims"). Dewey, the leading Progressive intellectual of his time, thus turned the Madisonian argument for rights on its head: government granted rather than recognized the individual right to property. Dewey did allow that private property could lead to an increase in power and freedom. But he at once evoked a darker side of property: "Over against these positive values of property are certain evils which moralists have always recognized, evils both to the property owner and to society. Avarice, covetousness, hardness toward others, seem to be the natural effects of the enormous possibilities of power offered by property, joined with its exclusive character."[22]

Dewey then recalls that the founders of Judaism and Christianity denounced the rich as immoral. He cites Plato's view that allowing a polity to be ruled by the wealthy led to "the perversion and disobedience of laws, the jealousies and class hatred, the evasion of taxes for public defense" as well as a general decline of virtue.[23] Private property along with "the rich" had no moral standing in a Progressive society.

Progressives also decried the immorality of the free market. As early as 1885, those who founded the American Economic Association stated: "[W]e hold that the doctrine of laisse [sic] faire is unsafe in politics and unsound in morals."[24] Left to itself, business concerned the selfish pursuit of profit and consumption, which the sociologist Albion Small called "mere economic achievement" and the Supreme Court would later deem "ordinary commercial activity." For that reason, business corrupted society and the state. More generally, the formalism of constitutional rights had "created a materialistic and immoral society divided by inequality and conflict."[25] Herbert Croly similarly complained that economic freedom leads to a "morally and socially undesirable distribution of wealth."[26] John Dewey and Roscoe Pound also emphasized the morally unacceptable character of economic inequality.[27]

That distribution in turn led to a concentration of wealth that created "money power," which Croly defined as "the malevolent social influence of incorporated and individual wealth."[28] Such alleged influence became a leitmotif of muckraking Progressive journalists, who took as their theme the corruption of politics by business. Their efforts found political success: by the early years of the twentieth century, politicians were regularly denouncing corporate bribery as well as business lobbying and campaign contributions. Then as now, Progressives argued that money in politics, licit and illicit, gave business "undue influence" over legislation. These attacks succeeded, in part because the politics of the era was marked by significant corruption.[29] By 1908, ten states had passed lobbying laws, nineteen had restricted corporate campaign contributions, and fourteen had banned free railroad passes for elected officials.[30] In 1907, Congress passed the Tillman Act, which banned contributions by federally chartered banks and corporations.[31]

As we saw, the Constitution grew out of the tradition of individualism and natural rights. For Progressives, the concept of the social contract was simply a mistake to be overcome by intellectual and political progress.[32]

They intended to overthrow what Croly called "the monarchy of the Constitution."[33] The victory of Progressivism thus "signaled the overthrow of constitutional government" and foreshadowed the "end of liberalism" in the twentieth century. That end—the end of government constrained by a constitution and individual rights—implied "extending the loss of constitutional protection over economic rights, which occurred in the 1920s and 1930s, to the entire system of governance."[34] The "constitutional language of checks and balances, of federalism, of jurisdictional rights, state's rights, property rights, and even individual rights" was merely "a rhetoric of evasion and bad faith."[35] A "constitutional declaration of rights" had little to do with "genuine liberty."[36]

The Progressives equated the constitutionalism of the founders with "legal formalism." Such formalism, Charles Horton Cooley argued, "goes very naturally with sensuality, avarice, selfish ambition, and other traits of disorganization." It reflected the individualism that Progressives identified with American political culture. Formalism allowed such disorder because it did not "enlist and discipline the soul of the individual, but takes hold of him by the outside."[37]

They sought to discredit the Constitution by reducing law to politics. They saw the Constitution not as framework for and constraint on political struggle but rather as "the effective distribution and actual exercise of power—a shifting complex of laws, formal and informal rules, governmental processes, and political philosophical understandings."[38] It was the outcome of, not a framework for, normal politics, and thus they repudiated the higher law and its power to constrain the ambitious. This depreciation of the Constitution also opened the door to fundamental changes in the basic law through normal politics rather than the amendment process of Article V.

This realism led them to examine the extraconstitutional, political foundations of the U.S. Constitution. Political parties, for example, were based on shifting coalitions and local interests, and so the parties supported all the other constitutional limits on government: individual rights, federalism, checks and balances, and a politics of bargaining and compromise. As we saw in chapter 1, Madison believed that the free political struggles protected by the Constitution would counter the concentration of political power. The Progressives agreed that the political parties, though absent from the Constitution, shored up the structure of the basic law. They disliked political parties largely for that reason. In their view, the parties precluded "critical inquiry and serious discussion of the common good."[39]

Many Progressive historians argued that political and economic interests created the Constitution to serve the economic and political interests of an exclusive minority. Thus J. Allen Smith, writing in 1907, asserted that "the American scheme of government was planned and set up to perpetuate the ascendancy of the property-holding class in a society leavened with democratic ideas."[40] Far from being the founding act of the American nation, in the eyes of Progressives the U.S. Constitution was a fraud perpetuated by the rich to the detriment of everyone else, a fraud that could be undone by scientific analysis.

They attacked the Constitution (and the idea of constitutionalism) as an outmoded institution that prevented social progress defined as the expansion of the federal government. Walter Hamilton, a law professor at Columbia University, warned that the Constitution imposed "outworn standards upon current activities."[41] For the Progressive, the belief in limited government "seemed hopelessly out of place in the face of social and economic needs requiring decisive governmental action."[42] If the Constitution of 1789 was hopelessly fraudulent or irrelevant to current circumstances, the United States needed a second founding, a new political order more in tune with the modern age.

Adherents of this philosophy tried to redefine individual freedom as the pursuit of self-interest and thus as greed or selfishness. Left alone, individuals act contrary to the social good by betraying their duties to society. In politics, the individual pursuit of self-interest corrupts the state by turning public power to private purposes. The elected agents of the people had betrayed their constituents in favor of "class control" and "the exercise of power by a parasitic class in its own interest."[43] As movement leader Eltweed Pomeroy put it, "it soon became evident that the interest of the ruler after election did not coincide with justice to all the people. It either was or could easily be the interest of a class, the corporations or organized wealth-owners."[44] The Progressive Party platform of 1912 was even more direct: "Behind the ostensible government sits enthroned an invisible government owing no allegiance and acknowledging no responsibility to the people. To destroy this invisible government, to dissolve the unholy alliance between corrupt business and corrupt politics is the first task of the statesmanship of the day."[45] For Pomeroy and his generation, the conclusion was clear: "Representative government is a failure."[46]

If representative democracy had failed, what should come next? Two paths seemed open. The people might bypass their corrupt representatives and rule directly. Or they might preserve representative democracy but change its rulers. If somehow people who were beyond self-interest came to control the government, representative democracy might yet be saved, but only by the suppression of the special interests and the ascendancy of those with the common good in mind.

The Progressives enunciated a revolution in ideas that sought to foster a revolution in reality.[47] They rejected root and branch the Madisonian vision of politics that undergirded the Constitution of 1789. They redefined freedom and natural rights as selfishness and class oppression. To guide the new world that was emerging, they articulated their own alternative vision of politics.

The Progressive Vision

Social collectives mattered first and last for this group. For example, Albion Small at the University of Chicago analyzed society entirely in collective terms. For Small, society was composed of social bonds that lead to collective achievements. Small's evolutionary view claimed that the first stage of human development was control over nature or "mere economic achievement" understood as control over material resources. The second stage was the control humans "have gained and may gain over themselves as individuals." Small's third and highest level reveals a control of "the types of co-operation which they have achieved and may achieve," a control that eventually leads to "progressively higher ranges of achievement."[48] Society comes first, and individuals gain meaning and value only by virtue of playing their part in the organic social whole. Indeed, the individual is subsumed within the larger collective adventure of achieving "progressively higher ranges of achievement." In contrast to such achievements, mere creation of wealth seemed trivial, an earth-bound concern presuming to limit the unlimited possibilities to be attained by "social co-operation."

Small was not alone among the Progressives. Fellow sociologist Charles Horton Cooley argued that society existed independent of the actions and choices of individuals. Society was best conceived as an organism that subsumes the individual: "Our life is all one human whole, and if we are to have any real knowledge of it we must see it as such."[49] For others, such as the political theorist Mary Follett, the group had primacy and society was a collection of groups.[50] The primacy accorded to collectives caused the leading Progressive publicist, Herbert Croly, to argue that Americans should value society as an end in itself.[51]

The Progressives set out a positive concept of freedom: the idea that individual liberty comes from society and its active element, government. They conceived of rights and freedom as powers, the ability to do this or that. Government could confer rights by providing the resources necessary for this positive liberty.[52] The Progressive economist Richard Ely saw "true liberty" as an "expression of the positive powers of the individual," which can develop only in a commonwealth ruled by a "social ethic" that unites "self and others, the individual and society . . . in one purpose." Hence, Progressives lauded the "freedom" to be part of the collective effort: "True liberty means the voluntary sacrifice of self for the common life."[53] A single sentence from the political theorist Arthur Hadley reveals much about this idea of freedom: "It is the ideal of a free community to give liberty wherever people are sufficiently advanced to use it in ways which shall benefit the public, instead of ways which promote their own pleasure at the public expense."[54] For Hadley, the community, not the individual, is free. Moreover, the community grants freedom to its people; individuals do not grant powers to government and retain rights against it. Indeed, liberty is not the natural state of mankind but rather a gift from the state contingent on providing benefits to the public.

Hadley was not the only Progressive demanding the subordination of the individual to the social whole. Albion Small called for an end to American individualism "and corresponding remolding of individuals. . . . We are demanding that each shall fall into the ranks of the social battle."[55] At about the same time Small was writing, a Progressive professor at Stanford University demanded that "industrial liberty, equality of opportunity, must yield in part, at least, to the organic sense of the nation—to fraternity."[56] For Cooley, the individual could be said to be free, "but it is an organic freedom, which he works out in co-operation with others, not a freedom to do things independently of society. It is team-work."[57] Once again, Follett gave direct expression to the Progressive desire to subsume the individual under the collective will: "An individual is one who is being created *by* society, whose daily breath is drawn *from* society, whose life is spent *for* society."[58] The freedom of an individual who lives *for* society could hardly be a freedom from the demands of the state: "Freedom then is the identifying of the individual will with the whole will—the supreme activity of life. . . . The heart of our freedom is the impelling power of the will of the whole." Not surprisingly, a page later Follett calls for "genuine collectivism."[59]

According to this view, the freedom to serve the collective is the freedom to realize one's "higher" or true self. Thus Cooley defined *freedom* as the "opportunity for right development, for development in accordance with the progressive ideal of life that we have in conscience."[60] Freedom does not mean choosing any life that a person might want; it means living in accord with the Progressive ideal of the self, "conceived as something wider than the individual (as the term is normally understood), as a social 'whole' of which the individual is an element or an aspect. . . .This entity is then identified as being the 'true' self which, by imposing its collective, or 'organic,' single will upon its recalcitrant 'members,' achieves its own, and therefore their, 'higher' freedom."[61]

We might pause to pursue the implications of this positive idea of freedom. The First Amendment offers a classic statement of negative liberty: it enjoins the government from abridging individual freedom. It does not "empower" the individual to achieve some good. It does not give the individual the means to speak or to persuade others. It does not direct the government to use speech as a means to some social end. It does not require "good speech" or "polite speech" or ban "negative speech." The language of the First Amendment, like that of the rest of the U.S. Constitution, does not express the Progressive vision of politics, in which a negative freedom of speech, like all other negative freedoms, would be an expression of selfishness and self-interest, the realization of the lower self, a corruption of both the individual and society. In time, Progressives would find this lower self running "negative ads" that advance the interests of candidates putatively at a great cost to democracy. A positive freedom of speech, on the other hand, would be the power to transcend selfishness in service to the social whole. From the start, Progressives saw true freedom of speech as a means to realize social ends, an instrument to achieve a higher social good. Conversely, speech in service to self-interest had no claim to protection against a government seeking the common good. For that reason, the Progressive vision was at odds with Madison's emphasis on speech and struggle as a means to discover the public interest.

The Progressives were "nationalist to the core."[62] The American nation constituted the most encompassing social whole that concretely affected individuals. It was a "living, formative political principle" that transcended mere legality.[63] It offered liberation from the nation's past and a "call to a larger life" that realized democracy and transcended individualism.[64] The Progressives "articulated an ideal of a national democratic community where equality was achieved more by sharing projects in common and by participating on the basis of equal respect than by being equally protected in one's rights against others."[65] In part, the national community was the social whole that they saw as encompassing all else in the society. They saw their mission as creating a unified American nation capable of great achievements and collective adventures. It would be a nation informed by Progressive public opinion.

Eldon Eisenach notes that during the Progressive Era Americans defined public opinion as majority opinion and majority opinion as the preponderance of individual preferences, expressed primarily through the market or elections.[66] Progressives rejected any entity founded on individual preferences. The sociologist Charles Cooley stipulated that "public opinion is no mere aggregate of separate individual judgments."[67] Rather, it would be a collective judgment and "an engine of social control and transformation" and "the authoritative will of the nation." According to Eisenach, public opinion became "a form of public conscience and therefore a shared commitment to a common good" which became "a new national ideal of American democracy."[68]

Some saw the state as the embodiment of the national community. Their devotion to the national state mixed freely with religious commitment and images. Thus we find the Christian Progressive Samuel Batten stating that "in the last analysis the State is the organized faith of a people" or a "sphere in which the religion of a people finds its full and final expression." As such, the national state would be the means to "the divine social kingdom."[69] Mary Follett provided the most concise, most intellectual, and most revealing account of the Progressive notion of the state:

> The old idea of natural rights postulated the particularist individual; we know now that no such person exists. . . . As an understanding of the group process abolishes 'individual rights,' so it gives us a true definition of liberty. . . . We see that to obey the group which we have helped to make and of which we are an integral part is to be free because we are then obeying ourself. Ideally the state is such a group, actually it is not, but it depends upon us to make it more and more so. The state must be no external authority which restrains and regulates me, but it must be myself acting as the state in every smallest detail of life.[70]

Others were far less mystical and saw a strong national state as a means to positive freedom and the common good. Herbert Croly argued that "genuine liberty"—positive freedom—"could be protected only by an energetic and clear-sighted central government, and it could be fertilized only by the efficient national organizations of American activities."[71] He proposed greater centralization of power in the national state in order to attain the national interest and welfare.[72] Indeed, Croly favored complete control of industry by government.[73] John Dewey believed that the state "must organize the life of its members where the cooperation of every member is necessary for some common good."[74] As the state improved its machinery for expressing "the common interest and purpose," Dewey hoped, Americans would lose their traditional distrust of government.[75]

This movement thus sought a nation bound together by a common good that constituted and guided its political life.[76] The good citizen in such a regime "spontaneously acts according to consciously held—and shared—ideas of the public good." He is "state-oriented" rather than concerned with his own good and seeks to "achieve a larger public good in his actions in every sphere of life."[77] As Dewey put it, "the moral criterion by which to try social institutions and political measures" is "whether a given custom or law sets free individual capacities in such a way as to make them available for the development of the general happiness or the common good."[78] Others identified the common good with a favored distribution of wealth. Croly thought the American state should become "responsible for the subordination of the individual to the demand of a dominant and constructive national purpose," thereby "making itself responsible for a morally and socially desirable distribution of wealth."[79]

Progressives believed that the national community, public opinion, and a strong centralized state would be tools of social reconstruction, created and nurtured by the most advanced thinkers, "a few exceptionally able individuals" who impose their "own purposes and standards" on the "plain people."[80] Public opinion and the government would be the object of which Progressive intellectuals would be the subject. The content of the national will—the nation politically engaged—would follow the "ascendancy of the wise."[81] They were not modest about their right to dominate public opinion. They fancied themselves to be ethical elite who "have at heart the general welfare and know what kinds of conduct will promote this welfare." This elite "stands for an order that is right, one that squares with their instincts of sympathy and fair play." They claimed "special learning beyond the common ken" and imbided a "tradition embodying the ethical elements that have been contributed by the prophets and elite of the past."[82] Similarly, William James, the pragmatist philosopher and Harvard University doyen, said of political reform: "[I]ndividuals of genius show the way and set the patterns, which common people then adopt and follow."[83] Albion Small also believed that the creation of a great nation demanded a common set of beliefs, a common religion created by sociologists to serve as a national bond.[84] Charles Horton Cooley was equally confident that the new social sciences would gradually create both "a system of rational ideals" and social knowledge that would inform the public will and realize Progressivism in practice.[85]

The power accorded educated elites by Progressives had implications for leadership of the new republic. Public offices should be held by those aptly trained in the latest methods of social science. Hence, Mary Follett says of Progressives: "We have long felt that city government should be concentrated in the hands of a few experts. The old idea that any honest citizen was fit for most public offices is rapidly disappearing."[86] Indeed, the Progressives "placed their faith in suprapolitical expertise, confident that management and planning could eliminate societal ills like slums and epidemics."[87] The regulatory state would require experts to understand society and the effects of government regulation. Power would accrue to the expert trained in and motivated by the Progressive vision.[88] The jurisprudence of natural rights thus should give way to a sociological jurisprudence whereby law remakes society with social science.[89] This move toward bureaucratic expertise came at a cost since "[m]odern liberalism was also a form of liberal democracy, but one in which the preexisting values and practices of democracy were attenuated."[90] In general, as Thomas G. West notes, "Progressive intellectuals were deeply suspicious of government by the people, except when the people and their elected representatives were kept far from the actual day-to-day operation of government."[91]

In place of the representative democracy, some Progressives sought "pure democracy, where the people rule themselves."[92] They helped enact the initiative and the referendum in several states, mainly in the West.[93] These devices aimed at providing a way around state legislatures that were presumably corrupted by business and other agents of self-interest. The Progressives did not limit their hopes for direct democracy to the states and localities. Herbert Croly longed for a national direct democracy in which the will of the people embraced a coherent national program of social justice.[94]

It might seem strange that thinkers dedicated to the rule of an ethical elite would embrace direct rule by the people. But it makes sense, all things considered. The will of the people would be a tool of the most advanced thinkers insofar as they had come to dominate public opinion via journalism and scholarship. As agents of the Progressives, the people would rule politics without limit: no longer would musty ideas about individual rights or constitutional government constrain the will of a Progressive majority. Herbert Croly lamented constitutional constraints on majority rule, the very constraints Madison had offered as a reason to adopt the Constitution.[95] No doubt Progressives believed that a suitably enlightened public opinion would guide majorities and thereby avoid the older concerns about tyranny.[96] Yet in their vision no one had any rights, especially not minorities. Croly's sanguine assessment of the possibility of majority tyranny is thus not surprising.

Progressivism and Free Speech

In the forty years prior to World War I, Progressive intellectuals had few occasions to deal with free speech issues. The Supreme Court largely denied free speech claims for much of this time, and the Progressives did not need to consider whether their general antipathy toward individualism and rights against government justified state control of speech.[97] They had enunciated a vision of politics that wholly denied the foundations of the First Amendment. Freedom of speech could not be a natural or constitutional right against government because no one had any rights against government, which itself had been redefined as the agent of the common good and the national community. Moreover, insofar as speech gave voice to self-interest (especially economic self-interest), they saw selfishness and the threat of corruption.

The question implicit in Progressive theory was how far government might go to organize political speech and bring it in line with the common good or social welfare. Roscoe Pound, a leading legal mind during the Progressive Era, argued that free speech was just another interest to be put on the judicial scale in the balancing of interests carried out by the law.[98] In cases involving dissent during wartime and the speech of the urban poor, Pound called for restrictions on free speech to attain the social interest.[99] John Dewey saw no value in free speech unless it was in service to what he called "positive social reconstruction." Dewey criticized pacifists who dissented against American participation in World War I, arguing that the struggle presented a fine opportunity to advance the Progressive cause. He specifically decried the pacifist reliance on "the sanctity of individual rights and constitutional guaranties." As the legal historian David Rabban puts it, Dewey "simply extended to free speech his general aversion to individual constitutional rights."[100]

Croly provided the most candid and insightful passage about the place of free speech in the Progressive vision. He noted that national policies will help and harm citizens "according to their special interests and opinions." Those who are harmed "have every right and should be permitted every opportunity to protest in the most vigorous and persistent manner." Yet for Croly that right to protest was not an unconditional right against government suppression; it "must conform to certain conditions." The protests must not lead to disobeying the law. Moreover, "when private interests are injured by the national policy, the protestants must be able to show that either such injuries are unnecessary, or else they involve harm to an essential public interest." [101] Croly took for granted the Progressive assumption that national policy represents the common good or public interest. Speech in defense of private interests must show that the public interest can be attained without harming those interests or that the private interests in question implicate some other public interest that is at stake. He began, in other words, with what might be called a presumption of the public interest, rather than a presumption of individual liberty.

Let us unfold the implications of Croly's conditions. Speech in defense of private interests per se—what might be called "selfish speech" in a Progressive lexicon—does not meet Croly's condition for legitimate protest. For his generation, citizens who wish to speak in defense of self-interest bear a burden of proof: they must show that their speech implicates some other public interest or is relevant to attaining the public interest at issue. For Croly political speech is not really free. In order to be permitted, speech must show how the private interest at stake conforms to some public interest. Individuals must prove that their speech is of social value; everyone must talk the language of the public interest and must do so in situations where the national policy at stake is presumed to represent the public interest. In fact, Croly misled his readers. He did not really favor "vigorous and persistent" protest against government action. He did argue for permitting speech that conforms to conditions set by Croly, speaking, presumably, on behalf of the nation. What happens to other speech? He did not say. But it did not serve the common good and thus played no useful role in society. Croly perhaps did not argue explicitly for suppressing such speech, but the conditions he sets for speech are little more than muttering, "Have I no friend will rid me of this living fear?" [102] Given that no one in a Progressive democracy had any right to speak out against government policy, "selfish speech" had no claim to toleration. [103]

The political vision set out to this point was written largely prior to World War I. It led Dewey and others to support suppression of speech in the national interest. The actions of the federal government after the war—the Red scare of the 1920s and the Palmer raids, conducted against dissent—alarmed Progressives; they came to see the state as a threat to civil liberties, a threat that should be limited by the social interest in free speech.[104] The experience of the 1920s fostered in them a commitment to freedom of speech for a number of years thereafter. But that commitment, like most if not all political commitments, arose also from other experiences. As one law professor has remarked:

> It is important to remember that for most of America's history, protecting free speech has helped marginalized or unpopular groups to gain political power and influence. The first amendment normally has been the friend of left wing values, whether it was French émigrés and Republicans in the 1790s, abolitionists in the 1840s, pacifists in the 1910s, organized labor in the 1920s and 1930s, or civil rights protesters in the 1950s and 1960s. We should remember too that during the ACLU's early years the organization represented mainly draft resisters and labor organizers. . . . So the historical connections between left politics and free speech in this country are obvious.[105]

As late as the Nixon administration, freedom of speech seemed to be in the interest of Progressive politics, as in the case of the Pentagon Papers.[106] Indeed, for much of that time, most Americans would have thought of free speech as a Progressive cause as a matter of conviction as well as interest. For some adherents of this cause today, a strong commitment to free speech, including a commitment to liberalism in campaign finance matters, remains. But they make up a small minority; to be Progressive now is to foster an expectation of support for restrictions on campaign finance.[107] That support for restrictions represents in part a triumph of theory over experience. In rejecting a right to free speech, Progressives today are affirming their older faith that governing means arranging a society, including its political activity, according to the correct idea of the common good. This dominant vision of governing has no room for limits on state power such as individual rights or freedom of speech. Understanding how this movement became so illiberal requires some attention to how the First Amendment relates to private property.

From 1890 to 1936, the Supreme Court often voided state and national regulations concerning economic activity on the basis of substantive due process. For example, the state of New York enacted a law limiting the number of hours a baker could work. In *Lochner v. New York,* a majority of the Supreme Court found that the measure was an arbitrary interference with the liberty of contract. The substance of the regulation—the legislative determination of how long bakers could work—unjustifiably violated a liberty recognized by the Fourteenth Amendment (which applied the due process protections of the Fifth Amendment to New York).[108] Such restraints on government regulation of the economy, of course, contravened Progressive doctrine and engendered much hostility from legislators. For three decades after *Lochner,* the Court continued in some measure to restrain government attempts to restrict economic liberty. Judicial resistance broke down, however, during the New Deal.[109]

In 1923 Congress passed the Filled Milk Act, which proscribed shipping via interstate commerce skimmed milk compounded with any fat or oil other than milk fat so as to resemble milk or cream.[110] The prohibition was challenged as a violation of the Fifth Amendment's due process provision. In other words, the plaintiffs contended that Congress had restricted economic liberty without justification. The Supreme Court rejected the challenge. In the famous fourth footnote to its decision in *Carolene Products,* the Court vindicated Congress's control over the fat content of milk by effectively denying all restrictions on state control of the economy: "[R]egulatory legislation affecting ordinary commercial transactions is not to be pronounced unconstitutional unless in the light of the facts made known or generally assumed it is of such a character as to preclude the assumption that it rests upon some rational basis within the knowledge and experience of the legislators."[111] After 1938, "ordinary commercial transactions" had no constitutional protections from sane legislators (in practice, no constitutional protections at all).

The *Carolene Products* footnote also adumbrated a new role for the Supreme Court in American politics. Rather than judging the wisdom of government regulation of the economy, the Court would be the umpire of the political process.[112] As such, the Court would strike down government actions "when legislation appears on its face to be within a specific prohibition of the Constitution, such as those of the first ten amendments."[113]

With this footnote, the New Deal Court had fashioned a two-tier theory of rights said to be in the U.S. Constitution. The lower tier, which henceforth would receive little, if any, protection from Congress, included the rights to own and use private property. The higher tier included rights such as free speech and other civil liberties along with protections against discrimination. The Court assumed that "the citizens' ability to engage in sustained social criticism and vote their rulers out would prevent a powerful state from becoming a tyrannical one."[114] It mattered little to the *Carolene Products* majority that "the distinction between property rights and personal liberties runs counter to the Framers' belief that rights are closely related and that the protection of property ownership is essential to the enjoyment of political liberty."[115] Instead of constitutional rights, Americans would have a guarantee of political self-help, though of course majorities bent on "wicked and improper projects" (in the words of Federalist no. 10) would not be constrained by the judiciary. As a later Progressive has written of the post–*Carolene Products* world: "No longer did constitutional principles enshrining limited government and the protection of property constrain the ability of politically dominant groups to reallocate resources in their favor [because] the Court in the modern era no longer feared that political power may be used to exploit the propertied classes."[116]

The First Amendment does specifically say that Congress shall "make no law abridging the freedom of speech" and other kinds of political activity. The New Deal Court and its progeny were thus committed to protecting free speech, a position fully in line with Progressive politics and interests after World War I. That support for speech, however, could not be cleanly separated from the Progressives' skepticism about private property, as a brief example shows. Once or twice per week David Broder is paid to write his *Washington Post* column on a computer owned by his employers. His column is printed at a factory owned by the *Post.* A *Post* employee who drives a truck owned by the newspaper delivers it to my apartment. David Broder's free speech implies at every point along the way a right to the unimpeded use of private property including the ordinary commercial transactions of paying Broder, the driver, and the employees of the printer. If the federal government declared that the *Post* could not use its property to print or deliver newspapers or prohibited paying Broder or the others anything more than one-half the minimum wage, the government would be regulating nothing but private property and ordinary commercial transactions. Yet such restrictions would certainly end Broder's column by hook or crook. Broder's property in his ideas requires the freedom of others to use their property as they wish if free speech in the United States is to be more than an empty promise.[117]

In politics, the way one frames an issue matters a great deal. The *Carolene Products* Court distinguished speech from property and promised protections for the former but not the latter. Yet as time passed and circumstances changed, many Progressives came to assimilate political speech to private property and concluded that the former should be as open to regulation as the latter. This revised understanding found public expression most clearly in the late 1960s and early 1970s in the writings of the most important entrepreneur of "reform" and of Supreme Court justices.

The Founding of the "Reform Community"

John W. Gardner was the nexus between the Progressive vision of politics and the political realities of campaign finance regulation. Gardner's life spanned almost all of the twentieth century, but it is fair to say that the height of his political influence and success came from 1965 to 1977. In 1965 Gardner became Secretary of Health, Education, and Welfare, the general overseeing the war on poverty at its height. He left the federal government in 1968 to head the National Urban Coalition, a group seeking solutions to the problems of race and poverty. In 1970 he founded Common Cause, a group that continues to influence Congress with regard to campaign finance issues.[118] Gardner wrote several books over the course of three decades. I consider two dealing with campaign finance: *The Recovery of Confidence* (1970) and *In Common Cause* (1972). These books share many themes and one large difference.

Both books are very much of their time. They are informed by a sense of impending apocalypse, a moment when the nation might become fundamentally and forever different. For Gardner, this crisis could be traced to a decline in shared values and common purposes, a decline that was not tolerable: "We are seeing the breakdown of established patterns without the emergence of viable new ones. . . . The consequences in loss of shared principle and purpose, in social and individual breakdown, in sheer disorder, are apparent to all."[119] More broadly, the decline of a civilization—even the American one—comes not from military defeats as much as "an erosion of shared commitment and an erosion of confidence."[120]

The most important response to this crisis should be a recovery of a sense of common purposes. Because "a nation is held together by shared values, shared beliefs, shared attitudes," Americans must "arrive at some common conception of what that civilization might stand for." The elements of this vision turn out to be "deep in our tradition and our being." According to Gardner, the nation wants "peace, justice, liberty . . . a society that honors the dignity of each person and proscribes the oppression of one by another . . . equal opportunity, equal access to the benefits of the society, an end to exclusion of some citizens . . . the fulfillment of the individual, the release of human potential . . . individual responsibility and the opportunities for participation . . . to restore a sense of community and to foster honest, open, and compassionate relations between people." The list of what citizens want becomes larger and more demanding: "We seek for each individual the chance to be a whole person, free of the fragmentation that plagues modern life . . . we want a society that puts human values above materialism, commercialism, technology, and the success ethic. We seek an end to the dehumanizing aspects of large-scale organization. We seek an end to the destruction of the natural environment." [121]

Gardner identifies the public interest with a concrete list of items on the Progressive policy agenda circa 1969: spending on education, housing, guaranteed employment, and job training. [122] At another point he lays out a policy agenda that includes peace in Vietnam, an end to discrimination, a "relentless attack on poverty," major tax reform, reallocation of resources among levels of government, an end to corruption, and "new solutions in housing, employment, education, health, pollution control, law enforcement, and the administration of justice." [123] He devotes more than 20 percent of *The Recovery of Confidence* to an appendix containing a policy agenda for the realization of "our" shared values. The agenda— tellingly titled "What to Do about the Cities"—offers essentially a Progressive policy wish list of the era. [124]

In Common Cause also contains much talk about the common good. Gardner seems to identify the public interest in Madisonian terms as the outcome of a process: "It is precisely in the political forum that free citizens can have their say, trade out their differences, and identify their shared purposes." [125] Gardner's idea of the common good does not appear to be known prior to a process of speech and bargaining that leads to a sense of shared purpose. Elsewhere, however, Gardner explicitly rejects Madison's political ideal because "[v]ery often the public interest is not served." What evidence does he offer for this claim? Political struggles in the cities "have not somehow balanced out to produce wise and far-seeing urban solutions." Similarly, struggle has not served "the public interest in clean air and water." [126] In other words, we know the public interest has not been served because the Progressive agenda enunciated in *The Recovery of Confidence* has not become law. Gardner was confused as a matter of logic: he argued that a substantive notion of the public interest is both an outcome of the political process and a prior standard by which we can judge the integrity of that process. Like earlier Progressives, he thus offered an incoherent idea of the common good.

Yet Gardner seems to go against Progressivism in his regard for the individual. His cardinal values include fulfillment of the individual. He also notes that "all discussions of the vitality of societies and institutions must eventually come back to the individual."[127] Moreover, he worries that all societies are headed for what he calls "the beehive model," which moves "toward ever greater dominance of the system's purposes over individual purposes." Yet these appearances of individualism are misleading. Gardner's ideal society, the society capable of continuous renewal, "will be one that develops to the full its human resources, that removes obstacles to individual fulfillment." Note the assumption: individual fulfillment is the means (human resources) to attain larger social purposes. Gardner quotes H. A. Murray approvingly to the effect that "individuality is something to be built for the sake of something else." In fact, the individual attains his fulfillment through "shared values, a sense of community, a concern for the total enterprise, a sense of identity and belonging, and the opportunity to serve."[128] Like Albion Small and other earlier Progressives, Gardner believed that individuals find their end in the social whole.

If the public interest is known but not realized in law, something has gone wrong with the political process. That something is, in fact, someone: "the innumerable vested interests frustrate and subvert plans for the common good."[129] In *The Recovery of Confidence* Gardner was far more concerned to elucidate his idea of the public interest than to denounce the special interests. But the older Progressive condemnation of selfishness and self-interest does appear in the book. Hence, we are told early on that America is threatened "by chiselers, by bigots, by extremists, by vested interests, and by the paralyzing lassitude of well-fed citizens."[130] The last term is interesting. In 1970 Gardner blamed "solid citizens" for blocking the changes he associated with the public interest for reasons of apathy and self-interest.[131] At that time, he was wary of blaming the ills of the country on a single miscreant, even a special interest.[132]

Two years later, he was more certain about the enemies of the public interest. Special interest groups and "behind the scenes operators" distort policy and subvert the common good.[133] The shortcomings of the solid citizen are not mentioned in *In Common Cause*. Instead, Gardner paints a picture of a wholly corrupted polity undone by money in politics: "[M]ost of the political process has become, behind the scenes, a vast game of barter and purchase involving campaign contributions, appointments to high office, business favors, favorable legal decisions, favorable location of defense installations."[134] Indeed, citizens no longer have any say in policymaking: "It isn't just that money talks. It talks louder and longer and drowns out the citizen's hoarse whisper." Hence democracy has been betrayed by unequal wealth: "All citizens should have equal access to decisionmaking processes of government, but money makes some citizens more equal than others." The rich are coming to have an "increased capacity to influence the public process through the power of money."[135] Gardner thus offers a story of decline and fall: a nation that should be constituted by a common commitment to the values of Progressivism has been undone by special interests and their money. What is to be done?

In 1970 Gardner had one solution to our political ills: leadership. He thought the middle class was not "a stubbornly conservative force" because "under vigorous and imaginative leadership [it] will support forward-looking policies."[136] By the time he wrote *In Common Cause,* he looked for leadership from a new elite of citizen action groups working outside the system: "Only on the rarest occasions are significant new directions in public policy initiated by the legislature, or by the bureaucracy, or by the parties. They are initiated by the people—not "The People" taken collectively, but by vigorous and forward-looking elements within the body politic. Or they are initiated by the special interests."[137] To be sure, Gardner points out that the citizen groups should not think of themselves as a new elite.[138] Caveats notwithstanding, Gardner echoes the Progressive call for an ethical elite to shape politics and public opinion. Now, however, the ethical elite will form citizens' action groups to advocate for the public interest, and above all, to replace the private financing of electoral campaigns with public financing.[139]

John W. Gardner was an accomplished political organizer and prolific writer. His affirmations and his negations show him to have been a quintessential Progressive in style and content. He disdained selfishness, private interests, affluent citizens, political apathy, and money in politics, all of which he believed to be fostering the decline and fall of the nation. The nation—or at least, Gardner's conception of the United States—is constituted by a conception of the common good or public interest that encompasses the values and policies of the Progressivism of the late 1960s. Finally, a reader searches in vain in Gardner's writing for any sympathy for the Madisonian vision. He simply ignores the whole tradition of individual rights and limited government in favor of the raw assertion that the tradition favors Progressive values.

He contended that Congress's failure to enact such an agenda was a sign of the corruption of representation by money and the special interests. This implies that most Americans prefer Progressive policies and yet have been frustrated by the political process. Another hypothesis that might explain the failure of that agenda would be that most Americans do not support it. For example, when Gardner was writing in 1972, only about 18 percent of Americans identified themselves as liberals, a proportion that on average would remain the same for the next three decades.[140] The number of Americans who were "afraid the government in Washington is getting too powerful for the good of the country and the individual person" had on the whole been rising and would continue to do so until 1980.[141] Support for health insurance provided by the government was falling and would continue declining for more than a decade.[142] The number of Americans who thought the government should provide every citizen with a job and a stipulated income was in free fall from a low level of initial support.[143] In 1970 and 1972, more people believed minorities should be expected to help themselves than believed the government should "make every possible effort" to improve their position.[144] The data do not even support Gardner's laments about low levels of political participation. Looked at over a fifty-year period, almost all measures of political participation were at their zenith just at the moment of Gardner's laments.[145] At the same time, the public did support a few of Gardner's positions, such as environmentalism.[146]

When he wrote *In Common Cause,* most aspects of John Gardner's conception of the public interest were not shared by a majority (or anywhere near a majority) of Americans. We therefore would not expect that in a democracy the legislature would enact a policy agenda that reflected Gardner's conception of the public interest. He concluded, however, that the failure of his political faith proved the corruption of the political process. For his "reformers," money and the special interests had become (and would remain) a convenient scapegoat for the political failure of the Progressive agenda in the early 1970s and thereafter.

Yet Gardner's story is somewhat more complicated. Although he clearly identified the public interest with his political views, he also thought the American people could be brought to share his views and values via leadership and citizen action. In a few cases, his preferred policies did attain public support. On the other hand, few if any politicians now run for office to enact the urban agenda or to fight a war on poverty. The public has little taste for such policies.

Therein lies the irony in Gardner's writings. In *The Recovery of Confidence,* the struggle against money in politics had nothing to do with the struggle to revive a sense of the common interest in the United States. Two years later, campaign finance law was a means to realize the larger Progressive agenda and to mobilize citizen action. It was a part (and far from the most important part) of Gardner's agenda. But the restriction of campaign finance was the part that survived the Darwinian struggle of political ideas and interests. Apart from environmentalism, the only aspect of Gardner's agenda that has garnered long-term public support and legislative action has been this restriction.[147] That result suggests that whether the nation extensively regulated money in politics has little bearing on the success or failure of the Progressive policy agenda. Absent his substantive policy agenda, his legacy to American politics has been a certain style of political struggle that has enjoyed considerable formal success. Gardner demonized the special interests and their money in pursuit of his ideal of the public interest. Campaign finance reformers in our time simply demonize the special interests and their filthy money. Abusing fellow citizens no doubt brings political victories. Whether such demonization will foster Gardner's original hope for "a common conception of what [American] civilization might stand for" remains doubtful.

In the end, Gardner was an optimist. The special interests and their money were a problem for the nation and an obstacle to realizing his idea of the public interest. But he did not call for their suppression. In fact, he argued, "We need the special interest groups, but we also need a strong voice for the public interest."[148] Some Progressives who would take up the struggle to restrict campaign finance were not so tolerant.

Contemporary Progressivism

In 1971 Congress passed the Federal Election Campaign Act, which restricted the amount a candidate for the presidency, the vice presidency, the House, or the Senate could spend on broadcasting time and on other political advertising; the law also mandated disclosure of campaign contributions and expenditures. In 1974, Congress greatly amended the 1971 law. Among other things, Congress replaced the limits on media spending with comprehensive limits on spending for each election by candidates and parties. The 1974 law also enacted limits on campaign contributions for groups, parties, and individuals.[149]

In *Buckley* the Court tried to have it both ways in assessing the 1974 campaign finance restrictions. On one hand, it decided that expending money on elections deserved the protection of the First Amendment, thereby invalidating Congress's effort to limit electoral spending. On the other, the Court decided that the freedom to give money to campaigns was rather like the economic liberties shorn from the Constitution in the late 1930s: campaign contributions did not enjoy the full protection of the First Amendment. Here we might pause to look at *Buckley* through the lens of *Carolene Products*.

In that light, *Buckley* is somewhat odd. The Court gave full First Amendment protection to political activity (campaign spending) that most resembles "ordinary commercial transactions" while denying any help to an activity (contributing to campaigns) that arguably least resembles "ordinary commercial transactions." In part, the Court managed that paradox by redefining donating to campaigns as an "ordinary commercial transaction," an exchange of a contribution for a political favor.

On the other hand, the Progressive commitment to equality fared poorly in *Buckley*. Defenders saw the law as a constitutional way of "equalizing the relative ability of individuals and groups to influence the outcome of elections." The Court emphatically disagreed: "[T]he concept that government may restrict the speech of some elements of our society in order to enhance the relative voice of others is wholly foreign to the First Amendment."[150] Promoting equality of influence could not justify limiting constitutional rights.

One could interpret the *Buckley* opinion as a compromise that sought to honor both the theory and the practice of Progressivism with regard to free speech. The voiding of spending limits spoke to free speech concerns while the affirmation of contribution limits regulated and restricted the use of private property. Progressives saw the decision quite differently:

> One could argue that free speech in a situation of radically unequal economic power is not free speech at all because it is skewed by the preexisting distribution of property. That is to say, in our country the power of persons to put their messages across loudly and repeatedly because of their economic power and influence effectively silences other, excluded and marginalized voices. The long term effect of the unequal distribution of power and property is an unequal exposure of particular ideas, and the stifling and co-opting of more radical and imaginative ideas about politics and society.[151]

This part of the decision redefines the interest at stake in Progressive political practice.[152] By permitting spending on speech, the state permits inequalities that effectively silence people with "more radical and imaginative ideas." Whereas the First Amendment assumes that no one possesses the truth prior to politics, Progressives embrace both equality and a hierarchy of truth in politics. Inequality marks the current system of speech: the economically powerful repress the excluded and marginalized. But the latter are also the bearers of truth. Some political ideas are more correct than others. Permitting freedom of speech means permitting the powerful (and incorrect) to triumph over the powerless (and correct), inequality understood as corruption. Governing well, on the other hand, means arranging political speech so that the last would be first and truth would win out over falsity. Important and influential Progressives came to believe in the 1980s that supporting free speech no longer advanced their political interest.[153] Absent that interest, their traditional theme of state control in pursuit of the common interest would be applied to political speech.[154]

This remarkable passage recalls the traditional Progressive hostility to a strong right to private property. But it does more than that. Contemporary Progressives tear down the wall built in *Carolene Products* between property and free speech. *Buckley* tied speech to property and concluded (so far as spending was concerned) that the government could not regulate speech. They agree that property is tied to speech but conclude the opposite: property that is speech should be as free of constitutional protections (and as subject to state control) as all other private property after *Carolene Products*. These theorists equate *Buckley*'s protection of free speech with the protection of private property as enunciated in *Lochner v. New York*. [155] They believe that *Buckley*'s limits on government control of campaign finance (like the limits on economic regulation in *Lochner*) will be eliminated as part of an emerging New Deal for speech and politics. Just as the New Deal expanded state control of economic markets and private property, contemporary Progressives call for expanding government control of speech to further "free speech values." [156] Several theorists have adumbrated this New Deal for speech, thereby articulating the Progressive vision of politics for our time.[157]

The New Deal for Speech

Contemporary Progressives, like their predecessors, reject the idea of individual rights as a limit on government. Government should be unlimited in its powers and its pursuit of the common interest, a mission that certainly includes subordinating property rights and might well include freedom of speech or political rights.[158] So defined, the central questions of politics become, what purposes will the plenary state pursue, and what justifies those purposes and not others? For a long time, Progressives thought of free speech as "an essential social instrument through which citizens could be assured of a continual ability to rationally and collectively plan for a better world."[159] They therefore supported protecting speech from state control. But what would happen if this freedom no longer helped people "rationally and collectively plan for a better world"?

They are much more forthright in rejecting the First Amendment as a prohibition on state action. Owen Fiss argues that free speech should be regulated to advance "the larger political purposes attributed to the First Amendment."[160] Similarly, Cass Sunstein asserts that the language of the First Amendment cannot be a restraint on power: "In a regime of property rights, there is no such thing as no regulation of speech; the question is what forms of regulation best serve the purposes of the free speech guarantee."[161] Consequently, Sunstein argues that restrictions on campaign finance should be assessed "pragmatically in terms of their consequences for the system of free expression."[162]

Fiss and Sunstein stand the First Amendment on its head. Instead of a right constraining government power over speech, the First Amendment becomes a rationale for expanding the ambit of the state with regard to political activities including political speech. This instrumental interpretation runs counter to the clear words and the prohibitions of the First Amendment, which does not mention Progressive goals, let alone make fundamental liberties a means to those ends. But Fiss's and Sunstein's arbitrary interpretations of the First Amendment fit well within the Progressive tradition both in their hostility to individual rights and limited government and in their pragmatic desire to make all of society a means to a common good attained by state action.[163] Once the Constitution became an instrument of, rather than a constraint on, political power, the only question became whether free speech advanced the Progressive project. Once it did not, its premises led to repressive conclusions.

Egalitarian Democracy

Owen Fiss argues that chief among "the larger political purposes" of the First Amendment should be "rich public debate" understood as "a debate on issues of public importance that is, to use Justice Brennan's now-classic formula, uninhibited, robust, and wide-open." Such debate is "an essential precondition for democratic government."[164] Yet democratic government is not the final purpose of restricting speech. Such restrictions and the ensuing debate are conditions for "true and free collective self-determination" that enables a people to be "truly free."[165] Sunstein believes that restrictions on First Amendment rights should seek the "central constitutional goal of creating a deliberative democracy."[166] In such a system, "new information and perspectives influence social judgments about possible courses of action." Beyond that, the system of free expression should sustain "broad and deep attention to public issues" as well as "public exposure to an appropriate diversity of view." Sunstein believes that contemporary America does not do well on either score: speech is rarely serious, and "dissenting views from the right and left" have a hard time being heard.[167]

Beyond the quality of speech, contemporary Progressives evince an abiding concern for equality. Sunstein's deliberative democracy is based on the norm of political equality, which means "every person counts as no more or no less than one." Practically speaking, that principle means that economic inequalities may not be translated into political inequalities "in the form of wide disparities in political expenditures."[168] Edward Foley assumes that electoral politics should "determine how wealth should be distributed among society's members." Elections, however, should be free of the influence of the existing distribution of wealth. Yet money pays for advertising that convinces undecided voters, thereby affecting the outcome of elections. If wealthy citizens are permitted to use their wealth in campaigns and elections, Foley argues, the outcomes will be biased in their favor and "against the political objectives of the poor." If they are to be fair, elections must provide equal resources for all citizens.[169] Fiss similarly complains that "the economically powerful" use their property to dominate and to distort (and thus depreciate) public debate.[170] For the new Progressives, a rich public debate will be one where the wealthy are heard less often, if at all.

Implications for Campaign Finance

What means are required to attain a rich, deliberative public debate? Contemporary Progressives often favor financing of campaigns and politics by the taxpayer. Sunstein calls for "full or fuller public financing."[171] Foley proposes that "the Constitution should guarantee that all voters receive equal financial resources for the purpose of participating in electoral politics."[172] Yet subsidies alone will not be adequate to attain political equality. If the poor receive public money to spend on elections, they will have to be forced to spend it for that purpose or equality will not be achieved. If some citizens (let us call them "the rich") decide to spend more than others even taking into account the public subsidy, the government will have to restrain the spending of the rich or give more money to the poor. Given the thin public support for taxpayer financing, the path of restriction will be the path of equality.

Fiss is candid about the restrictions he has in mind: "A commitment to rich public debate will allow and sometimes even require the state to act in these ways, however elemental and repressive they might at first seem. Autonomy will be sacrificed, and content regulation sometimes allowed, but only on the assumption that public debate might be enriched and our capacity for collective self-determination enhanced."[173] The liberty to engage in politics thus "may be protected, but only when it enriches public debate."[174] Fiss urges the Courts to allow or even require government to "restrict the speech of some elements of our society in order to enhance the relative voice of others." Indeed, he argues that "expenditures of political actors might have to be curbed to make certain all views are heard."[175] True to his analysis of the problem of speech, the elements to be repressed are "the economically powerful." He thus has a "clear view" of who if not what should be included in the public debate.[176]

The consistent egalitarian also faces the perplexity that newspapers and the media generally both spend money on political speech and enjoy First Amendment protections against government control of their speech. Like Fiss, Edward Foley is candid about his illiberalism. Political equality, Foley avers, requires forbidding "newspapers from using their resources to publish editorials that support or oppose a candidate or ballot initiative. In this respect, equal-dollars-per-voter [Foley's egalitarian proposal] treats newspapers and other media enterprises in exactly the same way that it treats all other nonelectoral organizations (including corporations and labor unions)." Lobbying of public officials would also be prohibited eventually as the next stage in progress toward political equality.[177] Citizens would be permitted to publish their views about justice and other political topics provided they did not support or oppose a candidate for office or a ballot referendum. Presumably if their discussions did concern both opinions about political topics and electioneering, they could not be published in an egalitarian society.[178]

Critical readers may suspect that I have misled them about the nature of the Progressive vision in our time. They might wonder whether I have chosen a few extreme views that do not represent Progressive thinking, thereby fashioning a straw man that later will be criticized and rejected. After all, political thinkers who end up openly calling for government repression of the political activities of their opponents or censorship of the media are, by most measures, extremists.

But I have not misled the reader. These contemporary thinkers are not marginal figures in American life. Fiss, Sunstein, and Foley are professors at leading law schools and count among the most respected authorities on constitutional law and campaign finance in the United States. These pillars of the legal establishment echo and explicate themes that have marked Progressive thought for more than century: on one hand, a skepticism about individual rights, limited government, and private property, and on the other, an aspiration to the common good via expansive government. To be sure, their subordination of free speech to the common good represents avant-garde Progressive legal thinking about money in politics, but that is exactly the point of examining their work in detail. We may reasonably expect that their innovations in theory may one day become the accepted practices of Progressive judges and politicians.

Their words and arguments have had influence. Supreme Court justice Stephen Breyer has argued that "the First Amendment's constitutional role is not simply one of protecting the individual's 'negative' freedom from governmental restraint." Instead, judges should put more emphasis on "people's right to 'an active and constant participation in collective power.'" For Breyer, the First Amendment fosters this right to collective participation by encouraging "the exchange of ideas needed to make sound electoral decisions and by encouraging an exchange of views among ordinary citizens necessary to their informed participation in the electoral process." Restrictions on campaign finance, in Breyer's view, serve the same purpose as the First Amendment. The laws "hope to democratize the influence that money can bring to bear upon the electoral process, thereby building public confidence in that process, broadening the base of a candidate's meaningful financial support, . . . encouraging greater public participation [and] help[ing] to further the kind of open public political discussion that the First Amendment also seeks to encourage, not simply as an end, but also as a means to achieve a workable democracy."[179] To be sure, Breyer appreciates negative liberty and is aware of the dangers of regulating speech and campaign finance.[180] In any case, political prudence might lead a sitting Supreme Court justice to avoid calling for suppression of disfavored groups. But if political speech is a means to the higher end of "rich public debate," one might wonder why the sacrifice of autonomy and content regulation would be impermissible, provided they bore a rational relation to fostering improved political participation. Fiss, unlike Breyer, had the courage to follow the premises of contemporary Progressivism to their logical and illiberal conclusions.

Knowledge, Interest, Power

Earlier we saw how the Madisonian vision addressed the problems of knowledge, interest, and power that confront humans engaged in political life. I now ask the same questions of the Progressive vision of politics. That might seem unfair. These questions are central to natural rights arguments, and Progressives rejected such thinking root and branch. In considering these questions, however, I am not demanding that they reach conclusions that support natural rights. But the questions do confront any political order, and it is fair to examine the answers to them offered by Progressivism.

Knowledge

Criticism of natural rights notwithstanding, the older Progressives, like Madisonians, seemed skeptical that anyone knows the answer to political questions apart from a process that provides answers that were not known prior to the process. John Dewey compared democracy to a continual scientific experiment, a collective adventure in learning informed by testing our commitments against experience.[181] This democratic and pragmatic effort would presumably make use of personal and local knowledge. Pragmatists argue that truth, including political truth, should be judged by what works. But knowing what works implies standards of success and failure which may be procedural or substantive. Let's imagine we are committed to majority rule. Whatever a majority decides is a proper process and its decision thus compose "what works." In contrast, if we are committed to the substantive goal of equality of wealth, a majority decision to cut taxes that leads to more inequality will be judged a failure. Progressives appear to be committed to procedures as the standard for what works in politics. On the other hand, from start they believed that an ethical elite comprising individuals of genius and social scientists both knew the common good and should shape the content of public opinion to conform to that ideal.

The tension between process and substance, between the many and the few, and between local and centralized knowledge continues in the Progressivism of our day.

Like Dewey, contemporary Progressives seem to focus on the process of democracy. They claim to know how we should go about democracy, not what should be said in our public debates or what conclusions should be reached by citizens. This focus on procedures appears compatible with the Madisonian view: both claim knowledge of the proper process for democracy but leave the debates and the conclusions to that proper procedure. For example, the call for a rich public debate and its sibling deliberative democracy seems to concern only the form and not the content of public debate. Accordingly, Owen Fiss asserts that "the duty of the state is to preserve the integrity of public debate—in much the same way as a great teacher—not to indoctrinate, not to advance the 'Truth,' but to safeguard the conditions for true and free collective self-determination." [182] Edward Foley also might say that his vision of political equality only requires giving citizens the means to participate in elections while not dictating what they do or say with the resources provided.

Professions of neutrality aside, Progressives did and do have a substantive agenda to impose on political debate. If Fiss foresees regulation of the content of speech, someone must know what the right and wrong content of speech is and act accordingly. Progressives are rather clear about who speaks falsely: the economically powerful and the wealthy, who promote views that distort the political process. They expect that repressing conservative views will advance nonconservative views, leading in the end to different outcomes in elections and policymaking. We should not be surprised to find two leading political theorists arguing that deliberative democracy requires taxpayer financing of campaigns, which would then cause a redistribution of wealth from the advantaged to the disadvantaged. [183] What seemed to be a reform of the political process is a means to a substantive political agenda focusing on the proper (that is, more egalitarian) pattern of the distribution of wealth in a society. [184]

These abstractions might seem far removed from the gritty realities of campaign finance. In fact, nothing is more important to understanding those realities. In politics, disappointment is a fact of life because of the old truth that "sometimes you win, and sometimes you lose" and because times change and those who once ruled must learn how to be ruled. By assuming they know the right answer to political questions, however much they obscure that assumption by talking about procedure, Progressives preclude the possibility of disappointment for themselves. If the political process leads to outcomes that vary from the Progressive ideal, the process must be distorted in some way, and the source of such distortion will be the rich and their money.

Interest

Contemporary Progressives directly attack the problem of interest in politics. They require anyone entering the political arena to articulate their positions in relation to the public good; assertions of what are called "naked preferences" are not political activity because they do not refer to some conception of the public good. Private interests in politics become "agents of corruption" and thus have no place in a deliberative (that is, true) democracy.[185] Given the history of Progressivism, it is not surprising that current advocates of that vision demand that all speech refer to the common good. Of course, such speech will not be free speech because citizens will not be able to say whatever they might wish to say.

Whatever else might be said about this requirement, it cannot be a solution to the problem of partiality in politics.[186] The question of whether speech is naked self-interest or fully clothed by the common good can only be answered if a person empowered to judge speech knows what such clothing looks like. The judge might apply a procedural standard that the speech must meet in order to be admitted. She could say that speech must refer not to naked preferences but rather to some conception of the public good. For example, she might demand that a trade union representative not say "We should protect our markets from competition to raise the total wealth of trade union members" in favor of saying "We should protect our markets from competition to advance the general welfare by raising incomes." This procedural demand would make dishonesty the price of admittance to the political realm. Indeed, in a world where political participants defend favored policies by evoking naked self-interest, the deliberative democrats would obscure or suppress important information about the true motives behind a policy proposal. But we might wonder whether the world of justification through naked self-interest exists. Those engaged in politics already seek to show how their favored proposals serve some larger national or public good. They do so because such appeals enlarge the coalition behind a proposal and because appeals to self-interest open the way to effective rebuttals.

Progressives might respond that the argument for protectionism might be dressed up in the language of the public good in current debates, but it really is an argument for harming consumers to benefit trade union members. In other words, it is naked self-interest wearing the clothes of the common good. But we know that protectionism masks self-interest because we believe, let us say, that the gains from free trade to consumers outweigh the losses to union members of increased competition. For these reasons, Progressives must either accept nominal professions of devotion to some public good (as a mask for self-interest) or apply a conception of the common good (to preclude self-interest from entering deliberations).

We might expect that a Progressive judge of speech will admit to the political arena an array of conceptions of the common good. But that is far from guaranteed. The philosopher John Rawls, for example, denies that libertarianism makes claims about the public good because the state is just another private association.[187] Having read Rawls, the committed Progressive might well decide that libertarianism has no place in a deliberative democracy seeking the common good. Similarly, Owen Fiss and Edward Foley are quite clear about who should contribute less to enrich public debate. Although Foley insists that his egalitarian proposal will be "fair to rich and poor alike," he and Fiss seek to redistribute speech from the rich to the poor, which means government is not a neutral arbiter among citizens but rather a friend taking sides on behalf of the least advantaged. A Progressive might be inclined to reply that the partiality on behalf of the poor in speech serves the larger common good of rich public debate. But the excluded and marginalized are also the putative bearers of the radical and imaginative truth of egalitarianism. That concern is not shared by the poor or, indeed, by any Americans except for wealthy citizens on the political Left.[188] Progressives are advocates for indifferent clients, and the good they seek is theirs alone.

The partiality of this vision goes deeper than its idea of the common good. The older Progressives were overtly partial to their own interests. Intellectuals and social scientists armed with the latest findings would dominate the new republic. The partiality of contemporary Progressives is similar but subtler. In an open political struggle, many factors will affect the outcome, including the political culture, the facts of the moment, and the resources the participants bring to the struggle. The resources in question would include money and various talents including, among others, capacities for organizing, motivating, and persuading others. In a deliberative democracy constituted by endless arguments about the public good, the primary and perhaps the only resource of value would be a talent for persuading others. Money and other resources would be of secondary importance. Because deliberative democracy favors a talent for persuasion and depreciates the resource of money (among others), we would expect Progressive intellectuals to dominate deliberations and those who have money but few talents at debate (say, leaders of businesses) to lose out.[189] The preference of Progressives for their interests is hardly surprising. To recall Madison, self-interest is an enduring feature of human life. We should not be surprised that self-interested proposals are accompanied by bold and apparently genuine professions of devotion to the common good.

Insofar as Progressives know the common good, they will also know who is actually exercising political speech. Insofar as their idea of the common good is true, their policing of speech might not trouble us. But if we can only attain the truth about the public interest by means of political struggle, any political theory that insists on imposing its conception of the common good on the substance or form of that struggle will also be insisting on its own interests, however much professions of altruism obscure that fact. By imposing their idea of the common good, Progressives would preclude the political struggle that is essential to discovering the public interest.

Power

The original Progressives were not very concerned about abuses of political power. Anyone who recommended, as Herbert Croly did, that private ownership of industry be eliminated in favor of government ownership has few doubts about the beneficence of coercion. John Dewey also considered the typical American distrust of government pathological, an anachronism to be overcome to meet the demands of changed circumstances. This faith in politics contravenes the Madisonian vision in interesting ways. Both Croly and Madison were ambitious men. Madison saw that the striving for fame and power—including his own—needed to be checked and limited by institutions and rights. Croly had no doubts about the potential risks of his own ambition. The Progressives of our time are more aware of the risks attendant on restricting freedom of speech,[190] and yet dangers notwithstanding they still speak of the need for repression and censorship. They are asking the rest of us, especially the rich and the Madisonian, to trust them and to trust that their power to restrict and control the political activities of their opponents will not be abused but instead directed toward a social good that favors rich and poor alike.

That desire to be trusted with power is not absurd, concretely considered. Individuals of a Progressive bent have been and are almost always well educated and highly intelligent and often express admirable sentiments including "the wish to make the world a better place, pity for human suffering, and hope for a better future than the past." These qualities will make the individual conservative happy to call the individual Progressive his friend and to be thankful that the bitter divisions of American politics have not infested all personal relations. But politics is not friendship writ large, and state power concerns coercion, not conversation. When the power to coerce is informed by a moral passion that "falsifies reality and demonizes critics," we have all the more reason to wonder whether Progressives would respect the right to disagree with their deepest commitments.[191]

From the start they have seen themselves as an ethical elite possessing special skills and a sure knowledge of the proper ends of society. They see the property and political activities of others as means to those ends, which implies that government has few if any constraints on the use of its monopoly on violence. Progressives would form a vanguard that uses censorship to liberate the oppressed and achieve equality.[192] Moreover, they have always seen those who disagree and oppose their vision as selfish obstacles to the common good. Foremost among those obstacles are citizens engaged in economic activity in markets free from government control. In light of the hopes and fears that mark the Progressive vision, a citizen might well ask whether Progressives fully empowered to govern the political speech of others are fated to abuse that power. Those who believe that humans are rarely as virtuous as they believe themselves to be will have no doubt about the answer to that question. They will not trust the Progressives (or anyone else) with the power to decide who speaks and who remains silent in political life.

The problem of power has another aspect. Progressives see society as an unequal struggle between haves and have-nots, oppressors and the oppressed. They assume that government will act on behalf of the have-nots and the oppressed. In Justice Breyer's more moderate language, government restricts spending on politics to advance ancient liberty and political participation. These different aspects of the same vision share a questionable assumption: government is both Progressive as to ends and rational as to means. A more realistic look at human history might suggest that those who hold power—Progressive or not—use government to preserve and augment their sway over others. In particular, campaign finance laws in the United States are intertwined with the narrow electoral interests of political parties and incumbent officials. We might reasonably doubt that such restrictions will transcend the power of those interests. Moreover, if Progressives lose power, government controls on political activities might not serve the cause of progress. Progressivism would be caught between its past and the future. As we shall see, this dilemma is not wholly speculative.

Criticisms aside, no one should doubt the appeal of the Progressive vision. Any political theory that pits morality against self-interest, the common good against selfishness, the poor against the rich, and intellectuals against businesspeople will not lack an audience among those who make their living making arguments. Rhetoric aside, this vision exudes an idealism that should appeal to even its harshest critics. It appeals to reason and altruism in pursuit of a higher good that transcends the mundane wants of daily life. The first Progressives were often overtly religious, and their progeny in our time practice a politics that is something more than secular, not least in their crusade against the social sin of corruption brought by private money in public affairs.[193] That admiration, however, should be tempered by the thought that they see society as an organization that they manage to attains goals that they alone know.[194] Managers cannot logically be denied the means to reach those goals, especially if all talk of rights exogenous to government is nothing more than an anachronism limiting human progress. Contemporary Progressives have been candid in acknowledging that among the things to be managed to attain the common good is the political speech and activities of some citizens. In doing so, they continue rather than betray the Progressive vision.

Conclusion

The struggle over campaign finance is ultimately a conflict between the Madisonian vision of the founders and the Progressive vision that undergirded a putative second founding. I have lingered in this chapter on aspects of that dispute—for example, the conflict between seeing society as a social whole and seeing it as the sum of individual choices—that may strike some readers as abstruse or irrelevant to the larger theme of campaign finance regulation. But attention to fundamental philosophical differences shows that struggles over campaign finance are more than the regulatory minutia and the content of the spreadsheets stored at www .fec.gov. These struggles reflect fundamentally different ways of thinking about and acting in political life. Campaign finance laws are informed by a political vision that is radically at odds with the philosophy undergirding the U.S. Constitution and the First Amendment. Whether the laws actually realize that vision (or are intended to do so) is a separate question that I address in subsequent chapters.

Of course, that opposition in itself does not refute the Progressive effort to restrict political speech. It is possible that Americans should sacrifice their rights to political speech (or to fund political speech), along with other rights, so that "we can know a good in common that we cannot know alone."[195] But most Americans believe in both the Constitution and campaign finance reform. Those two faiths can be sustained only at the price of incoherence. Restrictions on campaign finance are the fruit of a political vision whose differences with the Madisonian vision go all the way down. Forced to choose, Americans are unlikely to affirm state control of speech largely because campaign finance reform is an egalitarian island in the vast liberal sea of U.S. political culture.

Close attention to the Progressive vision also helps clarify what's at stake in debates on restricting money in politics. "Moderate reformers" who support such restrictions often say their handiwork does not threaten anyone's First Amendment rights.[196] Such affirmations are clearly wrong insofar as the First Amendment is understood as a limit on political power. After all, campaign finance laws seek to restrict the liberty of individuals to support political activity, thereby extending the ambit of government power over the very forces that are supposed to limit government. But Progressives deny that any such rights against state power exist. Their First Amendment is a means to the higher social good of self-government or rich public debate. Restrictions on the liberty of some are compatible with (or even required by) a First Amendment that empowers (rather than limits) the government. The repression of conservatives called for by leading contemporary Progressives would thus be fully compatible (and perhaps required by) the First Amendment, assuming that such repression attains some social good such as rich public debate or an egalitarian distribution of wealth.

Progressives saw themselves as bearers of a common good realized through history. The story of history was a story of "progress" and expanding government, despite the best efforts to the contrary of the selfish and the corrupt. For that reason, the original Progressives and John W. Gardner were optimists in many ways, not least in their conviction that they were winning a historical struggle to bring modernity and scientific reason to the backward American political culture defined by natural rights and limited government. In 1935 and 1972, history seemed to be on the side of the ethical and enlightened elite and moving sharply against Madison and his "horse and buggy" constitution.[197] This confidence was somewhat justified. Progressives did abrogate constitutional protections for private property and economic liberty and thereafter greatly expand the ambit of the national government. But the Madisonian vision did not pass away as expected under the march of modernity and enlightened governance, and by the 1980s Owen Fiss complained of the political ascendancy of the Right and advised repression of free speech as the proper antidote for changed political circumstances. Calls for repression and censorship of one's political opponents seem shocking in a liberal polity, but as we have seen, the extremism of Fiss, Foley, and Sunstein is consistent with, if not strictly entailed by, this vision. We might be inclined to see their demands as more academic than serious. After all, actually repressing conservatives (as opposed to talking about repressing them) is issuing an invitation to civil war. But we might still question the value of a political theory that did not preclude repression of political speech insofar as we wish to live in a society open to views that diverge from Progressivism. We might also question that vision all the more if such repression is undertaken in the name of deliberation and "true democracy."

This chapter has dwelt on aspects of Progressivism that should trouble not only Madisonians but anyone who believes in free speech. Certainly those troubling aspects have informed most of the history of Progressivism. But history has also complicated that vision, and it should complicate our thinking about its troubling aspects. Fiss, Sunstein, and Foley are points on an arc that rose up in the late nineteenth century, crested from 1935 to 1965, and crashed back to earth in 1994. They are thinkers living through a decline of their vision, and we should not be surprised that they offer remedies to stave off that decline.

I return to the question of the future of Progressivism in campaign finance in chapter 9. For the moment I suggest that an illiberal path forward remains the most likely for the men and women of the Left. But it is not the only possibility. A few Progressives have supported free speech even when it involved that mixture of private property and political activity we call campaign finance. We need not worry whether they have done so out of Madisonian convictions or political interests. Whatever their motivations, these few have combined a commitment to Progressive policies with an insistence on limiting state power over politics. For the time being Progressives are more likely to be the objects rather than the subjects of repression as they were for several decades after 1920. We may have entered an era of ideological drift in which their commitment to controlling speech has become an obstacle to the practical fulfillment of their vision.[198] If so, Progressives will have to choose between their anachronistic vision and their current interests. In making that choice, they may look to the few among them who have combined a commitment to Madisonian theory in First Amendment matters with a devotion to Progressive economic and social policies.

In the chapters that follow we shall see that the Progressive vision of politics has informed the justifications for limiting the liberty to finance political activities and speech, sometimes in ways that are both obscure and significant. But Progressivism is not simply a body of theory subject to the standards of clarity and logic. Its justifications for restricting money in politics depend on empirical assertions that may be prompted but cannot be evaluated by theory alone. In examining the case against a free speech, we should keep in mind both the vision that informs the claims and the reality that constrains the words that compose that vision. I turn first to the ubiquitous complaint that money corrupts politics.

PART II
Four Illusions

CHAPTER THREE

The Corruption of Representation

The Madisonian vision of politics that led to the First Amendment to the U.S. Constitution creates a presumption of liberty regarding freedom of speech. Progressives have abrogated the U.S. Constitution in several ways, but the presumption of liberty for free speech remains valid. Those who would restrict money in politics (and thus freedom of speech) still must overcome that presumption by showing that such liberties should be restricted in service to other government interests. Chief among these interests has been preventing corruption or the appearance of corruption.

The concept of corruption might be defined broadly as a decline from an ideal state. Corruption thus encompasses all of the justifications for limiting liberty to be discussed in the next few chapters. Here I wish to focus on the common claim that the use of private money in politics prevents government from achieving the democratic ideal of representation.[1] I look at the complexity of that ideal and the evidence for its corruption via campaign finance. As deployed in public and academic debates, that ideal is deeply informed by the Progressive vision of politics. Yet even by the standards set by that vision, the corruption case against contributions fails.

Legalized Bribery

People who want to restrict or ban campaign contributions often call such donations "legalized bribery."[2] The appeal of this condemnation cannot be denied. Bribery has few if any defenders. If contributions can be identified with it, Congress might outlaw private money in elections or, indeed, in politics generally. Moreover, bribery and campaign contributions both involve citizens' giving money to politicians (or to agents of a public official). But the law recognizes and condemns bribery while allowing campaign contributions, which many advocates of campaign finance restrictions do not seek to eliminate. The former must differ in some important way from the latter. The justification for limiting the liberty to donate money to campaigns depends on a third concept, "improper influence," that shares some elements of contributions and bribes.

Federal law proscribes giving money to induce a public official to commit fraud or "any act in violation of the lawful duty" of the official.[3] Federal law also condemns giving a public official anything of value "to influence any official act."[4] For the Progressive, bribes and contributions arise from self-interest.[5] The motives behind donating to politicians are not readily apparent to the law. Indeed, most people who are engaged in politics have mixed motives: their professed political ideals may well coincide with their material interests. We simply lack enough knowledge to regulate money in politics with regard to the motives of participants.[6] If we identify bribery with a self-interested motive, we will surely condemn political beliefs along with selfishness. We might seek more objective ways of distinguishing bribery from contributions.

Those who give and receive bribes are generally unwilling to publicize their transaction. This suggests that secrecy might be the distinguishing mark of bribery. Indeed, something like this assumption underlies the insistence on mandatory disclosure in all aspects of campaign finance and government ethics. But the secrecy of a payment to a public official cannot be a reliable way to identify bribery. If it were, almost all of the campaign contributions made prior to 1972 would have to be considered bribes. For example, the major contributors to Eugene McCarthy's presidential campaigns in 1968 and 1972 would be guilty of bribery because their donations did not become public until some time later. Identifying bribes as undisclosed payments to candidates for office (including those already in office) is overly broad: if that standard were accepted, a great deal of legitimate political activity would be condemned and punished, thereby sacrificing both the truth and fundamental rights.

One objective way of identifying bribery is examining how the recipient of the payment uses the money received. Those who receive bribes generally spend the money on private consumption: cars, big houses, the works. More generally, we might define bribery by what it is not: the money involved does not go to fund conventionally political or electoral activities. In other words, one sign that bribes are corrupting government is the absence of politics.

It is not difficult to find famous cases of bribery in American politics. *Congressional Quarterly* has published a list of government scandals from 1802 to 2003. They report three instances of bribery: the case of Interior Secretary Albert Fall during the Teapot Dome scandal, the cases of seven members of Congress during the Abscam scandal, and the case of Vincent A. "Buddy" Cianci Jr., the Democratic mayor of Providence, Rhode Island, who exchanged city contracts for bribes.[7] They might have added a few other cases. The Truman administration suffered bribe-taking Internal Revenue Service (IRS) officials, and the Eisenhower presidency saw the resignation of its chief of staff, Sherman Adams, for accepting gifts in exchange for intervening with a federal agency.[8] Former senator Daniel B. Brewster (D-MD, 1963–69) was convicted in 1972 on three counts of accepting money to influence his vote on postal rate legislation that was before Congress.[9] Randy "Duke" Cunningham (D-CA) recently pleaded guilty to accepting $2.4 million in return for defense contracts.[10] The United States judicial system collects comprehensive data about bribery convictions. In the calendar year ending September 30, 2001, the U.S. courts convicted and sentenced 221 individuals for the offense of bribery. Nine of these 221 felons were punished by a jail term greater than five years.[11] The data do not tell us how many of those convicted were public officials. The absolute numbers also tell us little. Is 221 a large number? This number was less than one percent of the number sentenced for drug offenses during the same period. Having nine major convictions for bribery in a nation of two hundred million adults suggests that bribery is relatively rare and imposes relatively little harm on society.

I might note in passing a certain asymmetry in the concept of bribery. The law properly forbids bribing legislators or public officials in general. It also prohibits spending campaign funds directly to buy votes. Anyone who tries to buy a vote with campaign funds or accepts such an offer may, if the violation was willful, be fined or imprisoned for not more than two years or both.[12] Yet if a member of Congress seeks votes by promising to increase the wealth of his or her constituents by, say, bringing to the district large public works projects (or otherwise redistributing wealth from citizens outside of the district to constituents), he or she has not broken any laws.[13] Indeed, the promises of enhanced wealth in exchange for votes might be seen as shrewd politics. Why is it a crime for voters to bribe politicians but good politics for politicians to bribe voters?

Some have compared campaign contributions to bribes by noting that such donations benefit the recipient.[14] That abstraction obscures an important distinction between bribes and donations. Unlike bribes, contributions can be spent legally only on political activity: getting out the vote, persuading voters by advertising, building political organizations, and other activities connected to elections. Contributions go toward political success, not personal gain: "Is there a difference in terms of democratic theory between a traditional bribe and an electoral contribution? The most important difference is that a contribution is effective only because it helps achieve electoral success, while a representative values a traditional bribe regardless of whether the bribe helps win elections."[15] On the other hand, if contributions are spent on private consumption, the individual who solicited the contributions is criminally liable. Consider the case of Roger D. Blevins III, who was accused of stealing $350,000 in campaign contributions from Senator Joseph R. Biden Jr. (D-DE). Authorities allege that Blevins spent the money on expensive cars and other luxury items.[16] The law appears to define campaign activity in a conventional way. Had Blevins spent the money buying broadcast ads to reelect Biden, he would not have faced charges.

Madisonians and Progressives diverge with respect to the meaning of politics and therefore the distinction between contributions and bribery. For Madisonians, the Constitution and other institutions define political activity. If a citizen spends money on activities recognized as political by the Constitution or by institutions that derive their authority from it, the citizen is engaged in politics. That understanding of politics encompasses self-interest and altruism along with points in between and relies on political struggle to bring forth a tolerable notion of the public good.

As we have seen, Progressives think otherwise. They define politics in the United States in relation to some idea of the common good or the public interest. Those entering the political arena must be able to articulate their positions in terms of the public good; assertions of what are called "naked preferences" are not political activity because they do not do so. Private interests in politics become in this conception "agents of corruption."[17] For Progressives, citizens must prove that they are engaged in something larger than themselves to gain admittance to the political realm. Money spent on activities that cannot bear that burden of proof are not political by definition. If such spending is not political, it must be bribery or some other form of corruption of the political process. For theoretical reasons, Progressives are inclined to exclude a broader range of activities from the political arena than are Madisonians. This relatively cramped notion of political activity is one important source of the general Progressive hostility to private donations to campaigns.

Apart from political theory, other considerations testify to the political character of contributions. Campaign contributions fund electoral struggle, thereby affecting the outcome of elections. Accordingly, banning or restricting donations might eliminate or hobble campaign activity, thereby creating a relative political advantage for those who advocate the restrictions or for their favored candidates or causes. For example, imagine that one political party received most of its contributions from donors giving less than $1,000 whereas its main opposition received almost all its funding in sums greater than $1,000. If the party of small donors had a majority in Congress, it would be tempted to enact contribution limits of $1,000 as a way to gain an advantage in the next election.

As long as parties and candidates differ in the way they finance their electoral struggles, incentives exist to enact apparently neutral restrictions on campaign finance to benefit the majority backing the restrictions. In other words, the authors of campaign finance law are unlikely to commit random errors in regulating money in politics. Given the overwhelming political incentives involved, we should be able to detect patterns of advantage and disadvantage in campaign finance laws. Far from random, the errors will be systematic, at least insofar as human knowledge and ingenuity can make them so. Use of the force of law to systematically bias elections does not exist when Congress legislates against bribery.

Voters need not discover such Machiavellian manipulations of the political process.[18] Campaign contributions involve giving money to public officials. Ambitious politicians may easily convince the public that such donations are actually bribes and thus corrupt. Voters have little interest in campaign finance and are unwilling to pay the costs of discovering whether contributions lead to corruption. Politicians who support restrictions on campaign finance can both manipulate elections in their favor and foster a reputation for righteousness among the public.

Much of the concern about the corruption of representation and politics by money depends on confusing bribery and contributions. But that is not the whole case against campaign contributions. Some argue that they can be used solely for political purposes and yet corrupt politics by improperly influencing representation. This argument begins by asking us to imagine a world that prohibited private campaign contributions. In that world "[e]ach legislator's position . . . would be determined by considerations such as constituency, ideology and party. The positions determined in this manner will be referred to as the legislators' 'natural' positions."[19] Now go back to our world, the one where individuals and groups may contribute to candidates and causes. In our corrupt world, it is argued, contributions drive a wedge between the natural and actual positions of legislators. Just as bribes cause public officials to do things they otherwise would not do, contributions induce legislators to vote in ways that are unexpected given their political ideology, their party identification, the concerns of their constituents, or other political variables. That difference indicates the improper influence of money in politics.

The improper influence argument distinguishes legitimate and illegitimate influences on legislative judgment. Constituent votes, ideology, and partisan differences fit in the legitimate category; campaign contributions are deemed illegitimate. The illegitimacy of money should not surprise anyone in light of the influence of the Progressive vision of politics in campaign finance debates. Progressives deem contributions illegitimate because they reflect self-interest (rather than the common good) and accord the wealthy unequal power (in opposition to political equality). The question of improper influence of contributions is in part a question of the validity of the Progressive vision of politics. But it is more.

The thesis that money improperly influences legislators may be empirically tested. Scholars can collect data about the actions of public officials (say, the votes of a member of Congress), their ideologies, their partisan identification, the concerns of their constituents, and their campaign contributions. If contributions were like bribes and had an improper influence, we would expect that statistically the donations would have a unique effect on the congressional votes, taking into account all the other factors (ideology and so on). On the other hand, if the study showed that contributions had no unique effects on congressional voting, we would have reason to believe that donations cannot be distinguished from other aspects of politics that are perfectly legitimate. Setting aside for the moment questions of propriety, we can determine whether contributions actually affect the judgment of legislators.

Improper Influence

Social scientists have extensively studied the influence of campaign contributions on lawmaking and on public policy. On the whole, they have concluded that contributions have little, if any, influence on policymaking. Those who worry about the influence of money on politics often dismiss these findings out of hand, citing the "common sense" view that money buys policy and elections. But common sense is hardly a firm guide to accurate beliefs. In the past it has led many people to believe false propositions: the earth is flat, the earth is stationary, objects such as the chair I am sitting in are solid.[20] All too often, common sense is nothing more than a complacent prejudice.[21] It should not be enough to justify restricting fundamental rights.

Some proponents of campaign finance restrictions reject these findings for somewhat more serious reasons. They claim these studies do not adequately measure money and its effects on policy. Perhaps that is true, but the studies I discuss are the best attempts we have to measure the influence of money on politics. In any case, it is not enough to simply say that studies contain measurement errors. You have to have a study to beat a study, and those who complain about measurement errors generally rely on anecdotes about the putative influence of money on politics. Anecdotes do not have statistical significance. Let's assume, however, that mismeasurement leads us to conclude that we cannot determine whether contributions affect policymaking. What should we conclude about campaign finance regulation? The advocate who rejects social science rushes to conclude that money corrupts politics and that more restrictions are needed. Notice the logical fallacy: social science provides no evidence about the influence of money, therefore more regulation is justified. If we accept that social science mismeasures the power of money, we can only logically conclude that we do not know whether money influences policymaking. But that conclusion cannot justify regulation of speech under current law. The advocates of restrictions bear the burden of showing that money corrupts politics. Not knowing whether it does is not enough. That said, the social scientific evidence leaves little doubt that campaign contributions have little influence on policy.

Scholars have researched and written dozens of studies of the influence of money.[22] Instead of recounting and assessing each one—a strategy that would surely try the patience of the reader—I have selected two general overviews of this literature, one published in 1988, the other in 2003. The author of the 1988 review, Frank Sorauf, a political scientist at the University of Minnesota, has worked in the field of campaign finance for at least two decades. The authors of the 2003 review, Stephen Ansolabehere, John de Figueiredo, and James Snyder Jr., are professors of political science, management, and economics, respectively, at the Massachusetts Institute of Technology.[23] Taken together, the two overviews cover the years of intensive regulation of campaign finance.

Sorauf identified three problems with assertions that money buys influence in politics, problems that have defined and complicated the scientific study of the issue. First, if contributions are political by nature, it is an open question whether money follows votes on a policy or the votes follow the money. Do contributions change votes or simply express support for a position already taken? If a legislator were to take a position absent the contribution, the money would hardly have any influence over him; the world of policymaking would remain the same.[24]

Second, the focus on money excludes other factors affecting legislative votes. Lobbying may affect the judgment of members of Congress along with contributions and constituency pressures. For example, the National Rifle Association has a powerful lobby, a well-funded PAC, and an effective grassroots organization. When it succeeds in political struggle, why ascribe the victory solely to campaign contributions? A number of other factors including political ideology, party affiliation, constituency concerns, and presidential persuasion can influence a vote. Unless an analysis of legislative action takes account of these other factors, we should not conclude that money has influence on policy.[25]

Third, the evidence for influence should be robust. The case for campaign finance regulation looks at particular cases, which are subject to the problems of misplaced causality. If money has influence in these particular cases, it does not follow that money is a general problem requiring general regulations.[26] Political struggle provides substantial incentives to bring to public attention the best policy examples to make the case that money buys policy. Consequently, the evidence the public knows best is likely to be unrepresentative; it is likely to be biased toward instances where money seems to have influence, telling us little about all the unobserved cases. This selection bias distorts our understanding of the overall effects of campaign contributions on politics and policy.[27] Given that bias, should legislators enact restrictions on an entire category of money in politics if we do not know about all cases? The standard quip notwithstanding, it is not true that the plural of anecdotes is data.

Frank Sorauf concluded that academic studies conducted prior to 1988 provided "no data" to support widespread assertions about the "buying of Congress." The strongest studies supporting the reform cause suggested only a modest influence for money, an influence far weaker than other factors affecting a legislator's vote. Even studies that showed some effect seemed biased by endogeneity. In other words, legislative votes might attract money rather than be a result of a contribution.[28] As we shall see, Sorauf's conclusions have not been seriously challenged by later research.

I might also pose a question to those who argue that contributions corrupt politics. If that is the case, why is there so little money in American politics?[29] The federal government affects the distribution of wealth in many ways. It directly gives money to some people and takes it away from others via taxation. Its regulations can protect businesses from competition or open up markets for new entrants. What the government does creates millions of opportunities for Americans to gain money or to lose it. Taken as a whole, those gains or losses certainly run into the hundreds of billions of dollars. Yet when Gordon Tullock posed this question in 1972, all campaign spending totaled $200 million. In 2002 total federal government spending was well over $2 trillion; consumption and gross investment of the federal government totaled $590 billion. In the 2000 election, in contrast, candidates, parties, and organizations spent $3 billion.[30] If the investment theory is correct, every dollar invested as a campaign donation yielded an average return of *at least* $200 in government benefits.[31]

In fact, some rates of return on contributions are much higher than two hundred fold (again, assuming contributions are investments). Ansolabehere, Figueiredo, and Snyder estimated the rate of return on one dollar's worth of contributions in five policy areas (see table 3.1).

These rates of return do not exist in any other market. Given these phenomenal returns on investment, we would expect capital to flow freely into the "political market." Yet 40 percent of Fortune 500 firms and one-third of industries in general do not have a political action committee (PAC) to make such investments. Moreover, PACs give far less than allowed. One study found the average contribution during the 1978–86

TABLE 3.1 **Imputed return on campaign contributions (selected policy areas)**

Policy area	Government favors (in millions of dollars)	Year of favors	Private contributions	Year of contributions	Imputed return on $1
Sugar production	5,000	1986–1991	$192,000	1985	$26,042
Defense procurement	134,000	2000	$13,200,000	2000	$10,152
Agriculture	22,100	2000	$3,300,000	2000	$6,697
Dairy prodution	1,000	2002	$1,300,000	2000	$769
Oil and gas industries	1,700	1999	$21,600,000	1998	$79

Source: Stephen Ansolabehere, John M. de Figueiredo, and James M. Snyder Jr., "Why Is There So Little Money in U.S. Politics?" *Journal of Economic Perspectives* 17 (Winter 2003): 110–11.

election cycles to be $1,500 for labor PACs, $1,300 for trade PACs, and $700 for corporate PACs. Even when those numbers are adjusted upward to account for inflation, it is hard to imagine that those sums could purchase anything of consequence.[32] Only 4 percent of all PAC contributions to House and Senate candidates are at or near the $10,000 limit. If all corporate, labor, and trade PACs gave the maximum sums allowed by law to all incumbents running for reelection in the House and Senate, the total PAC contributions in the 2000 election would have been forty times more than it was.[33] Moreover, PACs are not the most important source of campaign contributions; individual donations account for the largest part, and "it seems highly unlikely that the 21 million individual donors giving an average of $115 apiece were calculating the return that they would personally receive on this investment."[34] Business interests, for their part, spend far more on philanthropy than they do on campaign contributions. If businesses could make massive sums investing in politics, why do they spend so much more on charity?[35]

We might pose one other question about "missing money" in American politics. The president is the most powerful official in the government, and every administration makes decisions that involve billions of dollars in costs and benefits to various individuals and groups. Experts consider donations by PACs to be the most "interested" contributions because business associations or labor unions often establish these organizations; if that is the case, PAC contributions should represent a significant portion of all donations to presidential campaigns. In fact, such donations account for 1 percent of all PAC giving.[36] If money buys political favors, why do PACs spend so little on presidential campaigns?

Tullock's question thus raises profound problems for those who continually decry the corruption caused by money. It also informs this inquiry into the differences between bribery and campaign contributions. If contributions were bribes, the sums invested in purchasing political favors would be far larger than they are. On the other hand, if contributions were almost always a form of political participation, we would expect relatively small sums to be devoted to campaigns. That is what in fact happens.

Although the mismatch of "investments" and returns contravenes economic common sense, it does not definitively show that contributors do not attain influence. Perhaps the low level of spending relative to return reflects the low likelihood of receiving the favor. The exchange of a contribution for a favor is an unenforceable contract; the high rate of return may simply reflect the risk to the contributor that the contract will not be honored. This argument might be more persuasive if the rate of return on contributions were more uniform. The risk of a contract's not being honored presumably applies to all such "investments." Yet the rate of return on a contributed dollar ranges from $79 to more than $26,000. It is difficult to believe the range in risk is wide enough to fit the wide variation in the putative rate of return to campaign contributions. Again the investment theory runs counter to economic common sense.

Stephen Ansolabehere, John de Figueiredo Jr., and James Snyder (hereafter "the MIT Group") have recently provided an exhaustive review of studies examining the influence of money on policymaking. Most of these forty studies look at the effects of contributions by interest groups on roll-call voting. The studies most often examine the co-variation of contributions and legislative votes both in one period and over time. If money has influence, the political contributions of an interest group (a political action committee) and the desired legislative vote sought by a contribution will co-vary together. Because scholars have a great deal of data about PAC contributions and legislative votes, they are able to offer a robust examination of the claim that money has influence over policy. The MIT Group summarizes its review of the forty studies as follows: "Overall, PAC contributions show relatively few effects on voting behavior. In three out of four instances, campaign contributions had no statistically significant effects on legislation or had the 'wrong' sign—suggesting that more contributions lead to less support."[37] In other words, results may have been due to chance or the results directly contradicted the expected influence of money. Political scientists and economists have found little reason to reject the argument that money has no influence on policymaking.[38]

As the MIT Group notes, many of these studies suffer from methodological shortcomings similar to those cited by Frank Sorauf in the late 1980s.[39] To deal with these problems, the MIT Group did its own study of legislative voting using improved methods.[40] Its conclusion is worth quoting at length: "The evidence that campaign contributions lead to a substantial influence on votes is rather thin. Legislators' votes depend almost entirely on their own beliefs and the preferences of their voters and their party. Contributions explain a minuscule fraction of the variation in voting behavior in the U.S. Congress. Members of Congress care foremost about winning re-election. They must attend to the constituency that elects them, voters in a district or state and the constituency that nominates them, the party."[41] In other words, the evidence indicates that legislators take the "natural position" on issues before Congress.

Why do PAC contributions have so little effect on legislative voting? Such donations make up only a small part of all contributions; most money comes from individuals. If PACs try to withhold their contributions to gain leverage on a legislator, the legislator can raise money from individuals and need not grant the wishes of the interest group. Moreover, a contribution of between $1,000 and $5,000 will have essentially no effect on an incumbent's chances of winning election and thus "individual PAC contributions have little to no value at the margin to incumbents in either House or Senate elections." For this reason, a PAC contributor has no leverage to move policy in a particular direction.[42] Their money buys little influence, which implies they will spend little on contributions; this is what we observe.[43] If contributions are not investments, what are they?

The MIT Group argues that contributions are a form of participation (or, in economic jargon, consumption). If it is correct, personal income and national income should be strongly correlated with campaign contributions. The group found that rising income reliably predicted an increased likelihood of contributing to campaigns. They discovered that 94 wealthy corporate executives contributed about one-twentieth of one percent of their annual compensation to political campaigns (about $51 of every $100,000 of income).[44] More generally, the most significant factors affecting spending in congressional races are closeness of the election and the income level in the district.[45] The same is true of gubernatorial races since 1976, though the influence of income on total spending seems stronger in these elections.[46]

Seeing contributing as consumption also informs our understanding of total campaign spending. Many observers have long noted that total spending has risen sharply over time. Indeed, complaints about runaway spending were heard as early as the late 1960s, when Congress first embarked on the modern effort to restrict campaign finance. If, however, Americans spend a constant proportion of their wealth on political contributions (they do) and U.S. national income steadily increases (it has), campaign spending will also increase in absolute terms. The MIT Group found that the proportion of national wealth spent on campaigns has remained the same since 1976 (adjusted for inflation) and was roughly the same for most of the twentieth century.[47] Spending is not out of control. Americans spend more in absolute terms on politics, as with other goods and services, when they have more income. Their relative propensity to support campaigns, however, has not changed.

We might also consider more specific studies. Partisans of restrictions on campaign finance often focus on campaign contributions by unpopular industries to make their case. The tobacco industry is a favorite target, in part because it is politically active via contributions. The political scientist John Wright notes that two-thirds of the members of the House of Representatives received campaign contributions from one or more tobacco industry PACs during the 1995–96 election cycle. Moreover, sixteen tobacco industry PACs donated more than $2.3 million to congressional candidates during the 1997–98 election cycle. The largest of these, the Philip Morris PAC, gave almost $800,000.[48] A few older studies found that these contributions influenced policy concerning tobacco.[49] Wright did a comprehensive analysis of the influence of tobacco contributions on voting by members of Congress, taking other factors into consideration. His analysis revealed that "the strongest predictor of congressional voting on tobacco legislation is the ideology of incumbent legislators, not campaign contributions from the tobacco industry. Tobacco contributions, in fact, have the smallest statistical impact on voting of any of the factors considered. . . . Rather than purchasing votes with campaign contributions, the tobacco industry appears to succeed in Congress because many legislators adhere to a pro-business and antiregulatory philosophy on political matters affecting smoking interests."[50] The case of contributions by the tobacco industry, a putative exemplar of the influence of money, runs counter to reformer dogma.

If campaign contributions affect voting by members of Congress, a reduction in contributions by interest groups should lead to changes in voting by a member. John R. Lott and Stephen Bronars studied changes in the voting records of members of Congress who had announced their retirements. As it happens, members serving their last term receive many fewer contributions from interest groups. If the improper influence thesis were correct, the voting records of retiring members would change to reflect the decline in contributions. In fact, Lott and Bronars found no significant change in voting by retiring members, controlling for other factors. That finding indicates that contributors give to candidates who value their favored policies.[51] Contributions are consumption, not investment, political activity, not corrupt bidding.

We have another way to test whether contributions are investments or consumption. From 1979 to 2002, federal law permitted contributions (so-called "soft money") to the political parties that were unrestricted except for disclosure (after 1992). If individuals or groups were interested in investing in policy outcomes, soft money allowed them to spend as much as they might wish. Here's how a look at soft money helps us think about campaign spending.

Imagine you have a lot of money to invest in a politician's campaign in order to receive favors after the election. If you were sure a party or candidate would win, you would give all your contributions to them; money going to a sure loser would be money wasted. On the other hand, if you were not sure which party or candidate would win, you might spread the soft money around and donate to both parties. Such a hedging strategy will be familiar to readers managing their own investment portfolio for retirement or other purposes. If campaign contributions are investments in policy favors, we might expect to see political investors doing the same by giving to everyone. Indeed, one of the House sponsors of the McCain-Feingold law argued that the giving of soft money to both parties was evidence that contributions were investments in policy outcomes.[52] Did soft money contributors give to both sides?

Let us take a look at the election of 2002. In the summer of that year, this election looked evenly balanced. The Republicans had several disadvantages. First, they held the White House, and the party of first-term presidents in recent decades has generally lost twenty House seats in the off-year elections following their inauguration.[53] Moreover, the economic outlook of the electorate had been growing increasingly pessimistic. The Democrats looked set to gain enough seats to compose a majority in the House. In the Senate, the Republicans had to defend many more seats than did the Democrats; the odds suggested that the Democrats would retain their narrow majority in the upper house. The Republicans did have one advantage in retrospect: their leader, George W. Bush, was both popular and an effective campaigner. In the late summer and fall of 2002, however, the partisan outcome of the election was far from clear. A smart political investor would have hedged his bets and split his contributions between the parties.

Relatively few contributors of large sums in 2002 split their donations. Looking again at those who gave more than $100,000 we notice that 55 percent of them gave exclusively to one party (21 percent to the Democrats and 34 percent to the Republicans). Roughly another 22 percent of the donors gave 75 percent of all their soft money to one party or the other. All in all, about 77 percent of large soft money donors gave overwhelmingly to one party or the other, as reflected in figure 3.1. The donors do not seem to have been hedging their risks as good investors would have.

How many did hedge their bets? If we define it as giving less than 60 percent or more than 40 percent of their overall contribution to the Democrats, we find that only 11 percent of soft money donors split their contributions. If they were investing in policies, they were taking enor-

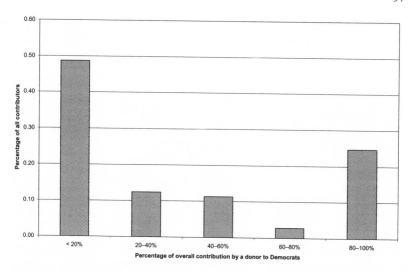

FIGURE 3.1   Soft money contributions, 2001–2. http://www.opensecrets.org (accessed June 9, 2003)

mous risks for highly uncertain payoffs. To put it mildly, such risk taking seems unlikely. Instead, the giving of soft money in 2002 tells a story of donors exclusively or predominantly supporting one party or the other at a time when neither party seemed certain to hold power in 2003. That does not fit the conjectures that large donors invest in politics or that big money buys public policies. Three in four soft money donors seemed to be pursuing an ideological agenda.

Indeed, at the highest levels of contributions, ideology seemed to play an especially large part. The top ten contributors of soft money in 2001–2002 gave 95 percent of their donations to the Democratic Party. Nine of these gave 99 percent or more of their contributions to the Democrats; only one donor split the contributions between the parties. Of course, that does not prove that the more soft money a donor gives the more likely he or she is to give exclusively to one party. However, major contributors of soft money who gave overwhelmingly to one party donated an average of $623,429, while those who hedged their bets gave an average of $357,677.[54] In the jargon of the MIT Group, the biggest of the "Big Money" donors seem to be consumers of, not investors in, politics. In more ordinary language, major contributors appear to be intensely partisan and ideological.

We have seen that most systematic studies of the influence of contributions on legislative voting have discovered that money has little effect and explored some of the reasons why that lack of influence makes sense. But not every study has reached this result. As noted above, the MIT Group found that 25 percent of the studies in the literature did find that contributions have some effect on roll-call votes, though this research had some methodological shortcomings. Recently a few studies have also argued that money changes legislative votes.[55]

Perhaps the most sophisticated and interesting study to back this claim concerns banking legislation before the U.S. House of Representatives in the 1990s. In 1933 Congress passed the Glass-Steagall Act, which forced banks to give up their investment banking operations. Banking interests tried to remove this constraint but had little success until the 1990s. Investment and insurance companies, in contrast, sought to keep the restrictions in place to limit competition. In 1991 Congress considered banking legislation including a title (Title IV) that allowed banks to enter the investment business, albeit under significant constraints. The limits were onerous enough that a supporter of the banks, Representative Doug Barnard (R-GA), offered an amendment on the House floor to strip Title IV from the legislation. The amendment was defeated. In 1998, the House returned to the issue of banking regulation and passed a bill allowing banks to enter the investment industry. The banks for the most part opposed this bill, however, because it included significant restraints on their ability to do so.[56]

The economist Thomas Stratmann used those two votes to test whether campaign contributions induced some members of Congress to change their votes on the issue. Stratmann discovered that 182 members of Congress cast a vote on both the Barnard amendment in 1991 and the House bill in 1998. He focused on members who had voted for the banking position in 1991 as well as the investment and insurance position in 1998 or vice versa. Stratmann found strong statistical evidence that campaign contributions were correlated with these shifts in voting from 1991 to 1998.[57] He concluded that in this case money did indeed change votes concerning legislation.

Stratmann realized that the two votes must be comparable if his conclusions were to be valid.[58] If the votes are about different subjects, we are comparing apples and oranges and cannot draw any conclusions about the meaning of a change in vote between 1991 and 1998. Stratmann argues that his paper "compares the 1991 vote that led directly to the abandonment of a bill allowing banks to merge with securities and insurance companies with the 1998 vote that led directly to the passage of a bill allowing such mergers."[59] Both bills, he asserts, were about the passage or defeat of legislation that liberalized banking rules. But the 1991 vote concerned an amendment to a bill allowing such mergers. Stratmann says the defeat of the amendment led to the abandonment of the bill, and thus the vote on the amendment was similar to the up-or-down vote on mergers in 1998. But the vote on the amendment was not the equivalent of an up-or-down vote on the bill. Two weeks after the amendment failed, a bill that in part allowed banks to enter investing was still alive.[60] Moreover, the vote on the Barnard amendment was not about banking interests versus investment and insurance interests. The outcome of that vote "was viewed largely as an expression of sentiment by the Democrats not to surrender control of the debate as well as a rallying cry around House Speaker Thomas S. Foley of Washington, who had been attacked by the Republicans."[61] The 74 Democrats who voted against the Barnard amendment may have done so for reasons of partisanship. If so, the inference that 38 Democrats changed their votes between 1991 and 1998 because of the influence of contributions is incorrect. The earlier vote appeared to be about partisanship, and the later vote was for or against insurance interests. The content of the two votes was different even though the subject matter of the two bills was similar, at least at first blush.

If we grant that the two votes are comparable, Stratmann's methods have one other problem. His study focuses on members who changed their votes. However, 69 legislators (38 percent of all members who voted in both years) did not change their votes. Stratmann excluded these legislators from his statistical analysis.[62] Technically, removing these cases can be defended.[63] Yet that technical defense depends on a crucial assumption that is surely false: it assumes that PAC contributions are distributed randomly. If they are not, two problems beset Stratmann's analysis. First, if PACs target legislators who might sell their vote (or who have already changed their vote between 1991 and 1998), his analysis will greatly exaggerate the extent of the influence of PAC contributions. Second, if that assumption is wrong, it may be informative to note that some legislators both received money and did not change their votes.

Finally, if we grant that Stratmann's analysis and conclusion are correct, what implications does it have for regulation of campaign finance? Those who support more regulation may see Stratmann's work as a "smoking gun" that justifies banning PAC contributions or perhaps private contributions to campaigns. We should keep in mind, however, that Stratmann selected his two votes because they would not be affected by either constituency pressure or the ideology of the legislator.[64] As a methodological matter, this makes sense: by removing factors that normally affect roll-call votes, Stratmann might more easily see the putative effects of money on policymaking. However, this decision greatly circumscribes the implications of his study. Recall that analyses of large numbers of roll-call votes find that contributions have little effect on policymaking once constituent preference and ideology (along with partisanship) are taken into account. In other words, Stratmann has chosen an odd, not a normal, case of congressional voting. Yet Congress regulates campaign contributions in general, not contributions related to financial services or other specific legislation. Let us say that on the basis of Stratmann's findings we ban PAC contributions to prevent corruption. To be sure, we would prevent the PAC contributions that, Stratmann argues, changed votes on the banking bill. We would also ban them in the much larger number of cases where ideology, constituent preferences, and partisanship determined the legislator's vote. The cost of these "false positives" [65] would be measured in the fundamental constitutional rights of the citizens involved in the affected PACs. All in all, it is far from clear that even if Stratmann is correct, we should restrict or ban PAC contributions.

Many Americans take for granted that campaign contributions are legalized bribery that corrupts representative government. But both logic and evidence indicate that campaign contributions are a form of political participation rather than a variant of bribery. These findings belie the Progressive tenet that money and business corrupt government. But that faith has other aspects.

Distortion of the Popular Will

The Supreme Court's opinion in *Buckley v. Valeo* redefines freedom of speech as a tool of the people rather than a restraint on government. As shown above, the framers of the U.S. Constitution believed freedom of speech was a natural right and that individuals created government to protect such rights. The *Buckley* Court disagreed. For its members, freedom of speech was a means to realize the will of the people. The justices noted that the First Amendment "affords the broadest protection to such political expression in order 'to assure [the] unfettered interchange of ideas for the bringing about of political and social changes desired by the people.'" [66] Implicitly the Court had abandoned the mixture of popular government and majority restraint adumbrated in Federalist no. 10. Freedom of speech is not a right but a means to realize the desires of the American electorate, whatever they might be.

In later cases, justices more explicitly subordinated freedom of speech to the popular will. In 1986 Justice William Brennan argued that large contributions are corrupt because they distort the political process. Raising and donating money to campaigns indicates support for a cause or a set of ideas. Such contributions deserve the protection of the Constitution, according to Brennan, but "[d]irect corporate spending on political activity raises the prospect that resources amassed in the economic marketplace may be used to provide an unfair advantage in the political marketplace. . . . The resources in the treasury of a business corporation, however, are not an indication of popular support for the corporation's political ideas. They reflect instead the economically motivated decisions of investors and customers. The availability of these resources may make a corporation a formidable political presence, even though the power of the corporation may be no reflection of the power of its ideas." [67] In 1990 Justice Thurgood Marshall expanded Brennan's idea of corruption to include "the corrosive and distorting effects of immense aggregations of wealth that are accumulated with the help of the corporate form and that have little or no correlation to the public's support for the corporation's political ideas." [68] Notice Marshall's extraordinary assumption: the protections of the First Amendment should only be offered to speech that has general support in the population. Thomas Burke argues that Brennan and Marshall created in these opinions a "distortion standard" of corruption: "The ideal behind this standard is that the decisions of officeholders should closely reflect the views of the public. Campaign contributions are corrupting to the extent that they do not reflect the balance of public opinion and thus distort policymaking through their influence on elections." [69]

With the distortion standard, the Court departed completely from both the Madisonian idea of corruption and from the bribery metaphor. Whereas Madison worried about the tyranny of the majority, the "distortion standard" makes the will of the people—as measured by current surveys—the benchmark for assessing corruption. This departure is not surprising. The Progressive vision made public opinion (and majority rule) central to politics.

Yet public opinion is not a reliable measure of the will of the people and therefore cannot serve as a firm benchmark to indicate corruption of the political process. What is the will of the people regarding a political issue? With respect to fundamental issues of law, we might say the Consti-

tution represents the aspirations of "We, the People." To resolve the daily
struggles over policy, we usually look to the will of majorities as expressed
in Congress. If the will of the majority equals the will of the people, any
policy that runs counter to the majoritarian preference distorts the political process.

Justice Thurgood Marshall, plaintiff's counsel in *Brown v. Board of
Education,* could not have believed that this majoritarian "distortion
standard" should govern the political process. Majorities supported racial
segregation of schools and limits on the voting rights of African Americans. Majorities have steadily opposed affirmative action since it began
in the 1970s. The practice of granting racial preferences in employment
and education has resisted the will of the majority during that period.[70]
Would Justice Marshall or his intellectual progeny decry such distortion
of policymaking? More broadly, public opinion opposes in practice many
fundamental rights embodied in the Constitution.[71] When Congress refuses to violate such rights, legislators are distorting policymaking, often
to the benefit of minorities. Should we decry such distortions? Even a
brief comparison of this distortion standard and our common moral intu-
ition reveals its emptiness.

The distortion concept of corruption also assumes that the will of the
people exists apart from the political process. Legislators have the job of
carrying out this independent will. If they do not, they are assumed to
have been corrupted by campaign contributions. Unfortunately for this
argument, the will of the people, however measured, is not separate from
politics. Political scientists have long known that the same set of popular preferences will lead to different outcomes depending on the voting
method chosen. The will of the people depends on the way they vote to
determine their will.[72] Scholars of public opinion have also found that
surveys affect the content of public opinion in many ways.[73] Those who
defend the distortion standard face a deeper problem. From the earliest
days, public opinion surveys found that many Americans simply did not
have attitudes or positions regarding politics and public policy.[74] Leaders
cannot follow the will of the people when individuals do not have views
that can be followed.[75] The political scientist John Ferejohn thus concluded, "In what sense, then, can the policies of any government be said
to reflect the will of the government when that will cannot even be said to
exist?"[76] If it does not exist, the distortion model of corruption falls apart
for lack of a benchmark.

Perhaps I am being too demanding. Most Americans have little reason
to become fully informed about politics and public policy. The people are

thus unlikely to have a detailed opinion, individual or public, about specific policies. If so, it makes no sense to demand that policy follow public opinion and then to cry corruption when the two diverge. A better, more realistic question might be whether the public exercises any constraint on policymaking.[77] The political scientists James Stimson, Michael MacKuen, and Robert Erikson have systematically studied whether policymakers respond to changes in the public mood. They defined the public mood as a general disposition toward more or less government, a disposition measured by public responses to a survey asking whether a respondent wanted to spend more or less in a certain policy area. These responses can be used to construct a measure of the public's mood and its shifts over time.[78] Stimson and his colleagues argue that politicians respond to shifts in the public mood in two ways. First, they adapt their views to changes in public mood to obtain reelection. Some representatives, of course, make mistakes or refuse to adapt and depart from office. Second, they rationally anticipate where the public mood is and might be going and adapt their positions accordingly. In general, Stimson and his colleagues expect that public officials will more or less closely follow public moods, if not every public opinion poll. Looking at everything from congressional roll-call votes to presidential actions and Supreme Court decisions, Stimson's group concluded that "there exists about a one-to-one translation of preferences into policy."[79]

This conclusion is unlikely to satisfy the partisan of campaign finance regulation. Even if Stimson and his colleagues are correct, the partisan will insist that regarding specific issues the will of the people will be ignored in favor of big money. We quickly run into a mismatch between the alleged problem and its solution. After all, Congress cannot ban only contributions from (let's say) drug companies or energy interests. It can lay down only general restrictions on money (and thus on political activity) to prevent the "distortion" of policy about drugs and energy. If policymaking follows public moods generally, however, such bans will incur enormous costs because of the acceptance in many cases of a false hypothesis, that is, the claim that contributions distort policymaking.

The Progressive Temptation

The empirical evidence reviewed in this chapter must come as a surprise to most readers who assume that campaign contributions dominate policymaking in Washington and elsewhere. When empirical evidence contradicts a cherished belief, reason suggests revising the belief in light of the evidence. Nothing of the sort has happened in struggles over campaign finance regulation. The evidence discussed here has had little or no effect on the faith of the believers in campaign finance restrictions. In part, the persistence of that dogma testifies to the common human desire for secure beliefs. Moreover, in politics, the closed mind contributes more often than not to victory; those who are most certain have an advantage over those who entertain doubts, both in persuading others and in bargaining. I might note a final irony: Progressivism began, as we saw, with a firm belief that experts should rule based on scientific evidence. Such evidence has been gathered about campaign finance, but it has had little effect on the effort to restrict money in elections.

Progressives of our time, like their predecessors, condemn private money in politics as a corrupting influence that bespeaks selfishness and moral decline. The affirmations that underlie that condemnation are more obscure and yet no less influential in current debates. As we saw with John W. Gardner, Progressive intellectuals have identified public opinion and the public interest with their vision of politics. It is one thing to say that their agenda should inform public opinion and quite another to claim it actually does. American politics has been moving away from Progressivism for some time. For that reason, it is neither surprising nor disturbing that Progressives are losing political struggles and that policy outcomes reflect a more conservative nation. These losses and outcomes reflect nothing more than an expected political response to changing times and views.

The concept of representation is easily abused in the exigencies of political struggle. Most generally, representation "means the making present *in some sense* of something which is nevertheless not present literally or in fact."[80] In campaign finance struggles, that something may be the will of the people, the common good, or the public interest. Being absent, these things are not subject to empirical investigation. For that reason, it is easy for the contemporary progeny of the Progressives to assume that their substantive ideal of the common good represents the true views of the public or perhaps the real interests of the people. Most people are probably inclined toward confusing their own hopes with what the people want, and Progressives have a long history of identifying themselves as an ethical elite who possess special insight into the common good of society. Once aspiration is confounded with reality, any policy outcome contrary to their political agenda becomes not merely a disappointment but a corruption of political representation. What should have been present again—their conception of the public good—was not, which implies that something has gone awry with the process of representing. Progressives then seek the causes of the "corruption" of the process, and money becomes the prime suspect given its associations in the Progressive view with selfishness, material interests, and business. Freed from the influence of money, the advocates of restrictions aver, the political process would realize true public opinion and the common good of a more equal distribution of wealth. Restrictions on campaign finance follow as the way to end the power of private money over politics. But the Progressive problem is not really the general problem of big money in politics. It is, rather, a problem of specific kinds of money that are said to lead to policy outcomes contrary to Progressive ideals.[81] We might wonder, however, why outcomes should comport with those ideals.

If one begins by assuming that a pure political process should produce specific results, empirical evidence about the process itself becomes irrelevant to policy struggles. If one assumes that a pure political process enacts Progressive policies, any other result is taken as a sign that something other than political factors (ideology, partisanship, constituent concerns, the public interest) has affected the process leading to the result. Of course, other explanations are consistent with policy results contrary to Progressivism. Indeed, the empirical evidence discussed in this chapter indicates that political factors can explain policy votes in Congress. But if the premise underlying charges of corruption concern the results of the policy process (and not anything about the process itself), this empirical evidence is irrelevant. Until Congress enacts Progressive policies, the political process will be corrupt and in need of reform.

The temptation to blame political defeats on the moral failures of other people holds dangers for Progressives as well as for the rest of us. That strategy denies the possibility that Progressives may be the cause of their own political problems by simply failing to appeal to a majority of Americans. By declaiming the corruption of politics, they direct their efforts away from the difficult business of winning elections. Moreover, this focus on the failures of politics may well persuade citizens that the national government is corrupt and hence unworthy of trust. If such distrust becomes habitual but remains essential to empowering an activist state, the temptation to see corruption everywhere may end up undermining the Progressive desire to use government as a means to transform society toward egalitarian ends. No one will trust the politicians to do anything, including realizing Progressivism.

Conclusion

Money corrupts politics.[82] Few Americans doubt that the truth of that charge. The burden of this chapter has been to raise doubts about this article of faith. Campaign contributions differ in important ways from bribery. Not least, contributions have little influence over legislators. If we equate the public interest with public opinion, the empirical evidence suggests that money does not distort representation in the United States. The concept of corruption itself is ripe for abuse. To discern corruption in politics we need to know the interests of a representative's constituents. Yet no one knows this public interest; it is, one hopes, the result of the political process. Advocates of restricting money in politics tend to identify their policy preferences with the public interest or public opinion. Consequently, they misidentify political differences as errors and policy disappointments as corruption. As a result, the language of moral condemnation has long since replaced logic and respectful argument in campaign finance debates. What is ignored in all this moral posturing is the cost of restricting campaign contributions, a cost wholly paid in the currency of First Amendment rights.

CHAPTER FOUR

Political Culture

Many critics of American politics who have been informed by the Progressive vision bemoan the low expectations we have of citizens. Americans do not appear sufficiently concerned about politics. Fewer of them turn out to vote than their European counterparts. Those who do vote or otherwise participate in politics are expected, some might say encouraged, to pursue their own interests instead of their ideal of the public good. In contrast, these critics say, republican political theorists argued that self-government demanded much of its citizens. They had to actively participate in the life of the polity and pursue the common good, the condition for private happiness. Self-government thus required individuals to practice civic virtues and a political culture—habits, practices, and ideas—that were conducive to citizenship and the common good. Leading Progressives such as John Dewey worried that Americans would become too concerned about private matters and too little devoted to "fundamental general concerns."[1]

Some contemporary critics say that private money in politics reduces public confidence in government and drives Americans away from participating. If trustful, participating citizens are ideal, they conclude, money is corrupting American political culture. These critics are partly correct. Americans do distrust government more now than they did in the 1960s, and they often turn out to vote in relatively smaller numbers. But the Progressive critics assume that the changes are wholly pathological and the result of a largely private system of campaign finance. Both assumptions are wrong.

Philosophical Differences

Trust in Government

Distrust of the national government has a long history in the United States, a tradition regretted by those on the Right and the Left who aspire to more collective guidance of society. Progressives believe deeply in the benevolence of government and democracy, at least insofar as both reflect public opinion guided by an ethical elite of experts trained in social science and law. Distrust of government casts doubt on the wisdom and benevolence of Progressives and complicates realizing their vision of the good society. For Progressives, as we have seen, distrust in government is as much an anachronism as the Constitution and natural rights.[2]

The advantages of distrusting government should not be overlooked. Public skepticism about the benevolence of the federal government has a valuable place in the political culture of liberty and limited government. It chastens those who possess the tools of coercion and collective violence. It serves as a check on both raw ambition and collective aspirations, as Madison noted in Federalist no. 10. Distrust signifies the health of a body politic. It is not an illness to be treated but rather a civic virtue to be celebrated, at least insofar as one accepts the Madisonian vision of politics.

Distrust of government is not so much a public problem as a problem for Progressives. Public faith in the federal government and Progressive control of American politics coincided about the time of John F. Kennedy's death. When critics decry the public's distrust of government, they may be longing for a time long past, a time when Progressives commanded majorities and passed sweeping laws. The complaint about money and mistrust may be nothing more than an understandable lament and aspiration misleadingly couched in the language of public concern. Yet that same golden age of trust should give us pause. Trust in the federal government reached its highest point just as the U.S. president led the nation with little criticism or questioning into the Vietnam War. At the same moment, public trust in Keynesian economic expertise led to mistaken policies that hurt the U.S. economy in the 1970s. Excessive trust in government might well serve as a leading indicator of oncoming catastrophes.

Progressives assume that no rational person would distrust the federal government. In the past, Progressives thus spoke of "the paranoid style in American politics" as a way to explain the political appeal of limited-government conservatism.[3] Another explanation has a definite appeal:

private donations in elections cause distrust in government. Once private financing is forbidden, citizens will regain their natural faith in their government. Bans on campaign finance are to politics what antibiotics are to medicine: a way of ridding the body of disease, thereby restoring health.

Distrust of the federal government is not an illness in need of a cure. It represents a reasonable, perhaps optimal response to the facts of history and American politics. The period of rising distrust included the following failures by national leaders: the Vietnam War, urban riots, rising crime, the Watergate scandal, the Iranian hostage crisis, the Soviet invasion of Afghanistan, rising inflation together with rising unemployment in the late 1970s, the Abscam bribery scandal, the Iran-Contra affair, and several economic recessions. Who would say that Americans are wrong to distrust the federal government? Indeed, an attitude of trusting the federal government to do what is right most of the time would be irrational in light of the events of the past few decades.

Voter Turnout

As we shall see, a little more than half of the eligible voters participate in presidential elections. Some decry this level of turnout, noting that voter turnout was much higher in the United States in the 1960s and that Europe has continuously enjoyed more participation at the polls than this country. Yet the turnout in the 1960s was as high as any in the twentieth century.[4] Does it make sense to use an extreme measure of a value to pass judgment on American democracy? Moreover, if the United States has never had turnout rates similar to those in Europe, why should we expect convergence now? In any case, the United States differs from Europe in many ways, not all of which are to be regretted. The implicit benchmarks for criticizing turnout in American elections seem misplaced.

Nonvoting might create an electorate that differs systematically from the population that is eligible to vote. Nonvoting would thus distort public choice on election day by assuring that a nonrepresentative sample selects public officials. Others have noted that those who vote are demographically different from those who do not: voters are more likely than nonvoters to be male, white, rich, educated, and residentially stable. The demographic differences, however, do not correspond to differences in political views. Voters are less liberal than nonvoters with respect to issues concerning the economic role of government; they are more liberal on defense, the environment, and social issues. The absence of some voters from the polls does not lead to "the communication of skewed and unrepresentative policy preferences" to elected officials.[5] In other words, those who vote reasonably reflect the political preferences of everyone. Even if contributors were skewed, however, one scholar has found that "if we follow considerable empirical evidence and assume that campaigns provide information and that there are multiple contributors with diverse policy preferences, then increasing campaign contributions increases social welfare in the model in many of the most reasonable cases."[6]

The concern about low turnout is more than a question of representation. It reflects the priority Progressives give to politics. Those who see government as a necessary but limited part of life, a condition for but not the purpose of civilized life, might not be terribly troubled by current rates of voting. Citizens have the right to vote, to be sure, but they also have a right not to vote if they wish. The decision to avoid the polls does not reflect badly on those who do. In contrast, the Progressive believes politics and government are essential to the good life. Those who refuse to participate in collective decisions are not simply ignoring the obligations of citizenship, they are choosing to be less than fully human. Low turnout is not merely a cultural difference between Europe and the United States but a sign of a failure by Americans to achieve an obligatory moral ideal. For Progressives, that failure justifies government efforts to raise turnout, including hectoring those who do not vote and imposing restrictions on campaign finance insofar as spending and contributions discourage voting.

Voter turnout has also come to play another part in the campaign finance struggle. As we saw, Progressives advanced a positive conception of freedom that implied a distinction between good and bad speech. That implication bore fruit in time in a relentless loathing of what came to be called "negative advertising." That loathing has attracted some support, not least from members of Congress who are often attacked by such ads when running for reelection. Beyond moral condemnation, the hostility to such advertising has been linked to declining voter turnout and thus to a weakening of democracy.

Once again we find a conflict of visions beneath the struggle over campaign finance. Those who believe in liberty and limited government see skepticism toward government as a civic virtue and the decision not to vote as an individual choice to be respected by the state and other citizens. Progressives see distrust of government and refusing to vote as vices to be discouraged. Empirically, the Madisonians have the better of the argument: Americans do distrust government and do vote less often than Europeans. Progressives are faced with the task of changing their fellow citizens by proscribing, punishing, and preaching. Yet the fight over political culture is more than conflict of visions. Progressives argue that money in elections causes distrust of government and low voter turnout. Presumably the proper restrictions on such money will bring an end to distrust of government. Neither the empirical claim nor the expected policy outcome bears scrutiny.

Empirical Evidence

Trust in Government

In *Buckley v. Valeo* the Supreme Court held that Congress may limit campaign contributions to prevent the "appearance of corruption." The Court defined the "appearance of corruption" as "public awareness of the opportunities for abuse inherent in a regime of large individual financial contributions."[7] Such awareness would harm the nation, the Court averred, by eroding "'confidence in the system of representative Government . . . to a disastrous extent.'"[8] The Court and later commentators assumed that the appearance of corruption provides a valid reason independent of the corruption or the improper influence standard to restrict campaign finance. For example, Anthony Corrado has written that "no presidential soft money donor has been judged guilty of any improper action or been shown to have received special consideration because of a donation." Large gifts of soft money have not "led to massive corruption in the political system." Yet such donations are a problem because they "encourage the appearance of corruption and widespread public perceptions that wealthy interests enjoy undue influence in the political process."[9] The appearance argument has nothing to do with proving corruption of policymaking.

On the surface, the idea that the appearance of corruption could justify restrictions on liberty seems mistaken. From the start, Western philosophers have tried to distinguish between appearances and reality in the faith that a life lived according to truth was better than a life lived according to lies. In his analogy of the Cave, Plato distinguished the illusions of everyday life from the truths available from philosophy. He argued that political life should be governed by knowledge and not the fickle and often false opinions of most people. Western religious traditions are similarly devoted to truth and reality although it is by way of revelation rather than reason. Natural rights arguments, whether secular or religious, assert that humans can know important truths about the purposes of government. If we are to permit restrictions on basic rights, surely we want the policy in question to be in service to an important and legitimate goal of government and to be certain to attain that goal. To attain the goal, the policy should be based on accurate premises.[10] The appearance of corruption argument cannot meet this standard.

Imagine that policymaking is corrupt and the public believes it is so. The appearance argument would be saved at the cost of collapsing into the actual corruption standard. Appearances would be reality. If policymaking is truly corrupt, we do not need the appearance rationale to regulate money.

Now imagine that policymaking is not corrupted by money, but the public nonetheless believes it is. In other words, the public has a false belief. The appearance rationale says that we should restrict fundamental rights to achieve some competing goal even though the purported cause and effect depend on a mistaken notion. The rationale thus vitiates the presumption of liberty, the foundation of a Madisonian regime. This presumption says that citizens may act unless others can show that their exercise of liberty would cause grave harms in fact. The rationale says that liberty may be restricted if enough people believe that an exercise of liberty causes harms and that that belief itself causes some harm although it is false. The presumption of liberty becomes less a matter of law and social science than a concern of public relations. Also, it is much easier to show that Americans distrust government than to prove that campaign contributions affect policymaking.

Moreover, we might wonder whether Congress can increase trust in government by enacting policies based on false premises. We have good reason to trust government if public officials are making policy based on accurate information and conclusions. We ought to distrust the competence or good faith of public officials who are making policies based on false assumptions about reality. The appearances rationale can hardly justify policies put in place to increase public confidence in government. Public distrust would be the only justified response to restrictions on campaign finance based on incorrect beliefs.

Consider, finally, a third possibility. We might not know for sure whether contributions corrupt politics. Given that uncertainty, one might argue, what people believe should be taken as a pragmatic truth for purposes of legislation. But this move accomplishes nothing. Uncertainty notwithstanding, money either corrupts representation or it does not. If it does, we do not need the appearance standard to restrict corruption. If it does not, the standard restricts basic rights in order to appease the populace. Neither course should be acceptable under the U.S. Constitution. For that reason, the appearance argument should be and has been distinguished from the more compelling actual corruption standard.[11]

The *Buckley* majority intimated that a public belief in political corruption, whether true or not, leads to bad consequences and specifically to a decline in public confidence in government "to a disastrous extent." The qualifier is essential. We are unlikely to restrict basic rights to increase public confidence in government by five percent. The defender of the appearance standard hopes to show that unregulated money calls into question the very legitimacy of the government. If citizens come to believe that money determines policy, it is argued, they will rationally lose faith in government because their representative will not be theirs but rather an agent for others. As a federal appeals court recently said, campaign contributions would allegedly create "a political system unresponsive to the needs and desires of the public, and causing the public to become disillusioned with and mistrustful of the political system."[12] Whether contributions have had that effect depends on empirical evidence, not armchair speculation, however appealing or apparently logical. What might count as evidence for the proposition that contributions drive down public confidence in government? Because campaign spending largely equals campaign contributions, we can measure our cause—contributions—by gathering data about campaign spending over time. We can examine the relation between campaign spending and measures of public trust in government.

Since 1964 surveys have asked, "Would you say the government is pretty much run by a few big interests looking out for themselves or that it is run for the benefit of all the people?" Taking responses to this question as a measure of the appearance of corruption, pure and simple, we find a moderate association since 1982 between Congress members' spending on campaigns and respondents saying government is run by a few big interests.[13] This finding hardly makes the advocates' case. They assume spending (or the contributions supporting such outlays) causes the public to believe that government is run by a few big interests. But such spending primarily supports campaign messages advocating election or defeat of candidates for office. Among the most common messages in elections dur-

ing my lifetime has been the claim that government is run for the benefit
of a few big interests rather than the benefit of all. The association we find
between money and a common belief in corruption may say more about
the efficacy of campaign spending than about the public's assessment
of the effects of money on governmental ethics. The "few big interests"
question may not be a useful measure of the effects of campaign finance
on public trust in government.

Over the course of the past forty years, the National Election Studies Center has asked the following question every two years: "How much
of the time do you think you can trust the government in Washington
to do what is right—just about always, most of the time or only some
of the time?" A response of "just about always" or "most of the time"
shows high trust in the federal government.[14] Since 1958, the proportion
of Americans showing high trust in the federal government has declined
overall (see figure 4.1).[15]

I begin with some general observations about the trend in trust among
Americans. Although the overall trend is downward, trust in government
has experienced two steady declines and two relatively brief increases
since 1958. The first decline began in 1964 and ended in 1980; the second
began in 1984 and ended in 1994. Commentators often attribute distrust

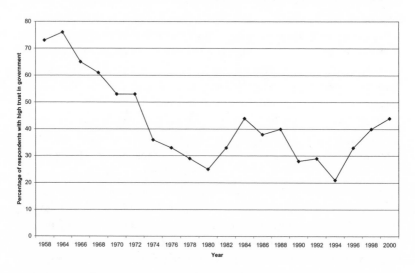

FIGURE 4.1 Trust in government, 1958–2000. National Election Studies, table 5A.1.
http://www.umich.edu/~nes/nesguide/gd-index.htm#3 (accessed August 1, 2003).

of government to the Vietnam War and the Watergate scandal, and it is true that both events occurred during the first long decline. But the decline began prior to 1968, the year that the general public began to have doubts about Vietnam, and long before Watergate.[16] Federal campaign finance legislation was passed in 1971 (nine years before the decline ended) and was amended extensively in 1974. Campaign finance regulation seems to have had little effect in curing the ill.

Proponents of restrictions might argue that the regulations did not increase trust in government because of loopholes, not least the soft money loophole, which allowed unlimited contributions to the political parties. The soft money exception came about in 1979.[17] Shortly thereafter, trust in government began to rise, which directly contradicts the conjecture that unregulated contributions cause distrust in government. Trust started downhill again in 1986 and continued to decline until 1994. The partisan of campaign finance regulation might be tempted to conclude that the "abuses" of soft money only became clear in 1986 and, along with the Iran-Contra scandal, caused a decline in trust. Unfortunately for this theory, soft money began to grow in 1995 when President Clinton and his advisors began soliciting such contributions to pay for an extensive advertising campaign designed to prepare the ground for his reelection.[18] In other words, just at the moment the alleged soft money abuses started, trust in government began to rise. In general, in presidential election years, we find a positive relation between soft money and trust in the federal government. In order words, *growth* in soft money spending tends to be moderately associated with *growth* in trust.[19]

Other public opinion data support a similar conclusion. For example, the number of Americans who agree with the statement "People don't have a say in what the government does" dropped like a stone during the period when soft money fundraising rose rapidly. By 2002 the number agreeing with the statement was near its all-time low point.[20] The same might be said of the number of people who believe that public officials don't care what people think or who answer "not much" when asked "How much does the government listen to the people?"[21] Public belief in the responsiveness of the government appears to have risen during a period of increased campaign spending and soft money fundraising.

Step back again from the trust data. When did trust in government increase? It did so in 1980 and 1994. What happened in those two years? Outsiders promising limits on government and lower taxes won the presidency and the Congress. Overall, increases in trust are strongly associated with declines in the federal government's share of the nation's wealth.[22] Moreover, both years saw victories by Republicans, the party that traditionally raises and spends more money on elections. If campaign finance causes distrust in government, why has trust increased only when the party associated with high campaign spending won watershed elections? Money apparently has little effect on public trust in government.

The numbers certainly support that conclusion.[23] The correlation coefficient between congressional spending on elections and trust in government from 1982 to 2000 is about zero.[24] We need not rely on general correlations alone. John J. Coleman and Paul F. Manna looked closely at the effects of spending on public trust in the 1994 and 1996 elections, taking all relevant factors into account through regression analysis.[25] They concluded that "spending by incumbents and challengers seems to have little substantive impact on trust and efficacy."[26] Gerald Pomper and Richard Lau conclude from their extensive study of the effects of negative advertising in U.S. Senate elections: "There is no hint whatsoever in the data that the tone of political campaigns has any effect on levels of trust in government. The data look no different if we consider just independents or just partisans. The logic that negative campaigns might lower trust in government is clear, but the evidence, at least in our data, simply does not exist."[27]

Nathaniel Persily and Kelli Lammie have recently examined the factors affecting public confidence in government. According to the appearance argument, Persily and Lammie should have found that some feature of the campaign finance system, taking all other factors into account, causes a decline in public confidence in government. They found instead that Americans' "confidence in the system of representative government" — specifically, their beliefs that officials are not "crooked" and that the government is "run for the benefit of all" — is associated with an individual's position in society, general tendency to trust others, beliefs about what government should do, and ideological or philosophical disagreement with the policies of incumbent officeholders. For Persily and Lammie, the regressions indicate that "trends in general attitudes of corruption seem unrelated to anything happening in the campaign finance system (i.e., a rise in contributions or the introduction of a particular reform)."[28] In lay language, other factors, not campaign finance, seem to cause declines in public confidence in government.

What are we to make of all these data about public trust and campaign spending? We should bear in mind that proponents of campaign finance regulation have the burden of proof on this question. They are required to show that campaign spending lowers public trust by creating an appearance of corruption. The evidence shows that spending has no effect on public trust, carefully measured and rigorously analyzed. Reasonable people have no reason to reject the conjecture that campaign spending has no effect on public trust. Indeed, multiple regression analysis suggests other factors account for changes in public confidence in government.

We should also recall the big picture. Advocates claim that unregulated private contributions to campaigns create an appearance of corruption that causes the public to mistrust government. Yet spending on campaigns (which roughly equals contributions over time) has little if any effect on whether people think the federal government does what is right most of the time. Thus the asserted line of causality from campaign finance to an appearance of corruption to distrust of government does not exist.

Political Participation

Pundits and professors have spent a lot of time and effort decrying the decline in political participation in the United States, especially as measured by voter turnout. Money in politics often serves as a general scapegoat for all political ills, but it seems an unlikely candidate for causing a decline in turnout. After all, candidates and parties spend money to convince people to vote for them and to get their followers to the polls to actually vote. Far from a suspect in the turnout mystery, campaign spending looks like a goad to participation. Nonetheless, some say big money campaigns focused on negative advertising disgust citizens and depress turnout. The best studies we have indicate that they are wrong.

Has voter turnout decreased? Most citizens probably assume Americans are voting less and less, an unexamined assumption often repeated but rarely proved. Some have made a profession of studying the putative failure of Americans to live up to their political obligations. Curtis Gans, an analyst often quoted with regard to this issue, has written of America's "disintegrating democracy," in which "the nation that prides itself on being the best example of government of, for, and by the people is rapidly becoming a nation whose participation is limited to the interested or zealous few."[29] Many political scientists in the past would have agreed with Gans's grim view.

The assumption that turnout has declined steadily has fostered a search for causes that has, in part, blamed campaign finance. If in fact turnout has not declined in recent decades, we do not have a problem.

Experts have measured voter turnout by dividing the number of voters by some measure of potential voters. Traditionally they gauged this number by the voting-age population of a state, a number easily obtained from the United States Census Bureau. That procedure does paint a picture of a nation slowly abandoning the polls. However, that way of measuring turnout is misleading.

The political scientist Michael McDonald has shown that the number of Americans who are actually eligible to vote has become progressively smaller than the number of Americans of voting age. In 2000, for example, the United States had more than nineteen million voting-age people who were ineligible. The voting-age population was more than 10 percent larger than the eligible population. In estimating voter turnout, this difference changes everything. Calculations based on the number of eligible voters show that turnout in presidential and off-year elections has not been declining. In fact, it has been flat or rising slightly for about thirty years (see figures 4.2 and 4.3).

McDonald's work indicates that voter turnout has been somewhat higher than previously thought. Nonetheless, his calculations confirm that turnout has decreased from its peak in the 1960s. The decline, however,

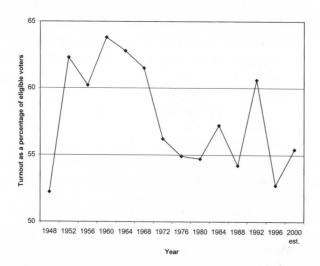

FIGURE 4.2 Turnout of eligible voters in presidential elections, 1948–2000. Michael McDonald, "United States Elections Project." http://elections.gmu.edu/voter_turnout.htm (accessed November 12, 2003).

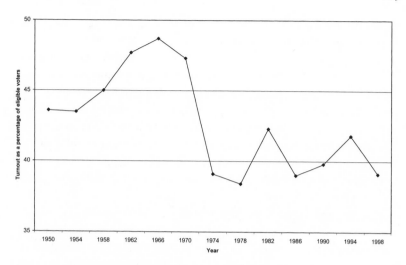

FIGURE 4.3 Turnout of eligible voters in off-year elections, 1948–2000. Michael McDonald, "United States Elections Project." http://elections.gmu.edu/voter_turnout .htm (accessed November 12, 2003).

has not been slow and steady. Instead, turnout followed a relatively high path in the 1950s and 1960s and a lower path after the mid-1970s, when the trend stayed flat or turned slightly upward. In sum, the decline in turnout by eligible voters looks like a shock that had a sharp effect on voting followed by a steady influence. Why would increases in campaign spending cause declines in voter turnout? One might expect that more money would lead to higher, not lower, turnout.

Some argue that increases in campaign spending alienate citizens and lead to lower turnout. The 1972 presidential election seems to support this proposition. That election saw both the highest spending by presidential candidates up to that time and the largest drop in turnout by eligible voters from one presidential election to the next.[30] Before concluding that increased campaign spending caused the drop in participation, we should consider two complications.

Spending would presumably have driven down turnout by changing attitudes. Specifically, we would expect to see a change in public attitudes during 1972. In fact, we find several measures of trust in government declining sharply from 1966 to 1970, remaining roughly level thereafter until Watergate.[31] Similarly, measures of voter efficacy—the feeling that one's vote or opinions matter—declined during the late 1960s but remained steady during the early 1970s.[32] If spending alienated voters, that feeling does not show up in public opinion surveys.

The timing of the declines in trust and efficacy also direct our attention to other causes for alienation from the political system. The late 1960s were a time of great turmoil regarding such questions as Vietnam and civil rights. Those struggles would have drawn Americans into the voting booth. By 1972 those issues had largely passed and their pull on the voters lessened. When we consider also that the 1972 presidential election was not competitive (Nixon ended up with a massive landslide victory), we have some plausible alternative explanations for the decline in turnout for that year.

A final point suggests that the influence of money on voting might be weak. No one doubts that after 1972 overall spending on American political campaigns rose steadily.[33] During that time, turnout has varied around a flat trend. Surely if money drove voters away from the polls, we would have seen a continuous steady decline in turnout since 1972.

Such general data can offer plausible but not definitive answers to the question of whether money drives down turnout. Political scientists have tried to specifically identify how campaign spending might affect participation. Their efforts have led to a useful and interesting body of research on political advertising that bears on our concerns about campaign finance.

Among intellectuals, television runs a close second to campaign contributions as the pathogen that causes public ills in the United States. Television ads attract most spending for communications by campaigns, which have "turned increasingly hostile and ugly." Attack ads, the argument continues, have "become the norm rather than the exception."[34] Aesthetics aside, critics have tried to link such advertising to declining turnout. Others claim private financing of campaigns fosters negative ads and that limits on spending would improve the tone of public discourse.[35]

What is a negative ad? The term is rarely defined overtly. Critics use the term to mean any advertising that attacks or is critical of an opponent. According to the political scientist William Mayer, "Negative campaigning focuses on the weaknesses and faults of the opposition: the mistakes they have made, the flaws in their character or performance, the bad policies they would pursue." As two other experts remark, "[N]egative campaigning is not lying and stealing and cheating, it is criticizing the opponent." Positive campaigning, in contrast, emphasizes the merits of a candidate and the beneficial policies he would pursue.[36]

Campaigns are not required to spend money on advertising that is critical of their opponents. Money is a means that advances (or retards) any content stated in any fashion, positive or critical. Candidates could spend their money on positive ads when doing so serves their interest in being elected.[37] When public financing and spending limits replace private funding of campaigns, candidates can and do run harsh ads critical of their opponents. For example, the first publicly financed Democratic guberna-torial primary in Massachusetts featured several negative ads by candi-date Warren Tolman. This reality clashed with the expectations of those who hoped public funding would improve the tone of campaign rhetoric.[38] Justified or not, partisans of campaign finance restrictions believe nega-tive advertising is the means whereby money harms democracy by driving down voter turnout. Are they correct?

If turnout had dropped into a lower path in the early 1970s, we would expect to see that campaigns turned negative at that time and remained so. In fact, advertising during presidential campaigns became progressively more positive from 1964 to 1976, the latter year having the highest tone of any campaign from 1964 to 1992 (see figure 4.4).[39] The year turnout col-lapsed—1972—was within that trend. Although the tone of presidential campaigning declined after 1976, turnout remained essentially flat. In fact, the 1992 election featured both the best voter turnout since 1970 and the worst tone of all the years measured. Put another way, the sharpest decline ever recorded in the tone of a presidential campaign is associated with the

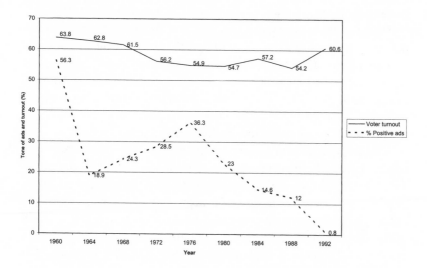

FIGURE 4.4   Voter turnout and campaign tone, 1960–92. Steven E. Finkel and John G. Geer, "A Spot Check: Casting Doubt on the Demobilizing Effect of Attack Advertising," *American Journal of Political Science* 42 (April 1998): 582, fig. 1.

largest rise in voting turnout in the thirty-year period studied. Negative campaigning does not correlate negatively with turnout by eligible voters. In fact, the data suggest the opposite conclusion, especially in the 1992 election: negative ads are positively associated with a rise in turnout. This simple bivariate analysis casts much doubt on the alleged harms done by negative advertising. Yet other factors could be at work. We have reason to consult the research done on the effects of critical advertising.

About a decade ago, a team of scholars conducted experiments indicating that attack ads drive down turnout. Their experiment exposed a treatment group and a control group to negative ads. Their results indicated that negative ads drove down turnout by 5 percent. They followed the experiments by looking at the effects of negative campaigns on turnout in the actual 1990 Senate contests. The scholars found that negative campaigns reduced turnout by 4 percent.[40] They concluded that negative campaigning drives down turnout by making "voters disenchanted with the business of politics as usual" and by lowering "confidence in the responsiveness of electoral institutions and public officials."[41] They argued that negative ads would in particular reduce participation by political independents whose disgust with the tone of campaigns would drive them away from the voting booth in disproportionate numbers. Following up on this conjecture, these same authors conducted experiments in the 1992 presidential elections that indicated that negative advertising led to an 11 percent decline in intention to vote among political independents.[42]

These studies have two small shortcomings and one big problem. First, the experiments did not use actual campaign advertisements. Their larger statistical study of the Senate campaigns measured "negativity" by press reports about the tone of a campaign. So, second, if the press reported campaigns as more negative than they were, their conclusions would be off target. What is the big problem? Subsequent studies have found that negative ads improve democracy in theory and practice.

A moment's reflection suggests several reasons why negative ads would boost turnout. They contain relevant information for a voter, and scholars have long known that more knowledgeable voters are more likely to participate. Negative information helps voters discriminate between candidates and thereby gives them a reason to go to the polls. Finally, it may stir up voters, creating more enthusiasm and involvement in an election and, perhaps, a desire to learn more about the candidates.[43] As two scholars point out, "Criticism of an opponent—particularly strong criticism—sends a message that something of substance is at stake in the election, that its outcome matters, and that this is a choice voters should care about."[44]

Tough critical electoral advertising does fall short of the norms of the seminar room, writ large as "deliberative democracy." But those norms are unrealistic for a nation where most people do not like politics or care much about participating in public affairs.[45] Scholars have long known that the costs of voting (and getting information about candidates for office) almost always outweigh the direct benefits of participation. Negative ads provide relevant, critical information in a brief, easily grasped format. Far from being pathological, the brevity and tone of electoral ads match the implicit demands made by American voters.

So much for theory. What about real life? Do the data support the theory that negative ads stimulate participation? That they do so has become the "emerging conventional wisdom" among scholars studying the question.[46] Why is this new conventional wisdom convincing experts? In part, scholars have not been able to confirm the broad findings of the experimental work done on the 1992 elections.[47] At the same time, several studies have looked at the effects of actual campaign advertising during real elections.[48]

Steven Finkel and John Geer studied closely most of the presidential campaign ads run in the United States since 1960. They decided whether each ad was positive or negative and constructed an index that measured the overall proportion of ads that were positive. Finkel and Geer then looked at the relation between the tone of the presidential campaign ads and turnout (including the participation of independents), controlling for many other factors that are known to affect turnout. Their findings are striking:

- Advertising tone has essentially no effect on turnout in the electorate, once other factors are taken into account
- Campaigns with more negative advertisements have a slightly higher rate of turnout among independents than more positive campaigns, again taking other factors into account.[49]

The authors conclude that "exposure to negative campaign advertisements has no demobilizing effect among the general public or among Independents."[50]

Finkel and Geer's study has some limitations. They have substantial data about the tone of campaign ads. They do not know, however, how often and where the ads were shown. Yet in their index each ad has equal weight and equal exposure. Other researchers have tried to estimate the effects of being exposed to political ads.

Paul Freedman and Kenneth Goldstein examined the advertising in the 1997 Virginia gubernatorial election. They not only evaluated the tone of the commercials but also closely tracked when and where campaign ads appeared. Their effort marks the most precise measure we have of voters' exposure to political advertising. Once again taking account of other factors that might affect turnout, they found that negative advertising strongly increased turnout. Strikingly, ads that conveyed a positive or more mixed message seemed to lower turnout. Freedman and Goldstein conclude that "it is primarily the negative spots that have a mobilizing effect on voters."[51]

Critics of negative ads might object that these are only two studies that are not representative of what we "know" about negative ads. Fortunately, four political scientists have considered all studies of negative ads up to 1999 to provide some general conclusions. They performed a "meta analysis" of 117 findings about negative ads drawn from 52 separate studies. Their work addressed three questions. Do citizens dislike negative ads? Are negative ads more effective than positive ads? Does negative advertising reduce electoral participation? Their statistical analysis of the research literature found

- no reliable statistical basis for concluding that negative ads are liked less than positive ones
- no evidence that negative political advertisements are any more effective than positive political ads
- little evidence that widespread use of negative ads imperils electoral participation.

The authors conclude that "participatory democracy may be on the wane in the United States, but the evidence reviewed here suggests that negative political advertising has relatively little to do with it."[52]

More recently, Goldstein and Freedman studied negative ads by using a commercial database that identifies where and how often a campaign commercial appears. Their research assistant then coded each ad shown during the 1996 presidential race as positive, purely negative, or contrasting (ads that have positive information about their sponsor and negative claims about his opponent). They also obtained data about when and where the ads ran and the television viewing habits of individuals in various parts of the country. All in all, Goldstein and Freedman have created the best measure we have of exposure to political advertising during an election. They found that increases in the overall volume of advertising slightly decreases turnout. Positive ads had no effect on turnout, but "negative ads have a significant and substantial mobilizing effect."[53] The increases in turnout brought by negative ads more than offset the decreases caused by the overall volume of ads. More concretely, Goldstein and Freedman looked at the progressive effects of negative ads on the likelihood that an "average voter" would go to the polls. Table 4.1 summarizes their results. Overall, exposing the average voter to heavy doses of negative advertising would, all things considered, increase their likelihood of voting by a little more than 10 percent. Lighter doses, an "average" exposure, for example, increase the probability of voting by 3 percent.

Other recent studies consistently support the conclusion that negative advertising does not suppress turnout. Joshua Clinton and John Lapinski constructed a large, controlled and randomized experiment to discern the immediate and long-term effects of ads on voting. The researchers found that "it is never the case that exposure to negative advertising decreases either the reported probability of voting or the actual voting." They also report "no evidence" that political independents are most susceptible to negative ads. Clinton and Lapinski found, in contrast to earlier studies, only limited evidence that negative advertising stimulates voting.[54] Similarly, Lau and Pomper conclude from their study of Senate elections that "the tone of the campaign *by itself* has almost no effect on turnout. We estimate a mobilization 'effect' (if one can call it that) of two-tenths of 1 percent, or at the extreme levels of campaign negativism observed in our data, campaign negativism will increase turnout by about 5.5 percent, all else equal."[55]

TABLE 4.1   **Effect of negative ads on propensity to vote**

Exposure to negative ads	Probability of voting	Effect of negative ads on turnout (%)
None	0.761	—
Average	0.789	2.8
One standard deviation above average	0.833	4.4
Two standard deviations above average	0.869	3.6

Source: Ken Goldstein and Paul Freedman, "Campaign Advertising and Voter Turnout: New Evidence for a Stimulation Effect," *Journal of Politics* 64 (August 2002): 721–40.

Social scientists have become increasingly skillful and sophisticated at measuring the effects of advertising on citizens. Their conclusions about negative ads are stark. It does not harm American democracy or its political culture. If negative ads did not exist, fewer people might well turn out to vote. If higher turnout is better for democracy than lower turnout, negative ads make a valuable contribution to American democracy. The same might be said about the money behind the ads.

Even if ads did reduce turnout, what could public policy do? Some argue that Americans should consider the tradeoff between free expression and voter turnout, suggesting that government regulation of ads may be warranted.[56] Americans may want to consider the tradeoff, but any government regulation of negative ads would involve controlling the content of speech, which the First Amendment forbids.

Even if we bracketed the constitutional questions, some research suggests that boosting turnout via regulation of advertising would require distinguishing "useful negative information" (which boosts turnout) and "shrill mudslinging" (which discourages voting).[57] Should government be given the power to distinguish good negative ads from bad ones? Would mudslinging ads simply be defined as any ad that effectively criticized the individuals or groups who have the power to regulate campaign advertising? This likely outcome highlights the wisdom of the phrase "Congress shall make no law" in the First Amendment. If negative ads are a public problem—and the evidence says they are not—the best policy response would be criticism and shame, coupled with vigorous media reporting and evaluation of campaign advertising.

Limits on negative ads would also make American elections less competitive because such limits inevitably favor incumbents. Those who already hold office begin their reelection campaign with enormous advantages in name recognition and resources (staff work, campaign money, and so on). Incumbents also benefit from the value that voters place on experience.[58] Incumbents do not lose unless challengers find some way to become known in a district and to call into question an incumbent's record. Challengers may use positive ads to make their names more easily recognized with voters, but calling the incumbent into question requires criticism that is sharp and memorable. According to Mayer, "Challengers certainly hope to convince people of their own virtues . . . but they are not likely to get far without directly undermining support for the incumbent." Not surprisingly, researchers have found that 18 percent of voters could name something they disliked about an incumbent who won reelection;

in contrast, in districts where incumbents lost, 46 percent of voters could name a reason to dislike the officeholder.[59]

A more recent study of Senate elections makes a similar point. Richard Lau and Gerald Pomper looked at United States Senate races from 1988 to 1998 to see who used negative appeals to voters. Taking all things in account, they found that challengers in general, candidates in open-seat races, Republican candidates, candidates with less money than their opponents, and candidates facing negative campaigns were more likely than everyone else to use negative appeals.[60] Lau and Pomper's conclusions suggest that negative advertising is a tool for candidates facing an uphill battle, candidates likely to lose unless something changes. Challengers and candidates with less money (often the same people) obviously need some weapon to fight their battles. Negative advertising is that weapon.

I have examined at length the common belief that big money campaigns based on negative advertising have reduced political participation. Candidates do spend money on ads criticizing their opponent, sometimes harshly. Such ads, however, neither bear any necessary relation to campaign finance nor harm American democracy. In truth, negative ads seem to make a valuable contribution to informing and mobilizing American voters. Here again, as elsewhere, logic and social science subvert the assumptions of those who would restrict money in politics. Here as elsewhere something more than conjecture about how the world works is driving the distaste for negative advertising.

Progressive thinkers see all critical advertising as an emotional appeal founded on falsehoods and thus as a corruption of political speech, which should make rational arguments in good faith. Negative ads both drive people away from politics and debase the debates among those who remain. Focused as they are on the personal and political failings of candidates, negative ads could never be speech about the common good or the public interest. Such ads, in the Progressive mind, are simply attacks designed to satisfy the self-interest of an ambitious candidate and lack the moral qualities that should define democratic talk.

What is the solution to "bad speech"? One answer would be more speech, good, bad, or indifferent. Freedom of speech would be the institutional response to bad speech. As we have seen, Progressives tend toward greater political activism in these matters. Government may both demand "good speech"—speech directed to a public good—and deny bad speech entry to the political realm through regulation and restrictions. In concrete terms, the government could enact and enforce content regulations to make sure electoral advertising is sufficiently public-spirited and not negative. Such restrictions would thus aspire to creating a rich public debate. Apart from the fact that such regulation would contravene the express language of the First Amendment, restrictions on negative advertising have two problems. First, no one would trust their political opponents to decide which advertising should have what content. Everyone would correctly assume that everyone else would use such regulations to advance their political causes and candidates and to harm those of their opponents. But if no one would trust opponents with such power, why should anyone have the power of forbidding speech? The answer might be that one group, an ethical elite, has the knowledge or the moral insight to apply ethically correct and impersonal standards to political speech. Does this elite exist? Does anyone other than the members of that group recognize their moral and intellectual superiority?

Critics, not least the U.S. Senators who support McCain-Feingold, tend to identify negative advertising with falsehood. The little evidence we have suggests they are not entirely wrong. John Coleman found that in House races where challengers spent the most money voters tended to have incorrect beliefs about the ideology or record of an incumbent.[61] But, as we have seen, Coleman also found that more spending (some of which would go to negative advertising) also led generally to voters' having more (and more accurate) information. If we constrain spending or spending on negative advertising, we will certainly suppress both true and false speech. Apart from everything else that might be said against suppressing electoral advertising, such regulations will deprive voters of some measure of truth about candidates for office. That would certainly harm voters and democracy, but it may not harm everyone engaged in politics, which brings us to a final point about negative advertising.

As we saw in the introduction, several U.S. Senators recommended McCain-Feingold as a solution to the "problem" of negative advertising. The provisions that complicate the funding of so-called electioneering communications sought to reduce issues advertising that had been highly critical of candidates for office, including, of course, incumbent members of Congress. Apart from the fact that no one likes to be criticized (especially if the criticisms are based on falsehoods or what one takes to be falsehoods), member of Congress may have other reasons to dislike negative ads. In the two cycles prior to the enactment of McCain-Feingold, ten members of the House of Representatives lost in the general election. In each of those contests, the voting turnout was higher in the loser's district than it was statewide. In the four such races in 2000, the turnout in the loser's district was 4 to 8 percent higher than the relevant statewide turnout. In 1998, the six races that incumbents lost saw turnout that was 7 to 12 percent higher than turnout statewide.[62] In those years, at least, higher turnout seems to be associated with a greater probability of an incumbent losing his bid for reelection, especially in the off-year elections. If members of Congress (correctly) see negative ads as prompting higher turnout, they may also believe that fewer ads will mean lower turnout, which in turn will increase their chances of reelection.[63] The distaste incumbents evince for critical advertising no doubt reflects concern about the tone of electoral discourse. But it may also reflect a presumed self-interest that contravenes the interests of voters who benefit from more rather than fewer choices on Election Day.

Conclusion

Distrust of the federal government and low voter turnout do not justify limiting spending on politics. Neither one is inherently bad or caused by money in politics. Critics of campaign finance—as well as a few Supreme Court justices—assume that money might foster a crisis of legitimacy for American government. In fact, most citizens have a high opinion of their nation, if not the federal government. In 2002 the Public Agenda Foundation asked whether the United States would be remembered in the future as the most democratic and free nation, as "right up there with the best of them," or as not standing out or falling far short of democracy and freedom. Eighty-six percent of those responding chose one of the first two options.[64] The legitimacy of American government remains strong. The same cannot be said for using the appearance of corruption to justify for restricting money in politics.

CHAPTER FIVE

Equality

Plato set out the first elaborate defense of inequality in political power. He argued that a class of guardians possessing knowledge should rule for the common good. Plato believed that democracy, the equal rule of all, would lead to corruption and eventually, tyranny. Similar doctrines have assured monarchs and aristocrats throughout history that nature or God or necessary circumstances have decreed that some people should rule over others.[1]

In contrast, the rule of the people—directly or via representatives—carries the assumption that no one has a special right or capacity for exercising political power for the common good. As Thomas Jefferson famously put it, "All eyes are opened, or opening, to the rights of man. The general spread of the light of science has already laid open to every view the palpable truth, that the mass of mankind has not been born with saddles on their backs, nor a favored few booted and spurred, ready to ride them legitimately, by the grace of God."[2] If no individual or group had the right to rule over others, individuals had an equal claim to their natural rights and to creating government.

We should understand what this idea of equality did and did not mean. Madisonians believed that citizens should be equal before the law in their rights. This notion excluded certain other ideas of equality. Individuals did not have a right to equality of property in part because bringing it about (or moving toward it) would require government to violate some individuals' right to property, violations that were both bad in themselves and sources of civil war, as Madison noted in Federalist no. 10. The Madisonian idea also did not imply an equality of political power in general or direct rule of the people all the time. Madison's idea of "popular government" did not entail equality of political influence in all matters.[3]

Indeed, Madison recommended representation of the people in part because he believed voters would choose well and select representatives marked by wisdom, patriotism, and a love of justice.[4] For Madison, the idea of political equality was compatible with political virtue and private inequality.

Progressives have offered a different and complex idea of equality. Like the founders, they rejected the older view that nature or God favors inequality of political power. At the same time, they were not egalitarians: they saw themselves as an ethical elite who should form public opinion and thereby influence government. This commitment to the rule of enlightened intellectuals existed alongside a faith in political equality. We might be tempted to conclude that Progressives offered an incoherent theory of equality or that their political practice subverted their political ideals. That temptation should not be indulged, at least not until we understand the complexity of their idea of political equality.

Progressives note that market economies lead to significant inequalities of wealth and income. Some acknowledge that such inequalities are perhaps necessary to provide incentives for individuals to produce wealth. They contrast economic life, a zone of inequality, with political democracy, which requires equality. Progressives argue that campaign contributions contravene democracy by transferring the inequalities of economic life to politics. Money is the bridge over which an economic elite enters and lays waste to the country called Democracy and raises up the new nation called "Plutocracy." At a minimum, the economy and the government should be separate spheres within a larger pluralistic society.[5] Given all that, the inequalities of influence claimed by Progressives might seem less troubling. If they use their power to create a public opinion and a polity that resist the inequalities generated by capitalism, the rule of an enlightened elite might comport with democracy and political equality.

We might note in passing the political appeal of the egalitarian argument. Few Americans identify themselves as upper class. In the past thirty years, 3 percent of Americans have identified themselves as "upper class" to survey researchers. In all these polls 87 percent of the respondents identified themselves as "working class" or "middle class."[6] Egalitarians attribute the corruption of democracy to a very small minority of Americans while allowing 97 percent of the nation to remain blameless for political problems. In a majority-rule polity, targeting the upper class or "the rich" seems to be a sure winner, especially if almost no citizens think of themselves as rich.

What should be done about the inequalities fostered by campaign finance? Egalitarians believe that regulations seeking to curb undue influence are inadequate to the task of assuring equality of influence. The contributor of $2,000 may be limited in his power to buy a vote, but his political power cannot be equal to that of others who are unable or unwilling to give as much to a campaign. Progressives originally looked to direct rule of the people to restore equality. Since the late 1970s, however, Progressives have become less happy with direct democracy.[7] The egalitarian strain in Progressivism always points toward eliminating private money from politics in favor of campaigns financed by taxpayers. Some Progressives have proposed more robust efforts to equalize political influence.

Until recently, the United States Supreme Court gave the principle of equality of influence little weight in considering the constitutionality of campaign finance restrictions. The *Buckley* Court had stated that "the concept that government may restrict the speech of some elements of our society in order to enhance the relative voice of others is wholly foreign to the First Amendment."[8] Since 2000 the Court appears to have imported a concern about political equality into its leading decisions in campaign finance cases, though under the guise of the older anticorruption rationale for such restrictions.[9] Equality of political influence, once deemed a threat to the First Amendment, may yet become the primary consideration in judicial evaluations of campaign finance law.

The Ambit of Equality

Forty years ago, the U.S. Supreme Court required the states to create congressional districts on the basis of the principle of "one person, one vote."[10] The decision initially affected state legislative districts that were often unequal in population within a state and across states, a malapportionment that accorded greater weight to some votes than to others. This decision recognized that the weight of votes in the directly representative institutions of American government should be equal; no single vote deserves to count more than any other vote.

Egalitarians in campaign finance see voting as the guiding analogy for allocating all political influence in the United States. They wish to expand the scope of the principle of "one person, one vote" to include campaign finance. They plump for a comprehensive "equality of influence" that includes spending on politics and elections as a way to realize "the egalitarian spirit of political democracy."[11] Egalitarians assume that contributions as well as spending create an inequality of influence. They argue that dollars are like votes and hence the freedom to donate to campaigns is something akin to stuffing the ballot box. Egalitarians claim that private financing of campaigns fosters an oligarchy where some citizens, the rich and powerful, have vastly more political power than others. A Madisonian would see a more constrained ambit for equality: votes would be allocated equally, but other forms of political participation would not have to meet the standard of equality in part because meeting that standard would impinge deeply on fundamental rights.

The egalitarian critique of campaign finance generalizes the Progressive concern about inequalities of wealth. Progressives believe that money is the most important resource in politics, the most potent source of inequality among citizens. The evidence presented in chapter 3 suggests that campaign contributions do not appear to have much influence, if any, on voting by members of Congress. Nonetheless, a look at the implications of political egalitarianism is revealing.

As some Progressives realize, the egalitarian project cannot stop at campaign contributions and spending. Money creates political inequality in other ways. For example, private political associations annually take in forty to sixty times the sums raised by political action committees.[12] Lobbyists spent $130 million a month lobbying Congress in 2001; in the first half of 2002, the monthly expenditure rose to $143 million.[13] If contributions have influence, surely interest group spending on lobbying creates as much or more inequality of influence. Why should the government regulate contributions and ignore lobbying, the right to petition the government for redress of grievances? If lobbying is free of regulation, the ambit of equality seems too narrow. Similarly, newspapers endorse causes and candidates for public office and spend millions propagating these attempts to influence the choices of voters. Surely such leading newspapers as the *New York Times* and the *Washington Post* have enormous and unequal influence on American political life. Why should their power be untouched by government? As we saw, the most thoroughgoing and consistent egalitarians advocate government control of lobbying and newspaper editorials.[14]

Money is not the only source of inequality. During elections both political parties depend on the efforts of thousands of volunteers. Federal law does not count those efforts as contributions to campaigns, although volunteers surely affect the outcomes of elections. Sometimes the volunteers have special talents to offer on behalf of a candidate. During the tight presidential election of 2004, the *Los Angeles Times* reported:

> In one of the most ambitious efforts by entertainers to influence a presidential election, a group of marquee-level pop musicians announced Wednesday an October concert blitz aimed at *mobilizing opposition* to President Bush. The tour will send more than 20 artists—including rock icon Bruce Springsteen—to perform more than 34 shows during a single week in nine states viewed as campaign battlegrounds. Concert organizers hope to not only raise money for efforts to defeat Bush, but *attract publicity to that cause and sway voters....* [Springsteen said,] "Hopefully, we have built up a lot of credibility with our fans over the years. There comes a moment when you have to *spend* some of it. This is that moment."[15]

The fame of celebrities gives them credibility with their fans, trust that translates into votes for a candidate favored by the famous. As Bruce Springsteen notes, fame, like money, can be saved and then spent on swaying voters. In an egalitarian world, why should such unequal influence over elections be free of government control?

The effort to restrict money in politics attracts people with the abilities to write well, to speak persuasively, and to manipulate the legislative agenda. Those talents certainly create an inequality of influence in American politics.[16] Freedom of speech, like other liberties, will permit inequalities in talents in writing and speaking to translate into inequalities in political power. If egalitarianism is a consistent doctrine, the expression of these talents, too, should be restricted by the state. In fact, such inequalities of talent are rarely mentioned by campaign finance reformers. Why?

Progressives might argue that economic inequalities are morally arbitrary because they arise from differences in social and natural assets that no individual deserves. Allowing private money into politics would both reproduce this injustice in the political sphere and prevent government from redressing the unjustified inequalities of the economic sphere. But this distinction does not help much. The talents that lead to fame or political influence are also distributed in a morally arbitrary fashion.

This diffidence toward political inequality is essential to the Progressive vision. Inequalities of wealth growing out of economic activity expressed as campaign finance perpetuate political inequalities, which in turn preserve all other inequalities in the society. In contrast, the expression of political inequalities may on the whole tend to lessen the other inequalities in the society. Political inequalities would be acceptable because they are a means to lessening the inequality introduced into politics by private economic activity. Some animals will be more equal than others, but only in service to the eventual equality of all. This argument distinguishes private wealth from political resources by abandoning the principle of one person, one vote. One group that enjoys unequal political resources gets to "stuff the ballot box" on the faith that such inequality will lead to greater equality. That faith in an ethical elite, of course, holds a central place in the Progressive vision of politics. For those who do not share that faith, toleration of political inequalities contravenes the egalitarian insistence on equality of influence and power.

Egalitarians may object that I am pushing a reductio ad absurdum. Surely the sphere of equality may be expanded, thereby improving American democracy, without equalizing the influence of the media or suppressing the effects of talent. In other words, could we not simply choose a different tradeoff in politics between liberty and equality, one that includes campaign finance but not other forms of political engagement? The most principled egalitarians do not believe that equality of influence should be limited. Indeed, the equality of influence standard admits of no limitation. If we equalize contributions to political campaigns and ignore the influence of endorsements by the *New York Times,* we are applying the demand for equality in a biased way to foster a system of inequality in which the media have more power and contributors have less. Indeed, the existing campaign finance system has fostered such inequality. To be sure, the First Amendment may require that exemption and those inequalities, but consistent egalitarians will not tolerate such exemptions because doing so would foment inequality of influence.

Finally, I should note that a rigorous egalitarianism would introduce a new kind of inequality of influence. Most egalitarians call for public financing of campaigns coupled with a prohibition on private donations to candidates. Egalitarians can hardly avoid banning private support because it is the putative source of the inequality of influence they abhor. If contributions are to reflect the equality of voting, each citizen should receive an equal sum to contribute to the candidate of his or her choice from the taxing authorities.[17] This effort to equalize political power thus ends by giving all power over the financing of elections to the government. By banning private contributions, egalitarians would end up creating a world where all power over elections lay with the state and none with civil society. Egalitarians may not be troubled much by this, perhaps because they trust that the government will use its new power to assure that each citizen receives an equal sum to contribute to a campaign; this inequality will be a necessary step toward the final equality of a voucher.

That trust seems misplaced. The government officials who assume power over the financing of elections will be tempted to use that authority to tilt election outcomes toward their favored candidates and causes. The authorities may simply abuse their power and favor their friends by means of clever interpretations and manipulations of the law. But they also might have egalitarian reasons for tilting the system. For example, the officials charged with the financing of elections might decide to award unequal sums to different groups of citizens. If anyone objected that such awards violated equality in campaign finance, the officials could say that just as nondiscrimination had to give way to affirmative action in racial policy, so formal equality in public financing of campaigns should favor those harmed by the older system of contributing. Of course, those who object to this reinterpretation of egalitarianism will have no outlet for resisting the authorities because all private financing of political activity will have been prohibited.

Apart from the franchise, all resources for influencing politics and government are unequally distributed. Applied rigorously—as it must be, according to its own inner logic—political egalitarianism inevitably restricts and ends freedom of speech and, indeed, the liberty to pursue any political activities. To escape that conclusion, egalitarians may argue that money is uniquely influential and harmful to democracy. But we have seen that campaign contributions have little influence on policymaking. Can the same be said of the unequally distributed talents for argument or political organizing? These problems indicate why American courts have limited political equality to the narrower ambit of the vote and refused to extend the logic of equality to other kinds of political participation. Beyond theory, the question remains whether campaign finance fosters inequalities of influence in the United States.

Elections and Representation

Do private contributions create significant inequalities of political power? In chapter 3 I cited studies that raise doubts about the policy influence of campaign contributions. If money has little influence, it follows that those who contribute to campaigns have little power. Of course, the critics of campaign finance do not accept such evidence. They believe that some combination of the rich, the Republican, and the conservative dominate American democracy. This egalitarian complaint comes in several versions.

A Conservative Bias?

The First Amendment denies Congress the power to abridge freedom of speech; it is a restraint on political power. As noted above, leading contemporary Progressives interpret the First Amendment as a grant of power rather than a restraint. It is said to be a means to foster a rich public debate to inform political life in general and elections in particular. A rich public debate creates opportunities for many voices to be heard in the public square. It is argued, however, that space in the public square is limited and scarce. If the government takes a hands-off approach to freedom of speech as the Constitution demands, the "rich and powerful" will buy up all opportunities to speak and "fill all available space for public discourse with their message." Be restricting the speech of "the rich" and permitting the arguments of favored groups, the egalitarian promises a public debate "sufficiently rich to permit true collective self-determination."[18]

The scarcity (or impending scarcity) of the means to make one's political case is an old canard in American politics. In the 1920s the federal government used the scarcity rationale to take over the broadcasting spectrum, thereby assuming power over broadcasters who kept their lucrative licenses so long as they served "the public interest" or at least did not threaten members of Congress. The scarcity rationale was more a pretext for political oversight than a necessity of nature.[19] Later the Supreme Court invoked scarcity as a rationale for regulating broadcasting in its *Red Lion* decision.[20]

Scarcity of the means to speak will always be offered as a rationale for greater federal control of political speech. More generally, the scarcity premise reflects a habit of mind that assumes all things of value are inherently limited and thus require distribution by government to attain justice or equality. The economic growth of capitalist nations in the past two centuries has belied the assumption of scarcity. Is the premise nonetheless true about the means to political speech?

The idea that the media for conveying political messages are scarce is patently absurd. The primary means for political discussion—television— has added hundreds of cable and satellite channels that continuously offer a myriad of political news and debates from domestic and international sources. Newspapers face declining audiences, but the Internet carries diverse opinions as well as news and continual argument. Talk radio programs often focus exclusively on politics for hours on end. Whatever problems the American republic might have, a lack of political argument and information is not among them. Moreover, individuals and companies seeking profits created this rich cacophony of news and information.[21]

But this conclusion begs the question raised by the political egalitarian who asserts that even if Americans have many channels of political argument and news, they nonetheless hear a single message bought and produced by the rich and powerful. That message, so the argument goes, promotes political conservatism and Republican dominance. Money and unrestricted speech lead to a lack of diversity in the content of speech.

Here again egalitarian premises contravene reality. Liberals dominate the newswriting and editing at the nation's three major newspapers, the *Washington Post,* the *New York Times,* and the *Wall Street Journal.*[22] They write the editorials and commission the opinion pieces at the *Post* and the *Times.* A similar political outlook informs the network news and CNN, the first all-news cable channel. Many if not most of the nation's leading magazines of political commentary also lean leftward: the *Atlantic,* the *New Yorker, Harper's,* the *New York Review of Books,* the *Nation,* the *New Republic, Newsweek,* and *Time* come immediately to mind. Indeed, economic and technological change have made mainstream liberal publications more liberal than in the past, when they had to appeal to a larger and less ideologically homogenous audience.[23] On the other hand, the editorial page of the *Wall Street Journal* has been conservative for a long time. Conservative opinion has also informed the largely successful programming of FOX News and much of talk radio. The Internet seems to be a guerrilla war of views and information. Common complaints about the polarization of American politics testify to this diversity. The Left may or may not be losing the battle of ideas, but it does not lack for venues for making its arguments known.

Yet even this diversity of media is unlikely to satisfy those who long for control over political speech. Most Americans have little interest in becoming more informed about politics. Given the choice between entertainment and political information, they will choose the former. In the older media world, Americans had fewer choices and often ended up watching political news. In the current environment, viewers of television, for example, have many choices other than political information. Most thus end up less frequently to political information, less knowledgeable about politics, and less likely to vote compared to the denizens of the older media world.[24] One way to promote a more knowledgeable and active electorate would be limiting the choices of consumers or forcing the media to carry political messages.[25] Yet we might wonder with the political economist Anthony Downs whether "the loss of freedom involved in forcing people to acquire information would probably far outweigh the benefits of a better-informed electorate."[26]

Some have complained that think tanks on the political Right have dominated policy debates, citing the influence of the Heritage Foundation, the American Enterprise Institute, and the Cato Institute. Let us grant the success of these institutions. One may, however, doubt that their success depends on having more money than their counterparts on the Left. The annual expenditures of the top three think tanks on the Left and on the Right favor the former (see table 5.1). Progressive foundations also have far more money to invest than do their conservative counterparts, as shown in table 5.2. The future also looks bright for the funding

TABLE 5.1   **Spending by selected think tanks**

Think tank	Annual operating expenses
Left-leaning	
Brookings Institution	$39,676,000
Urban Institute	$77,300,000
Center for American Progress	$11,000,000
Right-leaning	
Heritage Foundation	$34,615,493
American Enterprise Institute	$19,540,000
Cato Institute	$15,698,543

Source: Information for the most recent available year from the Web site of each organization except for Center for American Progress, which is an average of spending reported in David Van Drehle, "Liberals Get a Think Tank of Their Own," *Washington Post,* October 23, 2003.

TABLE 5.2   **Assets of selected foundations involved in public policy**

Foundation	Assets (in millions of dollars)
Left-leaning	
Ford Foundation	9,300
Rockefeller Foundation	2,600
Pew Memorial Trusts	4,100
Right-leaning	
Bradley Foundation	485
Koch Family Foundations	275
Scaife Family Foundations	250

Source: The Foundation Directory Online at http://fconline.fdncenter.org/.

of left-wing think tanks. Wealthy Progressives plan to spend more than $100 million by 2020 building an intellectual infrastructure for left-wing policy advocacy.[27]

 We might also consider the principle of indirect competition. The Madisonian vision assumed that competition among groups would both prevent tyranny and discover the public good. Egalitarians argue in reply that the wealthy and the business world have far more power than other groups, thanks in part to their contributions. Direct competition among groups, they say, leads to a bias in politics toward the wealthy. Business groups, however, often care about a particular issue. They might, for example, seek to shape regulation regarding their businesses rather than defend the free market. Skillful politicians can thus raise money from groups with a particular interest and spend the money informing voters about policies that putatively benefit the nonwealthy. In this way Bill Clinton raised money from groups while appearing to be responsive to their particular concerns and used the money to defend what he took to be the interests of the middle class and the poor. Other liberal Democrats— Ted Kennedy, Tony Coelho, Willie Brown, and Bill Bradley—followed a similar path. The same strategy marked Franklin Roosevelt's political projects.[28] "Big money" is compatible with big government and Progressive ambitions. Progressives have the funding to make their political case in the United States. We should not forget that over the long run their ample resources have translated into considerable influence over politics and public policy. To be sure, their successes have not equaled their aspirations. Yet we should not confuse having enough resources to make an argument with actually winning the argument *all the time*.

Who Gives?

We now leave the larger questions of public debates to focus on campaign finance. Egalitarians say that campaign contributors are overwhelmingly rich, conservative, and Republican. When money talks in politics, the egalitarian argument goes, this group has a megaphone that drowns out all other voices. Liberals and Democrats simply have little influence over elections and hence, over policymaking. Like most political rhetoric, these claims exaggerate and distort reality.

 Campaign finance law requires contributors to disclose their donations. It does not require donors to reveal much about themselves apart from their names and professional affiliations. Our knowledge of contributors comes from surveys. Scholars recently polled contributors of $200 or more to 1996 congressional races and to the 2000 presidential primaries. They found that 80 percent or more of such "significant donors" reported an annual family income of more than $100,000. The donors are also well-educated, with more than one-half holding postgraduate degrees, often JDs or MBAs. They also tended to be older than the general population, male, and white.[29] Because about 18 percent of all U.S. households earn more than $100,000 annually and about 9 percent of Americans hold an advanced degree, it follows that contributors are not an accurate sample of the U.S. population as a whole.[30] Of course, the same might be said of Congress, the people engaged in trying to restrict campaign finance, and those trying to stop them. All are likely to be more educated and richer than most Americans. Political egalitarians implicitly or explicitly assume that the data about the income, educational attainment, age, race, and gender, of donors justify restricting campaign finance. They claim, in short, that "demography is destiny." In fact, the rich as well as the near-rich are politically diverse.

Egalitarians falsely assume that wealthy people are monolithically conservative in outlook and Republican in partisanship.[31] The National Election Studies project has collected data about the political views of the top 5 percent of American households in terms of income. In 1998 that top 5 percent comprised more than 5.2 million households. The lowest earners among that 5 percent garnered just over $107,000 annually; on average, they made $143,000 each year.[32]

The NES found that in 1996 and 1998, the last years for which valid data are available, about one-third of the wealthy professed liberalism. In those years, 23 percent and 15 percent, respectively, identified themselves as moderates, and 42 percent and 48 percent, respectively, professed conservatism.[33] The number of wealthy Americans professing liberalism or a moderate view equals the number hewing to conservatism.

The politics of the rich surprises us in other ways. First, the rich have become much more liberal in the past decade. The median percentage of rich households identifying as liberal from 1972 to 1988 was 16 percent; the corresponding number for 1990–2000 was 26 percent. Now the number is 32 percent. Second, the richest Americans are more liberal than the poorest citizens, a difference that has grown remarkably in recent years. In 1996 and 1998 the rich were about 50 percent more likely than the poor to identify as liberal. Over the longer run, about 17 percent of the poorest U.S. households have identified themselves as liberal in the past thirty years. During that time, about 21 percent of the rich professed liberalism. As the rich became more liberal in the 1990s, the poor remained the same.[34]

Are the rich overwhelmingly Republican? In 2000, 36 percent of the rich identified themselves as Democrats, 54 percent as Republican, and another 10 percent as independents. In the past decade, up to 41 percent of the rich have identified themselves as Democrats; the number of Democrats among the rich rose sharply from 1988 to 1996 and declined modestly thereafter.[35]

What about the political views of the merely affluent, as opposed to the rich? The NES breaks down partisan and ideological identification by income; the second highest category has a lower limit of the 68th percentile of households, or about $70,000 in 2001.[36] The affluent are about as liberal as the rich (about 21 percent professed liberalism in the 1990s), but much more likely to be Democrats (50 percent identified as Democrats in 2000 and about 46 percent have done so in the past decade).[37]

What should we conclude about the ideology and partisan ties of the richest Americans? The top 5 percent are more heavily Republican and more conservative than the general population (a fact that should surprise no one), but they are also much more liberal than Americans in general and much more liberal than the poor. The political commitments of the rich and the affluent contradict the stark assumptions of political egalitarians.

How do donors compare politically to the larger population? Table 5.3 compares contributors by party and ideology. The pools of donors in 1996 and 2000 were both more heavily Republican and more conservative than the general population. Political independents and liberals are also overrepresented in the donor pool. Similarly, liberals and conservatives are about equally overrepresented among contributors; both groups are about 50 percent more likely to be found among donors than among the general population. This overrepresentation reflects an equal propensity to give among conservatives and liberals.[38] Democrats and political moderates are found more often among the general population than among contributors. Yet political moderates were almost as likely to be found among contributors as in the general population during the 1996 congressional elections. It is possible that a presidential contest draws more contributions from the ideological extremes than congressional elections.

Democrats make up a smaller portion of all regular contributors than they did of the general population in 1996 and 2000, but the difference is relatively small. Republicans are much more likely to be found among

TABLE 5.3   **Ideology and partisanship of contributors, 1996 and 2000**

	Congressional contributors, 1996[*]	Presidential contributors, 2000[*]	Average self-identification, 1996–2000
Partisanship			
Republican	50	54	35[†]
Independent/other	19	16	26[†]
Democrat	31	30	39[†]
Ideology			
Conservative	46	56	30[‡]
Moderate	22	15	23[‡]
Liberal	32	29	20[‡]
None			27[‡]

Sources: [*]Clyde Wilcox et al., "With Limits Raised, Who Will Give More?" in *Life after Reform*, ed. Michael J. Malbin (Lanham, MD: Rowman and Littlefield, 2003), table 4.2.
[†]Center for Political Studies, University of Michigan, *The NES Guide to Public Opinion and Electoral Behavior* (http://www.umich.edu/~nes/nesguide/nesguide.htm). Ann Arbor: University of Michigan Center for Political Studies, 1995–2000, tables 2A2, 3.1.
[‡]National Election Pool Data reported by the Pew Center for the People and the Press at http://people-press.org/commentary/display.php3?AnalysisID=102.

contributors than among the general population. This fits other knowledge we have about campaign contributions. Republicans have traditionally enjoyed a significant advantage over Democrats in hard money fundraising. Federal law limits contributions. Until recently more people identified with the Democratic Party than with the Republican. Accordingly, Republicans must outnumber Democrats among contributors. The parties are not equally represented among contributors. But this is an incomplete picture of partisan fundraising.

The foregoing relied on a survey of contributors whose donations fell within the ceilings established by federal law. In particular, they could donate up to $1,000 to any one candidate. That was not the only source of funding to fight elections. Until Election Day 2002, the political parties could raise so-called soft money without limits on contributions. In the 2001–2002 election cycle, sixty-one individuals and organizations contributed more than $1 million to a political party. Taken together, all those contributors gave a little less than $137 million. Of that sum, 63 percent went to the Democratic Party. The largest contributors, in short, were overwhelmingly committed to the Democratic Party. The BCRA did formally ban soft money fundraising by federal officials and the parties, but such contributions reappeared in national politics less than a year after the supposed prohibition took effect. The new soft money vehicles—called 527 groups, after a section of the Internal Revenue Code—raised large sums for the 2004 campaign. Thirty-five of the top fifty 527 groups as measured by contributions were affiliated with the Democratic Party. Altogether the top fifty groups raised slightly less than $500 million, a sum almost identical to the total of all soft money contributions made in 2000. Of that total, about $103.5 million was raised by the fifteen 527 groups associated with the Republican Party. The Democratic affiliates raised about $390 million, or 79 percent of all such fundraising. An examination of the top twenty-five individual contributors to these 527 groups is also revealing. Fourteen of the top twenty-five gave Democratic groups a total of $104 million, about 25 percent of the party's soft money in 2004.[39] In 2004, four individuals gave the Democratic 527s a little more than $73 million, slightly less than one-fifth of all the money the groups raised. That same year, eleven Republicans gave about $42 million, or about 40 percent of the Republican's much smaller 527 total.[40] Among those who, according to egalitarians, have the most influence and thus pose the greatest danger to democracy, the Democratic Party does much better than the Republican Party. The largest donors embrace Progressivism. This picture is also incomplete in another way. During the 2004 presidential campaign Democrats raised more money than did Republicans from smaller contributors, indicating that the party has expanded its donor base.[41]

Some groups appear more often among contributors than among the general population: committed Republicans, liberals, and conservatives. What do these groups have in common? Each comprises individuals with strong preferences about politics and policy. This suggests that the most important fact about campaign contributors may not be their partisanship or ideology but rather their activism and interest in politics. Wilcox and his colleagues found some data to support this guess. About one-quarter of contributors belonged to at least one ideological group on the Right or the Left.[42]

Some rough comparisons between contributors and the general population in terms of group membership are possible. Twenty-six percent of contributors belong to an environmental group. The leading environmental interest groups (the "Group of Ten") in recent years had a combined membership of no more than 8,676,157, or no more than 4 percent of the total adult population of the United States (209,279,149 in 2000).[43] Environmentalists are six to twelve times more likely to be found among contributors to campaigns than in the general population. Clearly, people concerned about the environment are wildly overrepresented among contributors.

On the other hand, NES found that 27 percent of Americans responded to a query about their political outlook by choosing the options "don't know" or "haven't thought about it." Americans lacking a political ideology are the second largest group in the population, just behind self-identified conservatives and just in front of political moderates.[44] Americans have long lacked interest in political ideology; as many as 36 percent chose "don't know" in 1980, and 23 percent responded this way in 1998. If we add together political moderates (23 percent of the population) and those who lack an ideology (27 percent), we find that half of Americans are either moderates or individuals without strong political beliefs. Because Wilcox and his colleagues did not include the "don't know/haven't thought about it" category in their surveys, we cannot know how often nonideological Americans gave to campaigns. Given their lack of interest in politics, it beggars belief that the nonideological would give significant sums. In general, the largest divergence between the contributor pool and the general population falls among those who lack strong beliefs about politics. This should surprise no one.

What does all this mean for campaign finance regulation? Egalitarians believe that Republicans and conservatives so dominate money in politics that the contributor class as a whole does not look like America. It is true that Republicans are more likely to be found among contributors than in the general population. But that is also true of liberals. Moreover, the Republican overrepresentation does not mean Democrats are severely underrepresented. Committed Democrats are somewhat less likely to be found among contributors than in the general population, but they clearly can raise more money than the GOP, as was proved in 2004. Like many of the assertions of those who would restrict campaign finance, the contention that Republicans and conservatives dominate contributions is overblown and misleading.

Campaign contributors are wealthier, more educated, and much more interested and involved in politics than most Americans. They participate in politics via group membership and by contributing to campaigns (and no doubt in other ways). Activists in general dominate the money game in American politics. Americans with little interest in politics or weak partisan commitments have a small role in financing political campaigns.

The Money Primary

Some egalitarians have argued that the need to raise money to run for office creates a "wealth primary" that restricts voters' choices by limiting the list of candidates available to voters.[45] They argue that the demands of funding a campaign discourage candidates representing the poor. This supposedly leads to a "plutocracy" in which only candidates representing the views of the rich attain public office, thereby creating "a tyranny of private wealth."[46] That "tyranny" should be ended, the critics conclude, by eliminating private funding of campaigns in favor of complete taxpayer financing. Bradley Smith has revealed the extensive constitutional shortcomings of this argument.[47] Does it bear up under empirical scrutiny?

The wealth primary argument is difficult to test. We do not have comprehensive data about the ideologies of candidates for Congress. More important to this argument, we do not have data about the views of candidates who would have run for Congress if they did not have to raise money from private donors. We also do not have data about the views of candidates in elections in which private financing has been eliminated because even the most rigorous public funding schemes permit continued private donations to campaigns. We do, however, have some evidence about the voting records of state legislators elected in Arizona, a state that recently enacted robust taxpayer financing of campaigns. The initial class of legislators elected under that system did not differ significantly in their voting records from the class elected without public money.[48]

We do have other data that bear on the wealth primary argument. We can determine the political outlooks of the poor and liberals in the electorate and compare them to the voting records of members of Congress. (Liberals and the poor are presumably the two groups most disadvantaged by the "tyranny of the rich.") A significant difference between the ideologies in the population and the voting records would be consistent with the wealth primary hypothesis or some other bias in the electoral system. Conversely, if the views of the population and of Congress members do not differ significantly, we have a reason to doubt the theory.

The poor make up about 16 percent of the American population. No member of Congress can be defined as poor given the salary associated with the position. It is also safe to say that few if any members of Congress were poor prior to their election. The most common former occupations of members of the House and Senate are law, business and banking, politics, and (in the Senate) education.[49] Keep in mind that the poor are also rarely found reporting at elite newspapers, professing at law schools, or directing large foundations.

We have seen that advocates of regulation offer a caricature of the political ideology of wealthy individuals. What about the poor? How do they identify themselves politically? For the past thirty years the National Elections Studies have asked Americans to identify their political ideology (liberal, moderate, or conservative). Figure 5.1 charts the responses

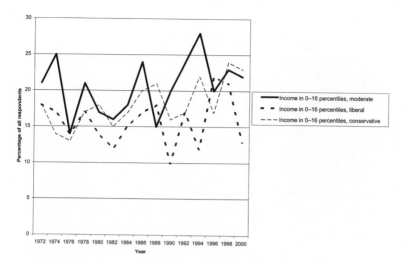

FIGURE 5.1 Ideological self-identification of the poor, 1972–2000. National Election Studies, table 3.1.1. http://www.umich.edu/~nes/nesguide/gd-index.htm#3 (accessed January 26, 2005).

from people in the bottom 16 percent of the income distribution in the United States. Far from being predominately liberal, the poor identify about equally with all three political persuasions. Looking at the median percentages over the entire thirty-year period, we find 21 percent of the poor professing liberalism, 17 percent saying they were moderate, and another 17 percent identifying as conservative. Like the rest of the United States, however, the poor have become more conservative in recent years. Considering the medians since 1990, we find that 23 percent of the poor identify as moderates, 20 percent as conservatives, and 16 percent as liberals. To round out this picture, I might add that a large proportion of the poor, like many Americans, do not profess a political ideology.

How do the ideological views of the poor compare to the voting records of members of Congress? An organization called Americans for Democratic Action has rated the liberalism of members of Congress since 1947. From 1972 to 1999, the ADA rated the voting records of 14,835 members of Congress on a scale from 0 to 100 where 0 is extremely conservative and 100 is extremely liberal. Figure 5.2 shows the distribution of members' voting records for the period by ideological outlook.[50] Here again we see a familiar story. The poor who professed conservatism, liberalism, and moderation were all overrepresented in Congress for the past thirty years. Poor conservatives and liberals were both strongly

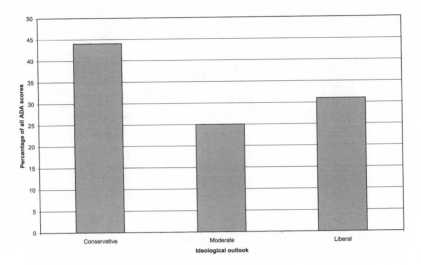

FIGURE 5.2   Ideological outlook of members of Congress, 1972–99. Timothy Groseclose.
Original on file with the author.

overrepresented, while the moderates in Congress about matched the
number of moderates among the poor. Those among the poor who had no
political ideology also had little representation in Congress.

Liberalism in general has been well-represented in Congress in the
past three decades. Once again we can turn to National Election Studies
surveys for data about liberal self-identification in the population. In 2000,
for example, these surveys found that 2 percent of Americans described
themselves as "extremely liberal"; another 9 percent said they were "liberal" and the same proportion identified their views as "slightly liberal."
Taken together, about 20 percent of Americans described themselves as
a liberal of some kind. From 1972 to 2000, the median self-identification
scores were 8 percent for either extremely liberal or liberal and 18 percent
for some variety (liberal, extremely liberal, or slightly liberal).

Let us again compare liberalism in the population to the ADA scores
for this period. Table 5.4 compares the proportion of the entire population professing liberalism with liberal voting records in Congress. The
table plausibly assumes rough correspondences between the category
"extremely liberal" and an ADA score of more than 90, between "liberal"
and an ADA score of 81 to 90, and between "slightly liberal" and an ADA
score of 71 to 80. Clearly Congress has been more ideologically liberal

TABLE 5.4 **Liberalism in Congress and in the U.S. population**

Level of liberalism	Population (%)*	Votes in Congress (%)[†]
Extremely liberal	2	11
Liberal	7	11
Slightly liberal	9	9
Totals	18	31

Sources: *National Election Studies, table 3.1. http://www.umich.edu/~nes/
nesguide/gd-index.htm (accessed January 21, 2005).
[†]Timothy Groseclose, ADA Scores, 1972–99, table 3.1, on file with the
author.

over the past three decades than has the population as a whole. Eleven
percent of members of Congress have had an extremely liberal voting
record, whereas only 1 to 2 percent of Americans identified themselves
as extremely liberal. Another 11 percent of members of Congress have
had a liberal voting record, whereas 7 percent of the Americans classified
themselves as liberal. Only the proportion of slightly liberal voting records corresponded to the views of the larger society. Overall, 31 percent
of members of Congress from 1972 to 1999 had a voting record reflecting
some degree of liberalism, whereas about 18 percent of the population
during that time professed some version of liberalism. The critics of the
wealth primary are not simply wrong about the poor, liberalism, and representation. They have the story exactly backwards. Liberals have been
overrepresented in Congress since 1972 compared to their strength in the
population.

Summary

My analysis suggests some curious policy implications. The most striking
inequality in campaign finance falls between the politically active and the
politically apathetic. Reducing this inequality would mean bringing nonideological and apolitical Americans into the contributor pool in large
numbers. If a lack of money were the obstacle to participating, government subsidies might well lead to a much larger contributor pool. But surveys indicate that Americans do not want to participate in politics most of
the time.[51] If we create a voucher system of contributions funded by general taxes, contributing the voucher to a candidate would have to be mandatory and backed by fines or other sanctions. Without the full force of
the law, the politically apathetic are unlikely to actually send their voucher

to a campaign. After all, they have shown a concrete lack of interest in politics. On the other hand, a citizen who does not contribute the voucher will foment political inequality. Egalitarians will eventually have to choose between coercion and inequality. They are likely, given their general intellectual framework, to choose the former and force the apathetic to engage in politics against their will.

The current pool of contributors overwhelmingly represents people who have intense beliefs about politics. In Federalist no. 10, James Madison argues that the intense concerns of minorities, as well as the numerical advantage of majorities, should play a role in both constitutional design and public policymaking. Similarly, "a modern Madison might argue that government should be designed to inhibit a relatively apathetic majority from cramming its policy down the throats of a relatively intense minority." [52] Campaign contributions do not fully achieve that goal because they do not determine either election outcomes or policymaking. Donations do, however, reflect the intensity of preferences among several minorities (for example, Republicans, liberals, environmental groups, pro-gun groups). The ability to make contributions means that the concerns of these groups will be heard though not necessarily taken into account. That sounds like a Madisonian echo in our politics rather than a single conservative voice drowning out all dissent.

Equality and Policymaking

Those who believe that the rich rule point to Republican tax cuts. In 2003, President George W. Bush proposed cutting taxes as promised during his campaign for the presidency. Eventually a tax cut of $350 billion over ten years passed Congress after largely party-line votes. The political Left had found more evidence for the satisfying story of rich Republicans taking from the vulnerable poor and the long-suffering middle class. A satisfying story, perhaps, but not a complete one.

That storyline would soon become more complicated by two developments in Washington. The cut expanded a tax credit for children of taxpayers. This expansion did not apply to poor families, however, because they do not pay income taxes and thus have nothing to claim a credit against. Critics of the tax cut immediately took the offensive, proclaiming the injustice of denying money to low-income families when the rich had taken so much from the mouths of poor children. "Faced with a choice between giving a tax break to an elite few or helping millions of working families, the Republicans once again chose to help their wealthy friends," said House Minority Leader Nancy Pelosi (D-CA).[53] "This bill will give millions to those who don't need it and very little to those who do," said Senate Minority Leader Tom Daschle (D-SD).[54] A more prosaic assessment of the critics came from the House Ways and Means Committee Chairman, Bill Thomas (R-CA), who said, "This is raw politics. Someone figured out a way to get on prime time in an impassioned way before the election."[55] Raw or cooked, the politics worked. Within days, the Senate expanded the child tax credit to low-income families by a vote of 94 to 2 at a cost to taxpayers of $10 billion over two years. Remarkably, this "credit" was a straight redistribution from taxpayers to people who pay no income taxes. Not to be outdone, the House, also controlled by Republicans, passed by a vote of 224 to 201 an $82 billion bill providing a tax credit for the poor.[56]

Meanwhile, Congress was hard at work expanding the prescription drug benefit offered under Medicare. The week after the entire Senate voted to transfer wealth to poor families via the child credit, the Senate Finance Committee approved a $400 *billion* plan to pay for prescription drugs for senior citizens. Although the plan did require seniors to pay some of prescription bill (at least for now), it also provided more money for poor seniors to pay their deductible and copayments. In contrast, the House plan for drug benefits, while relying more on competition and private insurance companies, required affluent individuals and couples to pay more of their drug bills before they could benefit from government largesse.[57] The final version of the entitlement included a deductible and a monthly premium for recipients who were not poor or nearly so. Taxpayers picked up the premiums and deductibles for those with incomes up to 135 percent of the poverty level. The poor and near-poor did have to make small copayments for each drug purchase; these, too, ceased after an annual ceiling had been reached.[58]

These two stories should make us wonder whether the rich really do rule. The tax credit story did not involve a large sum of money, at least when compared to the annual GNP of the United States. It did, however, directly pit the rich and the middle class against the poor in a competition for resources. Because the beneficiaries of the $10 billion in tax credits pay no taxes, their largesse came directly from those who do, especially those in the highest quintile of the income distribution. The poor got richer by making the rich poorer.

The Medicare story suggests that a policy outcome is more than a story of rich and poor.[59] The sum of $400 billion, large by almost any standard of comparison, grossly underestimates the actual cost of the entitlement; the net present value of the unfunded obligation is more than $21 trillion.[60] Current beneficiaries of the policy will pay for a small part of this benefit; current and future taxpayers will pay most of its costs. Who benefits? The first group of beneficiaries will be Medicare recipients who had no insurance that covered prescription drugs or had insurance that was inferior in benefits to the Medicare benefit. The second group of beneficiaries will be the companies that manufacture the medicines covered by the program. Medicare recipients who had no or inadequate insurance for prescription drugs will compose a large new market for these medicines and thus generate new sales and profits for the pharmaceutical companies. (This remains true even though the law provides that the medicines be sold at a discount.) The third group of beneficiaries has been and perhaps will be the policymakers who passed the Medicare benefit.[61]

Perhaps policymakers sold the benefit to the pharmaceuticals in exchange for campaign contributions. That simple explanation ignores some complexities. For example, the benefits to Medicare recipients with no or inadequate insurance equal the new sales to the drug companies. If campaign contributions bought the policy, then the money also bought the benefits for the Medicare recipients, an odd thought.[62] Second, the Medicare benefit passed only after great effort by the Bush administration. The resistance of House Republicans to expanding the welfare state suggests the influence of ideology on congressional behavior. Finally, policymakers face reelection and might be tempted to buy votes by offering policies that benefit large blocs of voters.

As it happens, Medicare covers forty million Americans. In 2002, an off-year election, a little more than seventy-five million Americans voted. In 2000, 72 percent of people aged sixty-five to seventy-four voted in the presidential election.[63] Putting it all together, we can see that those eligible for Medicare made up about 39 percent of the electorate in 2002, rich, poor, and middle class. This clarifies why a putatively conservative Republican administration pushed to enact the drug benefit and why the president had promised such plunder to voters in the election of 2000. Did the recipients of this huge entitlement buy their benefits with campaign contributions? The leading interest group representing Medicare recipients—the American Association of Retired Persons—neither formed a political action committee nor contributed soft money prior to the vote on the prescription drug benefit.[64] The benefits of this policy will come largely but not exclusively to those who vote. Its costs over the long term will be paid by those too young to vote or by people who do not yet exist.

Are these examples unusual and thus misleading? We have the data to paint the larger picture about the rich and the poor and the costs and benefits of government. The partisans of campaign finance regulation would have us believe that the rich rule to promote their own interests while the middle class and the poor do without, having been excluded from power and hence from the benefits that flow from the welfare state. Who benefits from government? Who pays the costs? Do the rich rule or benefit unfairly from government?

Like much else in campaign finance debates, political visions inform the answer to this question. Madisonians say government should protect life, liberty, and property from the depredations of foreign powers, other citizens, and the government itself. Government may tax citizens to provide for the collective good of protecting rights, but such taxes are limited to that purpose. Given those protections, individuals will engage in commerce that leads to inequalities of wealth. For the Madisonian, such inequalities come about from the choices of individuals rather than the actions of government. Such wealth remains with individuals after they have paid the necessary taxes for government protection of their rights. On the other hand, we should rightly condemn wealthy or powerful individuals who use government to take the property of others for their own use and enjoyment.

Progressives deny that individuals have any rights of property against government. They do not necessarily argue that government should eliminate private property in favor of collective ownership. Progressives do believe that insofar as government secures private property the wealth produced by individuals depends heavily on government action; the government may regulate or tax property as needed to attain the common good.[65] Because government is the cause of all effects in the private sector including inequalities in wealth, the rich by definition always benefit more than anyone else from government. Of course, apart from a state of primitive egalitarianism in which all wealth is divided equally, the rich under these assumptions would always benefit more from government than everyone else. But the Progressives' point here is that the private financing of politics makes the distribution of wealth more unequal than it would be otherwise, perhaps because campaign contributions allow the rich to prevent Congress from enacting high marginal tax rates to fund spending on the poor and the middle class.

This account of wealth and campaign finance runs up against two contrary considerations. Economists do believe that inequalities in income have grown modestly in the United States in recent decades. This trend shows up in pre-tax income, however, which suggests that public policy is not the source of the growing inequality. In fact, experts do not understand the causes of the increased inequality. The list of possible causes includes family composition and a shift in labor markets that offers increasing rewards for increases in skills and knowledge.[66]

Even if government did not cause the growing inequality, the egalitarian might still argue, as noted above, that campaign contributions by the rich prevent the government from redistributing the returns on education and thereby counteracting the growing inequality. The evidence that contributions have little influence on policymaking contravenes this conjecture. We might consider an alternative hypothesis. Perhaps the government's observed unwillingness to redistribute income as much as some might wish reflects public opinion. Americans do not care much about economic inequality. One poll found, for example, that only 27 percent of respondents agreed that "[i]t is the responsibility of the government to reduce the differences in income between people with high incomes and those with low incomes." Forty-six percent disagreed or strongly disagreed with the statement, and the rest either could not choose or neither agreed nor disagreed with the statement.[67] From 1983 to 1996, 31 percent of those surveyed agreed with the same proposition, and 46 percent disagreed.[68] From 1983 to 1998, the General Social Survey asked more than five thousand Americans, "On the whole, do you think it should or should not be the government's responsibility to reduce income differences between the rich and poor?" Fifty-four percent answered that it probably or definitely should not be the government's responsibility.[69] Perhaps Congress does not make incomes more equal because a majority does not support that policy.

We can look at the equality question by asking more tractable questions. How much does the federal government spend on the poor? In 2000, poor Americans received $436.9 *billion* in benefits from federal, state, and local governments. These benefits encompass a myriad of programs in the categories of medical benefits (such as Medicaid and insurance subsidies), direct cash aid, food benefits (such as food stamps), housing benefits, services, energy subsidies, and job training.[70] Even more revealing is the sharp rise in benefits going to the poor since 1968 (see figure 5.3).

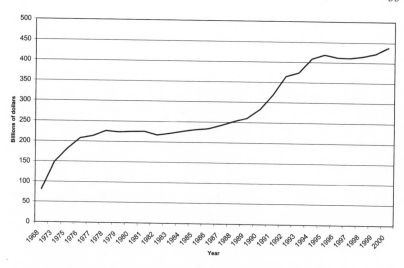

FIGURE 5.3 Government benefits for the poor, 1968–2000. Library of Congress, Congressional Research Service, "Cash and Noncash Benefits for Persons with Limited Income: Eligibility Rules, Recipient and Expenditure Data, FY1998–FY2000," CRS Report RL 31228, November 19, 2001 (Washington, DC: Government Printing Office).

Had spending on the poor in 1968 simply kept pace with inflation, government would have given about $81 billion in benefits to low-income people in 2000. The $437 billion actually provided to the poor is a *real* increase of more than $350 billion in benefits in about thirty years. More telling, since the federal government supposedly became more conservative with the advent of the Reagan presidency in 1980, the total real benefits given to the poor by government have almost doubled from $225 billion to $437 billion.[71]

Where does this money come from? Advocates of speech restrictions are fond of saying that the rich and corporations evade taxes and pay nothing. The reality is quite different. About one-half of all federal government revenue comes from the income tax; another 10 percent comes from taxes on corporations.[72] In 2002, households making $75,000 or more annually paid 86 percent of all income taxes though they composed 15 percent of all returns. This reflects the reality that high earners make more money than other Americans. That is not the whole story, however, as we can see from examining the group of households making more than $200,000 annually. This group's share of the income tax burden is 50 percent larger than its share of total income in the United States.[73] The rich and the affluent pay almost all of the income taxes, and they pay a much higher proportion of income taxes than their share of the income.

Let us set aside the question of whether this should be so. In fact, they do pay more. It is also true that much of the $437 billion in benefits the poor received in 2000 from the government comes from the rich and the affluent. The federal government extracts a lot of money from the rich and the affluent and gives it to the poor, directly or indirectly (by paying for services). If the rich rule, why have they continued for thirty years to increase the sums going to the poor at five times the inflation rate?

How might we account for the surprising fact that the poor pay little or no income tax and receive hundreds of billions of dollars in benefits and services? We might hesitate to ascribe those outcomes to the direct political influence of the poor, who participate in politics less than other Americans do.[74] Studies of policymaking for the poor have found that the poor do not participate in the political struggles that create social welfare policy. Instead, a series of proxies—intergovernmental lobbies and public interest groups—represent the interests of the poor in such policy battles.[75] Some might object that much of the government spending on the poor actually goes to funding services offered by everyone from health care providers to therapists. What seems to be spending on the poor is actually spending that benefits the middle class and the corporations that employ them. In a sense, this complaint must be true insofar as the government aids the poor by providing services rather than cash. That fact does not mean in itself that the poor do not receive more than $400 billion worth of services. Perhaps corruption and waste reduce the actual services provided to the poor or perhaps not. The challenge facing those who claim that the rich rule should be showing that the money spent on the poor actually provides little or no benefit to that group. Absent that, we might conclude that both the service providers and the poor benefit from government spending on the poor. These groups, in short, have formed a coalition to benefit from taxes levied (largely) on the rich.

Some might object that I have left out an important consideration: the benefits the rich themselves receive from the government. Advocates of campaign finance restrictions often decry "corporate welfare" and predict that limiting favors to special interests would save billions. In fact, Congress does spend about $90 billion a year on subsidizing various businesses in various ways. About a third of such subsidies go to agriculture interests.[76] To be sure, corporate welfare should be ended immediately. But we should again look at the larger picture. Spending on corporate welfare is about one-fifth the size of spending on the welfare of the poor.

Moreover, corporate welfare is classic pork-barrel spending that benefits interests in congressional districts. Members of Congress bring home the bacon to buy votes to get reelected. Every member faces the problem of getting other members to support such pork projects, which, after all, only help him or her. The solution of choice is log-rolling. Each member supports the pork projects of other members to obtain their assent to, say, dams and agricultural subsidies for his or her district.[77] Moreover, this practice attracts support from both parties in Congress; the majority party gives the minority ample pork so that that the latter cannot blame the former for "wasteful spending."[78] Wasteful pork-barrel spending, including corporate welfare, aims at winning votes from everyone and less at the welfare of the rich.

Sometimes partisans of speech restrictions focus less on inequality of influence over policy outcomes than on inequality of access. The assertion that contributions lead to access to public officials, thereby harming American democracy, played an important part in the U.S. Supreme Court's decision to uphold McCain-Feingold in 2003. Quoting a lower court opinion citing *Buckley v. Valeo,* the McConnell Court affirmed that "[l]arge contributions are intended to, and do, gain access to the elected official after the campaign for consideration of the contributor's particular concerns. . . . Senator Mathias not only describes this but also the corollary, that the feeling that big contributors gain special treatment produces a reaction that the average American has no significant role in the political process."[79] The *McConnell* majority concluded that soft money contributions to parties, like the large contributions of the *Buckley* era, led to access to public officials and thus could be regulated or banned by Congress. The nexus between money and access apparently threatens democracy in two ways. First, elected officials give special consideration to the concerns of their contributors. Second, public knowledge of this leads most people to think they do not matter in politics, a conclusion that presumably damages public support for democracy. I turn first to the second concern.

The National Election Studies has for some time asked three questions that bear on the asserted relation between large contributions and a feeling that the average American has no significant role in politics. Figure 5.4 shows the number of Americans who agreed with the statement "People like me don't have a say in politics" just before and during the soft money era in campaign finance.

Soft money came into its own in 1979. The number of people who felt they had no say rose shortly thereafter, then fell sharply, then rose again

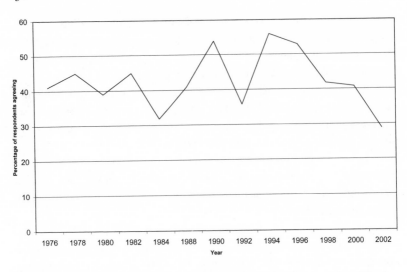

FIGURE 5.4 Agreement with the statement "People like me don't have a say in politics."
National Election Studies, table 5B.2. http://www.umich.edu/~nes/nesguide/gd-index.htm#3
(accessed January 21, 2005).

after 1994. That hardly offers evidence that large contributions make
Americans feel left out. More important, the era of soft money fundraising went into high gear after the 1994 elections, and such donations
rose rapidly until prohibited in 2002. A glance at figure 5.4 reveals that
the number of people feeling left out of politics fell steadily during the
era of rising soft money fundraising and widespread of criticism of such
practices.

Other measures of the political efficacy of the public show a similar trend. The NES has also asked whether Americans agree with the
proposition "Public officials don't care much what people like me think."
Figure 5.5 shows the results. Once again, the number of Americans who
thought public officials ignored their concerns dropped just as large contributions increased.

Finally, the National Election Studies surveys have also asked the following question: "Over the years, how much attention do you feel the
government pays to what the people think when it decides what to do—a
good deal, some, or not much?" Figure 5.6 shows the percentage of those
answering "not much" during the soft money era. Apart from a jump after
1996, the proportion of those choosing this response dropped throughout
the soft money era. By 2000 it attracted half as many replies as it did in 1980.

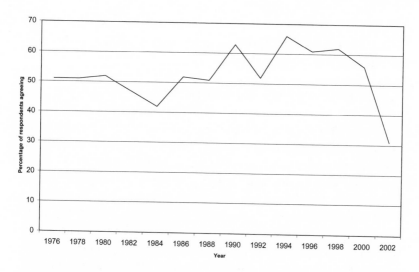

FIGURE 5.5 Agreement with the statement "Public officials do not care much what people like me think." National Election Studies, table 5B.3. http://www.umich.edu/~nes/nesguide/gd-index.htm#3 (accessed January 21, 2005).

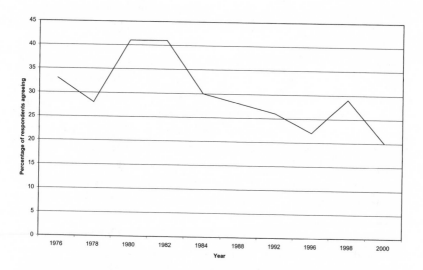

FIGURE 5.6 Belief that government pays "not much" attention to what people think. National Election Studies, table 5C.1. http://www.umich.edu/~nes/nesguide/gd-index.htm#3 (accessed January 21, 2005). I have omitted the years in which National Election Studies surveys did not yield adequate data for the "not much" response.

National Election Studies does high-quality surveys over long periods of time. The responses to these three questions bear directly on the claims that large contributions, perhaps mediated through access to public officials, decrease the sense of political efficacy of Americans. In each case, the data contradict the Supreme Court's assertion.

In *Buckley* the Court asserted that donors "gain access to the elected official after the campaign for consideration of the contributor's particular concerns." This consideration leads to at least the appearance of special treatment for the donor.[80] This version of the access argument really offers the corruption rationale while adding access as the intermediary between contributions and policy outcomes. Looked at that way, the empirical evidence about the improper influence of money bears also on the access argument; if money does not have much influence on legislative voting, that result does not change by adding the term *access*. That same evidence suggests, however, that the putative "consideration of the contributor's particular concerns" has little effect on legislative voting. As far as the "appearance of access" goes, the data about public confidence in government and voter efficacy cited above cast doubts on this claim.

In *McConnell v. FEC*, the majority of the U.S. Supreme Court seemed satisfied with the testimony of members and with anecdotes to carry Congress's burden of proof concerning access.[81] Social scientists have tried to be both more systematic and more rigorous in studying access. In the most famous study of the topic, Richard Hall and Frank Wayman argue that contributions from PACs affect not what members of Congress do but how vigorously they do it. They accept the dominant finding that money does not change legislative votes. Many factors—ideology, party, and constituency—affect votes. Since a member always has more issues to push than time or energy, he or she must choose which groups to help and how much to do on their behalf. Political action committees may believe contributions can affect how a member of Congress uses his or her time and energy; in political jargon, contributions may mobilize a member to advance a group's cause. A mobilized committee member might help a group by authoring or blocking a proposal, by negotiating compromises behind the scenes, by lobbying colleagues, by relaying intelligence about political developments, and by planning strategies to help the cause. Having activated a member, groups provide technical information, policy analysis, and even speeches to support the member back home.[82]

To test the mobilization thesis, Hall and Wayman examined congressional work concerning three issues: dairy price supports, natural gas regulation, and job training. They concluded that PAC money does affect how hard a legislator works on an issue even when constituency concerns are taken into account. They suggest that legislators see their district as divided into different constituencies. On one hand, organized economic interests matter more in the day-to-day work of a member; diffuse and unorganized interests matter less. Although money may not buy the votes of a legislator, they conclude, "it apparently did buy the marginal time, energy, and legislative resources that committee participation requires." This influence comes, they add, at the early stages of legislating, the stages that have a direct bearing on the laws that are enacted or rejected in roll-call votes.[83]

What is wrong with mobilizing legislators with contributions? Hall and Wayman argue that "by selectively subsidizing the information costs associated with participation, groups affect the *intensity* with which their positions are promoted by their legislative agents." This implies that not all preferences weigh equally in legislative deliberations and that "moneyed interests at least partly determine the weights."[84] Hall and Wayman presumably are not saying that all interests should be represented with equal intensity. Such equality would re-create the equality of the vote in the quite different forum of group struggle. Indeed, such equality, if possible, would make nonelectoral political activity superfluous. It would also deny the nation a way of reflecting the intensity of concerns among citizens. The complaint seems to be that variations in intensity of legislative effort fostered by private contributions to public officials contravene democratic equality. On the other hand, differences in legislative effort fostered by the concerns of a threatened minority group that made no contributions would presumably be acceptable, perhaps even laudable. Put that way, it becomes clear that Hall and Wayman's criticism assumes a traditional Progressive hostility to business ("moneyed interests") in politics. Contrary to Madison, private wealth is more predator than prey in contemporary democracy. We might also notice that this argument spreads well beyond policymaking. George Soros gave millions of dollars to the Democratic candidate for president in 2004 in the hope that a President Kerry would change foreign and domestic policy. The same might be said of most of Kerry's donors. Had Kerry won and changed those policies, his contributors would have used their money to make their preferences weigh more in presidential policymaking. If we assume that money changes the concerns of policymakers and that such variations are morally unacceptable, we will have to ban private funding of politics and elections. Such a prohibition will cover both alleged special interests and citizens seeking to get someone elected to public office to change policies.

Hall and Wayman's findings cannot justify the wide range of campaign finance regulations that now exist, even taking egalitarianism for granted. Their study concerned three policy areas at a specific time. By it nature, egalitarian restrictions on campaign finance would affect all political activity at all times. Taken on its own terms, we have no way of knowing whether their findings transcend their data and justify a broader regulatory regime. To make that judgment, scholars needed more general data.

We now have such data and such a study. Gregory Wawro, a political scientist at Columbia University, has studied whether campaign contributions affect legislative entrepreneurship, a concept quite similar to Hall and Wayman's idea of access.[85] Do members of Congress provide services (introducing and managing bills, doing committee work, and voting) to interest groups in exchange for campaign contributions?

To definitively answer the question whether contributions create access, Wawro collected data about donations and activities by members of Congress from 1984 to 1992. Using a sophisticated analysis that takes into account many factors that affect their work, Wawro concluded that they do not engage in "legislative entrepreneurship" to attract contributions from interest groups.[86] Gregory Wawro's work trumps Hall and Wayman's in two ways. Wawro's data are taken from several Congresses and issue areas; Hall and Wayman looked at three issues in one Congress. Wawro found no evidence that members of Congress provide service to interest groups in exchange for contributions. We thus lack persuasive evidence that money buys access understood as mobilization on Capitol Hill.[87]

We do have persuasive scientific evidence that constituents are more likely to gain access to a member of Congress than are contributors to interest groups. Three political scientists who devised an experiment to test this question asked sixty-nine congressional staffers, almost all of them schedulers, to fill out a schedule for their Congress member based on requests from PAC representatives and constituents. If the conventional wisdom were correct, the experiment would have found that the PAC requests were more likely to be scheduled (giving access to the Congress member) than the requests from a member. Instead, "Contrary to the perception that PACs buy access to legislators at the expense of constituents, these results suggest that constituency is a more important influence on scheduling requests than PAC status."[88] Another study found that groups with a PAC do have more contacts with legislators than groups without

a PAC but that contributions were not the reason for the differences between the groups. Rather, groups with PACs "have an organizational presence in a greater array of districts." For that reason, groups with PACs
may have a lobbying advantage, but "that advantage derives from their
ability to organize effectively in many regions of the country."[89] As one
scholar of interest groups notes, "[T]he constituency link remains particularly helpful when trying to gain access to a legislator's office. One can
only conclude that money may not be the most effective currency when
seeking access or lobbying for legislators' votes."[90]

The argument that campaign contributions lead to inequalities in access
to public officials comes up short. The presumption of liberty demands
that those who wish to restrict campaign finance must make a compelling
case that giving money leads to access and thus fosters inequality. They
have not made that case. The Supreme Court relied on a few examples
drawn from the testimony of individuals. The best study about contributions and access—indeed, the only study that can make systematic claims
about access based on general data—shows that leaders in Congress do
not sell access in exchange for contributions.

Conclusion

The vision of the founders led to a Constitution embodying a mixed regime that fragmented power as a way of avoiding tyranny. For Madisonians, *equality* meant equality before the law and not equality of outcomes
in politics or civil society. In contrast, some Progressives defined democracy as equality of influence throughout a broad ambit of society. Wealth
in the United States, and in any existing society, is not distributed equally.
Egalitarians say that inequality in holdings translates into inequality of
political influence, a perversion of true democracy that can be remedied
by excluding private money from politics and equalizing political power
wherever inequalities arise. This ideal of equality and the condemnation
of inequality that goes with it foster robust "reforms" that affect more
than the moneyed interests. In particular, the media, traditional supporters of restraints on money in politics, must eventually be subjected
to government control if we are to attain true equality of influence over
elections and politics.

Political egalitarians claim that conservatives, Republicans, and the
rich dominate elections and policymaking to the detriment of everyone

else and especially the poor. The moneyed few rule the many by deploying private money as a weapon in political struggle. The task is to disarm them by ridding politics of private money. For the egalitarian, the liberty to participate in politics by giving money inherently corrupts democracy and has no place in American political life.

The evidence shown in this chapter paints a different picture of American politics, one that focuses less on the contrast between rich conservatives and poor liberals than on the distinction between Americans who are interested and engaged in politics and others who are largely indifferent. It should not be surprising that the active are more likely to give to campaigns. If contributions reflect the intensity of political concern, the active will always be overrepresented among contributors. Although contributors as a group are more conservative than the general population, they are also more liberal and almost as likely to be Democratic. In any case, policy outcomes hardly suggest a plutocracy. The federal government transfers hundreds of billions of dollars from the rich to the poor (and from the young to the old), and liberalism has been overrepresented in Congress for the past three decades.

Electoral Competition

Jon Corzine spent $63,209,506 to win the 2000 Democratic Senate primary in New Jersey and the general election.[1] He won the general election against Republican Bob Franks by a vote of 50 percent to 47 percent. Many Americans saw Corzine's victory as vindication of the Golden Rule: "Them that have the gold, rule." In other words, candidates with the most money buy election to office. The people do not control who is elected to public office, contributions do, and the Golden Rule is ironic testimony to the corruption of democracy. Having more money does give a candidate an advantage. Yet money does not simply buy elections.

Jon Corzine raised most of his money from one contributor: Jon Corzine. Campaign finance law permits individuals to contribute as much as they wish to their own campaign. Because individuals cannot corrupt themselves, the Constitution does not permit regulation of such contributions. Large contributions and high spending, however, do not guarantee victory. Steve Forbes, the publishing magnate, spent $30 million of his own money vainly pursuing the Republican presidential nomination in 1996.[2] Two years earlier Michael Huffington had spent $28 million running for a senate seat in California, only to lose to Dianne Feinstein.[3] Forbes and Huffington both lost by large margins. Ross Perot also financed his first run for the presidency, which garnered 20 percent of the vote but did not lead to the White House. These three are not the only wealthy self-financiers to lose their bids for office.[4]

Corzine spent more than $30 million to beat a Republican challenger by 3 points in a predominately Democratic state. Democratic candidates won U.S. Senate seats from New Jersey in 2002 and 1996 by about 10 points and the governor's chair in 2001 by 14 points.[5] Would Corzine's spending have succeeded had he been a Republican? Perhaps not. Money does not magically overcome hurdles such as party affiliation. Moreover, spending often yields diminishing returns. Corzine's first $10 million would have made him a serious candidate; his next $10 million would have had less effect. His spending would also have been vitiated if his opponent had had dedicated volunteers, a first-rate organization, and a skillful campaign manager. Finally, Corzine's spending might have been overcome by a national recession blamed on the Democratic Party or a popular Republican incumbent running for reelection.[6]

Why did Corzine spend half of his $60 million in the primary? He faced James Florio, a former governor of New Jersey, well known throughout the state and the presumed frontrunner for the nomination. Corzine had to spend a lot of money to overcome Florio's inherent advantage in name recognition. Yet Corzine was also lucky. Florio was well known but not well liked because as governor he had broken a promise not to raise taxes.[7] Had Florio been both famous and popular, Corzine's money might have been wasted.

New Jersey Democrats are among the most liberal in the nation. Corzine was no centrist: "In March, three months before the primary, Corzine went up with TV ads in the New York and Philadelphia markets. He set forth his liberal stands on issues—for a universal health care system, for government payment of tuition to college or vocational or technical school for students with at least a B average, for gun control, for abortion rights."[8] Had he been an ideological moderate or conservative, Corzine might have lost his primary bid, lavish spending notwithstanding.

The Corzine example offers several lessons. Self-financing candidates for office are not certain of victory. Ideology and partisanship matters as well as fundraising. Even unlimited spending appears to yield declining returns on election day. One last lesson: had Corzine decided to remain in Congress, he would have been almost certain to win reelection in 2006.[9] The problem of electoral competition in the United States has become largely a problem of incumbent invulnerability.

The Importance of Competition

Apart from incumbents, does anyone defend this decline in electoral competition? After all, isn't everyone in favor of more competition for votes? The early Progressives were concerned about shirking by representatives and sought ways to make them responsive to their constituents, including direct democracy. More recently Progressives have been ambivalent about turnover in office. In the early 1990s one solution to incumbency advantage—term limits—gained continuing popular support. According to another argument, informed by the Progressive vision, turning out incumbents would sacrifice valuable legislative experience and expertise.[10] In this way, the arguments for the domination of experts now came to the defense of congressional incumbents.[11] Insofar as incumbents stand for expertise, the Progressive supports their long stay in public life and hopes for the professionalization of politics marked by the politician who makes a career out of public office. By implication if not by profession, the Progressive has doubts about inexperienced and inexpert outsiders coming to power.

The founders believed that elections were the primary means of controlling government.[12] If government has a monopoly on the use of violence, the possibility of tyranny always exists. Elections in some measure constrain that monopoly by forcing government officials—the people who control the use of violence—to face electoral competition. If that competition ceases to exist in theory or in fact, the Madisonian nightmare of government acting without effective restraints becomes possible. Madisonians also put limited trust in those who hold political power. The incumbent is as likely to be a threat to individual rights as a good representative seeking the public good within strict constitutional boundaries. Compared to the Progressive, the Madisonian is more likely to worry about electoral competition as a constraint on government.[13] That is true in large measure because the Madisonian has a more balanced view of government and its agents than the Progressive, who sees the monopoly on violence in the right hands as a means of improving the nation.

If we grant that the United States lacks electoral competition, the conflicting visions that dominate the nation suggest different remedies. Progressives see the advantage of incumbency as another example of the way freedom to spend money leads to monopolies, this time in politics rather than economics. In both areas Progressives economics turn to government itself to end the political monopoly of incumbents. Restrictions on liberty—limits on campaign spending or compulsory contributions to candidates for office—are a necessary means to achieve the collective goal of more competition in elections. The Progressive expects that those who benefit from a lack of electoral competition will adopt effective measures to increase voters' choices at the polls. Those who profess the Madisonian vision are likely to believe that restricting political liberty will increase rather than eliminate this lack of competition. In economic life, for example, restrictions on investments would prevent the creation of new products and services that would challenge the existing market leaders as well as efforts to spread information about the new possibilities. Such restrictions would lead to less market competition and create an effective monopoly. Madisonians would expect that Progressive efforts to control spending on politics would reduce electoral competition.

This chapter and the two following examine money as it relates to electoral competition. I start by asking whether campaign spending and fundraising reduce electoral competition and, if so, what might be done about it. In chapters 8 and 9 I critically consider whether those who write campaign finance laws seek to reduce electoral competition.

The Competition Problem

Incumbent members of Congress almost always win reelection when they run. Since 1998 they have been reelected more than 98 percent of the time. Like most numbers, this reelection rate should not be understood in isolation. Since 1945, members of Congress have generally won reelection more than 90 percent of the time.

Figure 6.1 shows in stark detail how successful House incumbents have been in gaining reelection. They have lost more than 10 percent of their races only three times in fifty years. This pattern continued after FECA passed in 1974. Clearly the new campaign finance regulations did not change the longstanding success of House incumbents at the polls as indicated by the trend line in figure 6.1. We can also "zoom in" and look at the small changes in incumbents' reelection rates. Figure 6.2 shows that incumbent electoral success has increased overall during the modern political era, but the upward trend has not been uniform. The average reelection rate before FECA was 93.3 percent; the average afterwards has been 95.7 percent.[14]

We can also ask whether the incumbent reelection rate rose or fell during this period. Figure 6.2 charts the increases and decreases in incumbent success from one election to another; for example, the first point shows that the rate rose 1.3 percent in 1952 compared to the election immediately preceding it. We notice immediately that after 1980 the range of change in incumbent success becomes half what it was in the previous

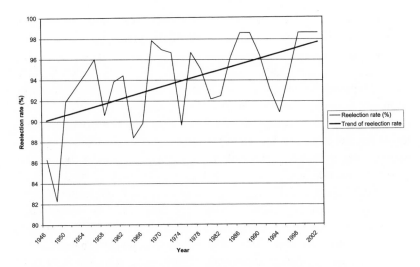

FIGURE 6.1 Reelection rate for incumbents in the House of Representatives, 1946–2002. Norman J. Ornstein, Thomas E. Mann, and Michael J. Malbin, *Vital Statistics on Congress, 1999–2000* (Washington, DC: AEI Press, 2000), 57; author's calculations for 2000 and 2002.

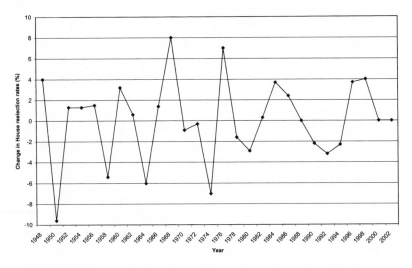

FIGURE 6.2 Change in House reelection rates, 1948–2002. Norman J. Ornstein, Thomas E. Mann, and Michael J. Malbin, *Vital Statistics on Congress, 1999–2000* (Washington, DC: AEI Press, 2000); author's calculations.

twenty years. After 1976, incumbent reelection rates were rising and oc-
curring within a narrower range than in earlier years.

We might also note that incumbent reelection rates had been declining
from 1968 to 1974, the latter year showing the single largest decline during the period. This sharp change reflects the electorate's response to the
Watergate scandal. The election of 1976 ran sharply the other way as more
than 96 percent of incumbents won. Thereafter we see a brief period of
declining rates followed by two longer trends: from 1984 to 1994, incumbent success declined (again, within a high range) and from 1994 to the
present, their rate of victory rose quickly and remained very high.

Over the course of the twentieth century, national congressional elections became less competitive. James Campbell and Steve Jurek found
that both the gross number of seats changing hands and the net partisan
gains or losses after 1970 were typically less than half of what they had
been prior to that date.[15] Specifically, in the thirty-eight elections held
from 1900 to 1974, thirty-three (or 87 percent) involved swings of at least
ten seats from one party to the other. Of the thirteen elections held from
1976 to 2000, only five (or 38 percent) resulted in double-digit shifts in
party control.[16] Indeed, House elections ended up being less competitive
in 2004 than they had been in 1994. A marginal seat in the House is subject to changes in party control. Seats whose incumbent received less than
55 percent of the vote in the previous election are the most vulnerable
to such changes. In 1994 the House had seventy-nine marginal seats.[17] In
2004 the House had thirty-five seats at stake. Over the course of ten years,
the number of marginals has declined by more than half. Other measures
also show that the number of competitive House seats declined from 1992
to 2000.[18]

Political scientists often define incumbency advantage in a single
legislative district as the difference between the proportion of the vote
received by an incumbent who runs and the proportion received by the
candidate of the incumbent party if an open seat exists and all major parties compete for the office.[19] In other words, the incumbency advantage is
the proportion of the vote that is due to incumbency itself.[20] The aggregate incumbency advantage may be estimated by looking at the average
of the incumbency advantages for all districts. Scholars have found that
although incumbency in itself has always increased the vote of an officeholder, the size of that advantage has increased rapidly since the 1960s.
Currently, incumbency seems to be worth about 10 percentage points at
the polls.[21]

The increasing advantages of incumbency have been extensively studied. Fifteen years ago, two students of the subject could say that scholars had been studying incumbency advantage for fifteen years.[22] Scholars and pundits have blamed everything from constituent services rendered by incumbents to favorable redistricting by state legislatures for the fortress around sitting officials. Some have also argued that the advantage of incumbency is a misleading statistical artifact created by the choices of officeholders.[23] Of course, campaign finance has been blamed for the decline of competition.

Incumbents do enjoy an overall advantage in campaign spending. A cursory glance shows that successful incumbents spend a lot more than do their challengers. On average incumbents who lose enjoy a much smaller advantage over their challengers.[24] Two scholars more systematically examined several House and Senate elections in the 1990s. During that period, House incumbents outspent challengers in 94 to 96 percent of the races; in a typical House election, the incumbent spent five times as much as the challenger. In the Senate during this era, the incumbent outspent the challenger 89 percent of the time, spending $2.70 for every dollar spent by a challenger.[25]

Does this advantage in spending explain the decline in congressional competition? The same two scholars related the decline in competition to five factors: campaign spending, the advantages of incumbency, the prior congressional vote, the most recent presidential vote, and the quality of the challenger in an election. Their analysis found that these five variables explain 90 to 95 percent of the variance in the House results and 77 percent of the variance in the Senate outcomes. They conclude that the typical spending advantage of incumbents "adds anywhere from seven to eleven percentage points to their vote shares compared to the expected vote if incumbents and challengers spent equal amounts." Compared to the four other factors affecting outcomes, "the campaign spending advantage was far and away the most important variable in determining the congressional vote."[26] Yet, as is often the case with scholarship, other studies cast doubt on the robustness of this conclusion.

Successful candidates for Congress sometimes do not spend all the funds they have raised for their campaigns. Some believe that incumbents use these leftover funds—so-called war chests—to deter challengers from contesting the election. They point in particular to wealthy candidates who are allowed to contribute as much as they might wish to their campaign. Why would this war chest deter a challenger?

In the mind of a potential challenger, the war chest might drive up the cost of winning an office. The challenger might see the war chest as money the incumbent would have to spend against a challenge. Such funds might signal to challengers that an incumbent has considerable capacity to raise money in the case of a hotly contested race. Finally, a war chest might tell a challenger something he might not otherwise know about an incumbent; it might say that the incumbent is tough, determined, or savvy.[27] Yet it need not deter a challenger. If it might be used for other purposes (such as retirement, prior to 1992, or seeking higher office), its deterrent effect would be decreased. Moreover, most challengers know the fundraising abilities or other characteristics of incumbents.[28] In theory, war chests may or may not deter challengers. We have to look at experience to figure out whether it does.[29]

The best scholarly study of war chests raises doubts about their influence. Jay Goodliffe examined races for the House of Representatives from 1984 to 1998 to see if war chests deterred challengers. He took into consideration incumbents' vote share during the previous election. Goodliffe's results are remarkable. If an incumbent faces a strong challenger and wins by 10 percent, that margin of victory, all things considered, decreases the probability of facing a high-quality challenger in the next election from .24 to .11. In contrast, if that same incumbent increases his war chest by $100,000, that increment, all things considered, decreases the chances of a high-quality challenger fighting his next reelection bid from .24 to .23.[30] In sum, Goodliffe finds strong empirical evidence that potential challengers considering a race examine how well an incumbent did in the previous election, not at how much money he or she has socked away to fight future elections.[31]

Do wealthy incumbents use war chests to scare off challengers? Two economists, Jeffrey Milyo and Timothy Groseclose, gathered data about the wealth of incumbents running for reelection in 1992. Controlling for all relevant factors, they found no evidence that wealthy incumbents raise or spend more money than nonwealthy incumbents, a crucial assumption of the war chest argument. Of course, the war chests of the wealthy may deter challengers even if the money is not spent. Testing the deterrence thesis leads to a problem: almost all incumbents in 1992 faced a challenger. Milyo and Groseclose decided to circumvent this problem by testing whether incumbent wealth was associated with low-quality challengers or with reduced challenger spending or vote share. They found "no evidence that the general election opponents of wealthy incumbents are less likely to have relevant prior experience or tend to either spend less or fare worse at the polls. In fact, if there is any relationship between wealth and challenger quality, it is that incumbent wealth weakly attracts experienced challengers."[32]

Such research once again raises doubts about conventional prejudices about campaign finance. It makes sense to average Americans that incumbents with lots of money scare off potential challengers. But average Americans rarely challenge incumbents or know much about electoral politics. Potential challengers know much more about incumbents and their strengths (and weaknesses). For them, an incumbent's election success matters a lot more than his or her funds.

We might also guess that soft money, the "big money" of the 1990s, increased the advantages of incumbents. That guess evokes three initial objections. First, the timing is wrong. Incumbents began enjoying inordinate success around 1970; soft money came into existence in 1979.[33] Some other factor must have been at work earlier. Second, soft money could only be donated to the political parties, not to candidates. During eras like our own of intense partisan competition, the parties would have every reason to focus their resources on contestable seats in Congress. Soft money, unlike hard money, might offer some competition to incumbents.[34] Third, the parties used soft money to mobilize voters through television ads and get-out-the-vote efforts. Incumbents might prefer lower turnout because their greater name recognition affords a decisive edge.

We lack sufficient data to definitively determine the relation of soft money to incumbents' reelection rates. Congress and the Federal Election Commission created soft money in 1979. The law did not require disclosure of soft money contributions until 1992. We have estimates, but not data, about soft money contributions prior to that date. The best estimates indicate that gifts of soft money rose from just under $42 million in 1980 to almost $100 million in 1992 (both figures are in 1998 dollars).[35] We can roughly estimate that soft money increased by a factor of 2.5 from 1980 to 1992 and by a factor of 4.5 from 1992 to 2002.

Here are the evident trends for soft money and for incumbent success. The amount of soft money that was given rose quickly in the era before disclosure and even more quickly in the decade afterward. From 1980 to 2002, incumbent reelection rates rose, fell, and rose yet again. We see, in short, no clear relation between rising soft money expenditures and rising incumbent success. From 1986 to 1994, incumbent reelection rates fell about as far as they ever have; during that same period, soft money must have at least doubled. On the other hand, incumbent success increased from 1994 to 2002, as did soft money fundraising and expenditures. The latter grew both when incumbent reelection rates were rising and when they were falling within a very high and very narrow range.

Finally, I might mention an assumption that informs the conventional wisdom about incumbency and campaign finance. If more fundraising translates into more incumbent spending, and if more spending translates directly into more votes, the general advantage in fundraising by incumbents would lead to a world where they outspend and thus almost always defeat challengers. In that world, restrictions on incumbent spending might break the connection between money and votes, thereby enhancing competition. This commonsense view of politics and policy, however, has little support from serious scientific analysis.

Increasing Competition

What might be done to increase competition? We should not rush to the conclusion that if campaign spending were equalized, incumbents would often lose. In 1998, 75 percent of House incumbents won with more than 60 percent of the vote in their district; equalization might reduce their margins but would probably not lead to their defeat.[36] Some of the 25 percent who won with less than 60 percent would perhaps lose under equalization of spending. In any case, equalization might induce more challengers to enter the lists, even if they ultimately lost. If more and better challengers did enter, we might surmise that elections would become more competitive thanks to an equalization of spending.

How might we achieve at least a closing of the gap between incumbents and challengers if not equal spending? As I noted at the beginning of the chapter, Progressives are inclined to try to reduce the advantages of incumbents via government action. The most common kind of government action, the institution of contribution limits, seems unlikely to enhance competition. Such limits make it harder to raise money to mount challenges by providing alternative sources of information to voters. More generally, in markets, controls on investment would not be expected to increase consumer choice or competition. As we have seen in national politics, the era since 1970 has seen a steady increase in incumbency advantage. That period has also seen a steady decrease in the real value of contribution limits in federal elections. In other words, the federal experience suggests an inverse correlation between contribution limits (they went down) and incumbency advantage (it went up). That experience might suggest that if contribution limits went up, incumbency advantage would go down. For these reasons, contribution limits are more often mentioned as an anticorruption measure rather than as a way to increase electoral competitiveness.[37]

In addition to limits, contemporary Progressives have advanced three alternatives. Government could restrict spending by candidates for office. Such limits would in most but not all cases affect incumbents more than challengers, putatively allowing challengers to overcome incumbents' spending advantage.[38] Government can also use tax revenues to subsidize candidates for office while allowing or prohibiting private spending on campaigns. Finally, government can both limit and subsidize campaign spending. As the law now stands, government can only insist on spending limits in exchange for public subsidies. Both limits and subsidies have serious drawbacks.

Spending Limits

Political scientists have looked closely at how campaign spending affects election results. They have found that the more challengers spend, the greater their share of the vote. Experts also found initially that the more incumbents spend, the smaller their share of the vote in an election. That was misleading. Incumbents spend more when they are in a close election with a strong challenger. Once scholars controlled for the challenger's level of spending, they found that the effect of an incumbent's spending was close to zero.[39] To most political scientists "these findings indicate that, in general, any policy restricting campaign spending is likely to protect incumbents and diminish electoral competition."[40]

The theory of spending limits assumes that if the government equalizes the outlays of incumbents and challengers, the latter will have an equal chance to win a seat. However, this logic is flawed. Incumbents' spending in a reelection contest is not limited to outlays during a current campaign. They also have spent money in the past on advertising and goodwill, investment that creates for them a brand name with voters.[41] The incumbent's brand name acts as an entry barrier to electoral competition. Those already in the "legislative industry"—incumbent officials—do not bear this cost in competition. Those seeking to enter the industry— challengers—must spend to create a brand name equal to the net present value of the incumbent's.[42] The implications of past incumbent spending for spending limits are stark. Imagine that election outcomes may be formalized with two equations:

$$I = IncB + IncC$$

and

$$C = ChB + ChC,$$

where I is the incumbent's share of the vote, $IncB$ is the net present value of past investment in a brand name by the incumbent, $IncC$ is the current campaign spending by the incumbent, C is the challenger's share of the vote, ChB is the net present value of past investment in a brand name by the challenger, and ChC is current campaign spending.

All things being equal, if $IncC = ChC$ the vote shares of incumbents and challengers will be determined by the difference between the net present values of the brand names of the two candidates. In almost all cases, we should expect that the brand name of the incumbent will be of greater value than that of the challenger ($IncB > ChB$). Hence, it follows that the incumbent will almost always win in a system with spending limits ($I < C$) insofar as the total vote is a function of relative spending. In short, spending restrictions bind challengers more than they do incumbents.[43] To avoid this conclusion, we must assume that other factors systematically favor challengers or that spending limits could reduce current incumbent spending by a sum equal to the net present value of the brand name. The former seems empirically wrong, the latter politically impossible. This theory does explain, however, why spending limits have continually been on Congress's campaign finance reform agenda since 1969.[44]

The effects of spending limits are more than theory. The political scientist Gary Jacobson has investigated the effect of campaign spending on a challenger's likelihood of winning. Looking at House elections from 1972 to 1984, he found that challengers needed to raise $660,000 (in 2000 dollars) to have a one-in-four chance of beating an incumbent. He then looked at the likely effects of spending limits on a challenger. If an incumbent and a challenger were limited to $200,000, the challenger would have .08 probability of winning. If no ceiling existed, and the same challenger raised an additional $100,000 while the incumbents raised $300,000 more, the challenger's probability of winning would increase to .13.[45] Jacobson concludes, "Competitive campaigns are unavoidably expensive. There is simply no way for most nonincumbent candidates to capture the attention of enough voters to make a contest of it without spending substantial sums of money."[46] Incumbents begin an election struggle with enormous advantages including money for staff and name recognition among voters. Challengers must spend a lot of money to overcome those inherent advantages of office. For this reason, spending limits complicate the lives of challengers more than the lives of incumbents. This truth should be kept in mind when I turn in the next chapter to the history of campaign finance regulation.

Other studies have shown that campaign spending has striking benefits both for electoral competition and, more generally, for democratic values. John J. Coleman and Paul Manna, political scientists at the University of Wisconsin, studied the effects of campaign spending on voters during elections in the 1990s. They found that incumbents begin a campaign with a large advantage in name recognition. They examined the empirical effects of campaign spending for challengers. Holding incumbent spending constant in the 1994 election, they found that increased spending by a challengers increases the probability of a voter's recalling his name; the average spending by a challenger ($180,000 in 1994) led to a .07 probability that a voter would recall his name; if a challenger spent $500,000, the probability increased to .14; if the challenger spent $1 million, the probability rose again to .33. (Only four challengers spent that much in 1994.) Spending by a challenger thus vitiates an incumbent's advantage in name recognition and introduces into an election an alternative to the status quo.[47]

Challenger spending increases the likelihood that voters will be able to learn about ideological alternatives in an election. Coleman and Manna found that increasing challenger spending from $180,000 to $1 million increased the probability that voters could place them on an ideological scale from .49 to .85; the probability that a citizen is confident of that placement also from .20 to .53 with an increase in spending. They found similar results for issues. Spending, especially by a challenger, increases voter knowledge about the ideologies and issue positions of candidates for Congress.[48]

The authors looked at how spending affects the way voters feel about candidates for office. Campaign spending did not help incumbents much. Their outlays did not clearly lead voters to like or dislike incumbents and did not increase their job approval rating. On the other hand, challenger spending reduced approval of incumbents; greater spending decreased the likelihood of finding something to like about an incumbent, and in the 1996 election, it increased the likelihood of voters' finding something to dislike about the current occupant of the office. Spending also increases the chances that voters will find something to like (and dislike) about the challengers. Overall, spending makes elections more competitive than they would be otherwise.[49]

Coleman and Manna found that incumbent spending did not confuse voters. As incumbents spend more, voters' beliefs about their ideology and stands on the issues become more accurate. It's a different story for challengers. Their spending tends to reduce the accuracy of voters' judgments about an incumbent's ideology or stands. At the same time, challenger spending has more effect than incumbent spending.[50]

The authors also show that spending affirms democratic values. But critics may still argue that increased knowledge and political efficacy go to "the haves" rather than "the have-nots." In a follow-up study, Coleman looked at the effects of spending on various groups who have a relatively large amount of political information (the haves) and those who have relatively little information (the have-nots). He found that increased spending by a challenger made it more likely that all groups (except racial minorities) would recall a challenger's name. Coleman finds that increases in spending equally help both groups accurately identify the ideologies of candidates. Note that this does not mean the two groups ended up with equal information; the increases did not eliminate the initial gap between them. If the challenger spends $1,000,000, however, the knowledge gap between the two groups goes away. In contrast, incumbent spending showed mixed results. Increased spending by an incumbent does not improve citizens' ability to recall his ideology or name. Yet for those who can identify his ideology, the spending makes their recall of ideology more accurate. It also improves voters' ability to accurately recall the incumbent's positions on government services and spending. These improvements apply to all groups in the study. Incumbent spending does not benefit only the haves. Spending by challengers improves knowledge of ideology and issues across all groups. At high levels, rarely achieved, spending by challengers improves the knowledge of the have-nots relative to the haves.[51] In general, campaign spending produces democratic benefits for all groups.

Coleman's findings are all the more important given the greater diversity of media today. As noted above, the political scientists Markus Prior has found that expanding choices in the media combined with a standing preference among many Americans for entertainment rather than political information tends to produce an electorate that is less politically knowledgeable, more unequally knowledgeable, and less likely to turn out on election day than in the past. Prior concludes, "[W]e might have to pin our hopes of creating a reasonably informed electorate on that reviled form of communication, political advertising." Since people rarely choose to expose themselves to political information, "their greatest chance for encounters with the political world occurs when commercials are inserted into their regular entertainment diet."[52] Such advertising, of course, would be reduced by spending limits.

On the whole, scholars who have studied the effects of spending on congressional elections believe that spending limits would help rather than hurt incumbents.[53] Certainly limits on spending would reduce the benefits to society identified by Coleman and Manna. Proponents of spending limits might protest, however, that they hope to have public subsidies along with spending limits. I turn now to the merits of taxpayer financing of campaigns.

Taxpayer Financing

For many years, Progressives argued that the solution to poverty was to redistribute money from the better off to the poor. Similarly, if challengers lack money, government can solve the electoral competition problem by instituting taxpayer financing of campaigns. When combined with spending limits, public subsidies would both limit incumbent outlays and increase spending by challengers. Most campaign financing in the United States comes from private sources. Public financing exists mostly in the states and then largely as a supplement to private sources of funding. In national elections, only presidential campaigns receive tax dollars, garnered from a voluntary checkoff system.

Public spending has had little effect on electoral competition at either level of government. The leading study of state public financing schemes offers some stark conclusions: "Low contribution limits, public financing, and spending limits all fail to do much to equalize political power among private interests, reduce the total amount of money spent on elections, or produce equal contests between challengers and incumbents." The authors also found that "full-blown public funding programs with spending limits do little to affect competition, if competition is defined as the number or percentage of candidates who are in close races."[54] Others have reached similar conclusions about states with full public financing.[55]

We might also consider the competitiveness of presidential elections.

The 1976 campaign finance law provided generous subsidies to those running for the party nominations and for the candidates in the general election. We would expect that the availability of public money would increase the absolute number of candidates for the presidency compared to elections prior to 1976. Has this "presidential system" led to an increase in candidates for the presidency?

We should begin by asking the correct question. The wrong question would be "Did the public fund significant candidates in the presidential primaries?" The correct question would be "Did the public funding lead to more presidential primary bids (and hence, more choice for voters) than would have occurred otherwise (that is, if the public funding did not exist)?" In short, we need to know what difference the public funding made by comparing what did happen to what would have happened (a counterfactual). In the case of presidential primaries, we know who ran, how much money they received, and the outcomes of the primaries. What we do not know is the counterfactual: who would have run in the absence of the presidential public matching funds program. [56]

Apart from the major-party candidates, nine presidential candidates in the general elections since 1948 have received more than 1 percent of the total vote. Five of those candidates ran after the presidential system was created in 1976. Not all five accepted public financing. Ross Perot did not accept taxpayer financing in 1992, preferring to spend $65 million of his own money on his candidacy.[57] Ed Clark, the Libertarian candidate in 1980, also did not take taxpayer financing. In all, six of the nine ran their campaigns without the help of the taxpayer. Moreover, the two top vote-getters during the period—George Wallace in 1968 and Ross Perot in 1992—made do without subsidies. The presidential system might be credited with three additional presidential campaigns in seven general elections (Ralph Nader's in 2000, Ross Perot's in 1996, and John Anderson's in 1980). The private funding system in place prior to 1976 produced four serious candidates apart from the major-party candidates in the previous seven general elections.

What about the party nominations? Most of the money paid out by the presidential system has gone to fund the conventions of the two major political parties (10 percent of all funding) and the campaigns of their candidates in the general election (61 percent of all funding). Candidates running in the primaries have received a little over $506 million, or about 29 percent of all outlays by the presidential system.[58] That money has funded eighty-three candidates in the primaries.[59] Of those, seventy-one were candidates for the nominations of the two major political parties. Of the seventy-one, fifty-five candidates received more than 1 percent of the total number of votes cast in a party's presidential primaries for a given year, an average of 7.8 candidates for each presidential election. How does that compare with the number of primary candidates prior to the presidential funding system? The seven elections prior to the 1976 election included an average of 10.7 candidates in the party primaries.[60] If we measure competitiveness by entry into a race, the years prior to the introduction of public subsidy of presidential campaigns seem somewhat more competitive than the years that followed it.[61] On the other hand, if we assume a bit of randomness in the data, we might conclude that the presidential system changed nothing: the number of entries into the presidential primaries was about the same before and after taxpayer financing began.[62]

We might also consider public support for taxpayer financing of campaigns. Scholars face several obstacles in determining public opinion concerning government financing of political campaigns. Polling organizations have not asked the same question about public financing over time. Hence, we lack a consistent time series of questions measuring the same aspect of public opinion. Asking the same question is important because the wording of the questions can affect responses.[63] In polling on campaign finance issues, questions that use words such as special interests and corruption can easily bias results. With these problems in mind, I have searched the databanks of the Gallup Organization and the Roper Center Archive of Public Opinion for surveys asking about public financing of campaigns.

The Gallup Organization first asked about this topic in December 1938. It found that 58.5 percent of respondents opposed federal financing instead of private contributions.[64] Gallup did not poll on this issue again for several decades. From 1973 to 1987, Gallup asked the following question eight times: "It has been suggested the federal government provide a fixed amount of money for the election campaigns of candidates for Congress and that all private contributions from other sources be prohibited. Do you think this is a good idea or a poor idea?[65] Figure 6.3 shows the percentage of respondents over time who thought federal financing along with a prohibition on private funding was a good idea.

The data suggest several observations. First, in the 1970s and early 1980s, majorities of the public looked favorably on federal funding of campaigns coupled with prohibitions on private contributions. Support was strongest, not surprisingly, during the Watergate crisis. Subsequently,

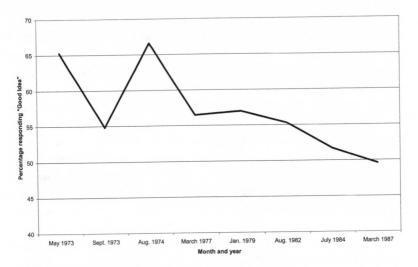

FIGURE 6.3 Percentage of people who believe public financing to be a "good idea," 1973–87. Question 6 (Gallup Poll #872); Question 8 (Gallup Poll #877); Question 6 (Gallup Poll #913); Question 6 (Gallup Poll # 971); Question 18 (Gallup Poll #121G); Question 9f (Gallup Poll #200G); Question 4 (Gallup Poll #237G); Question 9C (Ad Hoc Telephone Survey, March 13–18,1987). http://www.gallupbrain.com.

support for federal financing declined steadily; a decade after Watergate, a bare majority supported it.

This is not the entire picture of public opinion during this era. In 1979 and 1980, a survey organization asked whether respondents favored public financing for Congress campaigns three times. An average of 68 percent either disapproved or strongly disapproved.[66] Another question from 1980 set out the arguments for and against public financing of campaigns; in that context, 62 percent of the respondents disapproved or strongly disapproved of public financing.[67] From 1980 to 1985, an organization noted that "one way to prevent either business or labor unions, or any other group or person, from influencing politics by making contributions would be public financing of election campaigns—which is already done for the general election for President" and then asked whether the respondent favored or opposed public financing. The question itself is extraordinarily biased toward eliciting a favorable response. The wording associates public financing with preventing corruption (the first source of bias) by disliked groups (the second source of bias) and with a somewhat popular existing program (the third source of bias).[68] Despite this bias, an average of 39.9 percent of the respondents favored public financing and 40.3 percent opposed it; the remaining 20 percent did not know.[69] One can fairly say, in summary, that from Watergate to the end of the Reagan presidency, popular support for public financing declined. There is little evidence that by the 1980s a majority wanted taxpayers to fund campaigns.

Polling on public financing in the 1990s, on the whole, continued the trends established in the previous decade. To be sure, some polls showed support for this innovation. During the week of the 1996 election Gallup found that two-thirds of respondents thought it would be a good idea if government provided fixed amount of money for election campaigns and banned private contributions.[70] We have strong reasons for thinking this result is an anomaly appearing by chance.[71] Other polling offered what might be called favorable views of public financing. A majority in 1997 thought public financing would reduce spending on campaign advertising.[72] In the same year, half the respondents said public financing would reduce the influence of special interests and large contributors.[73] Another poll also found strong support for forcing the TV networks to give free air time to candidates for Congress.[74]

On the whole, however, polling in the 1990s and later showed a continued decline in public support for government financing of campaigns. Just two weeks after two-thirds of respondents said public financing would be a good idea, a Gallup poll found that 51.4 percent opposed public funding and a ban on private contributions.[75] Five months later, in March 1997, Gallup found that 60 percent of respondents opposed federal financing of presidential and congressional campaigns.[76] From 1990 to 2000, polling organizations asked seven straightforward questions about public opposition to or support for public financing of congressional or political campaigns. Five of the surveys indicated that more than 65 percent of the public opposed it. None of the seven showed more people favoring than opposing public financing.[77] Another three surveys asked about public financing while mentioning special interests, a sure way to bias the result in favor of public financing. Yet two still found majority opposition to public financing, and all three reported that more people opposed than favored government support for campaigns.[78] Even with the game rigged in its favor, public financing could not attract majority support in the 1990s.

Despite the limitations noted initially, one can draw some conclusions from this survey of polling about public financing. Support for the idea was highest during the Watergate era. It then declined steadily throughout the next two decades. In recent years, almost all evidence indicates strong public opposition to public financing, even when polling questions are biased to produce a favorable response. This conclusion is confirmed by another study of surveys.[79]

We might consider the public support question more pragmatically. For example, surveys could mention the costs as well as the benefits of public financing. When costs are mentioned in existing surveys, support for the idea goes down.[80] But even asking about costs does not actually reveal the preferences of the public regarding this issue: respondents are being asked to spend hypothetical money for expected benefits, a situation that inclines respondents to favor a policy.[81] Fortunately, we do have data about situations where people are asked to spend actual money to fund public financing programs. This evidence indicates that the public in fact does not support such schemes.

Rate of participation in public financing programs via tax checkoffs show little public support for such spending. Participation in the presidential system has declined steadily throughout its history (see figure 6.4). The highest participation rate came in the early years of the fund, when as many as 28 percent of taxpayers diverted money to the system. Recently, the rate has been slightly higher than 10 percent. This number is important. Survey research suggests that in 2000 about 12 percent of Americans

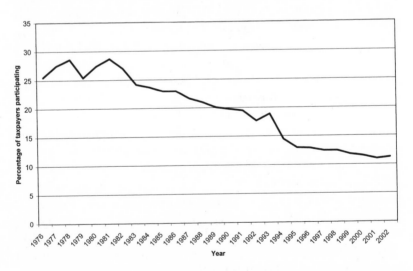

FIGURE 6.4 Participation in the presidential public financing program, 1976–2002. Federal Election Commission Press Office, "Presidential Matching Fund Income Tax Check-Off Status," March 2003.

over the age of eighteen gave to political candidates, party committees, or political organizations.[82] Compared to the private system, the presidential system does not broaden participation in donating to campaigns.

The lack of participation is not an aberration caused by the public's lack of knowledge of the presidential program. The public's apathy toward public financing is not limited to federal schemes. The thirteen states that had checkoff schemes for taxpayer financing saw a steady decline in participation from 1975 to 1994. The typical checkoff program dropped from 20 percent participation to 11 percent during that period.[83]

Public financing reflects the Progressive vision of its proponents. Progressives believe that government has the responsibility and the capacity to realize a multitude of collective goals. They see enhancing electoral competition as one such goal and redistribution from taxpayers to candidates as one vital means to achieve that goal. If public financing has not achieved that goal yet—and it has not—the solution lies in higher taxes and more money for candidates, especially for challengers. Presumably at some point the government could direct enough money to challengers to make a dent in incumbent reelection rates.

Even if electoral competition did increase, public financing would still have one serious shortcoming: it forces each taxpayer to contribute to candidates and causes they oppose. It is similar to compulsory levies for the benefit of specific religions. Both force taxpayers to support views they oppose as a matter of conscience or interest. This compulsion has long been recognized and condemned. The Senate Watergate Committee recommended that Congress stay away from public financing of presidential campaigns: "Thomas Jefferson believed 'to compel a man to furnish contributions of money for the propagation of opinions which he disbelieves and abhors, is sinful and tyrannical.' The Committee's opposition is based like Jefferson's upon the fundamental need to protect the voluntary right of individual citizens to express themselves politically as guaranteed by the First Amendment."[84]

Conclusion

When they decide to run, incumbents almost always win reelection in the United States. Their victories reflect their advantages including their raising of funds from private donors. Yet the use of private money does not tell the whole story. Incumbents are better known than most of their potential challengers simply by virtue of holding an office. An incumbent can use his influence over legislation to funnel money to his district, thereby purchasing votes that will contribute to reelection. To make it a race, challengers need a great deal of money and a bit of luck (the incumbent must be vulnerable in some way). In theory, money for challengers could come from the taxpayer, but that method has not enhanced competition and is unpopular, perhaps because such laws force citizens to support candidates they dislike or abhor. If challengers are to compete more effectively, the funding must come from private donors. If we are concerned about electoral competition, the question for public policy should be what system of campaign finance rules facilitates fundraising by challengers.

A deregulated system of campaign finance should be expected to increase electoral competition. Absent contribution limits, challengers could raise money quickly and easily from a small number of donors, if they wished.[85] When entry barriers are removed in economic markets, investors can provide the money needed to introduce competition, assuming that demand for a produce or service exists. Yet the freedom to spend money on elections does not guarantee increased competition. Even under a liberalized regime, incumbents might not be vulnerable all that often, perhaps because of partisan redistricting or because of the skills of the officeholder. A liberalized system of campaign finance, however, does offer more hope for challengers than spending limits (which complicate or preclude challenges) or public subsidies (which are politically unlikely and morally problematic).

From 1969 to 1974, Congress created the foundation of our current system of campaign finance law including limits on campaign contributions. Such ceilings were not adjusted for inflation and thus became progressively lower over time. Consequently, it became more difficult to raise large sums of money for a campaign than it had been in a system without contribution limits. Scholars date the largest decline in congressional electoral competition from 1970, the year Congress passed its first systemic campaign finance restriction. The decline in electoral competition and the new era of campaign finance regulation are virtually conterminous. In itself, this shared beginning does not mean campaign finance regulation caused the decline in competition. It does suggest that we should examine how and why Congress passed campaign finance laws. After all, those who enact legislation—members of Congress—have no interest in enhancing electoral competition; to the contrary, they have every reason to try to reduce their vulnerability to defeat at the polls. Did they act on that interest?

PART III
Realities

The Origins of Modern Campaign Finance Law

The stories reformers tell about campaign finance have heroes who practice politics or work for government, allegedly pursing noble purposes and the public interest. The villains in their tales are always in the private sector, often engaged in business and always pursing their private interests to the detriment of the common good.[1] One chapter of this narrative ended with Watergate, when idealists saved the United States from the Nixon gang and then passed campaign finance laws to clean up the corruption and restore the integrity of politics. But, of course, evil rarely remains at bay: Lucifer is always at hand to tempt the weak of will. Angels of reform must always attack his lures of selfishness and greed.

This story about campaign finance has satisfied its audience for a long time, but as we have seen, it is at best incomplete and at worst false. Apart from positing a battle of good and evil, the story assumes that Congress legislates in the public interest, a conjecture belied by "even the shallowest examination of congressional policymaking."[2] Another story, at once less charitable and fantastic, should be told about money in politics.

This alternative story begins with premises that are both realistic and Madisonian. Rather than assume that politicians and bureaucrats tend to be devoted to the public good, this story assumes that human beings, whether employed by government or by private concerns, are all pretty much alike, capable of benevolence but mostly self-interested. This shift in assumptions leads to a different narrative. Gone are the heroes and villains of the reform story, the victimizing moneybags and victimized politician. Instead politicians use political power to further their own goals rather than the public interest.[3] Campaign finance restrictions might well serve some especially powerful special interests and not the common good. Campaign finance laws might be, in other words, a form of corruption.

Politics is the struggle to obtain and hold power. In the United States, people obtain political power primarily by winning elections. Candidates run for office and, if successful, become representatives of their constituents. Candidates belong to political parties that assist their election campaigns and form a governing coalition in the legislature when their members form a majority. Those who hold office have a strong interest in retaining their power by winning reelection.[4] Incumbents also have an interest in retaining and increasing the power of their party because members of a dominant party have more power than the members of a minority party. Similarly, parties holding a majority have an interest in helping incumbents win reelection because victories by all their incumbents translate into control over the legislature. In most cases, the interests of the party and its members in Congress will not conflict. But conflict is possible. We must be alert to cases where the interests of the party may contravene those of some of the incumbent members belonging to the party.

This desire to hold and retain power creates serious conflicts of interest in a representative democracy. Members of Congress serve as agents of their principals, the voters in their district. They represent the views and interests of their principals in the legislature. A representative can win reelection by satisfying his principals that he has represented their interests well. But a representative might like to both follow his own preferences regarding policy and win reelection. He might wish to shirk his duties to his principals. The possibility of turning an incumbent out of office enables his constituents to control their agent's conduct and prevent shirking. Elections thus reconcile the interests of the representatives with those of his principals. Voters are better off if their representative fears defeat at the polls; they are more likely to fear defeat if vigorous competition exists for the job. The representative thus has an interest in reducing the competition for his job in order to reduce his vulnerability to electoral defeat thereby increasing his ability to do as he wishes. What's good for the people is bad for the representative, and vice versa.

This conflict of interest might not matter if incumbents did not have the ability to reduce competition for their jobs. Those who hold power, as individuals and as party members, create and enforce the rules for deciding who holds power; those already in office set the rules of the electoral game. We should expect that those rules would be set to increase the likelihood that officeholders or the members of the dominant party in Congress will retain and enhance their power. More prosaically, those who already have power will create election rules that maximize the likelihood they will win reelection whatever the policy mood of their principals.[5] If we doubt this, we must hold the implausible belief that officeholders are indifferent to their own interests.

How do campaign finance laws favor those who hold power? We have seen the way spending limits favor incumbents and the way the transaction costs associated with contribution limits complicate raising funds. We should also attend to the question of which resources for fighting elections fall within the regulatory net and which do not. Parties use different mixes of resources to fight elections. For example, the Republicans have until recently been "capital intensive": they rely more than Democrats do on fundraising and campaign spending. Democrats, of course, also depend on money to win elections, but they have other means to produce votes. Labor unions and other allies provide significant volunteer labor to get out the vote for the party.[6] The Democrats also rely on unpaid contributions from the media. Polls have found that most people who report for the national media support the Democrats, and the elite newspapers, editorially and to some degree in terms of reporting, lean leftward.[7] For the period treated in this chapter, the focus on money alone (as opposed to other resources) discriminated against the minority party in favor of the majority party.

In the 1960s and 1970s the Democratic Party controlled Congress. Members of the party often introduced bills to restrict fundraising and campaign spending, actions consistent with the theory that parties use campaign finance law to protect their control of the legislature. That history, however, should not be confused with the theory. Any party with a majority would have an interest in restricting challenges to its incumbents. The ideals of a party might constrain that interest, but the Democrats embodied Progressivism. Both major parties in the United States have been influenced by the Progressive vision of politics. We have no reason to believe, in other words, that only the Democratic Party will favor restrictions on campaign finance.

Some readers may object that this theory of campaign finance lawmaking ignores the constraints on incumbent lawmakers and party leaders. If incumbents rig campaign finance rules to favor their individual or partisan interests, voters would recognize that their representatives are acting against their interests by reducing electoral competition. Incumbents who use campaign finance laws to bias elections would thus end up losing their bids for reelection. This objection is not persuasive for several reasons. The voters who support a political party or an elected official may also support his efforts to avoid electoral defeat. The rest of the electorate will probably not recognize how campaign finance laws restrict electoral competition because they work in subtle ways. Most voters have few incentives to learn about the effects of money on elections. What they do learn from political debates has little to do with the actual working of campaign finance laws. Instead, voters hear emotional appeals about the corrupting influence of money on politics and elections. Such appeals are easier to understand than reasoned analysis about the origins of restrictions on campaign finance. Those who create such restrictions do well by doing good; they serve the special interests of incumbents and parties while being praised as foes of corruption and noble defenders of the integrity of government. Campaign finance restrictions constitute the perfect crime.

Enough of theory. We do need to understand why those who govern us might be the source rather than the victim of campaign finance corruption. But a plausible story is not necessarily a true one. In the rest of this chapter and in chapter 8, I examine how and why Congress enacted (and sometimes failed to enact) restrictions on campaign finance. In considering that story we should ask whether its particulars are consistent with the theory that campaign finance laws corrupt representative democracy.

The Powers That Were

The past forty years in the United States have seen both a persistent effort to enact campaign finance regulations and significant partisan and ideological change. The Democratic coalition formed during the New Deal and triumphant in the Great Society has slowly given way to Republican majorities in Congress and often a Republican president. For most of the past four decades, far more Americans identified with the Democratic Party. Partisan identification by voters now splits almost evenly between the two major parties (see figure 7.1). The period has also been marked by decline in trust in the federal government and a growth in self-identifying conservatives.

It would be a mistake, however, to focus only on ideological and partisan change in recent decades. The decade from 1960 to 1970 was a period of cultural and incipient political change. The upheaval that drove Lyndon

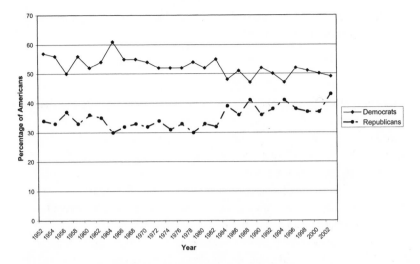

FIGURE 7.1 Partisan identification in the United States, 1952–2002. National Election Studies, "Party Identification 3-Point Scale, 1952–2002." http://www.umich.edu/~nes/nesguide/gd-index.htm#3 (accessed February 3, 2005).

Johnson from office in 1968 was a sign of the times. Senator Eugene Mc-Carthy's campaign for the Democratic presidential nomination that year was the work of outsiders attacking an establishment that had led the nation into the Vietnam War. In the late 1960s and early 1970s, big political changes seemed to be at hand. The direction of those changes was uncertain—after all, George Wallace had run a strikingly successful third-party campaign for the presidency—but one thing seemed clear: fundamental changes in American society would soon lead to changes in American politics. The effort to systematically restrict campaign finance began during this tumultuous period.

We should not expect to find a "smoking gun" indicating that the authors of campaign finance restrictions intended to slow political change by hobbling electoral competition. Absent statements of anticompetitive intent, what proof exists that the regulations sought to suppress challengers to the status quo? The most persuasive evidence would be affirmative answers to several questions. Did a coalition or party dominate American politics in the years prior to the start of campaign finance regulation? Was the power of this group threatened in some serious way? Did the group have the capacity to regulate challenges to their power? Did the group regulate electoral struggle in a way that weakened challengers or potential challengers? The empirical evidence from 1968 to 1974 supports an affirmative answer to each of these questions.

The Democratic Party

From 1960 to 1976, the national Democratic Party enjoyed great success. Lyndon Baines Johnson had won the presidency in 1964 in a landslide. The Democrats dominated Congress throughout the 1960s. Its members held 61 percent of all seats in the House of Representatives from 1959 to 1971; its majorities ranged from 68 percent (1965–67) to 56 percent (1969–71).[8] The same trends were evident in the U.S. Senate. The average Democratic share of Senate seats from 1959 to 1971 was 64 percent, with a range of 57 percent (1969–71) to 68 percent (1965–67).[9]

This electoral success obscures growing public discontent with liberalism that began about 1965. Public support for expanding the federal government began to decline. Trust in the federal government began to drop about the time of John F. Kennedy's death and would continue to decline until 1980.[10] Moreover, backing for increased spending by government began declining in 1961, fell until 1965, rose slightly, and then fell in 1969 to its lowest point in the decade. The public mood in the 1970s was worse for the partisan of expanded government. Support for increased spending and larger government dropped steadily throughout the decade (see figure 7.2).[11]

Politicians are skilled at sensing shifts in the public mood and public opinion. By the late 1960s—especially after the narrow Nixon victory in 1968—professional politicians would have guessed that the public was moving away from the New Deal and its progeny. They also would have sensed that this shift would threaten the long Democratic hegemony in American politics.[12] The disastrous congressional elections of 1966 might have reinforced those doubts.

The opponents of the Democratic Party had the means to act on this emerging weakness. Money, the means of translating shifts in public mood into changes in power, had always been a problem for the dominant party.[13] During most presidential elections in the twentieth century, the Republicans had more funding than the Democrats. In 1948 the Democrats enjoyed a substantial advantage. But in the six presidential elections held prior to the creation of the presidential funding mechanism, the Republicans enjoyed a consistent fundraising advantage.[14] From 1960 onward, that advantage grew rapidly (see figure 7.3).

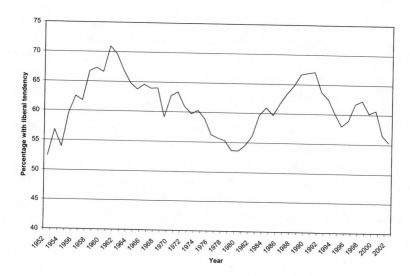

FIGURE 7.2 Policy mood of the American public, 1952–2002. James A. Stimson, "Public Policy Mood, 1952–2002." http://www.unc.edu/~jstimson/mood2k.txt (accessed October 22, 2003).

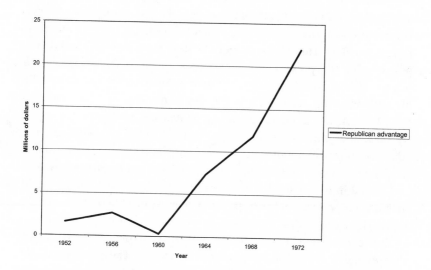

FIGURE 7.3 Partisan gap in presidential fundraising, 1952–72. Burton A. Abrams and Russell F. Settle, "The Economic Theory of Regulation and the Financing of Presidential Elections," *Journal of Political Economy* 86 (April 1978): 250, table 3.

If we assume that an antigovernment mood along with fundraising advantages would help the Republican Party, we may conclude that by 1970 the Democrats were looking at oncoming electoral difficulties. They had three choices if they wanted to avoid the disasters. They could change their programs and policies to adapt to the public mood. That was possible but unlikely; the party of active and expanding government could hardly forsake expanding the state. They could try to change the public mood. That might have seemed possible as late as 1968; thereafter the long decline in public support for more government must have been evident. The final and only real choice was preventing or at least hobbling the translation of the shifting public mood into electoral losses and policy changes. The Democratic majority in Congress pursued this strategy from 1969 to 1974 in passing restrictions on campaign finance.

Taming the Television Monster

The most recent period of campaign finance regulation began in 1966 when President Lyndon Johnson, previously an opponent of such restrictions, announced in his State of the Union address his intention to submit campaign finance legislation to Congress. Johnson proposed regulation of local and state fundraising committees, stricter disclosure requirements, tax incentives for small contributions, and a revision of the limits on campaign spending.[15] He did not propose limiting expenditures. He did propose revising "the present unrealistic restriction on contributions" as one way to "make it possible for those without personal wealth to enter public life without being obligated to a few large contributors." Four months later, Johnson sent Congress a bill that tightened contribution limits and *repealed* all expenditure limits. When that bill stalled in the Senate, the administration sent another version to Congress in 1967, again including a repeal of all expenditure limits. The 1967 model got through the Senate and stalled in the House.[16] Campaign finance regulations that loosened spending on politics could not pass in Congress in 1966 or 1967. A new approach was needed, and one would be found in the spring of 1969.

The year 1968 fell between the old approach and the new. It was a year when anything seemed possible in the United States. The assassinations of Robert Kennedy and Martin Luther King Jr., together with racial unrest and campus turmoil over the Vietnam War, suggested the United States might be experiencing profound political changes. For Democratic leaders, elections and the public mood had to be unsettling. Early in 1968,

Eugene McCarthy's campaign for the Democratic presidential nomination did surprisingly well in the New Hampshire primary, so well, in fact, that Johnson decided not to seek reelection. McCarthy's campaign was financed by a small number of large contributions donated by several wealthy individuals.[17]

Mainstream Democrats were also shaken from the other side of the political spectrum. George Wallace, a southern populist and renegade Democrat, received 14 percent of the presidential vote, the best third-party result since 1924 and the second best total in the Electoral College since the Civil War.[18] Most liberals believed at the time that wealthy conservatives and segregationists funded the Wallace campaign with large contributions: "For most liberals of the 1960s and 1970s it was an article of faith that Wallace was funded by such right-wing patrons as H. L. Hunt and Louisiana segregationist/oil man Leander Perez."[19]

Neither McCarthy nor Wallace won the presidency in 1968, but both had taught the Democratic establishment important lessons about the dangers to the status quo of unrestricted spending on elections. If citizens were free to spend their money, anything might happen, including the defeat of a sitting president (or an incumbent member of Congress) or the election of an outsider to the presidency.

In addition, more conventional partisan threats to the status quo ante emerged in the 1968 election. Richard Nixon's narrow victory convinced many people that the liberal Democratic era had reached a watershed. Although it was true that Democrats held 55 percent of the seats in the House of Representatives elected along with Nixon, they held fifty-two fewer seats than they had held only two years earlier, a decline that must have brought home a sense of waning power.

The Wallace, McCarthy, and Nixon rebellions all coincided with a sharp decline in support for expanding government. Public backing of this idea began decreasing at about the time John Kennedy took office. That decline, however, seemed to stop in 1965 and level off until 1968. During that chaotic year, the public mood went into a freefall against the government. In fact, the change in mood from 1968 to 1969 was the largest shift away from support for bigger government in the postwar period. In 1968 and 1969, however, the floor must have seemed as if it were dropping out from beneath the minders of the political status quo. McCarthy from the Left and Wallace from the Right had made impressive runs at the presidency fueled, it was thought, by unlimited contributions from wealthy individuals. The slow move away from the conventional pieties of 1965 seemed about to turn into an avalanche of discontent and electoral change. Something had to be done or the status quo would be overwhelmed, perhaps deeply and irrevocably. Something was done.

The Advent of Restrictions

After 1968, lawmakers and the incipient regulatory lobby complained often about rising spending on elections.[20] Spending on broadcasting in particular had risen rapidly, both in absolute terms and relative to other types of campaign spending.[21] In constant dollars, spending on presidential campaigns did rise in the 1960s, but expenditures did not exceed earlier peaks until the election of 1972. The record did not show a sustained growth in such spending.[22] Proponents of regulating campaign spending argued that such increases would lead to "a political system increasingly closed to all but the rich"[23] and that limits served the public interest by controlling rapidly growing spending on campaigns.[24]

We might wonder why increased spending became such an issue in the late 1960s. Rising spending (and the unlimited contributions that go with it) enables new candidates and causes to enter political markets. It enabled McCarthy to challenge a sitting president. It supported Wallace's outsider bid, which threatened to take away one part of the old New Deal coalition. The rising spending, especially spending on broadcasting, also fueled Richard Nixon's challenge to Democratic control of the presidency. In 1969 the complaints about rising spending were really complaints about challenges to those who held power and had done so for forty years. If spending were rising too fast, then government could restrict and suppress it, thereby protecting candidates and causes threatened by electoral defeat. In short, the complaints about rising spending offered a pretext for erecting barriers to entry into the electoral markets.

On the surface, spending limits might seem inconsistent with the struggle to maintain Democratic hegemony. After all, they applied to Democrats and Republicans, and Congress did not have a way to impose them only on the minority party. In 1974, however, Democrats held 55 percent of House seats and 57 percent of Senate seats. In October 1974, Democrats could well believe they would win overwhelming majorities in that year's elections. They did. In 1975 they held 66 percent of House seats and 60 percent of the Senate.[25] The authors of the 1974 law would have known that the systematic effects of any regulation that helped incumbents would tend toward maintaining a status quo marked by a large Democratic majority.

The first restrictions of the modern period date from 1969 to the end of 1971. This period is important in understanding the nature of campaign finance regulation. It was before Watergate. The legislative efforts of these two years were not responses to a massive scandal. They were normal legislative responses to threats posed by free-spending candidates and causes. During these two years, Congress struggled to gain control over campaign spending, especially spending on broadcast advertising. Following the scares of 1968, the Democratic Congress was trying to take away the means to challenge the political status quo: money, media, and information.

The Ninety-first Congress, 1969–1970

The Ninety-first Congress, which convened in early 1969, took up the regulation of campaign finance. Members introduced bills that were radically different from the proposals offered by LBJ in 1966 and 1967. The new bills focused on imposing, not removing, spending limits. In particular, the regulations aimed at restricting spending on broadcasting, the means to transmit information to the American electorate. The bill also required broadcasters to sell advertising time to candidates for office at the lowest commercial rates, a mandate that enjoyed bipartisan support.[26] President Nixon vetoed the bill, largely for partisan reasons. The veto was ultimately sustained.

The failure to find a supermajority in 1970 for campaign finance restrictions should not obscure an important point. Congress radically changed course on campaign finance in 1969. Whereas disclosure, tax subsidies, and liberalized spending limits had dominated the regulatory agenda before 1968, only restrictions on campaign spending passed Congress in 1970. Congress had moved from limited regulation to systematic suppression of spending. Those restrictions were attempted in response to the shocking and unsettling events of 1968: the presidential campaigns of McCarthy and Wallace as well as the presidential and congressional election results. In 1969, members of Congress were troubled by the idea that Americans might be free to spend money as they wished on politics. That concern would be enacted into law in 1972.

The Ninety-second Congress, 1971–1972

The Ninety-second Congress enacted the Federal Election Campaign Act in 1971 (hereafter FECA 1971). The bill was signed into law early the next year.[27] Most current debates about campaign finance concern contributions, the funding of presidential campaigns, or the Federal Election

Commission. But FECA 1971 did not deal with any of these topics. Like the 1970 bill, FECA 1971 dealt with political advertising, a perennial concern of lawmakers trying to regulate campaign finance. Title I of the 1971 law—the Campaign Communications Reform Act—restricted spending on what were called "communications media," defined as "broadcasting stations, newspapers, magazines, outdoor advertising facilities, and telephones."[28] Similarly, the Bipartisan Campaign Reform Act of 2002 (known more generally as McCain-Feingold) imposed restrictions on contributions for "public communication," defined as "a communication by means of any broadcast, cable, or satellite communication, newspaper, magazine, outdoor advertising facility, mass mailing, or telephone bank to the general public, or any other form of general public political advertising."[29] The more things change, the more they remain the same.

In 1976 the Supreme Court struck down spending limits as contrary to the First Amendment. Because these limits are not part of current law, the reader may wonder why they receive so much attention here. From 1969 to 1994, Congress sought to impose spending limits directly or in exchange for public financing of campaigns. Spending limits were Congress's main tool for regulating and restricting campaign finance. Such limits reveal much about the nature of campaign finance law. Congress's continual effort to pass spending limits suggests that campaign finance laws seek to restrict rather than increase electoral competition.

The 1971 law imposed two limits on communications media. In general, candidates had to limit their media spending to $50,000, or ten cents per member of the voting-age population of an area holding an election. The law also limited spending on television and radio to 60 percent of the limits for all media; a candidate could not spend more than $30,000, or six cents per voter, on broadcast advertising.[30]

The two major parties did not spend equal sums on radio and television advertising. In 1968 the Republican presidential candidate had spent twice as much as the Democrat on broadcasting. In 1972 the Republican would spend three times as much as the Democrat on broadcasting. There was indeed a growing problem with spending on broadcasting in 1971, but the problem was partisan, not national. The solution to that problem— the restrictions on broadcast spending in FECA 1971—was also partisan. Projecting the experience of the 1960s forward, the Democratic majority might have reasonably expected that their presidential candidates would be outspent by the Republicans in coming elections by a factor of four. The limits on media spending enacted in 1971 almost exactly track linear projections of Democratic presidential spending on media for a generation after the passage of FECA. At no time in the twenty years after 1971 would the limits on broadcast spending have been expected to be lower than projected Democratic broadcast spending. In other words, the majority chose a formula to restrict broadcast spending that had no expected effect on Democratic presidential campaigns while it lowered Republican spending by 70 percent from 1972 to 1992 (see figure 7.4).

For the Democratic majority in Congress, general restrictions on broadcast spending became a good solution to a growing problem for their presidential candidates. They imposed restrictions on broadcast spending that were apparently general and yet discriminated in favor of their party.

What of Congress? Its members, not the presidential candidates, created and enacted FECA 1971. Presumably, restricting spending on television and radio would make it harder for challengers to win a seat in Congress. At the time, incumbents had ample free access to television through "public service" announcements, a privilege denied most challengers seeking to establish name recognition.[31] By restricting how much a challenger could spend on broadcast time, members of Congress could

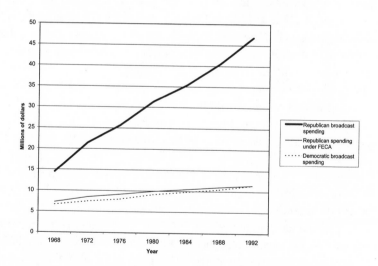

FIGURE 7.4 Effect of FECA 1971 limits on presidential spending on broadcasting by party, actual and projected. Figures for both parties for 1968 and 1972 are actual as reported in Lyn Ragsdale, *Vital Statistics on the Presidency: Washington to Clinton* (Washington, DC: CQ Press, 1996), 143, and per author's calculations.

increase the electoral value of their own unrestricted and costless access to the media.

Unfortunately, it is difficult to show exactly how the restrictions contained in FECA 1971 would have affected challengers who defeated incumbents in the election of 1970. We have data about campaign spending by congressional states for only two states, New York and California.[32] Moreover, few House incumbents lost in these states: of the seventy-nine seats at issue, only three challengers, all in New York, beat a sitting member of Congress. These states account for about 25 percent of House challengers who beat incumbents and one-third of Senate challengers who beat incumbents. These records do not indicate what proportion of campaign spending by various candidates went to broadcasting. As a result, we cannot conclude how much the FECA 1971 limits would have been expected to suppress the broadcast spending of successful challengers.

Limited data notwithstanding, we can discern some effects that the law would have had in 1970. It would have strongly limited the broadcast spending of two successful Senate challengers, John Tunney and James Buckley (the eventual plaintiff in *Buckley v. Valeo*). Both would have been prevented from spending more than half of their funds on broadcasting; Tunney would have been limited to spending only 29 percent of his funds on broadcasting. The law did not have as strong an effect on successful House challengers in New York, both of whom would have been limited to 55 to 60 percent of their overall fundraising. Only Samuel Stratton, a candidate who enjoyed some of the advantages of incumbency because he had represented another New York district earlier, would have been free of the effects of the broadcasting restrictions (see table 7.1). Those results are suggestive more than definitive. But they do indicate that the broadcasting restrictions would have large effects where the media mattered the most.

Shortly after its passage, Representative Morris Udall (D-AZ) said of FECA 1971: "It brings this television monster under control."[33] Certainly that was the intention behind the law. Unconstrained spending on television threatened incumbent members of Congress in general and majority control by the Democrats in particular. For all the talk about the public interest and out-of-control spending, the primary aim of FECA 1971 was to sustain the status quo by protecting incumbents and the majority party.

But the law also was a weapon in a struggle within the Democratic Party. It targeted the outsiders who had threatened the political status quo in 1968: Eugene McCarthy, George Wallace, and anyone who would

TABLE 7.1   **Potential effects of FECA 1971 broadcasting limits on successful challengers in 1970 elections**

Candidate	State/district	Chamber	Spent*	FECA limits[†]	TV limits	TV budget
Tunney	CA	Senate	$2,459,975	$1,177,100	$706,260	0.29
Ottinger	NY	Senate	$2,427,833	$1,145,000	$687,000	0.28
Buckley	NY	Senate	$1,495,060	$1,145,000	$687,000	0.46
Lent	NY/5	House	$54,547	$50,000	$30,000	0.55
Dow	NY/27	House	$49,744	$50,000	$30,000	0.60
Stratton	NY/29	House	$14,948	$50,000	$30,000	2.01

Sources: *Campaign Contributions and Expenditures California 1970* (Princeton: Citizens' Research Foundation, n.d.).
[†] *Federal Election Campaign Act of 1971*, §104(B) and author's calculations.

follow in their footsteps. The broadcasting limits in FECA 1971 applied to outlays in each state, not across the nation. Of course, the limits on each state taken together equaled a national limit on spending, and it was this number that mattered to the two major parties since their presidential candidates more or less contested every state. McCarthy and Wallace, in contrast, threatened the status quo by doing well in a few states (McCarthy in New Hampshire and, by implication, early primary states and Wallace in twelve states where he received 19 percent or more of the total statewide vote). To see the purposes of the restrictions we might consider the effects that FECA 1971 would have had on McCarthy and Wallace if it had been enacted in late 1967.

In 1968 the McCarthy campaign spent $110,000 on radio and television in New Hampshire and more than $150,000 on all communications media. If the limits set by FECA 1971 had been in effect in 1968, McCarthy would have been forced to spend about 80 percent less on the media in New Hampshire (see table 7.2).[34] The members who voted for the law would reasonably have believed that if McCarthy's broadcasting spending had been reduced by 80 percent, his challenge would have failed utterly. By restricting expenditures on electoral advertising, Congress would have effectively limited entry into the political marketplace and precluded McCarthy's challenge. Those who passed the 1971 law could well assume that the effect on future McCarthys would be the same.

What about George Wallace? His campaign spent at least $9 million in 1968.[35] I estimate that Wallace spent a little more than $5 million on broadcast advertising. The law's national limit on broadcasting ($8.4 million) would not have affected Wallace's overall spending. But Wallace threatened to win electoral votes in only twelve states. If he directed 75

TABLE 7.2 Communications media expenditures in the New Hampshire primary, Eugene McCarthy campaign 1968

Item	Outlay	FECA 1971 limits	Reduction of spending
Total media	$150,421	$30,950	0.79
Total broadcast media	$110,856	$20,600	0.81

Source: Herbert Alexander, Financing the 1968 Election (Lexington, MA: Lexington Books, 1971), 39.
Note: All figures are in 1968 dollars.

percent of his media spending toward those twelve states, his campaign would spend an estimated $3.9 million on broadcast media in those states. Because he would have been limited to $1.8 million in broadcast spending in 1968 in those states, his outlays on television and radio in his best states would have been reduced by 53 percent by the FECA 1971 restrictions (see table 7.3). Such a sharp reduction would have had predictable negative effects on Wallace's support in 1968.

Nixon reluctantly signed FECA 1971 into law in February 1972. That date helps explain his decision to sign the legislation. When running for reelection, most politicians prefer not to counter strong tides in public opinion. A November 1970 Gallup poll found that 78 percent of adult Americans favored a law limiting the total amount of money spent in political campaigns.[36] Moreover, Nixon would have known when he signed the law that the primary campaign of the Democratic frontrunner, Edmund Muskie, had collapsed in favor of the upstart candidate, George McGovern. Within four months of his signing of the bill, Nixon's campaign drastically reduced its broadcast spending compared to 1968 in favor of other forms of electoral communication.[37] In sum, Nixon's political instincts may have told him that on balance signing the bill would be popular with the public and do little harm to his upcoming campaign.

The law was serious business. Anyone holding a broadcast license who sold air time to a candidate who had not certified that his spending was beneath the limits set by Congress could be fined up to $5,000 or imprisoned for up to five years.[38] This is odd. The law prohibited candidates from buying advertising after reaching a certain dollar limit, and yet the penalty fell on the seller, not the buyer. Congress needed an enforcer for the new restrictions, and the media would both be effective and suitably intimidated.

TABLE 7.3   **Spending restrictions on broadcasting in Wallace states, general election 1968**

State	Wallace share*	FECA 1971 limits (in 1968 dollars)†
Alabama	65.8	$114,586
Arkansas	38.9	$65,921
Florida	28.5	$254,480
Georgia	42.8	$155,599
Louisiana	48.3	$117,837
Mississippi	63.5	$70,622
North Carolina	31.3	$174,705
Oklahoma	20.3	$89,578
South Carolina	32.3	$85,777
Tennessee	34.0	$135,543
Texas	19.0	$379,570
Virginia	23.6	$161,651
Total		$1,805,869

Sources: *Lyn Ragsdale, *Vital Statistics on the Presidency: Washington to Clinton* (Washington, DC: CQ Press, 1996), 110–11.
†"Campaign Spending, 1969–1972 Legislative Chronology." CQ Electronic Library, CQ Public Affairs Collection, catn69-0008168667. http://library .cqpress.com/cqpac/catn69-0000863968 (accessed December 5, 2005).

The Failure of the 1971 Law

Since Watergate, conventional opinion has claimed that FECA 1971 (and earlier laws) failed largely because their disclosure requirements had been flouted and then not enforced. In fact, FECA 1971 had failed at its larger and more important task of preventing and impeding competition in politics. The election of 1972 was a very good year for the political outsiders that the law had sought to suppress.

In his 1972 reelection effort, Nixon spent two-third less on political broadcasting than he had in 1968 and ended up well below the spending limits on media set by the 1971 law. His campaign manager decided in July 1972 to sharply reduce spending on broadcasting. Nixon was doing well in the polls and could count on a lot of free media attention by virtue of being the incumbent. In that context, spending on direct mail, mass telephoning, and storefront operations were more politically profitable.[39] Moreover, the Republicans still ended the cycle by outspending the Democrats by a factor of two to one.[40] Despite the drop in media spending, Nixon won every state but one in the 1972 general election.

The 1968 election indicated the danger to the Democratic Party establishment posed by outsiders in primaries and in the general election.

In 1972, similar threats appeared again in the primaries. George Mc-
Govern took up the insurgency effort pioneered by Eugene McCarthy.
George Wallace renewed his striving for the highest office by contesting
the Democratic presidential primaries. Both did well in those primaries—
McGovern eventually won the nomination—indicating that limiting
broadcast spending had failed to protect the political status quo.

The law's restrictions on broadcast spending did not enter into force
until April 7, 1972.[41] Therefore I divide my analysis into the pre-FECA
and post-FECA periods. As it turned out, McGovern and Wallace were
able to make solid runs at the nomination while spending much less than
the FECA limits on radio and television, both before and after April 7.

George McGovern's 1972 effort might be seen as the continuation of
Eugene McCarthy's 1968 primary campaign.[42] Like McCarthy, McGovern made the Vietnam War the centerpiece of his campaign and was
anathema to the leaders of his party. Having run briefly in 1968, he had
"virtually disappeared from public presidential speculation."[43] McGovern was expected to lose to the favorite candidate of party leaders, the
1968 Democratic vice-presidential candidate, Senator Edmund Muskie of
Maine.

McGovern's strategy to win the Democratic nomination focused first
on changing the rules of the primary game. After the 1968 election, Mc-
Govern chaired his party's Commission on Delegate Selection, which increased the influence of primary elections in selecting the party's presidential nominee. Second, he focused on a few primaries and depended
more on grass-roots organization than on media or endorsements by
party leaders. His financing strategy also had two aspects: major contributors and lenders provided seed money while direct mail appeals raised
funds from small contributors.[44]

He thus avoided the limits on media spending designed to stop a candidate like him. In New Hampshire he spent $65,000, almost twice the
FECA limit on radio and television but still spent far less than McCarthy had four years earlier ($110,000). Accounting for inflation, McGov-
ern in 1972 spent less than half the sum McCarthy had spent four years
earlier in New Hampshire. In three other states, prior to the new limits
on broadcasting, the McGovern campaign spent far less than the FECA
limits would have imposed. In the three states with primaries after New
Hampshire's (but before the passage of FECA), McGovern spent only
14 percent of the limits later imposed by FECA (see table 7.4). The restrictions on McGovern's spending did little to suppress his insurgent

campaign for the Democratic nomination or weaken his appeal to primary voters (see table 7.5).

Like McCarthy, he finished a strong second in New Hampshire, a showing that finished off the campaign of the party establishment's candidate, Edmund Muskie. As Theodore White put it, "On his home turf, in New England, in his first round in the open, Muskie had stumbled; nor did he know how to recover."[45] McGovern also won all the delegates from the traditionally Democratic state of Wisconsin, despite spending only one-half the permitted sum on broadcasting. In the end, victory in Wisconsin went to the candidate with the best organization, not the most media advertising.[46]

On April 8, 1972, the restrictions on broadcast spending in the FECA law of 1971 came into effect. The limits would complicate a repeat of the McCarthy insurgency against the party establishment in 1968. By April 8, McGovern had not won the Democratic nomination, but he had survived while largely staying within the FECA's media spending limits. Although he transgressed the limits in New Hampshire, he had spent half

TABLE 7.4   **McGovern media spending, 1972**

State	Broadcasting expenditure*	FECA 1971 limits†
New Hampshire	$65,000	$36,000
Florida	$28,000	$305,280
Illinois	$3,000	$453,780
Wisconsin	$95,500	$176,880
Total	$191,500	$971,940

Source: *Herbert Alexander, *Financing the 1972 Elections* (Lexington, MA: Lexington Books, 1976), 112–13.
† "Campaign Spending, 1969–1972 Legislative Chronology." CQ Electronic Library, CQ Public Affairs Collection: http://library.cqpress.com/cqpac/catn69-0000863968 (accessed December 5, 2005).

TABLE 7.5   **Democratic primary results, 1972**

Date	State	Humphrey	McGovern	Wallace	Muskie	Others
March 7, 1972	New Hampshire	0.4	37.1	0.2	46.4	15.9
March 14, 1972	Florida	18.6	6.2	41.6	8.9	24.8
March 21, 1972	Illinois	0.1	0.3	0.6	62.6	36.4
April 4, 1972	Wisconsin	20.7	29.6	22.0	10.3	17.4

Source: Lyn Ragsdale, *Vital Statistics on the Presidency: Washington to Clinton* (Washington, DC: CQ Press, 1996), 50.

as much as McCarthy and done as well as or better than he. Moreover, McGovern's insurgency sustained itself while staying well within the restrictions that FECA would impose. On April 8, 1972, the stakeholders in the status quo had strong evidence that restricting broadcast spending was not the answer to threats posed by such candidates as McCarthy and McGovern. The primaries held after FECA took effect made this completely clear.

By the time the law went into effect, the Democratic field had been narrowed to three candidates: McGovern, Wallace, and the new hope of the party stalwarts, Hubert Humphrey. A brief look at McGovern's vote share in the post-FECA primaries and his media spending in those states indicates how badly the law's restrictions failed to impede his campaign. He never spent more than 54 percent of the permitted sum on broadcasting in a state holding a primary. In most states, the campaign spent far less than half the limit, and overall, McGovern spent 25 percent of the permitted sums on broadcasting in post-FECA races (see figure 7.5). In Massachusetts he received a majority of the votes cast and yet spent only one-third of the limit on television and radio advertising. In Pennsylvania he spent almost nothing on broadcasting and received one-fifth of the votes. In Ohio, spending 29 percent of the limit yielded a virtual tie with Humphrey. The results were similar in Nebraska and Oregon. Prior to his victory in the California primary, which nailed down the nomination, the McGovern campaign spent 54 percent of the allowed sum on television and radio. This time the insurgent candidate opposing the party regulars had won the Democratic nomination, and constraints on broadcast advertising proved completely ineffective in preventing that outcome. The limits were even less of a problem for the other outsider of 1972.

George Wallace ran a surprisingly strong campaign for the Democratic nomination in 1972. He did not enter the New Hampshire primary in favor of concentrating all his initial efforts on Florida, which voted a week after New Hampshire. His huge victory in the Florida primary surprised everyone, Wallace included. He received twice as many votes as his nearest rival, Humphrey. Three weeks later, McGovern's victory in the Wisconsin primary was not the only rude surprise for the Democratic party establishment. Humphrey again lost second place to Wallace, although the Alabama governor had "almost no formal campaign or organization in the state."[47]

Scholars do not know how much Wallace spent on broadcast advertising in Florida. If we make the unlikely assumption that all his spending

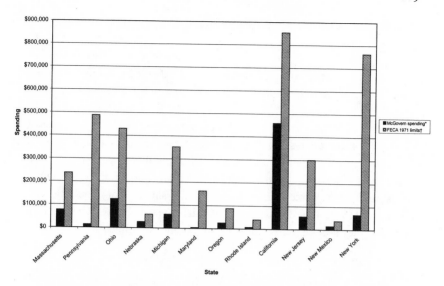

FIGURE 7.5 McGovern campaign spending, selected states, 1972. *Alexander 1976: 114–20.
†"Campaign Spending, 1969–1972 Legislative Chronology," in *Congress and the Nation,
69–72,* vol. 3 (Washington, DC: CQ Press, 1973). CQ Electronic Library, CQ Public Affairs
Collection: catn69-0000863968 (accessed December 5, 2005).

in that state went to television and radio ($200,000), his outlays would
still have been within the FECA limits. His strong showing in Wisconsin
required only $75,000 in broadcasting expenditures, much less than one-
half the FECA limit.

By the time the restrictions on broadcast spending took effect in early
April, the Democratic party had three serious contenders for their presidential nomination. McGovern and Wallace were outsiders intent on
overthrowing the party establishment and taking the party, if not the nation, along a radically different path. The two insurgents had become serious challengers largely without lavish spending on radio and television
advertising. The central assumption of FECA—outsiders threaten the
status quo via media ads—had been proved wrong before its restrictions
on broadcast spending went into effect.

Wallace did well in the primaries after FECA limited spending on television and radio up until the attempt on his life on May 15, 1972. In the
seven primaries held between April 25 and May 15, he won a majority of
votes in two (Tennessee and North Carolina) and finished a strong second in two others (Pennsylvania and Indiana). The day after the shoot-

ing, Wallace would win the Maryland and Michigan primaries (he had been leading both states in polls taken prior to the attempt on his life). In the six states that held primaries prior to May 15, the Wallace campaign spent a total of $20,000 on broadcast media.[48] The FECA limits allowed about $1.2 million to be spent on television and radio advertising in those two states.

After the election of 1972, the Democratic majorities in both houses of Congress continued to shrink. In the Senate, the Democrats emerged with fifty-four seats, a loss of three and the lowest number since the first Congress of Eisenhower's second term as president. The Democratic caucus had shrunk by 20 percent in only six years. A similar story could be told about the House. The Democrats lost thirteen seats in the 1972 election although they still held fifty more seats than the Republicans.

Summary

The four years between the New Hampshire primary in March 1968 and the reelection of Richard Nixon in November 1972 are among the most eventful in U.S. history and easily the most important in the history of U.S. campaign finance regulation. The year 1968 saw several threats to the political status quo, threats that seemed predicated on expansive spending on radio and television advertising. Following the shocks of 1968, Congress began considering restrictions on electoral spending on media, finally passing restrictions in late 1971. That initial attempt to deal with emerging threats to the political status quo failed in 1972. Unlike Gene McCarthy, George McGovern overthrew the Democratic establishment and did so largely without violating the spending limits contained in FECA. Richard Nixon sailed to reelection without testing the limits on broadcast spending. George Wallace's strong run at the Democratic nomination was stopped by an assassin's bullet, not the FECA restrictions. The story of the Campaign Communications Reform Act of 1971 offers three important lessons.

First, powerful people restrict the use of money in elections for political reasons. The usual proffered reasons—corruption, equality, out-of-control spending—have little to do with what the laws are supposed to accomplish. The events of 1968 made it clear that the Left and the Right threatened the dominant coalition in Congress. Faced with those threats, the majority fashioned campaign finance legislation designed to protect its power.

Second, those who restrict money in politics look to the past, not the future. The authors of FECA 1971 tried to deal with threats to their power in 1968 and perhaps also in 1970 (for congressional races). They assumed that their restrictions on media spending would do the trick. After all, in the late 1960s and early 1970s it was an article of faith among the establishment that television could "do it all" and force a "quantum leap" in campaigning techniques.[49] This assumption implied that restricting television advertising would impede changes in campaigning and perhaps changes in the political status quo.

Third, restrictions on campaign finance often fail because the targets of the regulations adapt and work around their strictures. By the end of 1972, that article of faith that television could do it all had begun to fade in the face of experience. The threats to the status quo who first appeared in 1968 returned in 1971 and easily adapted to the legislative obstacles put in their way. The future of politics need not be like the past, largely because being a successful politician requires overcoming challenges. So it was in early 1972.

By the end of 1972, stakeholders in the political status quo ante would have known that the 1971 law had not constrained the threat to their power. They might have guessed that the world was moving away from them, that absent stronger, more comprehensive restrictions on political activity, the political world would change decisively and not to their advantage. Observing the failure of FECA 1971 limits, "many in Congress" proposed "an overall spending limit for all campaign costs" with a broad scope and heavy enforcement. They believed an overall limit "would still limit any massive use of TV because a candidate would not be able to exceed his total campaign spending limit."[50] The law had focused too narrowly on broadcasting; other kinds of political activity had proved to be effective and thus in need of regulation.

Passing new restrictions, however, would be difficult; President Nixon had delayed and vitiated the FECA 1971. He and congressional Republicans would oppose broader measures aimed in part at slowing their momentum toward claiming power. The proponents of restricting money in politics needed a crisis that would become an opportunity to enact sweeping legislation. That crisis came their way.

Crisis and Opportunity

Upon signing the most systemic restrictions on campaign finance in American history, President Gerald Ford remarked, "the times demand this legislation."[51] The times in question may be summed up in a single word:

Watergate. This crisis for the republic has been analyzed in a thousand ways and has taken on the character of a salvation myth, with predictable heroes and villains. Campaign finance is certainly one of the villains. For the public, the Watergate scandal stands as a lasting justification for comprehensive government control of money in politics. It is the trump card played by those who plump for more restrictions on private funding of political activity. But Watergate was not primarily a campaign finance scandal. It refers to several concrete abuses of power carried out before and after the presidential election of 1972. I begin by recounting those abuses before turning to the political meaning attached to them.

Abuses of Power

The Watergate scandal began with the burglary of Democratic National Committee headquarters in Washington, DC, on June 17, 1972. Five men carrying electronic surveillance equipment were arrested for the break-in. In February 1973, the U.S. Senate voted 77–0 to create the Senate Watergate Committee to investigate abuses tied to the 1972 election. In May 1973 the Attorney General of the United States appointed a special prosecutor to pursue broad allegations of abuses of power. When it became clear that Watergate was more than a break-in, the special prosecutor's staff formed five task forces: Watergate, Political Espionage, Plumbers, Campaign Contributions, and ITT.[52] Watergate ended when Richard Nixon resigned the presidency and received a pardon from the new president, Gerald Ford.

The House Judiciary Committee's bill of impeachment against Nixon focused on abuses related to the Internal Revenue Service, the FBI, the Secret Service, the CIA, and the secret investigative unit set up to stop leaks from the White House. Campaign finance came into play twice in the bill of impeachment. The "plumbers" had been "financed in part with money derived from campaign contributions." Nixon was also accused of failing to faithfully execute the law regarding "the campaign financing practices of the Committee to Reelect the President."[53] These assessments suggest that Watergate may be divided into two topics: abuses of power and campaign finance abuses. I begin with the abuses of power by the Nixon administration.

The Senate Watergate Committee found that the Nixon administration and reelection campaign abused their power in several ways. They had broken into the offices of the opposition party and of opponents of the president's policy in Vietnam. The administration then covered up its complicity in the break-ins.[54] They had gathered political intelligence and derogatory information about individuals who were antagonistic to the administration, which had misused the IRS, the FBI, and the Secret Service "to obtain sensitive or derogatory information about their opponents."[55] They conducted "dirty tricks" in the Democratic presidential primaries in Florida, Illinois, and New Hampshire. By planting false information, the Nixon campaign hoped to damage Democratic candidates for the presidency.[56] The administration set up a "responsiveness" program "to politicize the executive branch to ensure that the administration remained in power." This program aimed at redirecting federal revenues to supporters of the administration, to encourage the support of target groups and geographic areas, to shape legal and regulatory action to further the goals of the Nixon campaign, and to use government employee hiring procedures to help the reelection effort.

Campaign Finance Abuses

While looking into the Watergate burglary, investigators discovered a number of real and alleged campaign finance abuses. Maurice Stans, the finance chairman of Nixon's Committee to Reelect the President (CRP), raised $60 million for the 1972 election. About a third of that sum came in before FECA 1971 went into effect on April 7, 1972.[57] Hugh Sloan, the treasurer of the reelection effort, later testified that he gave $100,000 to CRP official Herbert L. Porter to finance "dirty tricks" against the president's enemies.[58] Overall, it was variously estimated that between $423,000 and $548,000 was paid to the defendants for support and legal fees after the arrests, much of it raised from illegal contributions.[59] The special prosecutor's office found that eight corporations had admitted making illegal donations to the Nixon campaign. There was apparently "no evidence that the illegal contributions were made in response to promises of government favors."[60] By the middle of 1974, the Senate Watergate Committee concluded that the Nixon campaign had received illegal campaign contributions from thirteen corporations totaling $780,000.[61] The Watergate Committee found no evidence that any fundraiser directly solicited a corporate contribution. It did find that several fundraisers did not make an effort to ensure that a contribution did not come from a corporation. When the Watergate prosecutions wrapped up at the end of 1975, nineteen corporations had been convicted of making illegal campaign contributions.[62]

As the Watergate affair developed, prosecutors and the press uncovered what they thought were a few cases of favors being exchanged for campaign contributions. On October 23, 1973, the press published a leaked letter dated December 16, 1970, to Nixon promising a $2 million 1972 campaign contribution from a dairy industry group in return for action to curb dairy imports and thereby support the price of milk. The letter was signed by a representative of Associated Milk Producers, Inc., of San Antonio, Texas. Near the end of 1970, Nixon imposed import quotas on certain dairy products.[63] The price supports case ended up in the courts. In 1974 John Connally, the former Secretary of the Treasury under Nixon, was accused of perjury, conspiracy to obstruct justice, and accepting bribes in the case. In April 1975 Connally was found not guilty by a jury on charges of accepting illegal payments, and the remaining charges against him were dismissed.[64] Several other private individuals were convicted of making illegal campaign contributions.[65] The Senate Watergate Committee found no definitive link between the dairy producers' contribution and the Nixon administration's position on the milk supports but concluded that the contribution gave "the appearance of impropriety and provided circumstances that were ripe for abuse."[66] The contributions were not included in the articles of impeachment returned by the House committee.

In 1969 the Justice Department sued under antitrust law to force the International Telephone and Telegraph Corporation (ITT) to divest itself of two small companies and a larger one. Two years later, the suit was settled out of court. In 1972 Washington columnist Jack Anderson published a memo written by an ITT lobbyist. The memo said that the Justice Department had agreed to a settlement favorable to ITT in return for the corporation's paying for part of the 1972 Republican National Convention. The memo also implicated President Nixon and Attorney General John Mitchell. Early in 1974, the White House explained that the settlement had been reached because the president "had concluded the ITT litigation was inconsistent with his own views of antitrust policy because it was an attack on 'bigness' rather than an attempt to insure corporate competition." Investigators could not establish that the antitrust suit against ITT was settled in return for ITT's pledge of money for the 1972 Republican convention.[67]

The New Jersey financier Robert L. Vesco gave the Nixon reelection effort $250,000 just before FECA 1971 took effect. In May 1973, an indictment charged that the Vesco contribution had been obtained by Maurice Stans and John Mitchell in return for promises to intercede with the Securities and Exchange Commission on behalf of Vesco. The SEC was investigating Vesco for allegedly swindling investors. Vesco's contribution was returned to him in early 1973.[68] In 1975, Stans pleaded guilty to three misdemeanor violations of the Federal Election Campaign Act's reporting requirements and to two misdemeanor charges of accepting corporate contributions.[69]

The "selling" of ambassadorships also became an issue during Watergate. The Nixon campaign had garnered $1.8 million in campaign contributions from individuals later appointed as ambassadors. Nine of those whom Nixon appointed as ambassadors or heads of foreign missions had each donated more than $20,000 to the 1972 campaign.[70] In this case the evidence of wrongdoing went beyond the appearance of impropriety. Herbert Kalmbach, Nixon's former attorney and fundraiser, was sentenced to a minimum of six months in prison and was fined $10,000 for illegal fundraising activities. Kalmbach had pleaded guilty to promising a campaign donor an ambassadorship in exchange for a $100,000 campaign contribution to Nixon's reelection campaign.[71]

What might be said about the facts of Watergate thirty years later? In 1973 the nation was shocked by the abuses of power revealed by the Watergate investigations. The public and many policymakers perhaps harbored false expectations about the nobility of the presidency and its incumbent. Today Americans might be less surprised because Watergate and much else since have reiterated an old and important lesson: unchecked political power is bound to be abused. In a way, the shock and surprise often noted in the official Watergate reports seems odd. What did they expect?

In retrospect, the political intelligence and espionage activities of the Nixon administration seem like hardball politics run amok. Yet one need not share the partisanship or self-righteousness that motivated so many of Nixon's critics to see that the break-ins and other instances of political espionage crossed an important line.[72] Such activities in the Nixon White House constituted a gesture toward an American police state in which the president and his men harassed their enemies with the power of the federal government. To be sure, Nixon did not set up a police state; a gesture is not reality. But a gesture goes beyond fantasy and points toward reality.

Almost all of the campaign finance abuses identified or alleged during Watergate were already illegal. The contributions by corporations had been illegal for decades. The alleged trading of official decisions for campaign contributions in the Milk Producers and ITT cases would have been against the law had the charges been prove. Helping Robert Vesco in return for a contribution also would have contravened the law. Indeed, in Herbert Kalmbach's case offering an ambassadorship in exchange for a contribution led to jail time.

Without excusing these abuses, it may be that the passage of time will allow some perspective on Watergate and campaign finance. The illegal corporate donations composed a little more than 1 percent of Nixon's fund-raising in 1972; put differently, his campaign raised more than $59 million legally. In retrospect, one wonders why the campaign took such large risks for so little reward. The allegations of quid pro quo corruption in the cases of the Milk Producers, ITT, and Robert Vesco were not proved beyond a modest doubt. The Senate Watergate Committee admitted that Nixon's account of the Milk Producer affair was plausible: "[M]uch of what the President says is supported by surrounding events: the dairy lobby had successfully gathered the support of about a quarter of each House in support of bills to raise the support level and at least some dairy leaders had considered boycotting further Republican fundraising efforts because of the administration's position on price supports."[73] The real problem, the committee concluded, was "the appearance of impropriety" created when policymakers also acted as fundraisers.

This lesson of Watergate, however, applies more generally. Nixon's demise, however justified for his abuse of power, empowered the Democratic majority in Congress, who enacted comprehensive campaign finance restrictions within weeks of Nixon's departure from office. Watergate was not a scandal that revealed campaign finance abuses not covered by the law. Watergate was, rather, a scandal that revealed abuses of power and opportunity to extend the power of the federal government into political areas previously free of such coercion. Yet one question might have been asked (but was not) in the fall of 1974. If the powerful tend to abuse their authority, why should we not expect that the campaign finance law of 1974 would itself be an abuse of political power? After all, the circumstances of Nixon's fall might have meant that those who wrote the law had few constraints on *their* ambition.

What Watergate Came to Mean

American politics always has more policy proposals than public problems. Policymaking is not a rational attempt to devise solutions to public problems. Instead, policy advocates try to opportunistically attach their pet policy proposal to a problem that has come onto the public agenda.[74] Watergate was a crisis for the nation and an opportunity for advocates of campaign finance restrictions. As we shall see, they made the most of their chance. Yet we should also recognize that other policy roads out of Watergate existed and were not taken.

Why did the wrongdoing happen? The Senate Watergate Committee concluded that the scandal grew out of "an alarming indifference displayed by some in high places to concepts of morality and public responsibility and trust" along with "the belief that the ends justified the means, that the laws could be flouted to maintain the present administration in office."[75] The committee saw Watergate as a failure of personal responsibility marked by a lack of constraint on political activities in pursuit of Nixon's reelection. As the committee noted, "The evidence shows that, from the early days of the present administration, the power of the President was viewed by some in the White House as almost without limit."[76] Watergate was a new chapter in the old story of the human lust for power without end and the baleful consequences of such desires. As Senator Sam Ervin (D-SC) concluded, Nixon's men "apparently believed that the President is above the Constitution, and has the autocratic power to suspend its provisions if he decides in his own unreviewable judgment that his action in so doing promotes his own political interests or the welfare of the nation. They resorted to evil means to promote what they conceived to be a good end."[77]

This analysis and its policy implications were ignored in 1974, both by Congress in general and by the Senate Watergate Committee in particular. If humans have a lust for political power that leads to abuses such as Watergate, making it more difficult to accumulate and exercise power would be sensible, especially in the case of the U.S. presidency. Watergate might have reaffirmed the Madisonian vision of a limited federal government that did not, for example, control the price of milk.

Watergate might also have led to a combination of severe political punishment for the Republicans (the resignation of the president and massive losses in the 1974 midterm elections) with incremental policy changes. As noted, almost all of the campaign finance abuses revealed or alleged during Watergate were already against the law. Congress also might have prohibited executive branch policymakers from campaign fundraising. Most of the large contributions uncovered during Watergate would have been illegal whatever their size. The campaign finance problems revealed by the scandal could have been dealt with by relatively minor changes in the law; the reforms could have been episodic rather than systematic. But such changes would not have served the longstanding broader agenda of those who might benefit from more comprehensive restrictions on campaign spending.

Advocates of campaign finance restrictions made much of the size of the contributions revealed during the Watergate investigations. Yet the problem was the illegality, not the size of the contributions. While Maurice Stans was seeking some six-figure contributions for the Nixon campaign, Stewart Mott was donating $400,000 to the McGovern campaign.[78] No one, now or then, said much about the Mott contribution. Mott's donation supported an effort to win the presidency. The sheer size of the donation was morally meaningless, though it did reflect Mott's political commitment at the time. His money bought television ads that tried to convince citizens to vote for McGovern; a small part of Nixon's campaign funds was used for break-ins and other type of political espionage. Both the McGovern ads and the Watergate break-in were supported by large contributions. Logically, we should conclude that large contributions do not cause illegal or improper political activities.

Yet as the Watergate hurricane swirled in Washington, logic had little chance. The advocates of campaign finance restrictions recognized that the scandal offered an unprecedented opportunity to advance their cause. To seize that opportunity, they had to blame the abuses of Watergate on campaign finance. In other words, they had to blame the murder on the gun and not the murderer. Hence, John Gardner, the avatar of Progressivism discussed above, asserted: "Watergate is not primarily a story of political espionage, nor even of White House intrigue. It is a particularly malodorous chapter in the annals of campaign financing. The money paid to the Watergate conspirators before the break-in—and the money passed to them later—was money from campaign gifts."[79] Would the break-ins have been any different morally if the conspirators had been paid directly by the president or his political allies? Would the break-ins have been morally acceptable if H. R. Haldeman had simply persuaded the burglars to work pro bono or made them special assistants to an under secretary in return for their services? Gardner's position is logically untenable, but that hardly mattered. He was trying to set the political agenda, not win an argument in a university seminar. He was making an emotional connection between the illegal acts of the Nixon administration and the money it used to perpetuate those acts. Gardner was trying to blame campaign contributions for the abuses of the Nixon White House to advance his pet cause: restricting and eventually eliminating the private financing of political activities in the United States.[80]

In October 1974, a little over two months after Nixon's resignation, Congress greatly amended FECA 1971. The new president, Gerald Ford, signed the bill into law. He had little choice in the matter. The Watergate scandal and Nixon's resignation had created a political climate where congressional majorities could pass into law virtually any restrictions on campaign finance. Congress responded, in a bipartisan way, by enacting nearly every nostrum ever proposed by partisans of such restrictions. In different ways, each part of the amended law tried to suppress electoral threats to the political establishment.

The 1974 Amendments

The regime of campaign finance restrictions and regulations passed by Congress in October 1974 ostensibly amended the Federal Election Campaign Act of 1971. The 1974 act, however, was really a new law that today serves as the foundation of federal election law. Unlike the 1971 law, it was passed by overwhelming majorities in both houses of Congress. [81] The Republican minority and the Republican president wished to be on the side of reform and in any case could not stop or even slow the law. In the end, the 1974 law continued and broadened restrictions on campaign spending while introducing several new barriers to electoral competition.

Congress repealed the limits on spending on broadcast advertising in the 1974 law. It did not do so because of libertarian concerns. As we saw, the restrictions in the 1971 law had not done their job. They had to be broader if they were to suppress the challenges to the stakeholders in the political status quo. All spending had to be controlled and watched over.

The 1974 law limited spending in presidential primaries to $10 million for each candidate for all primaries. In a state presidential primary, spending was limited to $200,000, or sixteen cents for each eligible voter. In the general election, presidential candidates were limited to a total of $20 million.[82] We might once again compare the restrictions to the actual spending of the targets of the legislation.

In 1972 Richard Nixon's campaign spent a little more than $60 million in the primaries and the general election.[83] The 1974 restriction would have reduced his overall expenditures by 50 percent. The McGovern campaign spent $30 million in the general election (and another $12 million in the primaries).[84] The law would have cut McGovern's spending in the primaries by 17 percent overall. He probably would have remained within the spending limits in the first four primaries of the season.[85] In California, however, the state where McGovern wrapped up the Democratic nomination, the 1974 spending limits would have cut his 1972 expenditures by 30 percent.[86] In the fall, the 1974 restrictions would have cut McGovern's general election spending by more than 65 percent. George Wallace spent somewhere between $2.4 and $3.6 million on his 1972 effort, well within the overall 1974 primary spending limit.[87] His campaign also appears to have spent less than the state-by-state limits in primaries that he seriously contested. Of course, by the time the FECA amendments passed in October 1974 Wallace was finished as a political threat.

The 1974 law also put constraints on spending in races for the U.S. Senate and the House of Representatives. In a primary contest, a candidate for the Senate was limited to eight cents per voting-age resident of state represented or $100,000, whichever was greater. In the general election, a candidate could only spend the greater of twelve cents per voting-age resident or $150,000.[88] Candidates for the House of Representatives were limited to $70,000 in both the primary and the general election.[89]

If every candidate in the 1972 elections had spent the maximum allowed, the 1974 restrictions would not have constrained spending. But the authors of the 1974 law were not trying to restrain spending in general. In line with my overall hypothesis, the 1974 law sought to restrain spending that threatened the political status quo as personified by Senate and House incumbents. In 1972, five senators lost in the general election; four of the defeated were Republicans upset by insurgent Democrats.[90]

Indeed, seventeen of the thirty-three winners of Senate seats in 1970 and 1972 garnered less than 55 percent of the vote. In 1968, eighteen of the winners had garnered less than 55 percent. A majority of Senators who passed the 1974 amendments had been elected in a "zone of vulnerability" that raised questions about the success of their future campaigns. They had ample reason beyond partisanship to make their future campaigns easier.[91] Some specific Senate elections prior to 1974 might also have shown the danger to incumbents of unrestricted campaign financing. In New York, Congressman Richard Ottinger had spent a small fortune obtaining the Democratic nomination to run against the Republican Liberal incumbent, Charles Goodell. Ottinger split the liberal vote with Goodell, fostering a victory by the outsider, James Buckley, who ran on the Conservative ticket.[92]

In the 1972 House races, thirteen incumbents lost in the general election and eleven went down in the primaries. Another twenty incumbents experienced close calls in which a challenger received more than 45 percent of the total vote in a district.[93] Overall, incumbent House members received 60 percent or less of the vote in 22 percent of the elections of 1972.[94]

Do the data concerning elections indicate that the 1974 law would have helped incumbents? As with the presidential elections, we might assume that the congressional supporters of the 1974 law were trying to solve a political problem. It is reasonable to think they would have relied on their experience of the 1972 elections to set restrictions on campaign spending that would help those in power and harm those struggling to gain power. How would the 1974 restrictions have affected the 1972 elections?

In the general election of 1972, fourteen challengers beat sitting senators or House members (see table 7.6). Under the 1974 limits, twelve of those challengers would have been forced to spend less than they did in the victorious effort. The reductions in spending ranged from 5 percent to 66 percent of actual 1972 expenditures. The campaign spending by a victorious challenger in 1972 would have been reduced, on average, by 32 percent. The strength of the relation in this case reveals the intentions behind the 1974 limits. A *one-third* reduction in challenger spending was no accident. Congress mandated a steep cut in spending by the candidates most likely to unseat the authors and supporters of the 1974 law.

TABLE 7.6 **Victorious challengers in congressional elections in 1972**

House	Challenger	State	Expenditures	1974 Limit	Change
House	Young	Ilinois	$206,166	$70,000	−0.66
House	Hudnut	Indiana	$165,016	$70,000	−0.58
Senate	Biden	Delaware	$260,699	$150,000	−0.42
House	Owens	Utah	$118,252	$70,000	−0.41
House	Mezvinsky	Iowa	$113,546	$70,000	−0.38
House	Gilman	New York	$112,729	$70,000	−0.38
Senate	Scott	Virginia	$619,908	$390,840	−0.37
House	Beard	Tennessee	$105,022	$70,000	−0.33
Senate	Hathaway	Maine	$202,208	$150,000	−0.26
House	Schroeder	Colorado	$80,508	$70,000	−0.13
House	Sarasin	Connecticut	$80,251	$70,000	−0.13
Senate	Clark	Iowa	$241,803	$230,040	−0.05
House	Steelman	Texas	$69,581	$70,000	0.01
Senate	Haskell	Colorado	$176,234	$192,480	0.09
Total			$2,551,923	$1,743,360	

Source: Campaign Finance Monitoring Project, 10 vols. (Washington, DC: Common Cause, 1974). These documents are available in the Public Records Room of the Federal Election Commission.

How about strong challengers who nonetheless lost? Sixty challengers in 1972 got more than 40 percent of the vote in House elections.[95]
Six challengers for Senate seats also received more than 40 percent of
the vote in their state.[96] About two-thirds of all candidates who received
more than 40 percent of the vote *would not* have been limited by the 1974
spending restrictions. That should not be surprising. Incumbent members
of Congress might not have been terribly concerned about challengers
picking up this level of support. They would have been concerned about
more serious challengers. Half of the challengers who received more than
45 percent of the vote in the 1972 elections *would have* had their spending reduced by the 1974 restrictions. On average, the limits would have
reduced spending within this group of challengers by 60 percent. In the
Senate, half of the unsuccessful challengers who received more than
45 percent of the vote would have had their spending reduced.[97]

How likely is it that such an enormous reduction in spending by victorious and strong challengers accidentally found its way into a law written by the people who would face them (or people like them) in future
elections?

The 1974 law created extensive limits on campaign contributions from
individuals and organizations. Contribution limits had existed in federal
law prior to the 1960s, but they were largely ignored. The 1970 and 1971
laws that passed Congress, as we have seen, focused on spending restrictions rather than contribution limits. The 1974 law introduced systematic
contribution limits.

Why did it pass? The conventional answer is that the limits were instituted in response to the large donations uncovered during the Watergate
investigations.[98] Proponents of restrictions certainly did their best to demonize the large contributions to the Nixon campaign in 1972. Limits on
contributions would have appealed to Congress in 1974 for other reasons
that have little to do with equality and preventing corruption and a lot to
do with suppressing electoral competition.

Recall the reason why contribution limits may be expected to have the
same effects on electoral competition as spending restrictions. Consider
the example of a home equity loan. Imagine you need $30,000 to remodel
your home. Whether you take out a home equity loan for that sum depends on the interest rate and the ease of getting the loan. Banks try hard
to offer competitive interest rates and to make the process of getting a
home equity loan ever easier. Rates go down, agents of a bank come to
your house for your to sign the relevant papers, and the home equity market in general heats up.

Now imagine that the federal government prohibited all loans larger than $1,000. To get your $30,000 loan for home remodeling, you would have to go through the process of getting a loan thirty times. Of course, it is possible that you really want to remodel your house and you would put up with the bother of repeating the transaction thirty times. Across the nation, however, many people would be discouraged by the costs of repeating the loan process and would give up trying to get a home equity loan or perhaps seek other sources for the money that are not covered by the government ceiling on loans. The aggregate sum of home equity loans would nosedive because of the $1,000 limit.

Political fundraisers are seeking donations, not loans, but the logic of transaction costs remains the same. In 1972, George McGovern received a $400,000 donation from Stewart Mott. In 1976, McGovern or any other presidential candidate would have had to find four hundred people and persuade them to donate the maximum amount in order to equal Mott's 1972 contribution. In other words, a candidate would have to go through a process four hundred times that McGovern went through once. Some candidates would get through that process through sheer will or organizational acumen. On the whole, as with the home equity loans, contribution limits would mean that the total campaign contributions to all candidates for Congress or the presidency could be expected to be smaller than they would have been in the absence of the limits. Because campaign spending generally equals campaign contributions, limits on donations impede and limit campaign expenditures.

The 1974 law did not index contribution limits to account for inflation, as it did its spending. As a result, the limits became progressively more restrictive in real dollars. By the end of 2002, the 1974 contribution limit for individuals to a candidate ($1,000 per election) had fallen to a little more than $300 (measured in 1974 dollars). This meant, all things being equal, that the costs of the donation process had increased threefold from 1974 to 2002. Compared to a world where the real value of a contribution remained the same, the total sums raised for campaigns would have decreased proportionately.

It might be objected that contribution limits do not discriminate against challengers. After all, incumbents of all stripes as well as challengers would be subject to the limits. Yet limits need not discriminate perfectly against challengers to be effective. They would harm challengers more than they would incumbents. Officeholders, especially those who have held power for a long time, have lower fundraising costs, in part because they have a well-functioning system in place that includes donors from past elections. Over time, they learn how to negotiate the system. Inevitably, limits do less damage to their reelection efforts than they do to challengers, who lack experience. Moreover, the bar is lower for incumbents: given the advantages of office, they need less money than challengers to attain electoral victory. For these reasons, they prefer contribution limits, difficulties notwithstanding, to a world in which donations are free of government restraints. Such limits also had unexpected consequences that undermined their ostensible purposes.

On the surface, the contribution limits in the 1974 law sought to "create a more egalitarian system of campaign financing, one in which the concerns and interests of large publics were not 'drowned out' by the vast resources of small groups of wealthy individuals and economic institutions" by making sure money would be raised in small sums from private individuals.[99]

The political scientist Thomas Gais has analyzed the consequences of the 1974 limits for political representation. Gais begins with the fact that individual donations, especially small ones, do not happen out of the blue. Mobilizing small contributors is costly and difficult. Such donors give because they value political participation in its own right. A candidate or cause relying on small donations must first find citizens who value participation for its own sake. Even when found and persuaded to donate, small contributors may not persist beyond a time of political conflict and controversy, as conservative direct-mail organizations found in the 1980s. Disclosure regulations and attendant record-keeping add to the costs of getting small donations. Small contributors rarely produce the surplus needed to sustain an organization and attract a new group of contributors. Not surprisingly, Gais found that groups that depended on small contributors were ineffective and short-lived.[100]

Starting and sustaining an effective political action committee to represent the "little guy" requires a source of big money, which Gais calls a "patron." A patron—a wealthy individual, a foundation, or even the government—gives the money necessary to cover the costs of raising small contributions and to sustain an electoral organization. The patron acts as a capitalist would in funding a startup business and seeing it through tough times. For political patrons, of course, the payoff comes not in profits but in political change.[101] Experience has supported Gais's conjecture. The billionaire George Soros contributed $10 million to start an organization designed to get Democratic voters out in 2004.[102] Without the Soros contribution, the organization would have not gotten off the ground.

The federal contribution limits governing PACs prevented patrons such as Soros from playing the political game by criminalizing large donations to PACs or any other kind of electoral organization. A wealthy individual or group could no longer mobilize a group of Americans dissatisfied with the political direction of the nation. Yet not all political capital was excluded. This restriction primarily affected new and emerging interests seeking political change. Existing political interests—for example, businesses and labor unions—already possessed skilled and powerful institutions familiar with electioneering and fundraising. Those powers could be their own patrons by funding the overhead costs of their PACs through membership fees or economic activity. Gais found that such groups were much more likely to form PACs than were broader interests that were previously unrepresented in the system.[103]

The stakeholders in the status quo in 1974 became more powerful because contribution limits biased American campaign finance toward groups that could rely on an occupational or institutional patron to raise small contributions. Labor unions, an important component of the Democratic coalition, had created and exploited PACs to raise money for electoral activities. Union lobbyists pushed to have the PACs legalized as part of the 1974 law, expecting to gain a *permanent* fundraising advantage over business.[104] Reality eventually contravened that expectation.[105] From the point of view of the fall of 1974, however, the legal recognition of PACs in tandem with contribution limits complicated the life of political outsiders and thereby slowed political change.

Did the Democratic majority enact contribution limits and legitimize the PAC form knowing that these measures would slow political change? Thomas Gais thinks the combination and its effects were accidental.[106] That is possible. However, the authors of the law clearly aimed at impeding the raising and spending of money to fight elections. The contribution limits and the PAC format served that purpose independent of one another.

The 1974 law also subsidized campaigns. Congress had passed taxpayer financing of presidential campaigns as early as 1966. The program was repealed the following year.[107] The 1974 law offered subsidies to qualified candidates in presidential primaries, to the political parties to pay for national nominating conventions, and to the candidates in the general election. Those who accepted public funding also had to accept spending limits for their campaigns.[108] The presidential public funding system thus fit well within the persistent theme of campaign finance regulation circa

1968–74: enact spending limits to serve the interests of those formulating the regulation.

Before turning to what Congress did in enacting presidential public financing, I need to attend to what they did not do, which is, in some respects, as revealing as what they did. In 1974 Congress also considered but did not pass taxpayer financing of campaigns for the House and Senate.

In the summer of 1974, the U.S. Senate passed a campaign finance bill that included public financing of congressional elections. The House considered partial public financing and rejected it. In the crucial vote, a majority of Democrats (118 to 114) voted nay and were joined by a large majority of House Republicans. As a result, the 1974 law imposed public financing on only presidential elections. In conference, the Senate negotiators dropped taxpayer financing of congressional campaigns in return for higher spending limits and a strong commission to enforce the new law.[109]

Why did a majority of House Democrats oppose this plan? It would have provided funding for challengers to House and Senate incumbents. A late 1973 version of public financing, for example, would have given every qualified general election candidate for the Senate at least $175,000 and every House candidate $90,000.[110] The effects of this provision in the 1972 elections would have been startling. Fifty-nine challengers in House elections that year received between 40 and 50 percent of the vote. A $90,000 public subsidy would have increased the spending of forty-three of those candidates, or 73 percent of the group. The average challenger in this group would have seen a 121 percent *increase* in their expenditures with a $90,000 public subsidy. Though I have no data about House candidates who received less than 40 percent of the vote, we might safely surmise that virtually all of them would have had more money to spend on fighting the incumbents if public financing had been enacted in 1971. Congress enacted the conservative option if conservatism is understood as the choice that impedes change and preserves the political status quo. It rejected the public financing option that might have caused unwelcome political change for the authors of the 1974 law. Public financing of presidential campaigns, in contrast, served the partisan interests of the congressional majority.

The first serious proposals to publicly fund presidential campaigns date from the mid-1960s, though the current system was not enacted until 1974. As usual, supporters said spending limits served the public interest by controlling rapidly growing spending on campaigns.[111] In constant dollars, spending on presidential campaigns did rise in the 1960s, but expenditures did not exceed earlier peaks until the election of 1972. The record did not show sustained growth in spending on presidential campaigns. The public interest rationale for spending limits was and is not persuasive.[112]

By the time Congress began writing the 1974 law, the Democrats were looking at oncoming disasters in presidential elections. The presidential funding mechanism both equalized and restrained the spending by both major-party candidates for the office.[113] As with spending limits, a law that applied equally to both candidates would have unequal effects: it would considerably improve the competitive position of the Democratic candidate. It should come as no surprise that an overwhelmingly Democratic Congress mandated the equality and the improvement. The spending limits contained in the law and the presidential system were predictable responses to pressing political problems for the party; 80 percent of Democratic senators and 98 percent of House Democrats voted for the 1974 law.[114]

The presidential funding system was created to reduce competition that was eroding the status of the dominant party. The Democrats had reason to believe that the public mood was shifting away from them, a change that would eventually weaken or end their grasp on power. The presidency and its bully pulpit could either greatly enhance or retard the direction of political change. To preclude or at least slow down those changes—perhaps to buy time to change the direction of the public mood—the dominant party created a regulation and subsidy program aimed at equalizing spending between the major-party candidates in presidential campaigns and thus decreasing the Republican vote share (compared to what it would have been without the presidential funding mechanism). Indeed, the system probably handed victory to the Democratic candidate in 1976.[115]

The 1974 law also created an agency to carry out its strictures. To understand the Federal Election Commission (FEC), we should assume that "American public bureaucracy is not designed to be effective. The bureaucracy arises out of politics, and its design reflects the interests, strategies, and compromises of those who exercise political power." Creating an agency thus involves answering the question: "[W]hat sorts of structures do the various political actors . . . find conducive to their own interests?"[116] In practice rather than theory, independent commissions, and the federal bureaucracy in general, are anything but independent: they usually represent the interests of the groups or sectors they regulate, generally with the support of a congressional committee.[117] In the case of campaign finance, members of the Congress were the regulated group. A bureaucracy created by Congress was extremely unlikely, to put it mildly, to do things that threatened the core interests of its creators or to hand the fate of members over to "the reform community." The FEC, like campaign finance regulation generally, advances the welfare of its creators. In the case of the FEC, the most salient interests at stake belong to member of Congress. Why did they design the FEC the way they did?

In designing the commission, Congress had to choose between a high-risk and a low-risk strategy. The Democratic majorities in Congress in 1971 and 1974 might have decided on the former and created an election bureaucracy controlled by a majority of commissioners appointed by the majority party in Congress. Such a highly partisan FEC would need extensive powers to effectively discriminate against the candidates and campaigns of the minority party. Members of the commission, for example, would require the authority to conduct lengthy investigations of the financing of the campaigns of candidates from the minority party. The commission could use its authority to uncover and publicize information about the minority party or its candidates and follow up with charges of corruption or malfeasance. In politics, as in life generally, large benefits often involve taking significant risks. A congressional majority that creates an agency to harass a minority party runs the risk of being harassed if the minority becomes the majority. The benefits of harassing one's enemies may be equaled or outweighed by the future costs of being harassed.

The latter option would involve fewer risks and benefits to its creators. Congress would create an agency that had few powers and posed little threat to members of Congress. Legislators could also enfeeble the agency by dividing its leadership evenly by party as insurance for all members of Congress against politically motivated investigations of their past campaigns. Congress might also make sure the agency was tightly overseen by and responsive to the will of the legislature. If the congressional Democrats in 1970s decided the future benefits of harassment by the FEC were equal to or lower than the expected future costs of being harassed by an FEC under Republican control, they might rationally have decided to create a weak, divided agency closely controlled by Congress.

Congress created two election commissions in the early 1970s. Both fit the low-risk, low-return model of institutional design. The Federal Election Campaign Act of 1971 created a three-person commission to oversee implementation of its regulations. Two of the members, the clerks of the House and the Senate, reported directly to the leaders of the party that controlled Congress. These two members had exclusive administrative authority over the disclosure required of the members of the House and the Senate. The third member of the commission, the comptroller general of the General Accounting Office, handled disclosure of presidential campaign financing. In theory, the commission could act forcefully with the backing of a two-member majority. In fact, a majority of the commission would not have jurisdiction over the disclosures of the House or the Senate. The commission also had no subpoena powers and could not initiate legal action against suspected violators of the law.[118] In the political wars to come, the 1971 version of the FEC was a gun without any bullets. Of course, an unloaded gun cannot backfire. The passivity of the 1971 FEC largely realized the aims of its creators; it did not harm members of Congress.[119]

The Senate Watergate Committee recommended creating a seven-member "independent, nonpartisan Federal Elections Commission." No more than four of the members would come from the same political party.[120] Of course, an FEC with a working, partisan majority would hardly be independent or nonpartisan. It would have a loaded gun aimed at the minority of any era. Congress chose instead in 1974 to create an evenly divided FEC with three members from each party. The president would appoint two of the commissioners and Congress the rest; Congress would have a right to confirm all the appointments. Congress gave the new agency civil enforcement powers, the ability to fine violators, and the capacity to initiate civil suits. Criminal jurisdiction in campaign finance matters remained with the Department of Justice. Congress gave the FEC the power to write regulations to carry out the law but then required the agency to submit all proposed rules to Congress, where either house could veto them by a simple majority vote.[121] Not surprisingly, Congress had created an agency completely subordinated to the will of its creators. Rhetoric notwithstanding, Congress was not willing to create a Frankenstein's monster that turned on its creator and conducted endless investigations of the campaign financing of members targeted by the partisans of campaign finance restrictions.

In *Buckley v. Valeo,* the Supreme Court ruled that the design of the FEC violated the separation of powers in the Constitution. The Court found that the FEC's powers were judicial and executive in nature and could only be held by presidential appointees.[122] Congress went back to work and designed its third FEC within five years. It eventually reconstituted a six-member FEC appointed by the president and confirmed by the Senate. Congress did more, however, than simply respond to the unconstitutionality of the previous version. It also restricted the powers of the commission regarding advisory opinions and initiating investigations. Perhaps most important for our story, Congress strengthened its veto over FEC regulations by assuming the authority to strike down individual sections of any proposed rule.[123]

The majority party opted for an agency that would do no harm to members of Congress instead of doing harm to the minority party. Such a strategy benefited Democrats the most, given their large majority. It also protected them from harm if they ever became the minority party. All in all, the design of the FEC was a rational strategy for shoring up the political status quo.

The FEC was and remains a disappointment for the partisans of campaign finance restrictions. "The commission has a track record of having created, perpetuated and refused to prevent blatant, massive campaign violations," according one such partisan, Fred Wertheimer.[124] They judge the agency to be weak and beholden to Congress. Yet the ineffectiveness of the agency makes sense if we believe that Congress designed it to serve its interests (and not the interests or concerns of interest groups dedicated to suppressing political activity). Yet if that was the intent, it makes sense that the rest of the campaign laws of the early 1970s were created for the same purpose. The complaints about the FEC provide evidence for the thesis underlying this analysis of campaign finance restrictions generally: they serve not the public interest but rather the interests of their authors. Those interests require, above all, impeding changes in the political status quo.

Conclusion

From early 1969 to late 1974, Congress created most of the regulations that today govern the raising and spending of money in elections. Many people see the creation of these regulations as evidence that the system worked to correct abuses and advance the public interest. Americans moved Congress, perhaps against its will, to restrain the influence of money on politics and vindicate the rule of the people. In this chapter I have shown how badly this conventional story fits the facts of what actually happened from 1969 to 1974.

Beginning in 1968, outsiders began to threaten the power of the Democratic establishment that had dominated American politics for thirty years. The time was ripe for a challenge to the status quo. The public mood was shifting away from trust in Washington and the federal government. In 1968 three figures articulated that distrust and offered concrete challenges to the mainstream Democratic Party. Eugene McCarthy represented the antiwar Left that ended Lyndon Johnson's hopes for a second term. George Wallace stood for traditional blue-collar Democrats alienated by the racial policies and elitism of their party. Richard Nixon was a conservative Republican from California. Contrary to the conventional view of campaign finance laws, the regulations of 1971 and 1974 sought to preserve the political status quo by suppressing support for these candidates and other outsiders. Congress aimed to circumvent the natural translation of changes in the public mood into changes in electoral outcomes and policy.

This chapter has offered extensive evidence supporting the challenge suppression thesis. The emphasis on spending limits throughout the period fits the thesis well; outsiders need to spend a lot of money to effectively challenge the powers that be. Limits on electoral spending effectively discriminate against outsiders while preserving nominal equality in electoral financing. In 1969, the nature of the proposed regulations before Congress were different from that of earlier bills; spending limits—specifically, restrictions on media spending—became the core of the two bills passed by Congress in 1970 and 1971. The focus on the media reveals much about Congress. Spending on the media during an election creates competition by spreading information about candidates and causes. By limiting spending on the media Congress limited that spread of information and thus suppressed electoral competition. The effects that such spending would have had on the McCarthy, Wallace, and Nixon campaigns suggest the unspoken aims of Congress in passing these laws. The 1974 law contained more comprehensive spending limits that would have had predictable effects had they not been struck down by the Supreme Court. In 1972, the 1974 limits would have deeply reduced spending by outside presidential candidates (McGovern and Nixon) as well as victorious challengers of sitting members of Congress.

Some evidence from this era does not fit the hypothesis that Congress passed campaign finance laws to protect its members and its majority party. The 1974 spending limits would not have restricted McGovern's or Wallace's spending in the early primary states in 1972. In general, the state-by-state restrictions of 1974 would not have bound outsiders in 1972. They also would not have bound Wallace's overall spending in 1972. The thesis also cannot account for the Senate's initial preference for public financing of congressional campaigns in 1973. On the whole, however, the thesis explains almost everything about the creation of campaign finance regulation in those years and fails to explain very little. Compared to most theories, the theory tested in this chapter is strikingly consistent with the facts of political life from 1969 to 1974.

Did the 1974 law work as intended? Answering this question is a complicated task. The Supreme Court struck down the major tool of suppression in the law: spending limits. Congress was left with contribution limits and complex regulations to discourage challengers. On the surface, the restrictions worked fairly well. Democrats held a majority in Congress for another two decades after passage of the 1974 law. The presidential funding system probably threw the 1976 election to the Democratic candidate, Jimmy Carter. As noted in chapter 6, electoral competition in the United States has been in decline for three decades. Given that restrictions on contributions and spending serve as barriers to entry in elections, campaign finance laws have probably contributed to that decline in competition. We do not yet have a rigorous demonstration of that proposition.

In this chapter I have argued that history subverts the customary narrative of campaign finance regulation. In that story, private interests donate money to campaigns to gain control of policymaking, thereby corrupting elections and the political system. At the behest of reformers, Congress passes laws that restrict donations and campaign spending to protect the integrity of elections and policymaking. The influence of private contributions, as we have seen, is greatly exaggerated. This chapter should cast grave doubts on Congress's commitment to the public interest in passing campaign finance restrictions. The partisan leaders of Congress, and the members who serve, have strong partisan and individual interests at stake in such lawmaking. If corruption means using public power for private ends, then the campaign finance laws of 1974 are corrupt beyond all doubt. They sought the interests of the majorities (and the members who compose the majorities) that passed them and not those of the larger public who would benefit from greater electoral competition. Might the same be said of later lawmaking concerning campaign finance?

CHAPTER EIGHT

McCain-Feingold and the Market for Incumbent Protection

The decade of the 1990s was a time of surprises in congressional elections and in campaign finance legislation. The Democrats lost control of Congress in 1994 for the first time in forty years. One might have thought that they would have been aware of their vulnerability long before 1994 and responded with restrictions on campaign finance as a way to continue their dominance. Yet Congress did not act. The second surprise came eight years later when Congress passed and a Republican president signed the most restrictive campaign finance law since 1974. Because such restrictions are largely enacted for the advantage of those who write and enact them, we must ask two questions. Why did the Democrats fail to pass restrictions in the 1980s or early 1990s to prevent the loss of power in 1994? Why did a Congress with a Republican majority do so in 2004?

The End of Democratic Control

From 1974 to 2002, Congress passed only one major campaign finance bill. For most of that time Congress kept this issue on the back burner. Even when legislators returned to money and politics in the mid-1980s, they did not come close to enacting anything until 1992, when a bill went to President George H. W. Bush, who promptly vetoed it. In 1993 and 1994, when the Democrats held both Congress and the presidency but were dancing along the edge of an electoral cliff, no campaign finance legislation went to the president's desk.

On the surface the relative quiescence in campaign financing legislating in the 1980s seems odd. After Ronald Reagan's election in 1980, the
country appeared to be decisively moving away from the Democratic coalition that had ruled since the New Deal. If the Democrats in Congress
were threatened, we would expect them to pass campaign finance regulation to stop the threat to their power. Yet they had reason to feel secure
in their power.

Twenty-five years on, Reagan's 1980 victory looks like a harbinger of the
coming Republican dominance of national politics. But reading the past
in terms of the present can be misleading. Americans in the 1980s could
not know that Republicans would gain a persistent majority in Congress.
From 1980 to 1992, Republicans held the presidency and, for six years,
the Senate. But changes in the larger society were much more ambiguous. Americans were becoming slightly more conservative, but it is easy to
exaggerate those changes. Writing in 1997, the political scientist David C.
King summarized the views of Americans over the past two decades:

> The evidence from various conceptions of political ideology shows a gradual,
> slight, and recent trend toward conservatism. Looking at how Americans de-
> scribe themselves, the country has been growing more conservative, with the
> greatest change coming between 1992 and 1994. We saw no evidence of rapid
> swings in the self-identification of voters between the political extremes, and it
> could be that these labels are for many people just fashion statements with little
> real meaning. Moreover, when we examined public opinion on six conserva-
> tive issues, we found no marked trend, except for a recent appetite for cutting
> spending and rolling back affirmative action programs. Americans are becom-
> ing more conservative, gradually, but on core issues like the role and powers
> of the federal government Americans are about as conservative today as they
> were twenty-five years ago.[1]

A Democratic member of Congress in 1990 could also take heart from
signs of Democratic strength. The party gained twenty-six House seats in
the 1982 elections. For the next twelve years, the Democrats won 60 percent of all House elections. The party's candidates also won back the Senate in 1986 and for the next eight years held 55 percent or more of the
seats in the upper house.[2] And they had hope. The public mood favoring
increased government hit its all-time low in 1980, the year of Reagan's
victory. Thereafter it began to climb steadily, attaining its highest point
in thirty years (and second highest score ever measured) in 1991. Under-

neath the pulling and hauling of daily politics, the Democrats had reason to believe they could sustain and expand their influence in Congress, Reagan and Bush notwithstanding. They also could reasonably hope that the presidency would return to their party given the shifting mood of the nation.

Subsequent events belied that faith, but in the mid-to-late 1980s, it was perfectly reasonable for Democrats to think they had weathered the storm of Republican resurgence and could look forward to a new era of electoral victories and expansive government. In 1993, the threat to Democratic domination became increasingly clear. As we shall see, however, Democratic members of Congress ran out of time to pass legislation to avert the oncoming electoral disaster.

Shortly after the public mood peaked in favor of the Democrats, Congress did pass a campaign finance bill. The bill included public financing of congressional campaigns. If the Democrats expected change to go their way, why did they try to enact campaign finance legislation? In particular, why pass this bill, which would fund challengers? The 1992 bill seems to challenge the hypothesis that campaign finance laws protect incumbent officials and parties in Congress.[3]

The 1992 bill was not a serious effort at restricting campaign finance. Members of Congress often cast symbolic votes that have few concrete effects. For example, after a court decided the Pledge of Allegiance violated the principle of separation of church and state, both houses of Congress passed resolutions condemning the decision. They did not, however, pass constitutional amendments or a law affirming that the words "under God" should remain in the pledge.[4] Members thus affirmed popular revulsion for the decision without concretely violating the First Amendment. For members, symbolic votes offer benefits with few costs. Voters who feel strongly about a symbolic vote credit their representative for his stand while everyone else is indifferent.

In 1992 members knew that the campaign finance bill before Congress would never become law. President Bush promised to veto any such legislation, a threat he later carried out. For the Democratic majorities in Congress, the bill offered symbolic benefits without the costs of public financing of challengers or assuming other unknown risks. The Democrats could say they supported reform and blame the failure of the bill on the Republicans and their president. The House ended up twenty-four votes short of the two-thirds majority needed to override the veto; the Senate was nine votes shy of the constitutional requirement.[5] If Bush had changed his mind, the new law would still have been a symbolic gesture. The bill did not provide funding for the public financing of congressional campaigns. The conference report on the bill "contained a sense of the Congress['s] resolution that funding should not come from general revenues, increase the federal budget deficit or decrease spending on other programs."[6] It would be funded, in other words, by some special tax mechanism like the presidential campaign checkoff on IRS form 1040. Yet the legislation did not create that mechanism, which means the heart of the law, even if passed, would not go into effect.

The most conclusive evidence that the 1992 law was mere symbolism came a year later. In 1993, Democrats controlled both Congress and the presidency. Given that President Clinton had endorsed increased restrictions on campaign finance during the 1992 campaign, it would have been a simple matter to reintroduce the vetoed legislation and have it signed by the new president. At the end of April 1993, the Senate Rules and Administration Committee reported a measure identical to the bill vetoed in 1992. The bill went nowhere because of "growing apprehension within the Democratic Party over the provisions to provide public funding to candidates." On the House side, the leading proponent of the bill, Mike Synar (D-OK), admitted that public financing of congressional campaigns lacked the votes to pass. When public financing became a real possibility, it lacked a majority in a Congress controlled by the Democrats.[7]

To be sure, the 1992 bill dealt with a real problem for Congress. The Keating Five scandal had involved campaign contributions. The scandal had attracted public attention, throwing a bad light on Congress. As so often happens in Washington, something had to be done even if nothing really would be done. Voting for campaign finance regulation put members on the "right side" of the Keating Five issue without actually doing something that might jeopardize their reelection. The 1992 bill was a symbolic gesture rather than a real attempt to suppress electoral competition. Soon the majority would face more serious threats to their control of the legislature.

In the 1994 elections the Republicans picked up fifty-four seats and assumed control of that body for the first time in forty years. Six years earlier the Democrats had held about 60 percent of the House; afterward they had 47 percent. They lost almost a quarter of their caucus in one day. In the Senate nine seats changed hands as the Republicans assumed power again.[8]

Did the Democrats in Congress perceive a threat to their power in 1993 and 1994? In retrospect we can also see that the public mood shifted strongly away from a larger role for government from 1991 to 1995. The decline was as steep as any on record. Congress did try to meet the threat to Democratic hegemony by passing campaign finance restrictions in 1993 and 1994. The bills incorporated Congress's traditional tool for suppressing speech: spending limits. The Supreme Court decision in *Buckley v. Valeo* had invalidated spending limits standing alone. It did say spending limits could be imposed voluntarily as a condition for receiving public financing, as in the case of the presidential funding scheme. Spending limits constrain both incumbents and challengers, thereby helping mainly the former.[9] The combination of spending limits and public financing was an entirely different story; as we saw above, taxpayer financing could improve the prospects of challengers in relation to those of an incumbent. By linking spending limits and public financing, members of Congress predictably became more ambivalent about passing campaign finance regulations.

As the prospects for legislation concerning campaign finance dimmed in 1994, members began seeking a way to have spending limits without public financing. The Senate came up with an amazing scheme. The proposed law began with voluntary spending limits and no public funding as long as everyone observed the spending limits. But if a candidate exceeded the voluntary limits, his or her fundraising would be subject to a tax equal to the highest corporate tax rate of 34 percent. The revenue raised by this tax would fund communications vouchers (that is, broadcast spending) worth up to 100 percent of the spending limit for any candidate who faced an opponent spending more than the bypassed voluntary limit. This provision, which carried over into the conference version of the bill, thus allowed for two outcomes. If no candidate went over the spending limits, the effect would be identical to having spending limits and incumbents would have effectively discriminated against their most serious challengers. If, however, a challenger spent more than the limit, one-third of his or her fundraising would be taken and given to his or her opponent, the incumbent. In short, challengers would have to choose between abiding by spending limits or funding at the margin the media efforts of an incumbent up to 100 percent of the spending limit. Ironically and intentionally, this transfer of money from challengers to incumbents was the public financing element in the legislation. Challengers either abided voluntarily by spending limits or they would be forced to fund their opponent's campaign. Members of Congress, in other words, had concocted a bill in which incumbents said to challengers, "Heads, I win, tails, you lose." The Senate Republicans filibustered the bill; in a crucial late September 1994 vote, six Democrats joined the Republicans in a cloture vote.[10] The 1994 effort to pass campaign finance legislation died with that vote, and though no one knew it at the time, the era of direct spending limits on campaign spending had come to an end with a whimper. A month later the 1974 restrictions on campaign finance finally failed when Republicans won a majority in both chambers of Congress.

From a purely political perspective, the Democrats failed to use campaign finance restrictions to head off their 1994 electoral debacle. They settled for symbolism in 1992 and could not fashion their desire for spending limits into a viable bill in 1994. Yet passing restrictions requires time, and one thing the Democrats did not have in 1994, though they did not know it, was time. After 1994, the task became harder. The party that had traditionally supported these laws no longer enjoyed a majority in Congress. That did not mean, however, that the job would prove to be impossible.

The Market for Incumbent Protection

Some might see the passage of McCain-Feingold in 2002 as the triumph after many vicissitudes of good over evil. That story offers little insight about the actual reasons the law attracted majorities in the House and Senate and why President Bush decided to sign it. A better story of how McCain-Feingold passed begins with more realistic premises. The law had a number of co-sponsors, but for simplicity's sake I will refer to the principal sponsor, John McCain.[11] To pass his bill, McCain had to attract the support of a majority of House members and a supermajority of the Senate (where 60 members are needed to cut off a filibuster). How he put together his majority tells us a lot about his law.

McCain's Problem

After the 1994 elections McCain faced a big problem. Democrats had always favored campaign finance restrictions, largely because of ideals and partisan interest. Republicans had always opposed restrictions for the same reasons: they wished to avoid the electoral losses Democrats hoped to impose on them by restricting spending and access to the media. With Republicans holding a majority in Congress, the prospects of harming the GOP via passage of campaign finance legislation seemed bleak.

In 1995 McCain had two options. He could simply wait and hope that the Democrats regained the majority and then work from there. He might also accept the persistence of Republican control and try to attract enough GOP votes to pass the legislation. His appeals to GOP members, however, had to be tempered by the need to keep an overwhelming number of Democrats on board for the bill. His task was not easy.

What about the general public? Why couldn't McCain foment mass support for his bill, which would force members of both parties to vote his way? He might hope the public would demand that his bill be passed, but he must have known that experience contravened that hope. A majority of Americans support campaign finance restrictions in the abstract but care little about politics in general or such legislation in particular. For example, in late 1999, a Gallup poll found that 60 percent of respondents thought overhauling campaign finance law should be a low priority or not a priority at all.[12] Of course, McCain might also have hoped that a huge scandal similar to Watergate would enable him to drive congressional Republicans to vote for new restrictions on money in politics. Such a scandal was far from a sure thing. Accordingly, he set about attracting GOP votes for his bill with an eye on possible Democratic defections.

The Needs of Incumbents

How could McCain attract the necessary Republican votes? Clearly he would not promise them that the bill would harm the Republican Party and its candidates. Whatever else they might be, they were still Republicans, and inviting them to commit electoral suicide was not likely to put the bill on the president's desk. He also would have known, however, that the relative strength of partisanship varied a lot in Congress. Some Republicans might break party ranks for an important reason. McCain needed, in other words, to find something that might be more important than partisanship for enough of them.

What mattered more than partisanship? Congressional Republicans who voted for McCain-Feingold were more vulnerable to electoral defeat than those who voted against it. The vulnerable were in the market for protection from challengers, and McCain had a product that met their needs: the McCain-Feingold campaign finance bill.

As we saw above, political scientists have found that constituents' concerns offer a better explanation of Congress members' voting than campaign contributions.[13] The division of the vote for president indicates the underlying ideological and partisan preferences of voters in House districts.[14] In 2000, George W. Bush received an average of 57 percent of the votes in districts represented by Republican members who opposed McCain-Feingold. In contrast, Bush received on average 49 percent of the votes in districts where Republican members voted for McCain-Feingold. The latter represent districts that are far less Republican and conservative than the ones represented by the former. For example, the Republican sponsor of McCain-Feingold in the House, Christopher Shays (R-CT), was targeted by the Democrats for defeat in 2004 because Al Gore carried his district by 10 percentage points in 2000.[15] On the Senate side, we once again find a strikingly similar story. Republicans who backed McCain-Feingold came from states where Bush received on average 48 percent of the vote; those who opposed it came from states where Bush received 57 percent of the vote on average. These differences are large enough to be important.[16]

The Republicans who supported McCain-Feingold are always in danger because of the nature of their district or their state; their struggle for reelection might be a fight for survival simply because their party is often a liability with voters. They have more reason than most members of Congress do to run scared. These members must be aware that they are strangers in a strange land: all else being equal, their district would vote for a representative who is more Democratic and more liberal than they. The law's backers would like some help to make sure all else is not equal. McCain had something to offer them.

Other evidence shows that these Republicans are more vulnerable than those who voted against the bill. Looking only at the member's vote share in the previous general election, we find that those who voted for McCain-Feingold did slightly less well on average than those who voted against it (64 percent of the vote compared to 67 percent). Still, the difference is not as clearly marked as one might have expected given the differences in presidential voting noted above. This measure has a significant shortcoming, however. It does not tell us about the expectations of members. A Republican in a district where Bush received 47 percent of the presidential vote might reasonably feel vulnerable, whatever his success in the previous election.

One may also consult expert opinion about the competitiveness of a district (and thus the difficulties faced by a member). Charlie Cook, a well-known expert on American elections, rated the competitiveness of every House district for the 2002 elections for the biennial *Almanac of American Politics*. I collected Cook's ratings for each district represented by a Republican who cast a vote on McCain-Feingold.[17] Cook rates each district as highly competitive, competitive, potentially competitive, probably safe, and safe. Overall, 42 percent of House Republicans who voted for the bill came from districts Cook rated as highly competitive, competitive, or potentially competitive; in contrast, 22 percent of the members who voted against it came from such districts. If we look only at highly competitive and competitive districts—districts where incumbents are always endangered—the contrast is even more marked. Twenty-five percent of those who voted for the bill came from highly competitive or competitive districts. Only 9 percent of the Republicans who voted against the bill came from such districts.[18]

Other evidence confirms the vulnerability of the Republicans who supported McCain-Feingold. In ideological terms the group is only slightly less conservative than the Republicans who voted against the bill. A liberal interest group, Americans for Democratic Action, regularly rates the ideology of each member of Congress on a scale of 0 to 100, where 0 is very conservative and 100 is very liberal. The House Republicans who voted against the bill had an average ADA score of 5.6 in 2000 and 2001.[19] Those who voted for it had an average score of 20. The average Republican supporter was thus still quite conservative though not as conservative as most of the party caucus[20] but at the same time was probably more conservative than the district represented. His or her ideology in some ways was a compromise between the demands of constituents and the conservatism of the party.[21]

Congressional Quarterly calculates a "party unity" score for every member of the House of Representatives.[22] It measures how often a member votes with his or her party in roll call votes for which party matters. A party unity score measures whether a member is a strong or weak Republican (or Democrat) across the board on a wide array of votes. The average party unity score of the Republicans who voted for McCain-Feingold was lower than the same measure for those who voted against it. But it was on the whole still strongly Republican. The bill's backers voted the party line 81 percent of the time, whereas opponents supported their party 93 percent of the time. They were not mavericks or Democrats posing as Republicans. Their party allegiance was an electoral problem, a source of vulnerability.

Many experts argue that the 2000 presidential election revealed a nation divided between "red" and "blue" states. The red states went for Democrat Al Gore and were clustered in the Northeast and the West Coast along with a few Midwestern states. George W. Bush won almost all the blue states between the coasts. The 2000 result suggests the importance of regional differences in explaining political outcomes. Indeed, it provides us with another clue about the vote in the House. About 5 percent of the Republicans voting no came from the Northeast (Maine, Rhode Island, New Hampshire, Massachusetts, Connecticut, and New York). In contrast, a little more than one-third of the members of the GOP who voted for the bill came from the Northeast. The same regional differences appear with regard to the bill's Republican backers, though the overall number is much smaller. They were fish out of water, Republicans in a part of the country that is no longer hospitable to their party. The votes in favor of the bill came from members facing stiff electoral challengers, members who found themselves in states where Republicans were always swimming against the electoral tides.

Compared to Republicans who opposed McCain-Feingold, the typical Republican who voted for the bill was a conservative who represented a more competitive district in the Northeast that was far less supportive of George W. Bush in 2000. All of this adds up to one conclusion: the Republicans who supported the bill were electorally vulnerable. They needed every advantage they could get to continue their career in the House.

McCain offered these vulnerable Republicans the chance to vote for reform. They might have seen their vote as a means to both satisfy their more liberal constituents and to gain some distance from the national Republican Party. House Republicans who are electorally vulnerable have reason to vote for such legislation to please their constituents. Yet a vulnerable representative can have it both ways. By voting for reform he appeals to some of the voters he needs in his contested district; the vote is a "branding exercise" that is useful in attracting liberals and moderates.[23] At the same time, few of his constituents know much about the effects of the campaign finance bill he is supporting.[24] In other words, a vulnerable Republican can exploit asymmetries in knowledge between him and his constituents by supporting a "reform" whose specifics make him less vulnerable (the incumbent protection element). The agency problem means vulnerable members of Congress need not choose between reform and enhancing their chances of reelection. Indeed, the agency problem means that reform and suppressing electoral competition are two sides of the same coin.

Of course, I still must show that the specifics of McCain-Feingold offered considerable protection to the vulnerable Republicans who ultimately voted for it. That task requires recalling how McCain created his masterwork of suppression.

The First Failure

The first Congress to convene with the Republicans in the majority did not pass new restrictions on campaign finance. The proponents of restrictions did propose a bill that imposed spending limits, banned contributions from political action committees, and prohibited soft money contributions.

As we have seen, Congress had tried throughout the modern era of campaign finance regulation to limit spending as a way of stabilizing the political status quo; incumbents face fewer threats if spending is limited. Like all post-*Buckley* legislation, the 1995 bill proposed voluntary spending limits backed by incentives. In return for accepting spending limits based on voting-age population, a candidate would receive free media time in a state, a steep discount on all other media time purchased, and discounted postage rates. Except for the postage subsidies, all the costs of the incentives would be imposed on broadcasters, an easily demonized and unpopular minority. All candidates would have to raise 60 percent of their contributions from individuals in their home state.

As noted above, voluntary spending limits are de facto spending limits so long as no one violates the restrictions. As such, they benefit incumbents, who have no incentive to violate the limits. For them the crucial question becomes how to penalize challengers who violate the voluntary limits. In 1995, Senators John McCain, Russell Feingold, and Fred Thompson proposed a doubling of contribution limits for incumbents who faced challengers who violated the spending limits or wealthy challengers who spent more than $250,000 of their own money on a race. Apparently the $1,000 limit on contributions was necessary to prevent corruption except when a challenger posed a danger to an incumbent.

The 1995 bill also stipulated that only individuals could contribute to campaigns and prohibited contributions from PACs, which had long played a starring role in the demonology fostered by partisans of campaign finance restrictions. The desultory efforts to prohibit them had failed, however, in part because they were relatively more important to Democrats than to Republicans. In general, PACs had become (and remain to this day) vital to the fundraising done by incumbents. In 1995, an FEC study found that in a nonelection year PACs gave 95 percent of their donations to incumbents.[25] Later studies would find that PAC donations created most of the fundraising advantages possessed by incumbents.[26] The 1995 bill also proposed to ban soft money, donations to political parties that were free of restrictions. At that time, Republicans had begun to raise about 20 percent more soft money than Democrats.

The Senate bill ultimately ran into a filibuster led by Mitch McConnell (D-KY); its supporters came up at least six votes short of ending the filibuster. The failure of the Senate effort is not surprising. Only the spending limits served the interests of incumbents by harming challengers. The ban on PACs would cut off one stream of funds coming to incumbents and to Democrats. The prohibition of soft money would work against the interests of the new Republican status quo created by the election of 1994. McCain was unlikely to attract many vulnerable Senate Republicans with legislation that harmed both Republicans and incumbents. He had to make a new start.

McCain Goes to Market

The year 1997 marked the debut of McCain-Feingold in its original version. The bill proposed to ban soft money, provide free media time and postage in exchange for spending limits, reduce contribution limits for PACs, and provide for more disclosure and tougher penalties. The bill was supported by all Senate Democrats and three Republicans. The nature of its support turned out to be its weakness. Taken together, the major components of the bill (the soft money ban, spending limits, and stiffer limits on PACs) would improve the Democrats' fundraising position relative to the Republicans. At that time, the soft money ban alone was worth millions to the Democrats. Yet McCain and Feingold needed three Republican votes in the Senate for a simple majority and a dozen to invoke cloture and overcome an expected filibuster from Mitch McConnell. Perhaps the sponsors believed that their efforts to demonize fundraising and spending in the 1996 campaign would overcome partisan considerations and drive the dozen Republican votes toward the abyss of restrictions. The original formulation went nowhere.[27] As the 1997 struggle wore on and defeat became inevitable, McCain decided to radically change his bill in search of a majority and especially in pursuit of the necessary Republican votes.

Before I turn to McCain's revisions, recall the parts of the original McCain-Feingold that were deleted in pursuit of a Senate majority: limits on PAC contributions, free airtime for candidates, and voluntary spending limits. Incumbents had little interest in restricting a type of fundraising (PACs) in which they enjoyed a large advantage, although many consider such donations the quintessence of "special interest money."[28] They were also not likely to vote for a program that give challengers unpaid access to the media. Without the unpaid media as a carrot, the stick of voluntary spending limits—which members had long sought—could not become law.

The bill that debuted in 1997 eventually proved to be a winner with a majority of members of Congress. The new bill had three major components, two of which were passed into law in 2002: a ban on party soft money fundraising and restrictions on the funding of campaign advertising. Like the 1969 restrictions, those in the 1997 bill sought to restrict spending on campaigns (though they did so indirectly by suppressing fundraising) and control access to the media. McCain's 1997 bill was both new and quite old, a restatement of persistent themes in campaign finance legislation.

This new version of McCain-Feingold soon attracted significant Republican support in the House of Representatives. In August 1998, fifty-one Republicans voted for Shays-Meehan, the House version of McCain-Feingold, in a crucial vote on amending the basic bill. In the final vote, the House decided by 252-179 in favor of Shays-Meehan. Sixty-one Republicans voted for Shays-Meehan and eleven Democrats voted against it.[29] For one reason or another, almost a quarter of the House Republican caucus had voted to ban soft money and restrict political advertising. McCain had clearly made great progress with his target group: vulnerable House Republicans. Let us look at how the components of McCain's bill kept congressional Democrats on board and attracted enough Republicans to pass.

Soft Money and Hard Money

From 1980 onward, federal election law recognized two kinds of campaign contributions: hard money and soft money. Hard money contributions were fully governed by federal contribution limits, disclosure requirements, and other aspects of federal election law. Soft money was different. In 1979, Congress and the Federal Election Commission modified federal election law to allow the political parties to raise money outside normal contribution limits for purposes of "party-building activities." Both parties raised increasing sums of such soft money over time. The law did not limit soft money contributions. By 2000 a few hundred individuals and organizations were giving gifts of more than six figures to one or both political parties in a given election cycle. Overall, soft money accounted for a relatively small proportion of all fundraising; in the 2002 cycle for example, soft money made up $500 million of total fundraising of $5 billion.

Contrary to the intentions of the authors of the 1974 law, the GOP enjoyed an advantage in raising hard money for years. In the 2000 election cycle, for example, Republicans raised $466 million in hard money at the national level, and Democrats raised $275 million. In 2001 Republicans collected $131 million—a 35.2 percent increase over 1999—while Democrats raised $60 million, only 7.5 percent more than they collected in 1999.[30] For some time, Republicans also enjoyed a significant advantage on the other side, raising about 55 percent of all soft money from 1992 to 1998.[31] Not surprisingly, Democrats favored banning soft money during this period. All things being equal, if the Republican advantage persisted, a ban on soft money would improve the Democrats' relative capacity to fight elections.

Of course, McCain could not pass a bill that did nothing but ban soft money. The Republican majority would hold together well enough to prevent a law aimed at doing them harm from passing. McCain thus had to put something in the bill for the Republicans in general in exchange for the soft money prohibition. His 1998 bill proposed that members of labor unions be informed that they could ask for return of the portion of their union dues that went to political activity; such a law would probably reduce fundraising by the unions, a major source of Democratic support and therefore, McCain guessed, an appealing prospect for Republicans. However, Democrats (and some Republicans) refused to vote for the bill if the union provision remained. McCain began looking for something else to balance out the soft money ban.

The bill eventually included an increase in limits on hard money. Everyone in Congress could rationally assume that Republicans would benefit from such liberalization. In 1996 Clyde Wilcox, a professor of government at Georgetown University, surveyed about twelve hundred political donors to see whether they would contribute more or less money if the individual contribution limits were raised. Republican donors generally said they would give more money, but many Democratic donors, paradoxically, said they would give less.[32] Republicans would thus be compensated for the ban on soft money. They were not the only beneficiaries of the increase in hard money limits. Some Democratic incumbents who could raise hard money would also benefit from the change, the larger effects on their party notwithstanding.[33]

Vulnerable Republicans won on both ends of this deal. They were both Republicans and incumbents, two groups that were in a better position than any potential challenger to take advantage of an increase in hard money limits. Yet the soft money ban, though it hurt their party in general, must have been especially attractive to them. After all, the Democrats used soft money to attack Republicans in competitive or potentially competitive districts or states. The soft money prohibition was an especially valued form of incumbent protection for vulnerable Republicans. To be sure, Republican challengers and the party itself might benefit from soft money, but challengers did not get to vote on McCain's bill, and party leaders in Congress were asking vulnerable Republicans to vote against their own interests in voting for McCain-Feingold. Self-interest ultimately beat party spirit (and the threats of the Republican leadership in the House).

Partisanship, Part One

As the momentum for a Senate vote on banning soft money grew in 2001, congressional Democrats became ambivalent about the prohibition. Apparently they had privately worried for some time that a soft money ban would hurt their party more than it would harm the Republicans.[34] The Democrats had raised about the same sums of soft money as had the Republicans in the 2000 election cycle. The Democratic leadership could no longer assume that banning soft money would close a fundraising gap between them and their opponents. More partisan Democrats may have worried about the cost: to achieve a ban on soft money they would have to agree to an increase in hard money limits, a type of fundraising dominated by Republicans. Senator John Breaux (D-LA) opposed McCain-Feingold for this partisan reason: "It's sort of like unilateral disarmament. We're competitive with the Republicans in soft money, but there's a huge difference in hard dollars." Breaux said that many Senate Democrats shared his concerns. "When you're inside a closed room, [Democrats] are very concerned about the bill, the great majority of them, in terms of what it will do to Democrats," said a top labor union lobbyist. "The disconnect between what goes on behind closed doors and public utterances—I've seen a lot of it in Washington, but this one just about reaches the zenith."[35]

As it turned out, the Democrats voted overwhelmingly in favor of McCain-Feingold and its soft money ban. If the Democrat doubters were correct in 2001, the vote pursued the party's interest as it was defined from 1992 to 1998. Given these doubts, why did almost all Democrats nonetheless vote for the bill?

Members of the Democratic Party are profoundly influenced by the Progressive vision of politics. As we have seen, that vision counseled concern about private money in politics and extensive government control over political spending. Perhaps their commitment to these notions re-quired a sacrifice of partisan interest.[36] On the other hand, Progressivism and partisanship might long have gone hand in hand. Thus, in the 1990s a Democratic member of Congress could believe that large soft money con-tributions threatened Progressive ideals *and* favored the Republican Party during elections. After all, for a generation prior to passage of McCain-Feingold, Democrats had done well as a party by doing good as a political vision. They had reason to think a soft money ban made sense for them.

In deciding whether to vote for a soft money ban, Democrats had to predict how well they would do in future soft money fundraising relative to the Republicans.[37] If Congress banned soft money, only hard money would support the two parties. As it happens, Republicans had long en-joyed a substantial advantage in raising hard money; in fact, Democrats could reasonably assume, based on experience, that their party would raise 49 percent of the Republican total in hard money. Soft money fundraising therefore could improve the Democrats' relative position, *even if* Repub-licans also enjoyed an advantage in that category. For example, during the 1990s, Republicans had raised about 55 percent of all the soft money raised by the two parties. However, if the Democrats raised 45 percent of soft money in 2002 and the same relative sum of hard money, their total fundraising would be 62 percent of the Republican total. In other words, the Democrats would be 13 percent better off with soft money even if the Republicans raised more than they did. This relation is not true for all circumstances, however; if the Republicans raised a lot more soft money, the Democrats would be better off banning soft money. To understand McCain-Feingold, we need to know exactly how much more soft money Democrats had to assume the Republicans would raise in order to make a soft money ban appealing. Figure 8.1 provides an answer to that question.

The y axis in figure 8.1 shows the relative effect of a soft money ban on the Democratic Party. As noted, this depends on the Republican share of soft money, assuming that the Democrats' share of all hard money remains the same as in the past. The figure indicates that the value of a soft money ban to the Democrats increases as the Republican share of soft money fundraising grows. (The slope of the line shows the growth of the effects of Republican fundraising on the relative position of Democratic overall fundraising). A Republican edge in soft money per se did not mean, how-ever, that a ban on such fundraising would be in the Democrats' interest. The figure shows that a soft money ban improves the Democrats' position relative to the Republicans' only if one assumes that the GOP raises about

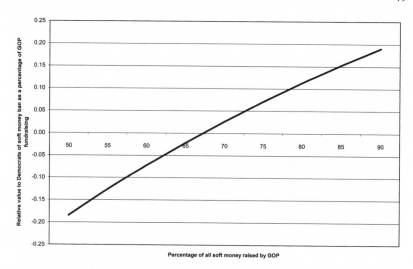

FIGURE 8.1 Democratic estimates of the value of a soft money ban

67 percent of all soft money. Below that level, a soft money ban would *worsen* the Democrats' overall position. If in 2002 they had assumed that the division of soft money in the 1990s (55 percent Republican, 45 percent Democratic) would continue into the future, the soft money ban would have made no sense. Yet Democrats had reasons to doubt that the future would be like the past. In late 2001, official Washington discovered that Republicans were pulling far ahead in soft money fundraising. They raised $100 million in George W. Bush's first year in the White House—a 67.8 percent increase over their soft money take in 1999—while Democrats raised $69 million, a 26.3 percent increase over 1999, according to the FEC. The 55-45 split now looked more like a 60-40 division in the Republicans' favor.[38] Moreover, no one knew what the trend might be. Was 2001 a sudden shift toward a long period in which Republicans raised 70 percent or more of all soft money? In the spring of 2002, when McCain-Feingold came up for a vote, a member of Congress could reasonably believe that Republicans would raise more the 67 percent of all soft money in the future.

Two other factors enabled Democrats to support the soft money ban. Having supported the prohibition for several years, the party would suffer some costs to its reputation if its members voted against it at a crucial moment.[39] Moreover, the Democrats could do what most investors do in the face of uncertainty: they could hedge their risk by buying insurance against the possibility that the Republican share of soft money would fall below 67 percent. As it happens, political professionals would have known that even if McCain-Feingold banned soft money, section 527 of the Internal Revenue Code allowed electoral organizations to raise funds not governed by federal contribution limits.[40] Section 527 allowed the Democrats in Congress to buy a put option, as it were, on McCain-Feingold. As we shall see, they decided to exercise that option once it became clear that Republicans would raise far less than 67 percent of all soft money. Given all this, the Democratic support for McCain-Feingold makes perfect sense. Progressivism and partisanship were reconciled.

Partisanship, Part Two

Early in 2001, McCain and Feingold attracted support from conservative senator Thad Cochran (R-MS), who added provisions requiring additional disclosure of contributions by outside groups. At the time, Cochran said that the 2000 election had taught him that "[w]e're defenseless against the juggernaut of huge, unregulated, undisclosed expenditures by groups."[41] Who exactly is the "we" that Cochran had in mind? Perhaps it is the same "we" that Barbara Boxer mentioned during these debates: members of Congress who are said to be defenseless against political spending.[42] Cochran and Boxer were not alone in fretting about the problems of incumbent members of Congress. Representative Clay Shaw was also worried. The Democratic Party and affiliated interest groups raised and spent large sums of soft money on advertising attacking Shaw (R-FL), a Republican leader in the House who was considered vulnerable. "After you've been a victim of soft money, you realize the magnitude of the problem," Shaw told the *Washington Post* in October 2000. "I'm determined to address this problem when we come back. It's really ripping at the fabric of our nation's political structure."[43] Shaw's complaint gives us an important clue about why McCain-Feingold passed.

To understand Shaw's problem, we must return briefly to *Buckley v. Valeo*. The authors of FECA had imposed tight spending and contribution limits on candidates and parties. They feared, however, that individuals and groups would find a way around the limits by buying advertising supporting a candidate. Such advertising would circumvent the purposes of FECA by allowing individuals and groups to support candidates indirectly. Congress therefore proposed to regulate political advertising. Yet this anticircumvention rationale was potentially very broad: all political advertising aired during an election could affect the outcome and hence function as a contribution or as campaign spending. In *Buckley,* the Supreme Court distinguished two kinds of advertising: express advocacy of the election or defeat of a candidate and issues advocacy. The latter composed all other advertising during an election and enjoyed the full protection of the First Amendment. Express advocacy, in contrast, had to obey the strictures of federal election law, including disclosure and contributions limits.

In the 1990s the political parties and interest groups found they could raise and spend soft money on ads that obliquely attacked vulnerable candidates for Congress, most of whom were incumbents. The ads would often discuss an issue (Social Security is endangered), identify a candidate's position (Clay Shaw wants to cut Social Security), and recommend a course of action other than voting (call Clay Shaw and tell him not to cut Social Security!). The ads did not expressly advocate the election or defeat of Clay Shaw. Thus the ads and the money raised to buy the airtime were free of the strictures of federal campaign finance law. The partisans of such laws quickly labeled the soft money advertising "sham issue ads" that in intention and effect were electioneering and thus subject to federal election law.[44]

The Annenberg Center at the University of Pennsylvania estimated that $509 million was spent on all issue ads during the 2000 elections. The major parties spent about $170 million of the total.[45] Advocacy groups spent about $340 million on advertising during the 2000 elections. Both parties had reason to believe that their opponents were benefiting from such nonparty spending. Interest groups supporting Gore spent more in the 2000 election than did Republican groups.[46] However, throughout the long struggle over McCain-Feingold, the Democrats often said they wanted limits on interest group ads because if soft money were banned, Republicans would simply shift their erstwhile soft money to friendly outsider groups. "I just worry that it may lead to some unintended consequences," said Evan Bayh, (D-IN), who said he feared that eliminating soft money contributions to parties would simply drive that cash into the hands of certain independent groups that can keep the source of their revenue secret.[47] For all the pious talk about corruption, members of Congress seemed primarily interested in the partisan consequences of prohibiting such funding.

Issues advertising funded by soft money posed a special threat to vulnerable incumbents. By and large, the parties and interest groups did not waste their soft money on ads attacking incumbents sitting in safe districts. They directed them at vulnerable candidates for Congress. The issues ads seem to have had their greatest influence on voters not affiliated with a political party. In other words, the ads "are successful with precisely those prospective voters who are in a position to tip the balance in close elections."[48] Vulnerable candidates in a close race had reason to fear their effects. Among those undecided about whether to vote for McCain-Feingold, vulnerable Republicans had the most reason to resent them. They were the most likely to appreciate restrictions on sham issue ads.

McCain sought the support of these vulnerable Republicans by including in his bill a provision that eliminated soft money advertising that mentioned a candidate for federal office. If a broadcast ad mentioned a candidate's name, the sponsoring group had to fund it according to the strictures of federal election law, including contribution limits and disclosure requirements. McCain's allies were quick to point out that the ad restrictions did not ban political advertising. That assertion was both true and false. It was true that the bill did not prohibit any group from running an ad saying Clay Shaw was against Social Security so long as it was subject to federal election law. It was false because the bill did prohibit running an ad mentioning Clay Shaw that was supported by soft money contributions that exceeded federal limits. By making it more difficult to fund ads, McCain could argue that the next election would see fewer ads attacking incumbents.

We saw in the introduction that several senators believed that McCain-Feingold would reduce attack ads that had been troublesome to incumbents. The whole purpose of the advertising restrictions was to make sure that fewer ads showed up in the weeks prior to an election. The sponsor of the restrictions *promised* that advertising that would have existed without McCain-Feingold would not exist after the bill passed. Whether we call that absence a ban seems beside the point. McCain aimed to create a political world with less speech, less information for voters, and thus, less competition. That world would serve the interests of incumbents in general and vulnerable Republican incumbents in particular. Their constituents, however, would have less information and hence less competition for their votes.

Final Payments

By the end of 2001, McCain was within sight of victory. The huge Republican advantage in soft money fundraising during that year had largely silenced Democratic concerns about banning soft money. McCain still was short of Republican votes. He had to put more incumbent-friendly planks in his bill to procure those votes.[49] To seal the deal, he also included a "millionaire amendment" that increased hard money contribution limits for candidates facing a wealthy opponent willing to spend large sums on a campaign. The provision also eliminated the limits on party spending on behalf of a candidate facing a wealthy self-financing opponent.[50]

On the surface, the millionaire amendment is neutral. Incumbents and challengers are subject to the same rules. If incumbent members of Congress decided to finance their own reelection efforts, their challengers would be freed from federal contribution limits. Yet incumbents rarely if ever finance their own reelection efforts; instead they rely on their own fundraising efforts along with party support. In practice, the amendment applies only to incumbents being threatened by a self-financing challenger. The amendment makes it easier to raise money quickly to head off a wealthy challenger. The provision will help vulnerable members of Congress of both parties, but only weak Republicans needed the extra push to vote for McCain-Feingold. The millionaire amendment was the last carrot of incumbent protection thrown their way. McCain believed (in the end, correctly) that adding this carrot to the stick of imagined incumbent vulnerability would provide the final push to get his bill through Congress.

A Puzzle

Democratic leaders must have known that McCain needed Republican votes to pass his bill and that to get them he would offer Republicans restrictions on campaign finance that would make their reelection more likely.[51] In that way, McCain's bill would protect the Republican majority by protecting some vulnerable incumbents. Why would the Democrats agree to this scheme? Again we must consider the alternative facing the Democrats. If soft money continued to exist, Democratic and Republican incumbents would be defeated. However, if the Republicans enjoyed a significant advantage in soft money (say, a 67 percent share), Democrats might well expect that more vulnerable members of their party would be defeated. Over time, what might be a small difference in survival rates could turn into a large increase in the Republican majority. Voting for a ban on soft money thus represented the better of two bad options for the Democrats.

Conclusion

Scholars tell us that "even the shallowest examination of Congressional policymaking" belies the belief that Congress acts in pursuit of the public interest.[52] The saga of how McCain-Feingold passed Congress provides no evidence to the contrary. Like earlier campaign finance restrictions, McCain-Feingold was a product of partisanship: congressional Democrats believed Republicans were likely to have an overwhelming advantage in soft money fundraising. Hence, more than 90 percent of Democrats in Congress voted to ban such fundraising. But McCain-Feingold also showed that incumbency could trump partisanship. The Republicans who supported the bill cared more about a ban on soft money advertising than they did about the fate of their party.[53] Differences aside, campaign finance law in 1974 and 2002 sought to sustain the status quo by proscribing or complicating electoral challenges.

For most voters, McCain was a man on a mission to clean up politics by prohibiting large contributions that were corrupting Congress. He was indeed a man on a mission. Over the course of five years he slowly put together a majority coalition of congressional Democrats and vulnerable Republicans in the House and the Senate. In the end, the Democrats could expect something from the bill (a ban on soft money), and Republicans in general could expect something (a minor liberalization of contribution limits), but vulnerable Republicans in both chambers of Congress could expect the most. Because of McCain-Feingold, these Republicans could expect to be much less likely to face soft money spending by Democrats, hostile advertising funded by the Democratic National Committee or interest groups, or a wealthy opponent with money to spare and a willingness to spend. What would be good for vulnerable Republicans, however, would not be good for American democracy. McCain bought these members' votes with the currency of incumbent protection. He corrupted American politics in the name of restoring its integrity.

CHAPTER NINE

A Liberalizing Agenda

The United States Supreme Court upheld McCain-Feingold almost completely in its decision in *McConnell v. Federal Election Commission*.[1] The *McConnell* decision may mark the beginning of the end of judicial efforts to limit the power of Congress over political speech. In the absence of constitutional constraints, politics will drive campaign finance regulation down one of two paths. We have already spent thirty years on the path of oversight and control of political speech marked out by the Federal Election Campaign Act of 1974 and by McCain-Feingold. The difficulties and dangers of that path may convince Americans of the need for an alternative way forward, a path that comports with the Madisonian vision of politics. In this chapter I look down the path of increased regulation and lay out an alternative.

Judicial Deference and Free Speech

Near the end of 2003 the Supreme Court upheld McCain-Feingold's most extensive restrictions on political speech. The decision embodies in many ways the Progressive vision of politics. Just as the *Carolene Products* footnote announced that economic activity no longer enjoyed constitutional protections, *McConnell* reveals for now that the Court will recognize only minimal protection for political speech in the face of congressional attacks.

The majority opinion stipulates that the constitutionality of McCain-Feingold's soft money prohibition requires a balancing of a lesser First Amendment interest (the right to contribute to campaigns) and the anticorruption rationale. Who strikes that balance? One justice had earlier

argued that the Supreme Court should strike the balance with due concern for both free speech and political participation.[2] The majority decided to show "proper deference to Congress' ability to weigh competing
constitutional interests in an area in which it enjoys particular expertise."
That deference is said to reflect "the respect that the Legislative and Judicial Branches owe to one another."[3] This deference fits well within the
Progressive vision of politics: the Court assumes that the expertise and
presumed objectivity of Congress justify its control over political speech.

But this deference calls into question the integrity of the political
process. James Madison stated, "No man is allowed to be a judge in his
own cause; because his interest would certainly bias his judgment, and,
not improbably, corrupt his integrity."[4] By allowing Congress to judge the
propriety of banning soft money, the Court allowed incumbent officials
to a judge in their own cause. Many members of Congress personally benefited from the prohibition of soft money. As we have seen, the political
parties and some interest groups had spent soft money on advertising that
criticized members of Congress. That created, as one member put it, a
"soft money problem."[5] Congress could not simply prohibit the ads or
jail its critics. But it could impose contribution limits and prohibitions
on fundraising to support the advertising. The restrictions contained in
McCain-Feingold make it relatively hard to raise money for any political
purpose. If groups find it harder to raise money to support advertising,
they will raise less money on the whole. If they raise less money on the
whole, less money will be available to fund speech. If less money is available, fewer ads criticizing members of Congress will run in the aggregate.
Money that does not exist cannot be spent on political advocacy. That is
why McCain promised his colleagues the bill would end attack ads. His
promise is a measure of the corruption caused by McCain-Feingold.

The *McConnell* majority argued that limits are acceptable if they permit enough fundraising to support "effective advocacy."[6] Absent regulatory harassment, citizens will be free to decide how much to spend and
thus how much speech is "effective." Congress or the Supreme Court
should decide how much speech constitutes effective advocacy. In truth,
almost all constraints on contributions would be judged constitutional by
the illiberal majority in *McConnell*.[7] For that reason, Congress and not
the American people will decide how much advocacy may be effective.
That judgment will involve being a judge in one's own cause regarding
speech criticizing members of Congress.

The decision in *Buckley v. Valeo* recognized the presumption of liberty in cases involving campaign finance. This presumption constrains

Congress by forcing it to show that banning soft money would prevent corruption or the appearance of corruption. The Supreme Court would then independently review that justification. In assessing Congress's determination about corruption, the *McConnell* majority relied on evidence created by . . . Congress. For example, the majority relies on a 1998 Senate report on investigations of Clinton fundraising to make the case against soft money.[8] They adduced the testimony of current and former members of Congress, all long-time advocates of increased restrictions on campaign finance. On the other hand, the Court completely ignored the social scientific evidence about hard money contributions and was "unbothered by the absence of any social science evidence whatsoever on whether unlimited soft money actually changed the policy positions of either party or any legislator in the period leading up to the passage" of McCain-Feingold. Deeply suspicious of the motives of campaign donors, the *McConnell* majority was deeply naïve about the source of evidence for corruption.[9] The decision shows that a Court that is deferential to Congress vitiates the presumption of liberty.

The majority also made it easier for Congress to restrict spending on elections. Its conception of corruption was not limited to "undue influence" on policymaking. The majority cited testimony that "various corporate interests had given substantial donations to gain access to high-level government officials." Moreover, "even if that access did not secure actual influence, it certainly gave the 'appearance of corruption.'"[10] The decision thus pushed corruption a step back from actual policymaking. If money leads to meetings with officeholders, money has corrupted the political process, and restrictions on campaign finance are constitutionally valid. But groups give money to candidates and officeholders who agree with them; it would not be surprising if those candidates or officeholders also met with their supporters. Those meetings, however, would be unlikely to change the mind of the officeholder about any issues or positions. After all, he or she already agreed with the contributors who are at the meeting.

Defining *corruption* as granting access to political allies lowers the bar on regulating campaign finance to the ground. When *corruption* meant exchanging policy favors for contributions, Congress had to prove that contributions had influence. As we have seen, there is little evidence of such influence. If access corrupts politics, however, every meeting of a member of Congress and a contributor justifies restrictions on campaign finance no matter what the content or consequences of that meeting. After *McConnell*, the corruption rationale no longer limited congressional restrictions on campaign contributions and spending.

Before *McConnell,* the Court had expanded congressional power over speech. In particular, it validated laws said to prevent the circumvention of measures (for example, contribution limits) designed to prevent corruption or the appearance of corruption. Congress thus had the power to regulate conduct that had not yet happened, putatively to identify and close prospective "loopholes" in laws justified under the anticorruption rationale.[11]

The majority relied heavily on the so-called anticircumvention rationale to validate McCain-Feingold. For example, the act prohibits the national political parties from raising or spending money not regulated by federal election law.[12] The defenders of the law attributed this prohibition to the government interest in preventing corruption or its appearance. The law also places a similar prohibition on spending "for Federal election activity by a State, district, or local committee of a political party." [13] In this instance the justification was different. Having banned the raising of soft money by the national parties, Congress expected that such donors would give to the state and local parties to avoid the national ban and garner influence with federal candidates. The Court deferred to Congress's judgment and the restriction on the state and local parties without offering any evidence that the latter in the past had been used to circumvent federal restrictions.[14] Similar reasoning justified a congressional ban on federal officeholders' raising money for nonprofit organizations.[15] In all these cases, the Court held that Congress need only have a "plausible" reason to legislate against a potential circumvention of campaign finance restrictions.[16]

The question remains whether congressional efforts to prevent circumvention have any limits apart from legislative lassitude and judicial fiat. As Chief Justice Rehnquist wrote in his dissent, the Court's identification of corruption and circumvention "has removed the touchstone of our campaign finance precedent and has failed to replace it with any logical limiting principle."[17] After all, almost all political activities involve spending money and therefore become potential paths for getting around the federal regulation of campaign finance. Many of these same activities may also threaten members of Congress in large and small ways. Given the Court's abject deference regarding these matters, Congress has an open invitation to judge its own cause and further corrupt our elections.

McConnell may also gesture toward the future of Supreme Court doctrine, a future in which campaign finance laws are said to enhance "participatory self-government." [18] Such a standard could easily embrace many of the values discussed in this book: increase voter turnout, rich public debate, and, of course, equality of political influence. According to this reading, the majority tried to fit its new "participatory self-government" standard into the *Buckley* precedent defined by the anticorruption rationale. *McConnell* is thus a transition away from *Buckley* and toward a future of more robust restrictions on money in politics. The Court's adoption of a participatory self-government standard could have profound consequences. For example, the Court might well replace the presumption of liberty in campaign finance with a presumption of equality. The burden of proof would fall on citizens, who would have to show that unequal spending on politics could be justified. In that light, a regulatory campaign finance regime that permitted inequalities of spending on elections might well be declared unconstitutional. An egalitarian Court might well prohibit private spending on politics and impose such remedies as public financing of campaigns. In the near future, the Supreme Court is unlikely to take such radical steps. But the future is a long time.

Interests and Ideals

The near future of campaign finance restrictions will be decided by Congress and the regulatory agency, the Federal Election Commission. The path Congress follows regarding campaign finance may well be affected by random circumstances that cannot be predicted reliably. One can, however, say something about the systematic factors shaping these regulations. The two parties and their incumbent officeholders have interests at stake in campaign finance, interests that inform and are informed by the two great political visions at work in the United States early in the twenty-first century.

I begin with the political parties. Campaign finance restrictions make it harder to challenge elected officials. Such laws thus benefit incumbents in general and therefore a party that holds a majority in a legislature. Throughout most of the era examined in this book the Democrats were the majority party in the U.S. Congress. They also relied less on fundraising to fight their political battles than on volunteers and a sympathetic media, resources that are not within the ambit of regulation. Consequently, legislation that restricted and hampered campaign fundraising and spending on the whole could be expected to improve the Democrats' prospects.

Not surprisingly, congressional Democrats supported the 1974 law and, with greater doubt, McCain-Feingold.

That era has now ended. The Democrats are no longer the majority party in the U.S. Congress. If that remains true, the Democrats will not have the votes to pass campaign finance legislation to benefit their party. The Democrats should expect that the campaign finance laws of the future will be like McCain-Feingold: insofar as Republicans support such laws, they are likely to harm the prospects of the Democratic Party's regaining control of Congress.

Two other factors inform the age of ideological drift for the Democrats.[19] First, the 2004 election (along with the two previous cycles) showed that sans contribution limits the Democrats could raise more than enough money to contest elections. Second, the 2004 election suggested that the Republicans, not the Democrats, were the party of volunteers. The Democrats used more paid workers funded by quite large contributions made to groups that were loosely affiliated with the party.[20] This experience suggests a distinctive characteristic of the Democratic Party: it is organized much more loosely than the Republican Party and depends more on the efforts of "outside groups."[21] Laws that force fundraising to stay within the party structure and complicate activity by nonprofits will harm the Democratic cause. Democrats will pay a price for favoring increased regulation of campaign finance.

Will Republicans become the party of reform? Their majority in Congress is vulnerable. Like the Democrats before them, they will seek ways to shore up their majority, and campaign finance restrictions inhibit political change. In early 2004 the Republican leadership began to advocate for broadening the restrictions on speech contained in McCain-Feingold. This turn against liberty reflected the harm being done to Republican candidates by Democratic 527 groups. As interests change, ideals may follow. The Republican Party has historical ties to the Progressive movement, and McCain sees himself as the proper reincarnation of Theodore Roosevelt.[22]

Nonetheless, the Republicans may hold firm. Having supported liberalization for much of the past decade, they may find it difficult to change course.[23] Many have taken up the party's Madisonian position regarding these issues. They may have the integrity to favor their ideals rather than their partisan ambition. More prosaically, the Republicans may simply find it difficult to come up with legislation that discriminates in their favor and against the Democrats. They may also conclude that over the longer term their interests and Madisonian ideals will converge.

This bright picture of the prospects for liberalization contains one large, dark cloud: the interests of incumbent officials. Unlike the political parties, whose interests may change as they gain or lose power, current members of Congress have a permanent interest in being reelected. Incumbents, especially those who are potentially vulnerable, seek ways to advance that permanent interest, not least via regulating and restricting campaign finance.

Also, we should not underestimate the persistence or power of the vulnerable Republican incumbents who provided the crucial votes necessary to pass McCain-Feingold. In the fall of 2005, the Federal Election Commission filed suit to force the Club for Growth to register with the FEC as a "political committee." If the group registered as a political committee, it would have to submit to federal restrictions on fundraising, ending its activities as a 527 group.[24] The Club for Growth "exists to encourage, and make possible, the enactment of pro-growth economic policies by the federal government." To realize that goal, it provides "financial support from Club members to viable pro-growth candidates to Congress, particularly in Republican primaries."[25] In other words, it funds primary challengers to incumbent members of Congress and especially to those who voted to enact McCain-Feingold. A Republican member of the FEC said the suit would decide "whether Club for Growth will be able to continue raising and spending millions of dollars in soft money for activities influencing federal elections."[26] Just as Democratic 527 groups posed a problem for a Republican presidential campaign, pro-growth 527 groups threatened the reelection of some Republican legislators. Congressional Republicans responded to these "problems" by trying to eliminate the threatening activity via administrative action.

Ideals and interests will influence the future of campaign finance restrictions. My prediction for that future incorporates the Madisonian vision by assuming a presumption of liberty. This means that the government bears a major burden of proof if it is to justify limiting the liberty of individuals. Conversely, individuals and groups do not have to show that their use of their liberty will serve some larger social goal to justify being free of government regulation. If the government does not carry its burden of proof with logic and evidence, citizens have a right to do as they wish. I have offered extensive evidence that the justifications for restricting money in elections are not convincing. One should therefore assume that existing restrictions should not continue absent some proof that they protect the rights of individuals better than the next alternative. Madisonian philosophy and social science findings converge to ask what, if anything, should be retained of the current body of campaign finance law. I turn first, however, to restrictions that are likely to be proposed in the near future.

Government Gains Ground

The immediate future of campaign finance regulation may be similar to its past. Groups spend money on elections, and Congress tries to stop them for reasons of partisanship and incumbency protection. Advances in technology threaten the political status quo and attract new laws to suppress that threat. Finally, the oldest restraint on free speech—spending limits on campaigns for office—may yet become law for the nation as a whole.

Outside Groups

Unincorporated political groups that register under section 527 of the Internal Revenue Code can raise money in unlimited amounts from corporations, labor unions, and individuals because they are not working with national party organizations. They must, however, report their donations and spending to the IRS in detail. Unincorporated 527 groups that do not accept funds from corporations or labor unions may buy broadcast ads within thirty days of a primary or sixty days of a general election, although they may not engage in express advocacy.[27] Not surprisingly, leaders of both major political parties began studying the potential of 527 groups.[28]

Democratic leaders moved to set up coordinated national and state-by-state operations similar to "a full presidential campaign, minus the candidate." Like the soft money operations of the Democratic Party prior to the passage of McCain-Feingold, the Democratic 527 organizations raised unlimited sums from wealthy individuals and groups. By early March 2004, a report indicated this parallel Democratic Party had spent $69 million to support its nominee for the presidency.[29] Clearly, big money had not been driven out of American politics. It was also clear that the speech supported by big money was wholly ideological; it was core political speech protected by the First Amendment.

Yet reality did turn out to be surprising in one way. The Republicans, who had enjoyed considerable success in raising soft money in the 1990s, failed to match the results of the Democratic 527 groups. Republicans raise much of their soft money from businesses, many of whom were unwilling to contribute in 2003 because of the uncertainty created by the new law and because President Bush had done an outstanding job raising hard money.[30]

To be sure, the law did suppress overall soft money fundraising. If McCain-Feingold had not become law, we might have expected the parties to raise $650 million in soft money in 2004. Shortly after the election, it became apparent that the 527 groups had raised about $400 million.[31] This might seem a success: McCain might say his law had reduced soft money by one-third. But McCain and his allies had stipulated that soft money corrupted American politics, and accordingly their law prohibited raising (and hence, spending) it. Given that stipulation and the concomitant aspiration, the spending by the 527 groups must count as a failure of McCain-Feingold, at least judged on its own terms. For his part, McCain argued the FEC had failed to enforce the law, thereby allowing outside groups to circumvent it.[32] Yet Congress did nothing to correct this "false" interpretation of the law by the FEC. Looked at another way, the 527 spending was a success. It undermined and may yet destroy efforts by Congress to suppress political participation and freedom of speech.

After the 2004 election, McCain and his allies moved quickly to prohibit fundraising by 527 groups. They enjoyed some initial success in the Senate. The House Republicans, on the other hand, sought to liberalize rather than restrict campaign finance. Incumbent Democrats were caught between their partisan support for 527 groups and their permanent worry that Republicans, too, would form such groups to attack electorally vulnerable Democratic members of Congress. It appeared possible that a bipartisan coalition in Congress might support both leaving 527 groups as they were and liberalizing the rules governing donations to the parties.[33] Outside of Congress, the world was also changing. Familiar with the logic of anticircumvention, nonprofit groups on the Left and the Right protested the assault on 527 groups, believing that their political activity would be McCain's next target.[34] The suppression of political speech via campaign finance laws has thus started to have random political effects that make bedfellows of the reform community and some Republicans while inducing resistance from erstwhile supports of restrictions on spending.

The Internet

The Internet had played a minor role in the 2000 election and in earlier contests.[35] By 2002 candidates had started to use their Web sites more effectively to raise money and disseminate their views about the issues of the day.[36] In 2004 the Internet became an important part of the presidential election. Democrat Howard Dean used it to support his presidential campaign. In the general election, John Kerry closed the traditional fundraising gap between the parties by using the Internet. Individuals also used their Web sites or Web logs ("blogs") to disseminate political views and information outside the established media. Late in the 2004 campaign, bloggers revealed the shortcomings of CBS News allegations about George W. Bush's National Guard service. Eventually the CBS scandal led to the retirement of Dan Rather, the network's longtime newsreader.[37] In 2004, as in 1968, a new technology for disseminating political speech shook up the status quo and threatened those who benefit from it. But another term for that threat to the status quo is free speech.

The Internet is mentioned seven times in the Bipartisan Campaign Reform Act of 2002. All seven mentions relate one way or another to disclosure.[38] Not surprisingly, in drafting regulations to implement McCain-Feingold, the FEC initially decided to exclude Internet communications from the web of campaign finance restrictions.[39] Subsequently a federal judge ordered the FEC to revise the regulations to include the Internet on the ground that the exemption opened a way to circumvent the strictures of McCain-Feingold.[40] Shortly after the 2004 election, the FEC began to write new regulations covering political activity on the Internet.

Since 1969, campaign finance regulators have tried to suppress political activity by controlling spending on the means of communicating with voters. The 1971 law set limits on spending on television and radio advertising, the 1974 law limited spending in general, and McCain-Feingold effectively banned unrestricted spending on ads that mentioned a candidate for federal office within a specified period of time before an election. The contribution limits enacted in all these laws offered indirect means to the same end of suppressing threatening speech.

In light of this history, it seems inevitable that Congress or the FEC will try to suppress political activity on the Internet. Some will argue that Web sites and blogs are "coordinated" with the campaigns and hence constitute contributions that should comport with federal election law. Other will note, as a federal judge has already, that allowing the Internet to escape the ambit of federal restrictions will undermine or circumvent the purposes of McCain-Feingold and other campaign finance laws. That is true. But the circumvention will not be in the service of corrupting public officials. Indeed, few argue now that Internet speech (and its funding) compromises the integrity of government. Some argue that regulation is needed now because an unrestricted Internet will corrupt the government at some future time. The presumption of liberty should not be overcome by assuming a future cost (or benefit), especially when history and logic suggest that the proffered regulation seeks to protect incumbents from electoral uncertainty and rough criticism.

The effort to regulate speech on the Internet may succeed if the restrictions systematically benefit political parties or incumbent members of Congress. Some Internet users have resisted the initial efforts to restrict political speech on the Web. That resistance has come from the Right and the Left, indicating that these restrictions may be expected to have a random ideological and perhaps partisan effect.[41] Incumbents will systematically benefit from less speech on the Internet. Congress may not have the will to impose such restrictions if the partisan consequences are ambiguous and the resistance to regulation remains widespread.

The Internet has until now been a domain of liberty including freedom of speech. Campaign finance laws provide a way to suppress challenges to some political status quo by limiting freedom of speech. By the nature of the case, the Internet will remain what it is and circumvent the campaign finance laws, or the campaign finance laws will restrict political speech on the Internet.

Limits on Expenditures

Congress has tried to impose limits on campaign spending throughout much of the history of campaign finance regulation. As we saw, restrictions on spending help incumbent members of Congress (and thus the majority party). Limits on spending were included in all the original laws passed in the 1970s. Once the Court in *Buckley* declared spending limits unconstitutional, Congress could only impose such constraints in exchange for public financing. What Congress wanted (limiting reelection challenges by limiting spending) could only be obtained by granting what it did not want to grant (public funding for challengers). Congress continued to seek ways to limit spending, but its aversion to capitalizing challengers prevented enactment of expenditure limits. This history does suggest, however, that it wishes to limit spending and has been stopped from doing so only by the Supreme Court's reluctance to grant that wish. The wish to suppress competition can hardly overcome the presumption of liberty, which depends in part on elections' offering alternatives to the status quo.

Soon the Supreme Court may validate limits on expenditures.[42] Absent legal constraints, Congress would almost certainly pass restrictions on spending. What Congress will not do is couple such limits with public financing for congressional campaigns. The public is, at best, ambivalent about taxpayer financing, and Congress has never shown much real interest in such legislation. The consequences of spending limits are predictable even now. Candidates and the parties will abide by the limits, but individuals and groups will set up organizations to spend more than they are allowed to spend. Congress will declare that these groups have circumvented the spending limits and will impose restrictions on them. Much of the campaign finance struggle will shift toward the question of coordination: do groups that are spending amounts in excess of the limits work with a campaign? Eventually the circumvention rationale will run headlong into the traditional protection afforded spending on politics that is independent of candidates and parties. In the larger picture, spending limits without public subsidies will make it even harder to challenge a member of Congress for reelection. The Court's deference to legislative judgment about spending limits will end by circumventing popular control of the legislature.[43]

We have little reason to think that future proposals to restrict campaign finance will overcome the presumption of liberty. Most proposals will be defended as necessary to prevent the circumvention of existing restrictions. That rationale, and the power Congress has to pursue it, suggest at first an area of law created at the expense of political speech. But as campaign finance laws engulf ever more political activity, their reach may yet prove their undoing, for restrictions may also engender resistance, especially when the law reaches those who once believed in "reform." The examples of the 527 groups and the Internet suggest that the politics of campaign finance regulation is changing in ways that may yet halt the expansion of the ambit of state power. Once it is halted, existing regulations will be undermined by normal political activity. Such liberalization will be preferable to the harassment and restrictions of current law. But working around current restraints involves wasted time, effort, and money. It would be better to simply liberalize the system via legislation. What would such an effort require?

A Madisonian Alternative

Libertarians often hear the following question about various policy issues: "We know what you are against. But what are you for?" By now the reader will know what I am against in campaign finance regulation and politics. But I have not addressed the question of what should be done to restore political liberty in the area of campaign finance. At first blush, the answer would appear to be simple. If laws require justification and if the rationales for current campaign finance law have been shown to come up short, we ought to simply get rid of all 221 pages of regulations and restrictions.[44] But the question of liberalization turns out to be more complicated than that and to require more arguments and considered judgments.

Limits on Campaign Contributions

I argued above that, like political spending generally, campaign contributions are central to freedom of speech in contemporary America. The reasons offered for such limits have proved to be unpersuasive given the evidence noted throughout this book. Individuals and groups should be able to give whatever sums they wish to candidates, organizations, and parties. This would require removing the contribution limits in the Federal Election Campaign Act of 1974 and the prohibitions on party fundraising in McCain-Feingold. As we have seen, Congress has tried for more than three decades to restrict spending on television and radio advertising during elections. Liberalization of our politics demands revoking all such restrictions. Of course, once all contribution limits have been revoked, McCain-Feingold's limits on the funding for certain kinds of electoral ads will be irrelevant.

The reader may object that the studies reported above regarding the influence of money on policymaking and political culture concerned a world with contribution limits. It might be argued that these studies tell us nothing about money and corruption in a world without contribution limits. In fact, I reported that few soft money donors split their donations between the parties. We also saw that those who donated to 527 groups in the 2004 election did so largely for ideological reasons.

But such an objection begins with a false assumption. The presumption of liberty means that if proponents of regulation, who carry the burden of proof, cannot show that some activity should be restricted, the regulation cannot be justified and should be removed. It is not up to those who propose deregulation to show that liberty will serve some higher end chosen by the partisans of regulation. Because the evidence suggests that contributions do not corrupt policymaking but rather merely complicate challenges to the status quo, contribution limits have to go.

Prohibitions on Campaign Contributions

Federal election law does not merely limit how much people and organizations can give; it also flatly prohibits contributions by various individuals and groups. Specifically, the law appears to forbid donations by national banks, corporations, labor unions, government contractors, minors, and foreign nationals.[45] Surely a flat prohibition on contributing infringes the right to freedom of speech more than do the limits on contributions. A liberalizing agenda would presumably eliminate all of these prohibitions. Is that presumption defensible? I consider first the prohibition on donations by individuals.

FOREIGN NATIONALS.   Federal law prohibits campaign contributions from citizens of other countries.[46] Should Congress revoke that ban? I should carefully set aside the political likelihood of such a revocation.[47] I have no illusions that permitting foreign contributions would be popular.

Campaign contributions provide a way to participate in politics. Other ways are voting and petitioning the government for redress of grievances, otherwise known as lobbying. Federal law now prohibits foreign nationals from voting or contributing to campaigns. On the other hand, the United States allows lobbying by foreigners. It does require that agents of foreign entities register with the attorney general.[48] Foreign diplomats are also permitted to lobby public officials on behalf of their nation. The United States seems to have decided to prohibit direct foreign participation in elections (voting, contributions) while permitting indirect foreign participation.

Natural rights theory tends to be cosmopolitan: individuals have natural rights whether or not their society recognizes them, and all governments have an obligation to respect the natural rights of their citizens. Madisonians are likely to believe that foreign nationals have a natural right to free speech, which implies a right to participate in politics by spending and contributing money. The ban on contributions by foreigners raises an odd question: Is the U.S. government obligated to recognize and enforce the natural rights of citizens of other countries? Perhaps not. Madisonians think natural rights should be realized in a nation created by individuals who agree to abide by a social contract. By definition, foreigners are not part of the U.S. social contract. Even if foreigners have background rights to free speech, it may not be unjust to refuse to recognize that natural right as a legal right.[49] If so, Congress may be unwise to ban contributions from foreigners, but the prohibition itself would not violate the fundamental norms of a liberal society.

CORPORATIONS AND LABOR UNIONS. The law forbids direct campaign contributions by corporations and labor unions. It specifically prohibits contributions by two kinds of businesses: nationally chartered banks and firms doing business with the federal government.[50] The prohibitions on donations by corporations, banks, and labor unions precede the 1974 campaign finance law by many years.[51] On the other hand, federal election law specifically allows corporations and labor unions to establish, administer, and solicit contributions to separate segregated funds to be utilized for political purposes. The law limits the types of persons who may be asked to contribute to these funds.[52] In other words, corporations and labor unions may now contribute to campaigns under certain conditions. The question of liberalization thus confronts two alternatives: (a) the status quo, which limits corporations and unions to the PAC format, or (b) direct donations by businesses and labor unions.

Many of the arguments for limits on contributions by corporations turn on the danger that private actors will corrupt public servants or create political inequality. The foregoing chapters have dealt with these allegations and concerns by examining studies of the influence of PAC contributions. Those studies show that generally such donations have little influence on policymaking. But those studies concern a world with the PAC format and limited contributions. Direct giving by businesses and unions without contribution limits may or may not yield different results. Again we come upon the question of burden of proof and the presumption of liberty. If the latter holds, the liberalizer is not required to show that direct donations by businesses and labor unions would harm the nation in some vital way. The danger associated with direct giving by businesses may be found elsewhere.

The U.S. government regulates much of the American economy. Regulations can help or harm businesses. The same might be true of labor unions via different means. The members of Congress who write the regulations are thus not helpless victims of big money. They have the power to harm individuals and groups who contribute to their campaigns (or choose not to contribute), a possibility known to potential contributors. Individuals, businesses, and labor unions face the choice of paying to avoid trouble or running the risk of being harmed by government regulation.[53]

Does such extortion exist? Given the temptation, we might expect that it does.[54] The Committee on Economic Development polled three hundred corporate managers in 2000 and found that "51 percent of business executives fear adverse legislative consequences to themselves or their industry if they turn down requests for campaign contributions from high-ranking political leaders and/or political operatives."[55] Some conservatives (and business leaders) have supported restrictions on large donations as a solution to the extortion problem. The Committee on Economic Development, for example, supported the restrictions on soft money donations contained in McCain-Feingold.[56] Conservatives might argue that such restrictions serve Madison's aim of "controuling government" by reducing the incentives for extortion by reducing the size of donations.

Why ban only large contributions? Perhaps conservatives assume that the likelihood of extortion correlates to the size of potential donations. Yet we have no reason to think members also would not extract smaller donations. Taken to its logical conclusion, the concern about extortion makes the case for banning private contributions altogether, hardly a conservative outcome.

Perhaps conservatives are actually arguing that contribution limits will restrict the harm done by extortion. Without the limits, so the argument might go, powerful politicians would demand campaign contributions up to the value of the potential harm they could do to the business in question. Of course, predatory politicians would stop extracting protection money at some point short of bankrupting the company; they would not kill the goose that laid the golden egg, except through miscalculation. In reality, many corporations do not contribute to campaigns even when the law does not limit donations to the political parties.[57] Businesses refused to contribute to groups supporting George W. Bush's presidential reelection effort even when his opponent was raising far more 527 money than Bush was.[58] Such evidence suggests that the incidence of extortion is nominal.

The proposal to restrict corporate donations loses sight of the moral problem of extortion of contributions. Why should the government be allowed to restrict the freedom of a person (or an organization) to prevent a crime by someone else? Should we tax away the profits of a business to prevent gangsters from offering them insurance? Do we prevent street crime by forbidding visits after dark to dangerous neighborhoods? Normally, in response to a crime, we apprehend and punish the criminal, not his victims. In campaign finance, the alleged perpetrator of extortion restricts the rights of his victim to reduce the likelihood that the perpetrator will sin again. Moreover, it restricts the rights of all potential victims whether or not they are likely to be preyed upon by the politician. The case for limiting or prohibiting contributions to prevent extortion seems morally confused. Can we deal with extortion in a normal fashion by punishing the criminal?

With most crimes, we place sanctions on the criminal post hoc, which deters the wrongdoing. The lower the likelihood of detection, the stronger the sanctions. The normal way of dealing with crimes, however, has problems in this instance. In the real world, an extortionist usually makes threats before doing harm to his victim. In politics, the extortionist need not say anything to threaten his victim. His threat or the potential harm to his victim is part of the way things are. To prevent extortion, we need to change the way things are. We should reduce the power of the state over the rest of society. Such limitations on government would reduce the leverage that legislators have over everyone else.[59] Anything short of that, such as restricting campaign contributions, simply violates the rights of innocent individuals or organizations. On top of everything else, restricting the liberty of individuals to contribute to campaigns makes powerful incumbents stronger, not weaker. Although intended to prevent political extortion, the limits end up punishing the innocent to empower the guilty.

If we allow corporations and unions to contribute to campaigns we run the risk that politicians will obtain money from them under duress. On the other hand, government can harm businesses and unions in many ways. Regulations can deprive a business of market share; unions might find their activities limited by law. Profits can be taxed away and given to constituents in exchange for their votes. "Big business" has become highly unpopular with the public and thus an inviting target for ambitious demagogues.[60] Given those incentives for exploitation and the government's monopoly on violence, we should be concerned that businesses and unions have the means to counterbalance the power of the state.

Currently businesses and unions spend money on lobbying to defend their interests. The freedom to directly contribute to election campaigns would allow business managers and union leaders to defend and advance the interests of their shareholders in a public and accountable way. The dangers of extortion notwithstanding, ending the prohibition on direct corporate and union contributions is, on balance, likely to limit rather than expand the ambit of government, thereby bringing us closer to a Madisonian vision of politics.

The Public Funding System for Presidential Elections

The presidential campaign funding system has accomplished very little for the public in the past thirty years while spending perhaps $2 billion. If we consider only its effectiveness, the program should be terminated. Yet some might object that liberalizing reforms need not touch the scheme largely because it does not violate rights by prohibiting freedom of speech. After all, contributions to the program are made voluntarily through the tax form check-off system. Only the taxpayers who want to support the system end up contributing to it.

The system does compel taxpayers to support candidates not of their choosing. The check-off on the tax form does not increase the taxes of those who decide to support the presidential campaign funding program. It simply allows those who check off the box to decide how some taxes raised from everyone will be spent. The system is an appropriations device that allows a small number of taxpayers (10 percent and falling) to force the others to fund their policy preferences. Looked at this way, the system seems similar to corporate welfare or other special interest provisions in the tax code.

The presidential campaign funding system also requires all taxpayers to support the costs associated with fundraising for the presidential candidates who benefit from the program. In particular, it forces all taxpayers to foot the bill for finding the contributors to the system, for the mechanisms for getting money to candidates, for administration of the system, and for related advertising costs. Without these taxpayer subsidies, the system would not exist.[61] Accordingly, because it is coercive, ineffective, and unpopular, we would better off without it. Chapters 95 and 96 of Title 26 of the Internal Revenue Code should be eliminated.

Disclosure

The federal government has mandated disclosure of campaign contributions and spending since 1974.[62] The Bipartisan Campaign Reform Act of 2002 expanded disclosure requirements for candidates, committees, and independent groups. The act also required broadcasters to keep records about requests to buy advertising time, records that include extensive information about the organizations seeking to purchase ads.[63]

Disclosure has few opponents. Even those who question the broader campaign finance regime often support disclosure as the least bad alternative.[64] Such broad support might suggest that the current disclosure regime is optimal, but it may be misleading. People who are inclined to oppose disclosure may believe they must support it because the only alternative is comprehensive restriction or prohibition of donations. If less coercive options existed, participants in the political process might support them instead of mandatory disclosure.

To illustrate, I begin with a paradigmatic case: an individual donates to the campaign of a candidate for federal office. In most cases, only two people will know that this contribution has been made: the contributor and the recipient (or an agent of the recipient). What happens next depends on individual choices or public policy.

1. The information about the contribution may remain known only to the donor and the recipient because they choose not to disclose it to anyone else (voluntary anonymity).

2. The donor and the recipient may choose to disclose the contribution to others including the public at large (voluntary disclosure).

3. The government may force the donor and the recipient to disclose the contribution to the public at large (mandatory disclosure).

4. The government may prevent the donor from credibly disclosing his contribution to anyone, especially the recipient (mandatory anonymity).

I turn first to the mandatory alternatives.

MANDATORY DISCLOSURE.   Forcing people to reveal their campaign contributions compels them to speak about a subject when they might otherwise choose to remain silent. In a liberal society, such compulsion demands extraordinary justification. *Buckley v. Valeo* set out four kinds of benefits provided by mandated disclosure. Three of these are deterring actual corruption, avoiding the appearance of corruption, and revealing information to voters.[65] I consider first whether mandated disclosure actually fosters these benefits. Even if they do, that does not settle the matter. That some people prefer to remain silent about their contributions indicates that mandated disclosure imposes costs. One must ask whether those costs outweigh whatever benefits mandated disclosure delivers.

Has mandatory disclosure deterred actual corruption? Studies have shown that contributions have little corrupting effect. Because these studies were conducted after 1974, we might conclude that disclosure vitiates the influence of money on the legislature. Such a conclusion would be unjustified. The studies of the influence of money were all done under a mandatory disclosure regime (indeed, many of the data in the studies resulted from that requirement). We lack studies of the influence of money absent mandatory disclosure, so we can conclude nothing about the influence of money when disclosure is required.[66] Moreover, we are unlikely to have studies that will be able to identify the effects of disclosure on corruption because they will not by their nature include any change in the disclosure variable.

We do, however, have data that bear on the deterrence argument. Disclosure deters corruption if voters punish candidates who receive questionable contributions. Voters must find and interpret the campaign finance data and then relate their conclusions to casting their ballot. Do they? Between 40 and 60 percent of the electorate in an election cycle does not vote. For those who plan to vote, the benefits of finding the information may not outweigh the costs of discovery. The benefits of discovery would be avoiding the costs of electing a corrupt legislator. But those benefits for each voter might be lower than the costs of finding the information. Oddly, for all the importance given to disclosure, we lack rigorous studies of whether and how voters use the revealed information. Public opinion polls have found that respondents are largely ignorant of campaign finance law and care little about finance reform.[67] Given their rational ignorance about the laws and apathy about the issue, it seems unlikely that voters use the data. If they do, their concerns about a donation may be outweighed by other considerations in voting for or against a candidate: "If a voter favors one candidate's substantive issue positions, discomfort with his or her campaign finance practices alone may not (and perhaps should not) alter that preference."[68]

The media spread the costs of discovering the information across a large number of readers or viewers, thereby changing the relative costs and benefits of obtaining the information. Once again we do not know whether the public learns this information. We do observe that newspapers in particular have consistently included contribution information in their stories for many years.[69] At the margins, this persistence suggests that the newspapers believe their readers are willing to pay for this information at the price at which it is offered. Given that the media have many customers and contain much information, the marginal value and cost of disclosed contributions may both be quite small to the individual though much larger in the aggregate if many individuals care about the disclosure. Even in that case, however, the cost of the information is lower than what it would have been if the mandate did not exist. That subsidy makes sense if it induces at the margin information about contributions that in turn reduces the costs of corruption to the point of equaling the opportunity cost of the mandate (that is, the difference in costs between imposing and not imposing the mandate). Insofar as we do not know whether disclosure deters corruption, we do not know whether the government mandate makes sense. The information in newspaper stories about contributions may be nothing more than corporate welfare that boosts private profits (by subsidizing production of newspapers) without increasing the public welfare. This way of looking at the issue also indicates that we should be concerned about the total opportunity costs of imposing mandates. Those costs, if known, should be put in the balance against the uncertain benefits of preventing corruption.

The uncertainty of the benefits of disclosure is important. If we could estimate the probability of corruption under a voluntary anonymity regime, we could speak of the risk of incurring costs (or forgoing benefits) by ending mandatory disclosure. We could come up with a discounted (risk-adjusted) estimate of the relative value of mandated disclosure. Since we do not have any knowledge of the counterfactual of voluntary anonymity, we remain uncertain about the costs and benefits of preventing corruption by mandatory disclosure; that is, we have no data to assign a probability to the costs and benefits of the policy.[70]

The defender of disclosure will not be impressed by this conclusion. He will be inclined to say that of course corruption would be rampant without mandatory disclosure. But that "of course" reflects untested assumptions and conventional dogma rather than knowledge. The defender might note that businesspeople act in the face of uncertainty to produce goods and services;[71] perhaps regulators of campaign finance might also need to act despite uncertainty. But businesspeople are different from the government. We do not presume they will not act unless they have knowledge about the risk of their ventures. Indeed, as Frank Knight pointed out, businesspeople inevitably act under uncertainty. Campaign finance regulators, in contrast, should not act unless they have knowledge of the risks of the costs posed by not acting and strong reasons to think their actions will mitigate those risks efficiently. This principle of inaction defines the presumption of liberty that underlies a liberal regime in campaign finance and in other areas. According to the presumption of liberty, uncertainty (and hence, ignorance) ought to be enough to justify inaction.

The appearance of corruption concerns the consequences of what people *believe* about campaign contributions. We can draw some empirical conclusions about the relation of mandatory disclosure and public confidence in government. Federally mandated disclosure of campaign contributions began in 1974. National Elections Studies has asked consistent questions about public confidence in government for almost fifty years. We have an interrupted time series of data about the effects of mandatory disclosure and the counterfactual, nondisclosure. We can divide the data into two periods: nondisclosure from 1958 to 1974 (FECA was amended in October 1974) and disclosure. The NES trust index indicated an average score of 49.2 for the nondisclosure era (the higher the score, the more trust among citizens). The corresponding average for the disclosure era was 33.5. Not surprisingly, the correlation coefficient between disclosure and the trust index was strongly inverse (−.74).[72] An increase in disclosure tended to be correlated highly with a decrease in trust in government. Individual questions bearing on corruption show the same relation. For example, disclosure is strongly associated with a decrease in the belief that government is run for the benefit of all.[73] Similarly, disclosure is strongly linked to the belief that "quite a few" government officials are crooks.[74] Disclosure clearly has not been associated with an increase in public confidence in the federal government.[75]

Its defenders justify disclosure by arguing that such revelations will deter questionable donations and thereby shore up public confidence. If that mechanism worked, presumably we would see an increase in the trust measures over time or perhaps an increase followed by a plateau at a higher level of trust (if all or almost all of the questionable donations disappeared in the light of disclosure). In fact, the passage of time during the disclosure era shows a weak though positive association with the trust-in-government index (.26). On the other hand, the same factor is weakly associated with an *increase* in the belief that the government is run by few big interests (.10). Disclosure also has a weak relation to the belief that quite a few officials are crooks (−.17).[76]

The analysis presented here does not exclude the possibility that the marginal effects of disclosure, all things considered, might have been to increase public trust in government. For example, factors unconnected to campaign finance law might cause a general decline in trust while disclosure (compared to an absence of disclosure) causes a slight increase in trust; the effect of disclosure would be lost in the general trend. We would never know that public trust is higher than it would have been otherwise during a period of general decline of trust. Unfortunately, there are not enough data to reach statistically significant conclusions from an analysis that takes into account all the factors that bear on public trust. We do have one multiple-regression study that indicates campaign finance regulations have little effect on public trust in government.[77]

All in all, there is little evidence that mandatory disclosure of contributions has reduced the appearance of corruption. Given what we know about public ignorance of politics as well as the lack of interest in the issue of campaign finance, it seems likely that mandatory disclosure has had little effect on public confidence in government. The case that disclosure combats the appearance of corruption and thereby increases public confidence in government remains unproved.

Experts have also studied the related question of efficacy. If citizens comes to believe that money determines collective choice (if, say, there is an appearance of corruption), they might be expected to doubt that they have a say in determining what government does. A recent study of mandatory disclosure in the states that offers a multifactor analysis of efficacy has some unusual results: public financing, for example, seems to reduce trust. The work does find the expected relation, all things considered, between mandatory disclosure and political efficacy: the former is positively and significantly related to the latter. As the authors note, the study found modest effects for mandatory disclosure. On average, it increased the probability of a favorable response by three percentage points when NES asked whether a respondent felt he or she "had a say" in what government does. Similarly, it increased by three percentage points the probability of disagreeing with the statement "Public officials don't care much what people like me think.["78]

Mandatory disclosure seeks to produce benefits as well as avoid costs (like those connected to corruption or the appearance of corruption). The *Buckley* Court argued that

> disclosure provides the electorate with information "as to where political campaign money comes from and how it is spent by the candidate" in order to aid the voters in evaluating those who seek federal office. It allows voters to place each candidate in the political spectrum more precisely than is often possible solely on the basis of party labels and campaign speeches. The sources of a candidate's financial support also alert the voter to the interests to which a candidate is most likely to be responsive and thus facilitate predictions of future performance in office.[79]

Elizabeth Garrett argues that mandatory disclosure enhances voter competence.[80] Some political scientists believe that voters manage the search for information by utilizing shortcuts or cues to help align their votes with their intentions.[81] Disclosure of contributions might be one shortcut indicating the actual views of candidates as well as predictions about their future performance in office. Improving voter competence might thus become the primary purpose of campaign finance regulation and mandatory disclosure the most apt policy to achieve that end.[82] Does it deliver the promised benefit of improved voter competence?

The voter competence argument assumes that voters use information about donations to vote for or against a candidate. The chain of events is not plausible given the other things we know about voters. They often do not know the names of public officials or candidates for office. How likely are they to use more esoteric information about contributors? Yet what might happen if voters focus not on contributors but rather on contributions? Absent knowledge of the donor, a contribution by itself would convey little information to a voter; it would simply be money, not money infused with information about the candidate.

According to the voter competence argument, competence is the ability to use disclosed information to match a voter's views with his or her vote. The quality of the information about contributions matters to this argument. If the information is poor, the voter's knowledge may not improve. Most people get information about contributions indirectly (if at all) from media reports that distort public perceptions of campaign finance. Stephen Ansolabehere and James Snyder Jr. rigorously examined reporting on campaign finance in major newspapers in the United States during the election years 1996, 1998, and 2000. They concluded, "If a reader were to treat the numbers reported in newspapers as the reality, he or she would carry a very inaccurate picture of campaign spending in America. Expenditures reported in the papers are approximately 3 to 5 times larger than the reality. The amounts spent on television advertising are much smaller than reported. And congressional challengers spend much, much less than is presented in the press."[83] Media reporting also misleads the public about the sources of contributions: individuals are the most frequent source, but "stories about PAC contributions are 5 times more numerous than stories about individual donors."[84] The public takes up the errors reported by the media.[85] This evidence does not indicate whether the media distort information about specific contributions. However, it does not inspire confidence about the quality of the information that reaches voters.

Disclosure also putatively helps voters predict the future performance of candidates for office. Elected officials are said to be creatures of the

interests that support their candidacy, and those interests are best measured prior to an election by their campaign contributions. Yet careful
studies of the relation of contributions to legislative voting and activities
indicate that donations have little predictive power, all things considered.[86]
If voters were acting rationally and fully informed, they would not use information about contributions as a proxy for future performance because
the available evidence suggests that donations are not good predictors of
what will happen. Party affiliation, professed ideology, and voting record
are much better predictors of voting and other activities.[87] For that reason, voters already have enough information to predict as well as possible
future performance in office. In this respect, the benefits of mandated disclosure at the margins are entirely illusory.

The case for compulsory disclosure rests on its purported benefits to
society understood legally as vital state interests. Those benefits are generally assumed to be large and uncontestable, thus overwhelming any
minor costs associated with the policy. We have little hard evidence that
such publicity has prevented much corruption or increased voter competence. There is some evidence that such disclosure has modestly increased
a sense of efficacy among voters. Insofar as knowledge matters, we may
conclude that the benefits of mandatory disclosure have been exaggerated. Public discussion of compulsory disclosure has focused myopically
on the putative advantages of the policy. With one exception, the costs of
such publicity have been ignored or assumed to be near zero. Given that
the benefits of the policy have been exaggerated, we might suspect the
costs have been underestimated.[88]

I begin with the costs to the privacy of individuals. *Privacy* has been defined as "the claim of individuals, groups, or institutions to determine for
themselves when, how, and to what extent information about them is com-
municated to others."[89] Giving publicity to donations thus violates privacy
by its nature. The costs of such publicity are paid at first in autonomy
and individual control. If disclosure is required, people lose their ability
to define themselves publicly or to shape "their identity in the world,"
which "is rooted in rights of dignity and autonomy."[90] After disclosure,
the donor may face ostracism because "political contributions label us,
and disclosure displays that label to others without our consent." Mandatory disclosure thus restricts the freedom to form personal relationships
by revealing aspects of a person without the person's permission.[91]

We might be tempted to think that such loss of control imposes few
costs on individuals. After all, donors contribute to a political campaign,
and that fact is merely reported to the public. Strictly speaking, the disclo-

sure does not put the donor in a false light or involve distortion because both of these actions involve falsehoods.[92] Yet how many of us would be indifferent if everything that were true of us were revealed to the public? Moreover, the disclosure of contributions, even if strictly factual, does show donors in a false light and present them to the public inaccurately. Mandatory disclosure is not a neutral act. We do not compel citizens to reveal their writings and speeches about candidates and campaigns, largely because such political activities are assumed to be valuable in a democracy. We do compel citizens to disclose their campaign donations, largely because such contributions are thought to be tainted or to be threats to the integrity of democracy. That presumption is strengthened by the context in which the disclosed information appears. That context shapes the expectations of those who receive the information about contributions. For two generations in the United States proponents of reform have claimed that money corrupts democracy and gives contributors undue influence. This context of abuse labels contributors, especially if they give the maximum, as malefactors. No doubt many people find these costs bearable and contribute anyway. That toleration of such costs does not mean they do not exist or that participation in politics would not be higher absent mandatory disclosure.

The requirement also impinges on more traditional political rights. The Supreme Court acknowledged that "compelled disclosure, in itself, can seriously infringe on privacy of association and belief guaranteed by the First Amendment."[93] In 1958, the Supreme Court prevented the state of Alabama from forcing the National Association for the Advancement of Colored People to divulge its membership list; the Court concluded that such information would endanger the rights of NAACP members.[94] Its decision in *Buckley v. Valeo* also recognized that compulsory disclosure of contributors' names could "subject them to threats, harassment, or reprisals from either Government officials or private parties."[95] The courts later used this standard to exempt the Socialist Workers Party and the American Communist Party from compulsory disclosure.[96]

The fame of the NAACP case may bias our thinking toward too high a standard for exemptions from disclosure, thereby increasing the costs of the policy. In the case involving the Communist Party, the United States Court of Appeals for the Second Circuit elaborated on the *Buckley* standard: "A minority party striving to avoid FECA's disclosure provisions does not carry a burden of demonstrating that harassment will certainly follow compelled disclosure of contributors' names. Indeed, when First

Amendment rights are at stake and the specter of significant chill exists, courts have never required such a heavy burden to be carried because 'First Amendment freedoms need breathing space to survive.'"[97] After all, disclosure may threaten freedom of association in less extreme ways.[98] Does it typically chill political activity? Is that chill significant?

Compulsory disclosure has in fact discouraged free speech and political participation. It achieves that end without posing anything like the dangers faced by NAACP members in Alabama in the 1950s. It may subtly and systematically suppress electoral competition. In a society where the state taxes and regulates most economic activity, incumbents are capable of harming (or benefiting) most individuals and organizations that might wish to participate in elections. Comprehensive mandatory disclosure indicates to elected officials which citizens have opposed their reelection and opens contributors to the possibility of retribution. Moreover, disclosure increases the risks of political participation. A contributor wishing to fund the opponent of an incumbent official may avoid the risks of publicity by not making a contribution. We might expect that few citizens would be brave enough to fund a challenger unless the challenger stood a good chance of winning. Of course, this is not likely unless he or she can raise enough money to overcome the previous spending by an incumbent. Disclosure, along with other factors, tends to nip challenges to incumbents in the bud.

Participants in elections also testify to the chilling effects of disclosure. Once donations are made public, those who oppose certain contributions will cast aspersions on the motives of the donor to prevent future contributions by that donor or others. For example, in 2003, Republican attacks on a large donation by George Soros discouraged several other contributions to Democratic 527 groups.[99] Perhaps the strongest testimony that disclosure inhibits political participation comes from McCain himself. During the debate over McCain-Feingold, McCain gave enhanced disclosure as a reason why his senate colleagues should support the bill. Such publicity, he noted, would reduce the number of ads paid for by soft money, which were often critical of incumbents: "If you demand full disclosure for those that pay for those ads, you're going to see a lot less of [such advertising]."[100] If we take McCain seriously—as we should—disclosure effectively abridges freedom of speech and association.

The chilling effect will fall most heavily on those inclined to associate with unpopular or unconventional causes or on marginalized individuals who have the most to lose from public disapproval of their views.[101] Indeed, those who adapt best to the costs of disclosure are likely to be those most often engaged in politics. Their political views, after all, are less likely to be a secret. Those who participate less often are more likely to be deterred by the prospect of publicity. Like many campaign finance restrictions, compulsory disclosure introduces a bias favoring the political status quo and against new players in the political game.

MANDATORY ANONYMITY. Egalitarians liken campaign spending to voting, an assumption that suggests that inequality in campaign finance is similar to stuffing the ballot box. Voting is now done in secret.[102] Law professors Bruce Ackerman and Ian Ayres have proposed a scheme that would extend the anonymity of voting to the act of donating to campaigns. They would require that all donations be made secretly through what they call "the donation booth." They argue that mandatory anonymity would resolve the hoary conflict between free speech and the prevention of corruption and break the putative link between donors and politicians; even if an elected official wanted to deliver favors in return for a contribution, he would not know whom to reward. Ackerman and Ayres's system would also set extremely high contribution limits, thereby allowing almost all individuals to contribute whatever sums they wish to campaigns.[103] The authors thus propose that citizens who wish to contribute to campaigns must do so via the donation booth (thus increasing coercion); those anonymous donations, however, will be less limited than under current law (thus increasing freedom). But Ackerman and Ayres permit donors (and everyone else) to say what they want about their donations. In fact, they are counting on such speech, true and false, to mislead and confuse elected officials about the sources of their campaign cash.[104]

The right to a secret ballot is an individual right instituted to prevent coercion of citizens. They may waive the right if they wish. Mandatory anonymity is not an individual right at all.[105] It is a condition imposed on the political system by the government. The authors recommend that the government impose mandatory anonymity to prevent corruption and to constrain the influence of "corporate America." This scheme does not seek to protect contributors from extortion (or other kinds of coercion) by politicians or employers; it is not an individual right designed to protect vital interests of a citizen. Similarly, the freedom of speech that it protects—the freedom to say that one has donated to a candidate—is a means to the end of preventing corruption by disrupting communication between donors and elected officials. If citizens use that freedom to reliably reveal their donations to elected officials, such speech will preclude the law from reaching its anticorruption goal. These reliable claims about the source of donations will constitute a loophole that will have to be closed by administrative fiat or by legislation. Ackerman and Ayres might argue that no one will be able to establish such reliable claims and thus freedom of speech will not run counter to the goals of their program. But that is unlikely. As the political scientist Kenneth Mayer notes, "Even under an anonymous system, committed donors will still have incentives to be honest with candidates, and non-donors will face compelling disincentives against misrepresentation. In a political environment where ongoing relationships are vital to both candidates and interest groups, the desire to be seen as credible will, over the long term, provide a powerful reason for interest groups to tell the truth."[106]

In the end, a strengthened FEC overseeing mandatory anonymity would be faced with a choice between allowing free and credible speech about donations and trying to suppress such claims by donors. The entire history of campaign finance regulation indicates that the FEC would choose the path of suppression.

VOLUNTARY DISCLOSURE AND VOLUNTARY ANONYMITY.   Most Americans, including many political professionals, find it difficult to imagine elections free of contribution limits and mandatory disclosure of donations. Yet such requirements have been enacted relatively recently in history. Although such disclosure has been a matter of law for almost a century, we have had systematic disclosure in fact only since the early 1970s.[107] Voluntary alternatives to mandatory disclosure would perhaps encompass a continuum from voluntary anonymity to voluntary disclosure. Having heard claims about the corrupt motives of donors for decades, we might assume that no contributions would be made public without coercion. It is not likely that mandatory disclosure may reveal too much information in light of the costs and benefits. A voluntary system might reveal the right amount of information and perhaps focus attention on questionable contributions.

Imagine that the law did not require disclosure. Once a contribution is made, the donor and the recipient will jointly possess information about that contribution (the donor's name, the amount, and so on). Assume that a significant number of voters wish to have information about the contributors to a recipient (a candidate for office). This demand for information will be expressed in at least two ways. The media, eager for an audience, will ask the candidate for such information, or a candidate opposing the recipient senses an opening and publicly discloses the names of her contributors. She challenges the recipient to do the same. Responding to the media or the challenger, the recipient then may either disclose or not disclose the identities of his contributors. To keep contributors happy, recipients will have reason to enter into agreements with donors about the use of donation information that they jointly possess. The disposition of the information about the donation would be a matter of contract between donor and candidate.

Now consider the political incentives. If a candidate discloses the names of contributors, the public will have as much information as it does now without mandatory disclosure. If the candidate does not disclose contributions or only discloses some of them, the public will also know that. This information and what the voter makes of it will become part of the decision to vote for or against the candidate. Voluntary disclosure would also reveal exactly how much voters care about campaign finance information. If a recipient did not disclose gifts and paid no electoral price, it may show that voters do not care much about who supports whom.[108] That indifference would be important information. If voters do not care much about such knowledge, why should citizens be forced to reveal it?

Next consider commercial motivations. If donors and recipients possess the information about the contribution, others would be free to try to induce them to disclose it for reasons other than political gain. For example, the news media—indirect consumers of contribution information—could pay the donors and recipients for it.[109] If the media are not willing to pay for the information, we might conclude that it is not worth much to them (or to their audience). Similarly, nonprofit organizations or foundations concerned about the influence of donations could pay the donors and recipients for the information. If they are not willing to do so, we might again wonder how much value the information really has.

Paying for contribution information might distinguish donors who otherwise refuse to disclose gifts because of attendant privacy costs from those who do not disclose gifts because of corrupt motives. The cost of purchasing the information from those concerned about privacy loss would presumably be much smaller than the costs related to obtaining the data from people who are trying to corrupt government (given the potential gains from such corruption). Information customers could set the price high enough to compensate donors for their loss of privacy but not so high as to buy off those seeking to corrupt government. As a result, the public would have data from those who disclosed them for reasons of principle, of politics, and of commerce. The contributions of the remaining donors would remain undisclosed.[110] The existence of undisclosed donations could itself be made public, however, and voters would be free to draw their own conclusions about the candidate who receives such contributions.

A system of voluntary disclosure and anonymity would work if the public wanted disclosure enough to motivate candidates and parties to make donations public despite the costs associated with doing so. If sufficient demand for disclosure exists, candidates will supply the information desired. If voters do not, in fact, care much about such information, it will not be supplied. The absence of such information might be thought to be a major disaster for democracy. But it may be nothing more than an accurate assessment of the value of disclosed contribution data.

For the time being, Madisonians face the brute political reality that mandatory disclosure will inevitably accompany any realistic liberalization of campaign finance regulation. The costs to be paid, however, need not be as high as they are now. Some might object that rights should not be subject to calculations of costs and benefits. In fact, traditional natural rights analysis took into account both rights and consequences.[111] If the perfect need not preclude the good, mandatory disclosure may be a part of a liberalized campaign finance regime.

The disclosure requirement means the government decides who must reveal the names of their contributors. Currently the law requires disclosure of the identity of everyone who gives more than $200 in total to a campaign within a calendar year.[112] It also requires disclosure of the names of contributors who pay for electoral communications that refer to a candidate for federal office within sixty days of a general election and in total cost more than $10,000 in a calendar year.[113] Taken together, these rules mean that information about the supporters of all significant speech during an election must be disclosed to the federal government.

The ambit of mandated disclosure does not fit its stated purposes of informing the public and preventing corruption. A contributor whose views might inform other voters is likely to give far more than $200, particularly in the absence of contribution limits. It is also absurd to think a $200 contribution would influence a member of Congress. As William McGeveran notes,

> Most donors are small fry. Their negligible influence poses little danger of corruption, however defined. As one of the lawyers for the *Buckley* plaintiffs wrote a few years before the decision, "it is flatly unbelievable that a contribution of [$100] could have an undesirable impact." *Buckley* itself acknowledged that many small contributions "are too low even to attract the attention of the can-

didate, much less have a corrupting influence." Rather than serving as one side
of a corrupt trade or influencing the candidate excessively, the typical small
contribution earns only a thank-you card and subsequent appeals for more
money.[114]

Because we have strong evidence that donations that do not exceed
current limits do not on the whole influence congressional deliberations,
in a world without contribution limits a reformed disclosure regime might
begin at the earlier ceilings: individuals who gave more than $1,000 to a
candidate would have to make their contributions public, and so on for
other categories of donors.[115] In such a world, pre-2002 limits should become the floors for disclosure at various levels of giving.

Political organizations also must disclose contributions. Before
McCain-Feingold became law, most experts and politicians assumed that
federal election law applied to support for advertising that clearly advocated the election or defeat of a candidate for federal office. All other
speech was free of federal restrictions. McCain-Feingold applied federal
law (including disclosure requirements) to ads that mention "a clearly
identified candidate for Federal office" within sixty days of a general election or thirty days of a primary.[116]

A liberalizing agenda for campaign finance would reduce the ambit of
disclosure for electioneering to the minimum necessary to serve an anticorruption rationale.[117] Currently, contributors to an "electioneering communication" must disclose their gifts if they spend more than $10,000 and
the ads refer to a federal candidate. In 1998, the sum of $10,000 composed
less than one-tenth of one percent of all independent expenditures in congressional races.[118] Such a small portion of overall independent spending
hardly represents a threat to the integrity of representation. If the disclosure threshold were raised to one percent of independent expenditures,
we might have an acceptable tradeoff for the near future between political
reality and a liberalizing agenda. Who should disclose their spending? Ads
that expressly advocate the election or defeat of a candidate for federal office would have to disclose the names of their contributors assuming that
they met the minimum standard for expenditures. Speech that does not
engage in express advocacy would not involve disclosure of anything.

The Federal Election Commission

The Federal Election Commission has a plethora of powers related to
the campaign finance laws including the power to hold hearings and is-

sue advisory opinions.[119] It also receives and records campaign finance disclosures by federal candidates. Partisans of additional restrictions on campaign finance wish to eliminate the FEC in favor of a kind of FBI of campaign finance.[120] Given the FBI's record on civil liberties, this proposal should concern Americans who care about a free and open political system.[121]

Under a liberalized campaign finance regime, the FEC would be largely replaced by an agency that collects and makes public disclosed information about the financing of federal campaigns for office. (The agency might do this both for a system of mandatory disclosure and for a successor system of voluntary disclosure.) Once the FEC as we now know it ceased to exist, it would become no more of a threat to political liberty than a large library. The successor agency could be called the Election Information Division (EID) in the Public Services Collections of the Library of Congress.[122] The head of the EID would report directly to the Office of the Associate Librarian for Library Services. Since a reformed FEC would only be in the business of managing and disseminating information, it would make sense for the new agency to be run by information professionals. Perhaps most, if not all, new employees of the EID would have advanced degrees in library science. The information collected by the EID (along with historical data) would move to the Internet.

Particular attention should be given to eliminating the office of the general counsel at the FEC. Most agencies in Washington are captured by the interests they purport to regulate. The Department of Education advances the special interests of the teachers' unions, the Department of Commerce provides corporate welfare, and so on. As I mentioned in my discussion of the 1974 law, the FEC is a creature of Congress. The commission has long been an agent of Congress under conditions of partisan competition. The office of the general counsel, however, has often represented the ideals and interests of the partisans of additional restrictions on freedom of speech and political activity (the so-called reform community). It was the general counsel of the FEC who proposed widening the ambit of McCain-Feingold to small political organizations that might be involved in electioneering in minor ways; the effect of such regulations would be to eliminate these organizations and their political activity.[123] Here as elsewhere in the government, there is a revolving door, in this case between the general counsel's office and the interest groups that petition the agency.[124] By eliminating this position, Congress could reduce the baneful influence of special interests on constitutional rights and liberties.

Conclusion

Campaign finance laws are political realities informed in part by political ideals. The realities are much less inspiring than the ideals. Politicians who are threatened by electoral defeat or some other loss of political power fashion campaign finance laws to complicate challenges to their power. Beneath all the pious talk about equality, fairness, and the integrity of the process lies this unpleasant truth: those who write campaign finance laws seek primarily to repress and harass those who would challenge their power. Sometimes they do it to preserve the power of their party and almost always they do it to sustain the power of incumbents.

Yet the struggle over campaign finance is more than a battle to preserve political power. It is also a struggle of ideals and political visions, a conflict more than a century old that defines and divides Americans. The effects of the ideals can sometimes be seen through the smoke of political battle. The Democrats are the bearers of the Progressive vision. They tend to support restrictions on campaign finance even when their leaders are uncertain of the consequences of such laws. But in the Progressive view money, especially in the form large campaign contributions, corrupts politics, the struggle to define and impose the common good. So soft money had to go even if the Democrats paid a price at the polls. The Madisonian vision has strongly influenced the Republicans. No doubt they found the ideas of liberty and limited government attractive during their long sojourn in the wilderness of political impotence; being free of regulation is appealing if you are the target of the proposed restrictions. Over time, however, the ideals have taken on a life of their own, and the Republicans, like the Democrats, ended up professing and acting on ideals that harm their interests, at least in the short term. In early 2004, two Republican members of the Federal Election Commission who had long defended deregulation of campaigns voted to delay regulations on fundraising by 527 groups, votes that certainly helped the Democratic effort to defeat a sitting Republican president.[125] In these ways, ideals matter to campaign finance struggles.[126]

In the struggle over political visions in campaign finance, the Progressives seem to have the upper hand. Just as in the *Carolene Products* decision the Court announced that the federal government had plenary power over the economy, in *McConnell* the Court all but said that Congress has complete control over funding of the political process. Public opinion polls continue to show widespread general support for restricting political speech. Those who profess the Progressive vision remain well-funded and politically powerful. They may yet eliminate all rights to spend money on politics and elections.

Yet history also offers hope to those who espouse the Madisonian vision. In 1941, when the decision in *Carolene Products* came down, informed citizens believed that government should and could control the economy to achieve the general welfare and "the great society." In the 1970s that belief crested and began to decline, a slow fading that has engulfed both the developed and developing worlds in the past thirty years. The idea that rulers could be trusted to collectively control political activity to achieve the common good never had as much public or intellectual support as did economic collectivism. It is possible that the global move toward individual liberty and away from political collectivism may yet reach American politics.

What about those who hold to the Progressive vision of politics? Will they not be the chief losers in the liberalization of spending on politics? Certainly the logic of Progressivism suggests reasons for concern for its adherents. As we have seen, Progressives often believe that campaign finance laws will lead to egalitarian policy outcomes. If restrictions were removed, they would be apt to believe that the rich would rule, thereby fostering increasing inequality in wealth. To preclude that outcome, Progressives of late have spoken in favor of repression of free speech as a means to enrich public debates. We have also seen that Progressives have at times opposed government regulation of speech in pursuit of interests and ideals. We have reason to hope and to believe that the liberal aspects of Progressivism, so long in abeyance, will be revived in coming years.

The progeny of Progressivism need not fear the political results of liberalization. The Democratic Party dominated American politics before the era of restrictions on campaign finance. The soft money era and the 2004 presidential election suggest that many wealthy Democrats are willing to put their money behind their beliefs. Indeed, after liberalization American politics may end up looking a lot like it did in the 1990s, an era of partial deregulation of contributions to the political parties. That period was closely fought and uncertain, a time of waiting for both Progressives and conservatives. It was also a time when congressional Democrats raised huge amounts of soft money and moved distinctly to the left.

Liberalization of campaign finance might even advance the Progressive cause in an unexpected way. Progressives often believe that private money in politics has caused their decline in American politics in the past two generations. Fix the process, and Progressivism will return to power. Once deprived of that argument, Progressives will have to make the case for the policy outcomes they think best for the nation. They will also have to do the hard work of facing their past failures and preparing for future electoral successes.

Yet it is interest and not ideals that may ultimately convince Progressives to support liberalizing campaign finance laws. Such laws are weapons in political struggle. To use those weapons, a party or individuals must have control of the legislature. At this writing Progressives do not have control of Congress and may not have it for some time. They and their political activities are likely to be the objects rather than the subjects of campaign finance restrictions. Their older faith in the value of government action to restrict money in politics will continually run up against this hard reality. Progressives will sooner or later realize that their faith in reform is an ideological atavism.

For the time being, the future of campaign finance law lies with the Republican majority in Congress. Until 1994, Republican thinking about campaign finance reconciled partisan interests with ideological commitment. Republicans were correct in thinking that restrictions on campaign finance were actually restrictions on their ambition. Like the Democrats, they did well by doing good: opposition to reform advanced their partisan interest in gaining a congressional majority. But the GOP has been in the majority for a decade now, and McCain-Feingold may have sustained its control by protecting the most vulnerable of its members in Congress. The Republican experience will thus be a natural experiment that answers the question of whether ideals can trump interests in partisan political struggle.

We cannot know the future of campaign finance struggles, but we do know the history of related restrictions and regulation. Campaign finance reform is a delusion. It purports to reform the world for the better but in reality affirms the status quo for better or worse. Many Progressives say they wish to clean up the political process by restricting the influence of private money. Yet they also expect such procedural reforms to bring about their favored policy outcomes, especially an egalitarian distribution of wealth. But those Progressives are wrong in thinking that the morass of restrictions imposed on money in politics will bring about a realization of their egalitarian hopes insofar as such aspirations require political change. Restrictions on campaign finance are about preventing political change. Indeed, they could hardly be otherwise because the restrictions are written by people who have the most to lose from unrestricted fundraising during elections. Campaign finance reform, in practice if not in theory, will always be conservative in the narrow sense of affirming the existing order. That affirmation, however, has no necessary relation to progress, equality, freedom, or virtue, the final ends that now inform our politics. It sustains whoever has power to achieve their chosen ends. Progressives do not now have power. Indeed, we seem to be living in a post-Progressive America. In that world, Progressives may yet awaken from the dream of reform to live in a Madisonian reality that may advance both their interests and their ideals. They may find, in short, that the words "Congress shall make no law . . . abridging freedom of speech" bespeak both a constitutional requirement and our common good.

Notes

Introduction

1. I refer to the law throughout this book as McCain-Feingold; this has remained the most common term for it. For details of the roll-call vote, see "Campaign Finance Overhaul/Passage. (in Sen.) HR 2356." http://library.cqpress.com/congress/wr20021130-0000000037 (accessed November 29, 2005). Originally published in *CQ Weekly 2002,* vol. 60 (Washington, DC: Congressional Quarterly, 2002).

2. Karen Foerstel, "As Groups File Lawsuits, Bush Spurns Signing Ceremony for 'Flawed' Fundraising Law," *CQ Weekly,* March 30, 2002, 868.

3. For example, in late 2004, 44 percent of respondents to a Pew poll said that "books that contain dangerous ideas should be banned from public school libraries." See Pew Research Center, *Mapping the Political Landscape 2005* (Washington, DC: Pew Research Center, 2005), 88. As for free speech and campaign finance, William Mayer notes that "the public strongly supports limits—of just about any kind—on campaign contributions and spending." See William Mayer, "Public Attitudes on Campaign Finance," in *A User's Guide to Campaign Finance Reform,* ed. Gerald C. Lubenow (Lanham, MD: Rowman and Littlefield, 2001), 53–59.

4. A more extended argument connecting money and speech may be found in chapter 1.

5. See the analysis of survey data in J. Tobin Grant and Thomas J. Rudolph, "Value Conflict, Group Affect, and the Issues of Campaign Finance," *American Journal of Political Science* 47 (July 2003): 453–69.

6. Senator John McCain, 107th Cong., 2nd sess., *Congressional Record* (2002), 148:S2109.

7. Ibid., S2139.

8. Senator Fred Thompson, 107th Cong., 2nd sess., *Congressional Record* (2002), 148:S2110.

9. Senator Thomas Daschle, 107th Cong., 2nd sess., *Congressional Record* (2002), 148:S2110–1.

10. Senator Maria Cantwell, 107th Cong., 2nd sess., *Congressional Record* (2002), 148:S2117.

11. Senator John McCain, 107th Cong., 1st sess., *Congressional Record* (2001), 147:S3116.

12. Senator Jean Carnahan, 107th Cong., 2nd sess., *Congressional Record* (2002), 148:S2100.

13. Senator Thomas Daschle, 107th Cong., 2nd sess., *Congressional Record* (2002), 148:S2111.

14. Senator James Jeffords, 107th Cong., 2nd sess., *Congressional Record* (2002), 148:S2117.

15. Senator John McCain, 107th Cong., 2nd sess., *Congressional Record* (2002), 148:S2138.

16. Senator Jean Carnahan, 107th Cong., 2nd sess., *Congressional Record* (2002), 148:S2100.

17. Senator Paul Wellstone, 107th Cong., 2nd sess., *Congressional Record* (2002), 148:S2097.

18. Senator Barbara Boxer, 107th Cong., 2nd sess., *Congressional Record* (2002), 148:S2101.

19. Senator Olympia Snowe, 107th Cong., 2nd sess., *Congressional Record,* (2002), 148:S2134.

20. Senator Russell Feingold, 107th Cong., 2nd sess., *Congressional Record* (2002), 148:S2102.

21. Senator Fred Thompson, 107th Cong., 2nd sess., *Congressional Record* (2002), 148:S2110.

22. Senator Charles Schumer, 107th Cong., 2nd sess., *Congressional Record* (2002), 148:S2111.

23. Senator John Kerry, 107th Cong., 2nd sess., *Congressional Record* (2002), 148:S2150.

24. Senator Fred Thompson, 107th Cong., 2nd sess., *Congressional Record* (2002), 148:S2110.

25. Senator Thomas Daschle, 107th Cong., 2nd sess., *Congressional Record* (2002), 148:S2111.

26. Senator Susan Collins, 107th Cong., 2nd sess., *Congressional Record* (2002), 148:S2134.

27. Senator John Kerry, 107th Cong., 2nd sess., *Congressional Record* (2002), 148:S2150.

28. Senator Maria Cantwell, 107th Cong., 2nd sess., *Congressional Record* (2002), 148:S2117.

29. Robert Bauer notes that "different members argued at different times that the bill would provide for 'equality' in the political process, help to reduce the total amount of money in the political process, reduce the fundraising demands on federal officials, and limit negative campaigning." See Robert F. Bauer, "When 'The

Pols Make the Calls': *McConnell's* Theory of Judicial Deference in the Twilight of *Buckley,*" *University of Pennsylvania Law Review* 153 (2004): 5, 18.

30. Ibid., 19.

31. I have adapted the idea of visions from Thomas Sowell, *A Conflict of Visions: Ideological Origins of Political Struggles* (New York: Basic Books, 2002). A vision may be defined as "a cluster of ideas describing how the political process works—and how it should work," according to Daniel H. Lowenstein, "The Supreme Court Has No Theory of Politics," in *The U.S. Supreme Court and the Electoral Process,* ed. David K. Ryden (Washington, DC: Georgetown University Press, 2000), 246. The concept of "political frames" is similar. *Framing* is the use of words, images, and presentation style to define and construct a political issue or public controversy; see Grant and Rudolph, "Value Conflict," 454.

32. Lowenstein notes "two opposing models that have been pervasive in American political thought and debate: pluralism and progressivism." See Lowenstein, "Supreme Court," 247. The concepts deployed here differ in one important way from Lowenstein's: he associates progressivism with a concern for the individual and pluralism with a focus on the group. This work does the opposite. After finishing this book, I discovered an essay that offers a similar analysis of the visions behind the campaign finance struggle. See Tiffany R. Jones, "Campaign Finance Reform: The Progressive Reconstruction of Free Speech," in *The Progressive Revolution in Politics and Political Science: Transforming the American Regime,* ed. John Marini and Ken Masugi (Lanham, MD: Rowman and Littlefield, 2005), 321–46.

33. See Richard L. Berke, "Congress Moves on Ethics, but Stalls on Campaign Spending," *New York Times,* October 24, 1989.

34. Grant and Rudolph, "Value Conflict," 465. These authors also found that framing the issue in terms of rights tended to mitigate the political or group concerns of many citizens.

35. Quoted in Thomas B. Edsall, "McCain-Feingold Unmade? New Election Regulator Opposes Campaign Finance Law," *Washington Post,* February 5, 2004.

36. Senator Barbara Boxer, 107th Cong., 2nd sess., *Congressional Record* (2002), 148:S2101.

Chapter One

1. By "Madisonian vision" I do not mean simply the political thinking of James Madison, as opposed to, say, the Jeffersonian vision or the Hamiltonian vision or perhaps a Rawlsian vision. If I could, I would call the current chapter "The Liberal Vision of Politics," but the term *liberal* in ordinary political language has come to mean almost the opposite of the theory I set out in this chapter. Identifying the

theory with James Madison makes sense in several ways. He drafted much of the U.S. Constitution and actually wrote the original version of the Bill of Rights. Although he was not the author of the Constitution in the strict sense, the basic law does strongly reflect his political philosophy and political science. Madison thus embodied the liberal republicanism that informed the U.S. Constitution, though my interpretation perhaps downplays the more populist Jeffersonian element in that mixture. See Michael P. Zuckert, *The Natural Rights Republic: Studies in the Foundation of the American Political Tradition* (Notre Dame, IN: University of Notre Dame Press, 1996), 240.

2. Michael P. Zuckert, *Natural Rights and the New Republicanism* (Princeton: Princeton University Press, 1998), 70. For the influence of Locke's natural rights theory on the founders, see ibid., 5, and Steven M. Dworetz, *The Unvarnished Doctrine: Locke, Liberalism, and the American Revolution* (Durham, NC: Duke University Press, 1994).

3. Aristotle, *The Politics*, sec. 1253 in Aristotle, *The Politics and the Constitution of Athens*, ed. Stephen Everson (New York: Cambridge University Press, 1996), 13.

4. See Galileo Galilei, *Dialogue Concerning the Two Chief World Systems: Ptolemaic and Copernican,* trans. Stillman Drake, 2nd rev. ed. (Berkeley: University of California Press, 1967).

5. The numbers of deaths from fighting and from disease were similar to those of World War I and significantly greater than those of World War II. See Peter Gaunt, *The English Civil Wars, 1642–1651* (London: Osprey, 2003), 8.

6. See Thomas Hobbes, *Leviathan,* ed. J. A. Gaskin (New York: Oxford University Press, 1998), 114–15.

7. The individual could disobey commands "to kill, wound, or maim himself; or not to resist those that assault him; or to abstain from the use of food, air, medicine, or any other things without which he cannot live." See ibid., 144.

8. The Declaration of Independence says that humans are endowed by their Creator with certain unalienable rights. The initial author of the declaration, Thomas Jefferson, did not include the reference to the deity. He adapted the language from a draft of the Virginia Declaration of Rights, written by George Mason. The Virginia document refers to "inherent natural rights" without reference to a deity. See Pauline Maier, *American Scripture: Making the Declaration of Independence* (New York: Vintage, 1998), 165.

9. Randy E. Barnett, *The Structure of Liberty: Justice and the Rule of Law* (New York: Oxford University Press, 1998), 12.

10. Ibid., 14.

11. Alan Gibson notes "the Founders' essentially deontological understanding of the purposes of government." See Alan Gibson, "Ancients, Moderns and Americans: The Republicanism-Liberalism Debate Revisited," *History of Political Thought* 21 (Summer 2000): 295. A deontological theory of government would say its aims are intrinsic (to protect rights) rather than teleological (to add to national

welfare) or perfectionist (to help citizens act virtuously). See Gerald Gaus, "What Is Deontology? Part One: Orthodox Views," *Journal of Value Inquiry* 35 (2001): 2.

12. The extent of Locke's influence has been much disputed. For a useful brief survey, see Zuckert, *Natural Rights Republic,* 202–10, and the works mentioned therein.

13. See Leonard W. Levy, *Origins of the Bill of Rights* (New Haven: Yale University Press, 1999), 24.

14. James Madison, *Writings,* ed. Jack Rakove (New York: Library of America, 1999), 441.

15. James Madison in *The Federalist,* ed. Jacob E. Cooke (Middletown, CT: Wesleyan University Press, 1961), 349. All subsequent references to this work are to this edition.

16. For the development of Locke's thinking regarding toleration, see Philip Abrams, introduction to John Locke, *Two Tracts on Government* (New York: Cambridge University Press, 1967), 98–107.

17. For a useful selection of these letters, see David L. Jacobson, ed., *The English Libertarian Heritage: From the Writings of John Trenchard and Thomas Gordon in The Independent Whig and Cato's Letters* (Indianapolis: Bobbs-Merrill, 1965).

18. Some historians have argued that Cato's Letters were not Lockean. That claim seems incorrect. See Ronald Hamowy, "Cato's Letters, John Locke, and the Republican Paradigm," *History of Political Thought* 11 (1990): 273–94. For Cato's skepticism about government see Thomas Pangle, "The Federalist Papers' Vision of Civic Health and the Tradition out of Which That Tradition Emerges," *Western Political Quarterly* 39 (December 1986): 579.

19. For the influence of Cato's Letters on the American colonists, see Hamowy, "Cato's Letters," 290, and the references cited in n. 66. Clinton Rossiter writes that the series Cato's Letters "was the most popular, quotable, esteemed source of political ideas in the colonial period." Clinton Rossiter, *Seedtime of the Republic* (New York: Harcourt, 1953), 299. See also Leonard W. Levy, introduction to Leonard W. Levy, ed., *Freedom of the Press from Zenger to Jefferson: Early American Libertarian Theories* (Indianapolis: Bobbs-Merrill, 1966), xxiii. Gary L. McDowell remarks that "the influence of John Trenchard and Thomas Gordon on political thinking in colonial Anglo-America is one of the few matters on which there is near universal agreement." See Gary L. McDowell, "The Language of Law and the Foundations of American Constitutionalism," *William & Mary Quarterly* 55 (July 1998): 375. Cato's Letters were well-known to newspaper readers in the American colonies. See Gary Huxford, "The English Libertarian Tradition in the Colonial Newspaper," *Journalism Quarterly* 45 (1968): 677–86.

20. Jacobson, *English Libertarian Heritage,* 38.

21. Hamowy, "Cato's Letters," 290.

22. James Madison outlined this argument when he introduced the Bill of Rights in Congress. See Madison, *Writings,* 447, and Levy, *Bill of Rights,* 16, 20–21.

Levy adds, "The overwhelming majority of the [Constitutional] Convention believed, as Roger Sherman of Connecticut succinctly declared, that bill of rights 'is unnecessary'" (19).

23. Levy, *Bill of Rights,* 30.

24. Cincinnatus to James Wilson, November 8, 1787, in Herbert J. Storing, ed., *The Complete Anti-Federalist* (Chicago: University of Chicago Press, 1981), 6:11–12 (emphasis in original).

25. Madison, *Writings,* 439. Madison's opposition to a Bill of Rights had damaged his political position in Virginia. See Levy, *Bill of Rights,* 32.

26. Madison, *Writings,* 442.

27. According to Owen Fiss, "Classical liberalism presupposes a sharp dichotomy between state and citizen. It teaches us to be wary of the state and equates liberty with limited government. The Free Speech Tradition builds on this view of the world when it reduces free speech to autonomy and defines autonomy to mean the absence of government interference." Owen Fiss, "Free Speech and Social Structure," *Iowa Law Review* 71 (1986): 1405, 1413–14.

28. Barnett, *Structure of Liberty,* 17.

29. Madison, *Federalist,* 60.

30. Friedrich A. Hayek, *The Constitution of Liberty* (Chicago: University of Chicago Press, 1960), 29–30.

31. Barnett, *Structure of Liberty,* 31.

32. Ibid., 34–35.

33. Ibid., 137.

34. Madison, *Federalist,* 59.

35. James Madison, speech of August 10, 1787, during the debates in the Federal Convention of 1787, quoted in Christopher B. Mann, "'A Personal Interest Distinct from That of Their Constituents': Congressional Alignments and the Development of Campaign Finance Regulation" (paper presented at the annual meeting of the American Political Science Association, Washington, DC, September 1–4, 2005), 1.

36. Madison, *Federalist,* 60.

37. See Drew R. McCoy, *The Elusive Republic: Political Economy in Jeffersonian America* (New York: Norton, 1980), 16. For example, Zabdiel Adams, a first cousin of John Adams, believed liberty depended on virtue, as shown by the Spartan example. See Zabdiel Adams, "An Election Sermon Boston, 1782," in *American Political Writing During the Founding Era 1760–1805,* ed. Charles S. Hyneman and Donald S. Lutz (Indianapolis: Liberty Fund, 1983), 1:557.

38. Darren Staloff, *Hamilton, Adams, Jefferson: The Politics of Enlightenment and the American Founding* (New York: Hill and Wang, 2005), 82.

39. McCoy, *Elusive Republic,* chap. 3. See also Noah Webster's remark that the self-denial of the Spartans constituted "a rigor of despotism which no free nation would now bear." Webster, "An Oration on the Anniversary of the Declaration of

Independence, New Haven 1802," in *American Political Writing*, 1226. Indeed, as McCoy notes, the founding generation might have looked back to David Hume, for whom "Sparta stood as a warning to modern societies, not as a model, for it demonstrated that men could not be governed by a disinterested passion for the public good without an unacceptably tyrannical enforcement of perfect equality and austerity" (*Elusive Republic*, 29).

40. Madison, *Federalist*, 58.

41. He may have been influenced in this regard by David Hume, who wrote that "every man ought to be supposed a knave, and to have no other end, in all his actions, than private interest." Quoted in Staloff, *Hamilton, Adams, Jefferson*, 83.

42. Madison, *Federalist*, 62.

43. Ibid., 63. See Bradley A. Smith, "Hamilton at Wits End: The Lost Discipline of the Spending Clause vs. the False Discipline of Campaign Finance Reform," *Chapman Law Review* 4 (Spring 2001): 117, 138.

44. Madison, *Federalist*, 58.

45. Ibid., 57–59.

46. One scholar has noted procedural theories of democracy in James Madison, Robert Dahl, Joseph Schumpeter, and Anthony Downs. See Bruce E. Cain, "Moralism and Realism in Campaign Finance Reform," *University of Chicago Legal Forum* 1995:111, 122.

47. Madison's reliance on Adam Smith and the idea of competition is set out in David Prindle, "The Invisible Hand of James Madison," *Constitutional Political Economy* 15 (2004): 223–37.

48. The endogenous quality of a spontaneous order is noted in Friedrich A. Hayek, *Law, Legislation and Liberty*, vol. 1, *Rules and Order* (Chicago: University of Chicago Press, 1973), 36.

49. NAACP v. Alabama, 357 U.S. 449, 460 (1958).

50. Roberts v. United States Jaycees, 468 U.S. 609, 622 (1984).

51. Madison, *Federalist*, 60.

52. See, e.g., Mancur Olson, *The Logic of Collective Action* (Cambridge: Harvard University Press, 1964).

53. See Barnett, *Structure of Liberty*, 242–43, and the reference to Locke therein.

54. Madison, *Writings*, 446.

55. Madison, *Federalist*, 349.

56. Jacobson, *English Libertarian Heritage*, 42.

57. Quoted in Marvin Meyers, ed., *The Mind of the Founder: Sources of the Political Thought of James Madison* (Hanover, NH: University Presses of New England, 1981), 340–42.

58. Levy, *Bill of Rights*, 129–30.

59. Meyers, *Mind of the Founder*, 341.

60. Robert Rutland, *James Madison: The Founding Father* (New York: Macmillan, 1987), 11.

61. Keith Whittington, *Constitutional Construction: Divided Powers and Constitutional Meaning* (Cambridge: Harvard University Press, 1999), chap. 1.

62. Buckley v. Valeo, 424 U.S. 1, 19 (1976).

63. The reader may confirm this claim by searching *Buckley v. Valeo.* The complete text of the decision may be obtained at http://laws.findlaw.com/us/424/1.html. Later, a Supreme Court justice did say that money was property and not speech. See Nixon v. Shrink Missouri Gov't PAC, 528 U.S. 377, 398 (2000) (Stevens, J., concurring). But Justice Stevens did not develop that comment, and it remained "more epigram than program." See Robert F. Bauer, "Judicial Deference to the Legislature in Campaign Finance Regulation: Justice Breyer's Concept of 'Active Liberty.'" http://moresoftmoneyhardlaw.com (accessed November 29, 2004).

64. Stephen Breyer, "Madison Lecture: Our Democratic Government," *New York University Law Review* 77 (2002): 245, 252.

65. Buckley v. Valeo, 25.

66. Ibid., 3, 26–27.

67. Ibid., 21.

68. This was the task faced by the National Association for the Advancement of Colored People in 2000. See Katharine Q. Seelye, "Both Parties Break Records for Donations at This Stage," *New York Times,* October 14, 2000.

69. Thomas Gais, *Improper Influence: Campaign Finance Law, Political Interest Groups, and the Problem of Equality* (Ann Arbor: University of Michigan Press, 1996), chap. 6.

70. As Gais shows, campaign finance law pushes the speech of grassroots groups into the sphere of petitioning the government for redress of grievances, otherwise known as lobbying. See ibid., 103ff.

71. The FEC had earlier taken a dim view of pure issue advocacy based on its interpretation of the 1974 Federal Election Campaign Act. See FEC v. Central Long Island Tax Reform Immediately Committee, 616 F.2d 45 (2d Cir. 1980).

72. B. Holly Schadler to the Federal Election Commission, February 4, 2004, available online from the FEC at http://www.fec.gov.aos/2003/aor2003-37com4.pdf. It begins on p. 55 of this file. The letter comments on Draft Advisory Opinion 2003-37 of the Federal Election Commission.

73. Senator John McCain, 107th Cong., 1st sess., *Congressional Record* (2001), 147:S3116.

74. Senator Maria Cantwell, 107th Cong., 2nd sess., *Congressional Record* (2002), 148:S2117 (emphasis added).

75. Senator Barbara Boxer, 105th Cong., 1st sess., *Congressional Record* (1997), 143:S10208.

76. See McConnell v. FEC, 540 U.S. 93, 137 (2003).

77. Joel Gora, "No Law Abridging," *Harvard Journal of Law and Public Policy* 24 (2001): 841, 858. On Mott's contribution, see James L. Buckley, "Why I Sued in 1974," *Wall Street Journal,* October 11, 1999.

78. "Ninetieth Congress (January 3, 1967, to January 3, 1969)," http://library.

cqpress.com/congress/lmkleg-121-6508-375479 (accessed November 29, 2005). Originally published in Stephen W. Stathis, *Landmark Legislation, 1774–2002* (Washington, DC: CQ Press, 2003). Later we shall see that Congress sought to suppress campaigns such as McCarthy's by limiting spending on television.

79. Donald Wittman, "Why Democracies Produce Efficient Results," *Journal of Political Economy* 97 (1989): 1400–1401.

80. See John H. Alrich, "When Is It Rational to Vote?" in *Perspectives on Public Choice: A Handbook,* ed. Dennis C. Mueller (New York: Cambridge University Press, 1997), 377–78.

81. Arthur Lupia, "Shortcuts versus Encyclopedias: Information and Voting Behavior in California Insurance Reform Elections," *American Political Science Review* 88 (1994): 63–76.

82. We need not consider at this point whether information about contributions is disclosed voluntarily or by government mandate. I return to this question in chapter 9.

83. Dhammika Dharmapala and Filip Palda, "Are Campaign Contributions a Form of Speech? Evidence from Recent US House Elections," *Public Choice* 112 (2002): 89–91.

84. Ibid., 95ff.

85. Robert F. Bauer, "*McConnell,* Parties, and the Decline of the Right of Association," *Election Law Journal* 3 (2004): 199, 200.

Chapter Two

1. Eldon J. Eisenach, *The Lost Promise of Progressivism* (Lawrence: University Press of Kansas, 1994), 2.

2. On the continuing influence of Progressive ideas today, see ibid., 205–14; the essays in Stanley B. Greenberg and Theda Skocpol, eds., *The New Majority: Toward a Popular Progressive Politics* (New Haven: Yale University Press, 1997); and Michael J. Sandel, *Democracy's Discontent: America in Search of a Public Philosophy* (Cambridge: Harvard University Press, 1998). The historian Wilfred M. McClay has written of Herbert Croly's book *The Promise of American Life*: "Its fundamental ideas still flow through our national political discourse, permeating the agendas and rhetoric of both political parties." See Wilfred M. McClay, "Croly's Progressive America," *Public Interest* 137 (Fall 1999): 57. Alonzo Hamby writes of Progressivism, "Worn thin by the end of this century by the excesses of its ambitions and by cultural upheavals, it nonetheless remains an often powerful presence in American political life." See Alonzo L. Hamby, "Progressivism: A Century of Change and Rebirth," in *Progressivism and the New Democracy,* ed. Sidney M. Milkis and Jerome M. Mileur (Amherst: University of Massachusetts Press, 1999), 41.

3. The Progressives "saw in constitutional interpretation the opportunity to re-

write a Constitution that showed at every turn the influence of John Locke and James Madison into a different Constitution, which reflected the wisdom of the leading intellectual reformers of their own time." Richard A. Epstein, *How Progressives Rewrote the Constitution* (Washington, DC: Cato Institute, 2006), 135.

4. Eisenach, *Lost Promise,* 187.

5. Herron is quoted in ibid., 188.

6. Mary Parker Follett, *The New State, Group Organization the Solution of Popular Government* (New York: Longmans, Green, 1918), 164.

7. Eisenach, *Lost Promise,* 113.

8. John Dewey and James H. Tufts, *Ethics,* in *The Middle Works, 1899–1924,* ed. Jo Ann Boydston and Paul F. Kolojeski (Carbondale: Southern Illinois University Press, 1978), 5:422 (hereinafter *Ethics 1908*). Dewey supported a "generalized individualism," which he contrasted with "American individualistic convictions." Ibid.

9. John Dewey, "Experience and Nature," in *The Later Works, 1925–1953,* ed. Jo Ann Boydston, Patricia Baysinger, and Barbara Levine (Carbondale: Southern Illinois University Press, 1981), 1:357.

10. Eisenach, *Lost Promise,* 187.

11. James T. Kloppenberg, *Uncertain Victory: Social Democracy and Progressivism in European and American Thought, 1870–1920* (New York: Oxford University Press, 1988), 288–89. See also Thomas G. West, "Progressivism and the Transformation of American Government," in *The Progressive Revolution in Politics and Political Science,* ed. John Marini and Ken Masugi (Lanham, MD: Rowman and Littlefield, 2005), 14–18.

12. Albion Small, "The Evolution of a Social Standard," *American Journal of Sociology* 20 (1914): 15. A leading contemporary Progressive sees constitutional law as functional in that it seeks "to promote human dignity and community need." See Stephen Breyer, "Madison Lecture: Our Democratic Government," *New York University Law Review* 77 (2002): 246

13. Dewey and Tufts, *Ethics 1908,* 394.

14. Follett, *New State,* 172.

15. Ken I. Kersch, "The Reconstruction of Constitutional Privacy Rights and the New American State," *Studies in American Political Development* 16 (Spring 2002): 75.

16. Eisenach, *Lost Promise,* 189; see n. 4 for citations to numerous critiques of individualism by Progressives. Similarly, Justice Stephen Breyer emphasizes positive liberty (participation in governing) rather than negative liberty (freedom from government). See Breyer, "Madison Lecture," passim.

17. Follett, *New State,* 164.

18. Herbert Croly, *The Promise of American Life* (New York: Capricorn Books, 1964), 44.

19. John Dewey argued that "by one of the paradoxes of history, the principle

[of natural rights] is now most often invoked in favor of 'vested interests.' 'Natural' easily loses the force of an appeal to reason and to social good, and becomes merely an assertion of ancient usage, or precedent, or even a shelter for mere selfish interests. Natural rights in property may be invoked to thwart efforts to protect life and health." Dewey and Tufts, *Ethics 1908,* 143–44.

20. Eisenach, *Lost Promise,* 187. See also Croly's criticism of the Bill of Rights in Herbert Croly, *Progressive Democracy* (New York: Macmillan, 1914), 217–19.

21. Dewey and Tufts, *Ethics 1908,* 435.

22. Ibid., 439.

23. Ibid.

24. The American Economic Association's initial platform spoke of "the state as an educational and ethical agency whose positive aid is an indispensable condition of human progress." Eisenach, *Lost Promise,* 139.

25. Small is quoted in ibid., 55. The Supreme Court refers to "ordinary commercial activity" in United States v. Carolene Products, 304 U.S. 144, 146 n. 4 (1938). David M. Rabban, "Free Speech in Progressive Social Thought," *Texas Law Review* 74 (1996): 951, 958.

26. Croly, *Promise,* 22.

27. Rabban, "Free Speech," 992.

28. Croly, *Promise,* 23.

29. See Richard L. McCormick, "The Discovery That Business Corrupts Politics: A Reappraisal of the Origins of Progressivism," *American Historical Review* 86 (1981): passim.

30. Ibid., 260–66.

31. Bradley A. Smith, *Unfree Speech: The Folly of Campaign Finance Reform* (Princeton: Princeton University Press, 2001), 24.

32. Follett, *New State,* 75.

33. Croly is quoted in Eisenach, *Lost Promise,* 216.

34. Ibid., 216.

35. Ibid., 129.

36. Croly, *Promise,* 44.

37. Charles Horton Cooley, *Social Organization: A Study of the Larger Mind* (New York: C. Scribner's Sons, 1909), 349, 351. See also Eisenach, *Lost Promise,* 189.

38. Herman Belz, *A Living Constitution or Fundamental Law? American Constitutionalism in Historical Perspective* (Lanham, MD: Rowman and Littlefield, 1998), 57.

39. Eisenach, *Lost Promise,* 111–12.

40. See Belz, *Living Constitution,* 60; J. Allen Smith, *The Spirit of American Government* (1907; reprint, Cambridge: Harvard University Press, 1965), 65–66, 97–98, 298–300. Charles Beard later formulated a more famous version of this indictment of the Constitution. See Charles A. Beard, *An Economic Interpretation of the Constitution of the United States* (New York: Free Press, 1935).

41. Hamilton is quoted in Belz, *Living Constitution,* 69.

42. Ibid., 58.

43. Eisenach, *Lost Promise,* 87.

44. Quoted in David S. Broder, *Democracy Derailed: Initiative Campaigns and the Power of Money* (New York: Harcourt, 2000), 31.

45. Eisenach, *Lost Promise,* 137. See also John M. Allswang, *The Initiative and Referendum in California, 1898–1998* (Stanford: Stanford University Press, 2000), 5.

46. Quoted in Broder, *Democracy Derailed,* 32.

47. Eisenach, *Lost Promise,* 2.

48. Small is quoted in ibid., 55.

49. Cooley, *Social Organization,* preface. On the subordinating of the individual to social purposes, see Cooley's orchestra metaphor, ibid., 3. See also Cooley, *Human Nature and the Social Order* (New York: C. Scribner's Sons, 1902), 36.

50. Follett, *New State,* 120.

51. Eisenach, *Lost Promise,* 79.

52. Ibid., 193.

53. Ely is quoted in ibid., 189.

54. Arthur Twining Hadley, *The Relations between Freedom and Responsibility in the Evolution of Democratic Government* (New York: Charles Scribner's Sons, 1903), 82.

55. Small is quoted in Eisenach, *Lost Promise,* 55.

56. Ibid., 56 n. 13.

57. Cooley, *Human Nature,* 48–50.

58. Follett, *New State,* 66, emphasis in original.

59. Ibid., 71–73.

60. Eisenach, *Lost Promise,* 190.

61. Thus the Progressives fit Isaiah Berlin's famous definition of positive freedom. See Isaiah Berlin, "Two Concepts of Liberty," in *Liberty,* ed. David Miller (New York: Oxford University Press, 1991), 45.

62. Eisenach, *Lost Promise,* 5.

63. Croly, *Promise,* 273.

64. Eisenach, *Lost Promise,* 5.

65. Ibid., 219.

66. Ibid., 74.

67. Cooley is quoted in ibid., 75.

68. Ibid., 78.

69. Batten is quoted in ibid., 130.

70. Follett, *New State,* 137–38.

71. Croly, *Promise,* 44.

72. Ibid., 273–74.

73. See Edward L. Glaeser and Andrei Shleifer, "The Rise of the Regulatory State," *Journal of Economic Literature* 41 (June 2003): 417.

74. Dewey and Tufts, *Ethics 1908,* 31.

75. Ibid., 425.

76. Eisenach, *Lost Promise,* 121. Eisenach remarks, "Progressive intellectuals and academics invented a conception of citizenship that stipulated that the possession of social knowledge entailed the duty of reflecting on and articulating ideas of national public good unmediated by party, interest, region, or sectarian religion" (7).

77. Ibid., 132.

78. Dewey and Tufts, *Ethics 1908,* 431. Notice that Dewey contrasts this criterion to the doctrine of laissez-faire.

79. Croly, *Promise,* 23.

80. Ibid., 449.

81. Eisenach, *Lost Promise,* 76. See also Franklin Giddings, *Elements of Sociology* (New York: Macmillan, 1898), 155–57.

82. Edward A. Ross, *Social Control: A Survey of the Foundations of Order* (New York: Macmillan, 1904), 363, 369, 376; Eisenach, *Lost Promise,* 87.

83. See Broder, *Democracy Derailed,* 30.

84. Eisenach, *Lost Promise,* 59.

85. Cooley, *Social Organization,* 411.

86. Follett, *New State,* 175.

87. See William M. Wiecek, *The Lost World of Classical Legal Thought: Law and Ideology in America, 1886–1937* (New York: Oxford University Press, 1998), 187.

88. Progressives hoped to set the agenda and monopolize the information intended for powerful government bureaucracies and executives who were independent of electoral and legislative majorities. That domination of government, in turn, came from Progressive control over enlightened opinion through journalism, teacher training, and social science. See Eisenach, *Lost Promise,* 135.

89. Roscoe Pound was associated with sociological jurisprudence; see Rabban, "Free Speech," 994.

90. See Nancy Cohen, *The Reconstruction of American Liberalism, 1865–1914* (Chapel Hill: University of North Carolina Press, 2002), 224. Cohen continues, "The administrative mandate at [modern liberalism's] core proposed that decisions about regulation should be removed from their traditional locus in the legislative and judicial branches and transferred to new expert-staffed administrative agencies, divorced from partisan politics, legislative direction, and popular participation." Ibid. On expertise, see the views of James Landis, a leading New Dealer, quoted in West, "Progressivism," 20.

91. West, "Progressivism," 19.

92. Broder, *Democracy Derailed,* 32.

93. Allswang, *Initiative and Referendum in California,* 3.

94. Eisenach, *Lost Promise,* 115.

95. Croly, *Promise,* 34–35.

96. Croly, *Progressive Democracy,* 244.

97. David M. Rabban, *Free Speech in Its Forgotten Years* (New York: Cambridge University Press, 1997), chap. 3.

98. Rabban, "Free Speech," 990.

99. Ibid., 1000–1001.

100. Ibid., 955–56, 964. The "reconstruction of society" was a central conception of the founders of modern socialism, Comte and Saint-Simon. See Friedrich A. Hayek, *Law, Legislation and Liberty,* vol. 1, *Rules and Order* (Chicago: University of Chicago Press, 1973), 53.

101. Croly, *Promise,* 286. See also Rabban, "Free Speech," 987.

102. William Shakespeare, *Richard II,* act 5, scene 4. David Rabban raises concerns about Croly's words but reaches few conclusions because of what he sees as the "ambiguity of this passage." Rabban, "Free Speech," 987. Croly's conditions for speech are clear. True, he does not say explicitly what measures should be taken against speech that does not meet his conditions. Yet Croly's silence in that respect is ambiguous only if we ignore the larger vision: Progressivism is essentially communitarian and antagonistic to liberal individualism. Speech, like all other aspects of society, should serve the common good. That premise leads to Croly's conditions for speech. Speech that does not serve the common good has no claim to exist in a Progressive democracy.

103. Rabban argues that Croly's reasoning led the Supreme Court to uphold the convictions under the Espionage Act of socialists for sending antiwar circulars to soldiers called up for duty. See Rabban, "Free Speech," 988.

104. Ibid., 1017–18.

105. J. M. Balkin, "Some Realism about Pluralism: Legal Realist Approaches to the First Amendment," *Duke Law Journal* 1990:375, 383.

106. See the account of the case by a participant, the Progressive First Amendment lawyer Floyd Abrams, *Speaking Freely: Trials of the First Amendment* (New York: Viking, 2005), chap. 1.

107. Abrams reports that a group of Progressives in New York were shocked by his support for liberty with respect to campaign finance. See ibid., 231–32.

108. Lochner v. New York, 198 U.S. 45, 56–57 (1905).

109. For a concise overview of this period see James W. Ely Jr., *The Guardian of Every Other Right: A Constitutional History of Property Rights,* 2nd ed. (New York: Oxford University Press, 1997), chap. 7; and John Nowak and Ronald Rotunda, *Constitutional Law,* 6th ed. (Minneapolis: West, 2000), 408–16.

110. United States v. Carolene Products Co., 304 U.S. 144, 146 (1938).

111. Ibid., 154.

112. Some scholars have also seen this footnote as a justification for a more general and aggressive judicial review of the political process. See Daniel H. Lowenstein, "The Supreme Court Has No Theory of Politics," in *The U.S. Supreme Court and the Electoral Process,* ed. David K. Ryden (Washington, DC: Georgetown University Press, 2000), 259–60.

113. United States v. Carolene Products Co., 152.

114. John O. McGinnis, "The Once and Future Property-Based Vision of the First Amendment," *University of Chicago Law Review* 63 (1996): 50.

115. Ely, *Guardian,* 134.

116. Bruce Ackerman, *We the People,* vol. 1, *Foundations* (Cambridge: Harvard University Press, Belknap Press, 1991), 129.

117. The example is not fanciful. The history of the struggle for freedom of the press is tied up with the struggle to preserve property rights. See McGinnis, "Once and Future Property-Based Vision," 92–93.

118. For a useful short biography see "About John W. Gardner," in John W. Gardner, *Living, Leading and the American Dream,* ed. Francesca Gardner (San Francisco: Jossey-Bass, 2003), xxiff.

119. John W. Gardner, *In Common Cause: Citizen Action and How It Works,* rev. ed. (New York: Norton, 1973), 25. On the loss of shared values, see ibid., 40, and John W. Gardner, *The Recovery of Confidence* (New York: Norton, 1970), 55.

120. Gardner, *Recovery,* 52.

121. Ibid., 128–29.

122. Ibid., 131–32.

123. Ibid., 22.

124. Ibid., 147ff.

125. Ibid., 30.

126. Ibid., 80–81.

127. Ibid., 60.

128. Ibid., 66, 60, 65, 69.

129. Ibid., 86–87.

130. Ibid., 22.

131. Ibid., 34, 88, 143.

132. Ibid., 142. Gardner writes of the "individual who has committed himself to the fight for a better future." Such a person "does not waste time looking for scapegoats. He does not indulge in moral posturing. He does not entertain the mind-poisoning conviction that all the nation's difficulties stem from the actions of people morally less worthy than himself. He does not imagine that the main point is to show how angry he is."

133. Gardner, *Common Cause,* 20, 81.

134. Ibid., 33.

135. Ibid., 54–55, 69.

136. Ibid., 48.

137. Ibid., 77; see also ibid., 92–93, where Gardner writes, "The perception of the need for significant change begins with a few individuals who are sufficiently far-sighted to comprehend the problems that lie ahead and to propose solutions."

138. Ibid., 96.

139. Ibid., 86.

140. Center for Political Studies, University of Michigan, *The NES Guide to*

Public Opinion and Electoral Behavior (Ann Arbor: University of Michigan, Center for Political Studies, 1995–2000), table 3.1. http://www.umich.edu/~nes/nesguide/nesguide.htm (accessed January 21, 2005).

141. Ibid., table 4A.1.

142. Ibid., table 4A.3.1.

143. Ibid., table 4A.b.1.

144. See the survey response in Robert Y. Shapiro, Kelly D. Patterson, Judith Russell, and John T. Young, "The Polls: Public Assistance," *Public Opinion Quarterly* 51 (Spring 1987): 130.

145. Center for Political Studies, *NES Guide,* tables 6B.1–5, 6A.1.

146. The exception might be his references to the environment. See Helen Erskine, "The Polls: Pollution and Its Costs," *Public Opinion Quarterly* 36 (Spring 1972): 120–35.

147. Environmentalism was hardly a unique or signature issue for Gardner.

148. Gardner, *Common Cause,* 81.

149. "Campaign Finance Reform, 1974 Legislative Chronology." CQ Electronic Library, CQ Public Affairs Collection, catn73-0009170395. http://library.cqpress.com/cqpac/catn73-0009170395 (accessed August 15, 2003). Originally published in *Congress and the Nation, 73–76,* vol. 4 (Washington, DC: CQ Press, 1977).

150. Buckley v. Valeo, 424 U.S. 1, 49 (1976).

151. Balkin, "Some Realism," 379.

152. The Left worries that instead of protecting dissenters from state power the First Amendment is "now being invoked by the economically and politically powerful to prevent regulation of campaign financing, the media, and harmful speech directed against minorities, women, and children." See Rabban, "Free Speech," 953.

153. As Owen Fiss put it, in First Amendment cases during the 1970s, "capitalism almost always won." Owen Fiss, "Free Speech and Social Structure," *Iowa Law Review* 71 (1986): 1407.

154. The Progressive free speech theorists to be discussed below hold academic positions in higher reaches of the academy and thus enjoy an influence over political culture that is similar to that of forebears who held similar positions. Some contemporary Progressives are aware of the continuity of their tradition, especially in regard to legal realism. See, e.g., Balkin, "Some Realism," 384, and Cass R. Sunstein, *The Partial Constitution* (Cambridge: Harvard University Press, 1993), 204. That said, a leading scholar of Progressivism has noted that contemporary thinkers overlook the similarity of their ideas with the older Progressive tradition. See Rabban, "Free Speech," 1026.

155. Cass R. Sunstein, *Democracy and the Problem of Free Speech* (New York: Free Press, 1993), 97; Owen M. Fiss, "Why the State?" *Harvard Law Review* 100 (1987): 781, 782.

156. Fiss, "Why the State?" 783.

157. Sunstein, for example, calls for applying the "New Deal reformation" to freedom of expression. See Sunstein, *Democracy,* 34.

158. Foley notes that no one has any right to property prior to the decisions of a majority realized through government: "The electorate may determine that the money currently held by Bert (and other wealthy citizens) properly belongs to Amy (and other impoverished citizens). Thus, until the electoral process is complete, all claims of entitlement are necessarily in limbo." See Edward B. Foley, "Equal-Dollars-Per-Voter: A Constitutional Principle of Campaign Finance," *Columbia Law Review* 94 (1994): 1204, 1242.

159. McGinnis, "Once and Future Property-Based Vision," 51.

160. Fiss, "Why the State?" 785.

161. Sunstein, *Partial Constitution,* 206.

162. Sunstein, *Democracy,* 98.

163. In this respect Progressives agree with the legal positivists, who make law the will of the sovereign. So interpreted, law becomes an instrument of political power rather than a limit on it. See Hayek, *Law, Legislation and Liberty,* 1:91–92.

164. Fiss, "Why the State?" 785.

165. Ibid., 1416, 1425.

166. Sunstein, *Democracy,* 18. Sunstein identifies this goal with "the Madisonian conception" of the Constitution. Two commentators who share Sunstein's Progressive political sympathies reject his evocation of Madison, citing his lack of evidence for the link. See Rabban, "Free Speech," 1034 and n. 659, and J. M. Balkin, "Populism and Progressivism as Constitutional Categories," *Yale Law Journal* 104 (1995): 1935, 1954–56. Both suggest that Sunstein asserts the tie to Madison to borrow from the authority of the founder to fund his own anti-Madisonian vision. As Balkin puts it, "Sunstein's 'Madisonian' theory of the First Amendment is about as Madisonian as Madison, Wisconsin. It is a tribute to a great man and his achievements, but bears only a limited connection to his actual views. . . . Madison was more likely to believe that the state existed to protect individual rights or natural rights than that such rights existed to serve the just interests of the state" (Balkin, "Populism and Progressivism," 1956).

167. Sunstein, *Democracy,* 19, 21–23.

168. Ibid., 20, 98.

169. Foley, "Equal-Dollars-Per-Voter," 1205.

170. Fiss, "Social Structure," 1412.

171. Sunstein, *Democracy,* 99–101. Sunstein does speak favorably of Bruce Ackerman's voucher system of public financing, in which "regular money" (i.e., private funds) "could not be used at all." Ibid., 101.

172. Foley, "Equal-Dollars-Per-Voter," 1205.

173. Fiss, "Social Structure," 1415.

174. Fiss, "Why the State?" 786.

175. Fiss, "Social Structure," 1425, 1415.

176. Fiss notes that the Marxist philosopher Herbert Marcuse has a "clear view of what should be included in public debate," which makes it easier to "attain true collective self-determination." Ibid., 1412. Marcuse argued that achieving true liberation required suppressing the political activities and speech of capitalists. See Herbert Marcuse, "Repressive Tolerance," in *A Critique of Pure Tolerance*, by Robert Paul Wolff, Barrington Moore Jr., and Herbert Marcuse (Boston: Beacon, 1969).

177. Foley, "Equal-Dollars-Per-Voter," 1251–52.

178. Foley sets the condition for publishing opinion journals; ibid., 1249. It is a fair inference that if the condition is not met, the publication could not appear, because that is the conclusion Foley himself draws for newspaper endorsements of candidates.

179. Breyer, "Madison Lecture," 246–53.

180. See ibid., 253–54.

181. See Dewey's comments on state action as an experiment in John Dewey, *The Public and Its Problems*, in *The Later Works, 1925–1953*, ed. Jo Ann Boydston (Carbondale: Southern Illinois University Press, 1981), 2:256–57. For Dewey's skepticism, see Benjamin R. Barber, *Strong Democracy: Participatory Politics for a New Age* (Berkeley: University of California Press, 1983), 47.

182. Fiss, "Social Structure," 1416.

183. Amy Gutmann and Dennis Thompson, *Why Deliberative Democracy?* (Princeton: Princeton University Press, 2004), 49. Robert Fogel has noted that modern egalitarianism has three elements: a conviction that society would be better off if wealth were redistributed from the rich to the poor, the belief that the state is the instrument to carry out such redistribution, and a commitment to developing public policies to bring about such redistribution. See Robert Fogel, *The Fourth Great Awakening and the Future of Egalitarianism* (Chicago: University of Chicago Press, 2000), 84.

184. Anyone who doubts that public financing is tied to a substantive policy agenda should listen to its proponents, as I have done in many debates over the years. These advocates invariably recommend public financing because it will bring about a rapid shift to the Left in policy outcomes or because it will bring about a preferred demographic distribution of legislators.

185. Dennis F. Thompson, *Ethics in Congress: From Individual to Institutional Corruption* (Washington, DC: Brookings Institution Press, 1995), 113–14. See also Cass R. Sunstein, "Political Equality and Unintended Consequences," *Columbia Law Review* 94 (1994): 1390, 1392.

186. The Progressive identification of individual freedom with selfishness is not persuasive. As Friedrich A. Hayek remarked, "The freedom to pursue his own aims is, however, at least as important for the complete altruist as for the most selfish. Altruism, to be a virtue, certainly does not presuppose that one has to follow another person's will." Hayek, *Law, Legislation and Liberty*, 1:56.

187. John Rawls, *Political Liberalism* (Cambridge: Harvard University Press, 1993), 265.

188. Alberto Alesina, Rafael di Tella, and Robert MacCulloch, "Inequality and Happiness: Are Europeans and Americans Different?" NBER Working Paper no. 8198, April 2001, 4. In an earlier poll of eleven nations, 19 percent of U.S. citizens agreed with the egalitarian statement "The fairest way of distributing wealth and income would be to give everyone equal shares." This was the tenth lowest level of agreement among the nations surveyed. See Toril Aalberg, "Achieving Justice: Comparative Public Opinion on Income Distribution," International Comparative Social Studies, no. 7 (Boston: Brill, 2003), 44.

189. For a milder version of this argument, see Smith, *Unfree Speech*, 206.

190. See the sources noted in Rabban, "Free Speech," 1036.

191. John Kekes, *The Illusions of Egalitarianism* (Ithaca: Cornell University Press, 2003), 6, where he discusses the optimistic faith, sentiments, and moral passion of the egalitarian liberal.

192. Herbert Marcuse, who advocated intolerance in the service of equality, never answered the question of who should operate the system of censorship he proposed. The system would not be directed by the people because they were indoctrinated to favor capitalism. Only a vanguard who knows the true interest of society should both censor and liberate. See Andrew Altman, "Equality and Expression: The Radical Paradox," *Social Philosophy and Policy* 21 (Summer 2004): 12.

193. Robert Fogel has delineated the religious nature of modern egalitarianism in what he calls the Second and Third Great Awakenings, whose content I have called the Progressive vision: "Much of the ideological foundation for modern egalitarianism was laid during the Second Great Awakening, when holiness and virtue were equated with disinterested benevolence. That doctrine gave powerful impetus to the social reform movements of the nineteenth and twentieth centuries. The Third Great Awakening completed the ideological foundation for modern egalitarianism by making social rather than personal corruption the chief source of sin." See Fogel, *Fourth*, 85. At the same time, contemporary Progressives, unlike the original thinkers, no longer assume Protestantism should guide political reform. See Hamby, "Change and Rebirth," 72–74.

194. The misunderstanding of society as an organization to be rationally ordered has a long history. See Hayek, *Law, Legislation and Liberty*, 1:53–54. See also Michael Oakeshott, "Rationalism in Politics," in *Rationalism and Politics and Other Essays* (Indianapolis: Liberty Press, 1991), 6–42.

195. Michael J. Sandel, *Liberalism and the Limits of Justice* (New York: Cambridge University Press, 1982), 183.

196. See, e.g., Norman J. Ornstein, "McCain-Feingold: No Cause for Alarm," *Washington Post*, April 24, 2001.

197. Franklin Roosevelt in 1935 denounced the Supreme Court's "horse and buggy definition of interstate commerce." See Ely, *Guardian*, 126.

198. Ideological drift is the disconnection between principles and interests. For example, as J. M. Balkin argues, the Left's commitment to free speech ended up

in the 1970s serving the interests of their political opponents. See Balkin, "Some Realism," passim.

Chapter Three

1. Thomas F. Burke, "The Concept of Corruption in Campaign Finance Law," *Constitutional Commentaries* 14 (Spring 1997): 140: "The debate over the place of corruption in campaign finance ultimately turns on the theoretical foundations of representative democracy." The "appearance of corruption" standard, which concerns political culture, is treated in chapter 4.

2. The charge is found among academics as well as politicians. See G. Calvin MacKenzie, *Scandal Proof: Do Ethics Laws Make Government Ethical?* (Washington, DC: Brookings Institution Press, 2002), 172.

3. 18 U.S.C. § 201(b) (2000).

4. 18 U.S.C. § 201(b)(1)(A) (2000).

5. Some commentators, informed perhaps by the Progressive emphasis on collectives, focus on the corruption of institutional practices rather than the intentions of individuals; see Dennis F. Thompson, *Ethics in Congress: From Individual to Institutional Corruption* (Washington, DC: Brookings Institution Press, 1995), chap. 5. Thompson admits the possibility that money can corrupt Congress even though no individual member is corrupt (ibid., 121). According to Thompson's account, Congress appears to have an existence apart from the wills of its members.

6. "Motive-based regulation is the attempt to distinguish appropriate from inappropriate motives in political representation and to weed out the latter through prohibition or limitation." Bruce Cain, "Moralism and Realism in Campaign Finance Reform," *University of Chicago Legal Forum* 1995:113.

7. "Scandals." CQ Electronic Library, CQ Encyclopedia of American Government, elaz2d-156-7495-402910. http://library.cqpress.com/eag/elaz2d-156-7495-402910 (accessed November 30, 2005). Originally published in John L. Moore, *Elections A to Z* (Washington, DC: CQ Press, 2003).

8. Kenneth Jost, "Political Scandals." *CQ Researcher Online* 4, no. 20 (May 27, 1994). http://library.cqpress.com/cqresearcher/cqresrre1994052700 (accessed October 15, 2004).

9. "Sen. Daniel B. Brewster Conviction, 1972." CQ Electronic Library, CQ Congress Collection, catn69-0008168692. http://library.cqpress.com/congress/catn69-0008168692 (accessed December 7, 2005). Originally published in *Congress and the Nation, 69–72*, vol. 3 (Washington, DC: CQ Press, 1973).

10. Charles R. Babcock, "Prosecutors Urge 10-Year Sentence for Cunningham," *Washington Post*, February 18, 2006.

11. Administrative Office of the U.S. Courts, "U.S. District Courts—Criminal Defendants Sentenced after Conviction, by Major Offense, During the 12-Month

Period Ending September 30, 2001 [Part 03: General Offenses; Special Offenses]," in *Judicial Business of the U.S. Courts, 2001* (Washington, DC: Government Printing Office, 2002), 216.

12. 18 U.S.C. § 597 (2000).

13. "It should of course be kept in mind that these payments [i.e., campaign contributions] are not actually for the purpose of buying votes. The votes are bought by the bills passed by Congress, or the Legislature, which benefit voters." Gordon Tullock, *Public Goods, Redistribution and Rent Seeking* (Northampton, MA: Edward Elgar, 2005), 95.

14. Daniel Hays Lowenstein, "On Campaign Finance Reform: The Root of All Evil Is Deeply Rooted," *Hofstra Law Review* 18 (1989): 301, 313–22.

15. Cain, "Moralism and Realism," 117.

16. See the short report in the *Washington Post*, August 8, 2003. Similarly, Earl Allen Haywood pleaded guilty to taking $187,000 in campaign contributions raised for Elizabeth Dole's North Carolina Senate campaign and spending it on personal items. See "Washington in Brief," *Washington Post*, March 18, 2004.

17. Thompson, *Ethics in Congress*, 113–14. See also Cass R. Sunstein, "Political Equality and Unintended Consequences," *Columbia Law Review* 94 (1994): 1390, 1392.

18. Machiavelli writes that a ruler must have a reputation for virtue that is set aside to achieve his ends. See Niccolò Machiavelli, *The Prince*, trans. George Bull (New York: Penguin, 2001), 57.

19. Lowenstein, "On Campaign Finance Reform," 318. He writes, "If the political system did not allow for contributions, each legislator's position on the scale would be determined by considerations such as constituency, ideology and party. The positions determined in this manner will be referred to as the legislators' 'natural' positions" (ibid.).

20. The examples are taken from Benjamin Radcliff and Amy Radcliff, *Understanding Zen* (Boston: Tuttle, 1993), 45–46. In truth, the earth is spherical, traveling through space, and rotating on its axis. Solid objects are composed mostly of the empty spaces between molecules, atoms, and subatomic particles.

21. See, e.g., the concept of "common sense racism" in Ian F. Haney López, *Racism on Trial: The Chicano Fight for Justice* (Cambridge: Harvard University Press, Belknap Press, 2003).

22. Stephen Ansolabehere, John M. de Figueiredo, and James M. Snyder Jr., "Why Is There So Little Money in U.S. Politics?" *Journal of Economic Perspectives* 17 (Winter 2003): 105–30. The authors mention forty studies of roll-call voting.

23. The authors of these reviews have been skeptical and supportive of campaign finance regulation. Sorauf supported the McCain-Feingold legislation of 2002. Ansolabehere has done research suggesting that campaign ads drive down voter turnout, a conclusion welcomed by those who wish to restrict such advertising. See Stephen D. Ansolabehere, Shanto Iyengar, and Adam Simon, "Replicating

Experiments Using Aggregate and Survey Data: The Case of Negative Advertising and Turnout," *American Political Science Review* 93 (December 1999): 901–90.

24. Frank J. Sorauf, *Money in American Elections* (Glenview, IL: Scott Foresman, 1988), 310. Readers might also consult Sorauf's later work, *Inside Campaign Finance: Myths and Realities* (New Haven: Yale University Press, 1992).

25. Sorauf, *Money,* 310–11. This is an example of a standard problem in social science research: omitted variable bias. See the helpful discussion in Gary King, Robert O. Keohane, and Sidney Verba, *Designing Social Inquiry: Scientific Inference in Qualitative Research* (Princeton: Princeton University Press, 1994), 168–81.

26. Sorauf, *Money,* 311.

27. King, Keohane, and Verba provide a thorough discussion of selection bias in *Designing Social Inquiry,* 128–38.

28. Sorauf, *Money,* 312.

29. Gordon Tullock, "The Purchase of Politicians," *Western Economic Journal* 10 (1972): 354.

30. Ansolabehere et al., "Why Is There So Little Money?" 110.

31. John W. Gardner notes the huge alleged return on contributions: "A thousandfold sounds like excessive return on an investment, but the senator was not exaggerating as much as one might think. The campaign contributions in a presidential election year run to a few hundred million. The return flow of political favors to donors must be reckoned in the scores of billions." Yet he misses the challenge this assertion raises for his faith that money corrupts politics. See John W. Gardner, *In Common Cause: Citizen Action and How It Works,* rev. ed. (New York: Norton, 1973), 39.

32. Jeffrey Milyo, David Primo, and Timothy Groseclose, "Corporate PAC Contributions in Perspective," *Business and Politics* 2 (2000): 82. The reader should bear in mind that the most frequent contribution from PACs was zero.

33. Ansolabehere et al., "Why Is There So Little Money?" 108–9, 111.

34. Ibid., 111.

35. Milyo et al., "Corporate PAC Contributions," 84–85.

36. Ibid., 80.

37. Ansolabehere et al., "Why Is There So Little Money?" 114.

38. Recently Thomas Stratmann reported the results of an unpublished meta-analysis of the studies cited by Ansolabehere and his colleagues. Stratmann argues that his study reverses the traditional finding that contributions influence policy. Yet he notes that this conclusion should not be overstated since it assumes that all the studies surveyed in the meta-analysis have properly controlled for the simultaneous determination of contributions and votes. See Thomas Stratmann, "Some Talk: Money in Politics; A (Partial) Review of the Literature," *Public Choice* 124 (2005): 146. Ansolabehere et al. ("Why Is There So Little Money?" 114) report that "most of the studies" in their data set are plagued by simultaneity bias.

39. Contributions may influence votes, but votes may also influence contributions (the endogeneity problem). Most of the studies also fail to account for other factors that are highly correlated to campaign contributions and to legislative votes (the omitted variable problem). Once those omitted variables are included in the analysis, it is possible that the influence of contributions may disappear. Ibid.

40. For a description of their methods, see Ansolabehere et al., "Why Is There So Little Money?" 115–16.

41. Ibid., 116.

42. Jeffrey Milyo, *The Electoral Effects of Campaign Spending in House Elections* (Los Angeles: Citizens' Research Foundation, 1998), 1; Milyo et al., "Corporate PAC Contributions," 83.

43. Ansolabehere et al., "Why Is There So Little Money?" 116–17.

44. Ibid., 119.

45. Ibid., 124.

46. Ibid., 122.

47. Ibid., 120, especially fig. 1.

48. John Wright, "Campaign Contributions and Congressional Voting on Tobacco Policy, 1980–2000," *Business and Politics* 6 (2004): 1.

49. Thomas Stratmann, "Campaign Contributions and Congressional Voting: Does the Timing of Contributions Matter?" *Review of Economics and Statistics* 77 (1995): 127–36.

50. Wright, "Campaign Contributions and Congressional Voting on Tobacco Policy," 11.

51. John R. Lott Jr. and Stephen G. Bronars, "Do Campaign Donations Alter How a Politician Votes?" *Journal of Law and Economics* 40 (October 1997): 317–50.

52. In the run-up to the ban on soft money in 2002, Christopher Shays (R-CT) asked of the Enron Corporation: "Why did they give to both sides? They did it for access and influence. They wanted to influence energy policy, and they did in a big way." See Karen Foerstal, "Opponents of Shays-Meehan Bet It All on a Conference," *CQ Weekly* 60, February 9, 2002, 393.

53. Norman J. Ornstein, Thomas E. Mann, and Michael J. Malbin, *Vital Statistics on Congress, 1999–2000* (Washington, DC: AEI Press, 2000), 54.

54. I defined *overwhelmingly* in this case to mean contributors who gave 90 percent or more of their total contribution to one party or the other.

55. In addition to the Stratmann article discussed in n. 38, work by Matthew Fellowes and Patrick Wolf suggests that business contributions procure indirect benefits (in the form of regulatory and other favorable policies) rather than direct benefits (explicit public spending). They believe that the risks of appearing to offer quid pro quo benefits in exchange for PAC contributions lead public officials to offer more obscure favors for their donors. Even Fellowes and Wolf find that ideology has a much greater effect on indirect aid to business than do contributions. This work runs counter to the general trend of research discussed in the text and

depends on changes in measurement. Whether Fellowes and Wolf's work stands up over time remains to be seen. See Matthew C. Fellowes and Patrick J. Wolf, "Funding Mechanisms and Policy Instruments: How Business Campaign Contributions Influence Congressional Votes," *Political Research Quarterly* 57 (June 2004): 315–24, esp. 319–21.

56. Thomas Stratmann, "Can Special Interests Buy Congressional Votes? Evidence from Financial Services Legislation," *Journal of Political Economy* 45 (October 2002): 351–52.

57. Ibid., 357–62.

58. Ibid., 348. He notes that his time-series research design "requires the existence of two votes that are taken at different points in time but that are comparable, meaning that the contents of the votes are very similar."

59. Ibid., 352.

60. See Stephen Labaton, "Congress Takes up Banking Bills," *New York Times,* November 14, 1991.

61. Stephen Labaton, "White House Loses a Vote on Bank Bill," *New York Times,* November 2, 1991.

62. In "Can Special Interests Buy Congressional Votes?" Stratmann writes: "69 legislators did not change their voting behavior. Thus, those legislators will not contribute to the determination of whether or not money influences votes" (355).

63. Jeffrey Milyo outlines this defense: "Assume members of Congress differ in the firmness of their position on the first vote. Some are right on the fence, while others will never change their mind, and everything in between. Next assume some randomness in voting on roll-calls. Consequently, we can imagine that each member has some probability that they will change their position on the second vote, with some having very low probabilities and some having very high probabilities. Next, suppose PAC contributions are given randomly, and that PAC contributions really do affect the probability that a member changes their vote. Finally, even though some member will have their probability of changing a vote affected by contributions (say from .00001 to .00002), we won't observe such changes in probability. Because we only observe actual changes in votes, and because contributions are random, it is acceptable to omit the members that don't change votes." Pers. comm., July 25, 2003.

64. Stratmann writes: "Legislators do not typically take clearly articulated positions on financial services legislation in their election campaigns, simply because voters do not demand that they do so. Most voters care little about the details of financial services regulation; thus the contributions' potential influence may be larger in this area than on issues voters feel more intensely about. Moreover, financial services legislation is not highly ideological in that candidates must commit in their election campaigns to their position on the Glass-Steagall Act reform" ("Can Special Interests Buy Congressional Votes?" 348).

65. That is, contributions that were regulated even though they would not affect outcomes.

66. Buckley v. Valeo, 424 U.S. 1, 14 (1976), quoting Roth v. United States, 354 U.S. 476, 484 (1957).

67. FEC v. Massachusetts Citizens for Life, 479 U.S. 238, 257–58 (1986). See also Burke, "Concept of Corruption," 133.

68. Austin v. Michigan Chamber of Commerce, 494 U.S. 652, 659–60 (1990); Burke, "Concept of Corruption," 134.

69. Burke, "Concept of Corruption," 131.

70. Elaine B. Sharp, *The Sometime Connection: Public Opinion and Social Policy* (Albany: SUNY Press, 1999), chap. 3.

71. For a general overview of the evidence, see Thomas R. Dye and Harmon Ziegler, *The Irony of Democracy* (New York: Harcourt Brace, 2000), 141–45.

72. William Riker, *Liberalism against Populism: A Confrontation between the Theory of Democracy and the Theory of Social Choice* (Glencoe, IL: Waveland, 1988).

73. Ironically, the will of the people about the will of the people depends on how the survey question is asked. A small majority (54 percent) believes that public officials should do what the majority wants even if it contravenes the judgment of the official. But if a mistake by a past majority is mentioned, a small majority (51 percent) of respondents say the official should rely on his or her own judgment and 40 percent say the majority should get what it wants. See Mollyann Brodie, Lisa Ferraro Parmelee, April Brackett, and Drew E. Altman, "Polling and Democracy," *Public Perspective,* July–August 2001, 12.

74. See Philip Converse, "The Nature of Belief Systems in Mass Publics," in *Ideology and Discontent,* ed. David E. Apter (New York: Free Press, 1964), 206–61.

75. See pp. 23–26 in Jeff Manza and Fay Lomax Cook, "The Impact of Public Opinion on Public Policy: The State of the Debate," in *Navigating Public Opinion: Polls, Policy, and the Future of American Democracy,* ed. Jeff Manza, Fay Lomax Cook, and Benjamin I. Page (New York: Oxford University Press, 2002), 17–32.

76. Ibid., 24.

77. I am not offering a comprehensive assessment of scholarly examinations of the influence of public opinion on public policy. Here the experts disagree. Some say that a power elite controls public policymaking and that public opinion has little influence. See G. William Domhoff, "The Power Elite, Public Policy, and Public Opinion," in Manza, Cook and Page, *Navigating,* 124. In his essay Domhoff admits that most correlational studies show some influence of public opinion on public policy. He offers no hard evidence to rebut these studies. Others argue that the effects of public opinion on policy depend on the political institution in question, the salience of any issue to the public, and the number of interest groups that are active with regard to a policy. See Manza and Cook, "Impact of Public Opinion," 28–29. See generally Manza, Cook, and Page, *Navigating,* pt. 1 for a good overview of the literature.

78. James A. Stimson, *Public Opinion in America: Moods, Cycles, and Swings,* 2nd ed. (Boulder: Westview, 1998).

79. James A. Stimson, Robert S. Erikson, and Michael MacKuen, "Dynamic Representation," *American Political Science Review* 89 (1995): 557.

80. Hanna Fenichel Pitkin, *The Concept of Representation* (Berkeley: University of California Press, 1967), 8–9, emphasis in original.

81. Foundations spent $123 million from 1994 to 2004 supporting a lobbying campaign to persuade Congress to pass additional restrictions on campaign finance. See Political Money Line, "Campaign Finance Reform Lobby: 1994–2004," http://www.fecinfo.com. According to the lobbyist who designed the strategy, "The idea was to create an impression that a mass movement was afoot—that everywhere they looked, in academic institutions, in the business community, in religious groups, in ethnic groups, everywhere, people were talking about reform." See Ryan Sager, "Buying Reform," *New York Post,* March 17, 2005. The spending included subsidies to supportive media outlets; see Robert F. Bauer, "Pew: Day Two." http://www.moresoftmoneyhardlaw.com (accessed March 22, 2005).

82. Some argue that contributions buy access to public officials. I have not evaluated this version of the corruption charge in this chapter. The access issue may also be viewed as a problem of inequality; unequal giving leads to unequal access to a public official. The evidence concerning access is treated in chapter 5. However, the evidence reviewed there is relevant if the reader wishes to see the question of access as a problem of the corruption of representation.

Chapter Four

1. John Dewey and James H. Tufts, *Ethics,* in *The Middle Works, 1899–1924,* ed. Jo Ann Boydston and Paul F. Kolojeski (Carbondale: Southern Illinois University Press, 1978), 426.

2. Some conservatives display considerable trust in government. Patrick Devlin, for example, argues that government should enforce morality that is constitutive of society: "What makes a society of any sort is a community of ideas, not only political ideas but also ideas about the way its members should behave and govern their lives; these latter ideas are its morals." Patrick Devlin, *The Enforcement of Morals* (New York: Oxford University Press, 1965), 9. This argument assumes that government may be trusted to enforce the morality that constitutes society and not the preferences of an eccentric minority. Hence, the skepticism about distrust of government is not unique to Progressivism. Because I am concerned primarily with campaign finance issues, I focus on Progressivism.

3. Richard Hofstader, "Goldwater and Pseudo-Conservative Politics," in *The Paranoid Style in American Politics and Other Essays* (Chicago: University of Chicago Press, 1978), 93–141.

4. William H. Flanigan and Nancy H. Zingale, *Political Behavior of the American Electorate,* 9th ed. (Washington, DC: CQ Press, 1998), 33, fig. 2-1.

5. Ruy A. Teixeira, *The Disappearing American Voter* (Washington, DC: Brookings Institution Press, 1992), 100–101.

6. Michael Bailey, "The (Sometimes Surprising) Consequences of Societally Unrepresentative Contributors on Legislative Responsiveness," *Business and Politics* 6 (2004): 1–34, 22.

7. Buckley v. Valeo, 424 U.S. 1, 27 (1976).

8. Ibid., quoting CSC v. Letter Carriers, 413 U.S. 548, 565 (1973).

9. Anthony Corrado, *Paying for Presidents: Public Financing in National Elections* (New York: Twentieth Century Fund Press, 1993), 72.

10. The U.S. Supreme Court thus applies the "strict scrutiny" standard to laws that impinge on fundamental rights. Ordinary policies, however, need only show a rational relation between means and ends.

11. It may be that the appearances standard serves as a substitute for proving actual corruption. Nathaniel Persily and Kelli Lammie note that few campaign finance laws would pass constitutional scrutiny if their sponsors had to actually prove the corrupting influence of money. The appearance of corruption, however, relies on responses to public opinion polls. See Nathaniel Persily and Kelli Lammie, "Perceptions of Corruption and Campaign Finance: When Public Opinion Constitutes Constitutional Law," *University of Pennsylvania Law Review* 153 (December 2004): 119.

12. See David Stout, "Court Upholds Alaska Limits on Soft Money in State Races," *New York Times,* August 14, 2003.

13. The correlation coefficient is .33.

14. The NES has asked other questions related to trust in government. For example, since 1964 it has asked, "Would you say the government is pretty much run by a few big interests looking out for themselves or that it is run for the benefit of all the people?" Responses to this question have a 98 percent correlation with responses to the general trust question noted in the text. The two questions clearly tap into the same set of attitudes and may be treated for present purposes as identical.

15. I have excluded from this chart the results of the 2002 polling on this question by NES. Those surveys showed that 56 percent of Americans highly trusted the federal government. I have excluded the 2002 results because I believe the high level of trust reflects the aftermath of the September 11, 2001, attacks on the United States.

16. A majority in all age cohorts did not consider the Vietnam War a mistake until late 1969. See Hazel Erskine, "The Polls: Is War a Mistake?" *Public Opinion Quarterly* 34 (Spring 1970): 134.

17. Anthony Corrado, "Party Soft Money," in *Campaign Finance Reform: A Sourcebook,* ed. Anthony Corrado, Thomas E. Mann, Daniel R. Ortiz, Trevor Potter, and Frank J. Sorauf (Washington, DC: Brookings Institution Press, 1997), 171–72.

18. Michael Kelly, "Soft Money, No Crime?" *Washington Post,* November 27, 1997.

19. The correlation coefficient is .37. I focus on presidential election years to produce comparable data. Soft money spending in off-year elections was much lower than in presidential years, so it is necessary to control for the presidential race.

20. The National Election Studies, *The NES Guide to Public Opinion and Electoral Behavior* (Ann Arbor: University of Michigan, Center for Political Studies, 1995–2000), table 5B.2. http://www.umich.edu/~nes/nesguide/gd-index.htm#3 (accessed August 1, 2003).

21. Ibid., tables 5B.3, 5C.1.

22. Since 1964 the correlation between trust in government and federal spending as a percentage of GDP has been .61. This is an intriguing though not definitive result. Other factors may have affected the trust measure during that time.

23. A similar argument about soft money can be found in Persily and Lammie, "Perceptions of Corruption," fig. 2, which indicates the relevant trends in soft money and public opinion.

24. The actual number is .013. David Primo reports a similar finding; see David Primo, "Public Opinion and Campaign Finance: A Skeptical Look at Senator McCain's Claims," Cato Briefing Paper no. 60 (Washington, DC: Cato Institute, 2001).

25. Coleman and Manna's methods, data, and variables are discussed in John J. Coleman and Paul F. Manna, "Congressional Campaign Spending and the Quality of Democracy," *Journal of Politics* 62 (2000): 763–65.

26. See ibid., 766. This conclusion reflects the minuscule coefficients for candidate spending reported in ibid., table 1, p. 767.

27. Richard R. Lau and Gerald M. Pomper, *Negative Campaigning: An Analysis of U.S. Senate Elections* (Lanham, MD: Rowman and Littlefield, 2004), 88.

28. Persily and Lammie, "Perceptions of Corruption," 123.

29. Curtis Gans, "Table for One, Please: America's Disintegrating Democracy," *Washington Monthly* 32 (July–August 2000): 44.

30. For the presidential spending, see Lyn Ragsdale, *Vital Statistics on the Presidency: Washington to Clinton* (Washington, DC: CQ Press, 1996), 143. For the turnout, see figure 4.1 in this text.

31. See National Election Studies, *NES Guide to Public Opinion,* table 5A.5. http://www.umich.edu/~nes/nesguide/gd-index.htm#3 (accessed August 1, 2003).

32. Ibid., table 5B.4.

33. Stephen Ansolabehere, John M. de Figueiredo, and James M. Snyder Jr., "Why Is There So Little Money in U.S. Politics?" *Journal of Economic Perspectives* 17 (Winter 2003): 120.

34. Stephen Ansolabehere, Shanto Iyengar, Adam Simon, and Nicholas Valentino, "Does Attack Advertising Demobilize the Electorate?" *American Political Science Review* 88 (December 1994): 829.

35. Ronald Dworkin, "The Curse of American Politics," *New York Review of Books*, October 17, 1996, 19–24.

36. William G. Mayer, "In Defense of Negative Campaigning," *Political Science Quarterly* 111 (1996): 440–41. See also Richard Lau and Gerald Pomper, "Negative Campaigning by US Senate Candidates," *Party Politics* 7 (January 2001): 81.

37. For example, John Kerry and John Edwards used positive ads to gain an advantage in the 2004 Iowa Democratic presidential caucuses. See Ronald Brownstein, "Victors Show Wide Party Appeal; Positive Messages by Kerry, Edwards Pushed Them Ahead in Most Groups, Poll Finds," *Los Angeles Times,* January 20, 2004.

38. "As Clean Elections candidate Warren Tolman blankets the airwaves with ads criticizing his rivals—paid for by the people of Massachusetts—some voters are joining Tolman's rivals in wondering: What does it mean to be clean? The Democratic candidate for governor, whose campaign is being underwritten with public money, has poured hundreds of thousands of dollars into negative ads targeting his three rivals in the Sept. 17 primary. Nothing in the Clean Elections Law prohibits that use of the funds, but the reality of public financing is beginning to clash with some voters' expectations that the new system would change not only the funding of elections, but the tone of them." Stephanie Ebbert, "Tolman's Ad Blitzes Test Clean Elections: Negative Spots May Sink Funding Law," *Boston Globe,* September 8, 2002.

39. Steven E. Finkel and John G. Geer, "A Spot Check: Casting Doubt on the Demobilizing Effect of Attack Advertising," *American Journal of Political Science* 42 (April 1998): 582, fig. 1. Lau and Pomper (*Negative Campaigning,* 77) found no systematic trend in the use of negative ads in their study of Senate races from 1988 to 1998.

40. Stephen Ansolabehere and Shanto Iyengar, *Going Negative: How Political Advertisements Shrink and Polarize the Electorate* (New York: Free Press, 1995), 833.

41. Ibid., 835.

42. Ibid., 111.

43. Finkel and Geer, "Spot Check," 577.

44. Paul Freedman and Ken Goldstein, "Measuring Media Exposure and the Effects of Negative Campaign Ads," *American Journal of Political Science* 43 (October 1999): 1190.

45. John R. Hibbing and Elizabeth Theiss-Morse, *Stealth Democracy: Americans' Beliefs about How Government Should Work* (New York: Cambridge University Press, 2002), 3, write: "Participation in politics is low because people do not like politics even in the best of circumstances."

46. Freedman and Goldstein, "Measuring Media Exposure," 722.

47. Some of this work has found a generally positive though nuanced effect of negative advertising. One study of United States Senate campaigns concluded that people distinguish between relevant negative information presented in an

appropriate manner and irrelevant, shrill, and pejorative ads. Ads seen as legitimate criticism draw people into the voting booth. In contrast, "harsh and irrelevant" negative messages seemed to discourage voting. The study also found that "mudslinging"—the harsh and irrelevant information—discouraged turnout more among political independents, people with little interest in politics, and political novices. See Kim Fridkin Kahn and Patrick J. Kenney, "Do Negative Campaigns Mobilize or Suppress Turnout? Clarifying the Relationship between Negativity and Participation," *American Political Science Review* 93 (December 1999): 877–89.

48. These are not the only studies supporting the "mobilization thesis." Martin Wattenberg and Craig Brians concluded that "in 1992, recollection of negative campaign ads was actually associated with significantly higher turnout, and in 1996, there was no significant relationship." Martin Wattenberg and Craig Brians, "Negative Campaign Advertising: Demobilizer or Mobilizer?" *American Political Science Review* 93 (December 1999): 892. Critics have noted that this conclusion depends on voter recall of ads, which is subject to distortion and error. Stephen D. Ansolabehere, Shanto Iyengar, and Adam Simon, "Replicating Experiments Using Aggregate and Survey Data: The Case of Negative Advertising and Turnout," *American Political Science Review* 93 (December 1999): 901–9.

49. Finkel and Geer, "Spot Check," 584–86.

50. Ibid., 587.

51. A change of one standard deviation in exposure to negative ads resulted in an increase of three points in the probability of turnout. Freedman and Goldstein, "Measuring Media Exposure," 1198–2000.

52. Richard Lau, Lee Sigelman, Caroline Heldman, and Paul Babbit, "The Effects of Negative Political Advertisements: A Meta-Analytic Assessment," *American Political Science Review* 93 (December 1999): 856–58. According to Gene V. Glass, "Meta-analysis refers to the analysis of analyses . . . the statistical analysis of a large collection of analysis results from individual studies for the purpose of integrating the findings." Gene V. Glass, "Primary, Secondary, and Meta-analysis of Research," *Educational Researcher* 5 (1976): 3.

53. Ken Goldstein and Paul Freedman, "Campaign Advertising and Voter Turnout: New Evidence for a Stimulation Effect," *Journal of Politics* 64 (August 2002): 733.

54. Joshua D. Clinton and John S. Lapinski, "'Targeted' Advertising and Voter Turnout: An Experimental Study of the 2000 Presidential Election," *Journal of Politics* 66 (February 2004): 92.

55. Lau and Pomper, *Negative Campaigning,* 86 (emphasis in original).

56. Ansolabehere, Iyengar, Simon and Valentino, *Going Negative,* 836.

57. Kahn and Kenney, "Do Negative Campaigns Mobilize or Suppress Turnout?" 887.

58. Mayer, "In Defense of Negative Campaigning," 451, n. 29.

59. Ibid., 451, quoting research by Gary Jacobson on the 1980 and 1982 elections.

60. Lau and Pomper, *Negative Campaigning*, 79.

61. John J. Coleman, "The Distribution of Campaign Spending Benefits across Groups," *Journal of Politics* 63 (August 2001): 928.

62. These figures are based on state turnout numbers available from Michael McDonald's United States Elections Project Web site, http://elections.gmu.edu/voter_turnout.htm (accessed November 12, 2003), on the voting-age population of districts in 1998 and 2000, available from the U.S. Census Bureau, Census 2000 Summary File 1, Matrix P12, http://factfinder.census.gov/, and actual turnout in the loser's district, which is available from the Federal Election Commission at www.fec.gov.

63. I am not claiming that this line of reasoning is correct. For example, higher turnout may be correlated with other unknown factors that actually increase the probability that incumbents will lose their bids for reelection. I am arguing that it is plausible that members of Congress would associate negative ads with higher turnout and thus with an increased chance of defeat.

64. Steve Farkas, Jean Johnson, and Ann Duffett, with Leslie Wilson and Jackie Vine, *Knowing It by Heart: Americans Consider the Constitution and Its Meaning* (Philadelphia: National Constitutional Center, 2002), 9, 49.

Chapter Five

1. S. E. Finer suggests that social stability depends on congruence among a society's belief systems, social stratification, and political institutions. See S. E. Finer, *The History of Government from the Earliest Times*, vol. 1, *Ancient Monarchies and Empires* (New York: Oxford University Press, 1999), 28ff.

2. Thomas Jefferson to Roger C. Weightman, 24 June 1826, in *Writings*, ed. Merrill D. Peterson (New York: Library of America, 1984), 1517.

3. Madison receives support from a leading study of comparative politics. S. E. Finer says of the Forum (i.e., popular government): "To conform to the Forum type of polity, the government must be accountable to the people who have conferred on it the right to govern. In practice this means periodic renewal of its mandate by such processes as elections and the like." See Finer, *History*, 43.

4. James Madison in *The Federalist*, ed. Jacob E. Cooke (Middletown, CT: Wesleyan University Press, 1961), 62.

5. See Michael Walzer, *Spheres of Justice: A Defense of Pluralism and Equality* (New York: Basic Books, 1984), chap. 12.

6. Another 5 percent identified themselves as "lower class." National Opinion Research Center at the University of Chicago, *General Social Survey*, Codebook Variable: Class, Question 185A, available at http://webapp.icpsr.umich.edu/GSS.

7. This dissatisfaction is discussed in David S. Broder, *Democracy Derailed: Initiative Campaigns and the Power of Money* (New York: Harcourt, 2000), chap. 4.

8. Buckley v. Valeo, 424 U.S. 1, 48–49 (1976).

9. See the discussion of the post-2000 line of decisions in Richard L. Hasen, "*Buckley* Is Dead, Long Live *Buckley*: The New Campaign Finance Incoherence of *McConnell v. Federal Election Commission*," *University of Pennsylvania Law Review* 153 (2004): 31, 42–46.

10. Baker v. Carr, 369 U.S. 186 (1962).

11. Alexander Heard, *The Costs of Democracy* (Chapel Hill: University of North Carolina Press, 1960), 48.

12. Thomas Gais, *Improper Influence: Campaign Finance Law, Political Interest Groups, and the Problem of Equality* (Ann Arbor: University of Michigan Press, 1996), 76.

13. "How much do lobbyists spend?" CQ Electronic Library, CQ Encyclopedia of American Government, qho60031. http://library.cqpress.com/eag/qho60031 (accessed August 5, 2005). Originally published in Bruce Wetterau, *CQ's Desk Reference on American Government,* 2d ed. (Washington, DC: CQ Press, 2000).

14. Edward B. Foley, "Equal-Dollars-Per-Voter: A Constitutional Principle of Campaign Finance," *Columbia Law Review* 94 (1994): 1204–52.

15. Ronald Brownstein, "Musicians Banding Together to Beat Bush," *Los Angeles Times,* August 5, 2004.

16. Bradley A. Smith, *Unfree Speech: The Folly of Campaign Finance Reform* (Princeton: Princeton University Press, 2001), 206–7.

17. Egalitarians are drawn to voucher schemes. See Ian Ayres and Bruce Ackerman, *Voting with Dollars: A New Paradigm for Campaign Finance* (New Haven: Yale University Press, 2002), 142.

18. Owen Fiss, "Free Speech and Social Structure," *Iowa Law Review* 71 (July 1986): 1405.

19. Thomas W. Hazlett, "Assigning Property Rights to Radio Spectrum Users: Why Did FCC License Auctions Take 67 Years?" *Journal of Law and Economics* 41 (October 1998): 529–70. The interference between broadcasters noted in the 1920s could have been dealt with by the courts under common law.

20. Red Lion Broadcasting v. FCC, 395 U.S. 367 (1969).

21. Judge Richard Posner notes a "vertiginous decline in the cost of electronic communication and the relaxation of regulatory barriers to entry, leading to the proliferation of consumer choices. Thirty years ago the average number of television channels that Americans could receive was seven; today, with the rise of cable and satellite television, it is 71. Thirty years ago there was no Internet, therefore no Web, hence no online newspapers and magazines, no blogs. The public's consumption of news and opinion used to be like sucking on a straw; now it's like being sprayed by a fire hose." See Richard A. Posner, "Bad News," *New York Times Book Review,* July 31, 2005.

22. See Pew Research Center for the People and the Press, *How Journalists See Journalists in 2004: Views on Profits, Performance and Politics* (Washington, DC:

Pew Research Center, 2004), 24. Thirty-four percent of the national journalists surveyed profess liberalism. As Fred Barnes notes, "Since 1962, there have been 11 surveys of the media that sought the political views of hundreds of journalists. In 1971, they were 53 percent liberal, 17 percent conservative. In a 1976 survey of the Washington press corps, it was 59 percent liberal, 18 percent conservative. A 1985 poll of 3,200 reporters found them to be self-identified as 55 percent liberal, 17 percent conservative. In 1996, another survey of Washington journalists pegged the breakdown as 61 percent liberal, 9 percent conservative." Fred Barnes, "Liberal Media Evidence," *Weekly Standard,* May 28, 2004.

23. Posner remarks, "[S]uppose cost conditions change, enabling a newspaper to break even with many fewer readers than before. Now the liberal newspaper has to worry that any temporizing of its message in an effort to attract moderates may cause it to lose its most liberal readers to a new, more liberal newspaper; for with small-scale entry into the market now economical, the incumbents no longer have a secure base. So the liberal newspaper will tend to become even more liberal and, by the same process, the conservative newspaper more conservative." See Posner, "Bad News."

24. See Markus Prior, "News vs. Entertainment: How Increasing Media Choice Widens Gaps in Political Knowledge and Turnout," *American Journal of Political Science* 49 (July 2005): 557–92.

25. One proposal to require diversity of content may be found in Cass Sunstein, *Republic.com* (Princeton: Princeton University Press, 2001).

26. Quoted in Prior, "News vs. Entertainment," 589.

27. James Harding, "Billionaires Add to Left-Wing Funds," *Financial Times,* January 12, 2005.

28. See Michael Bailey, "The Two Sides of Money in Politics: A Synthesis and Framework," *Election Law Journal* 3 (2004): 662–64.

29. Clyde Wilcox et al., "With Limits Raised, Who Will Give More? The Impact of BCRA on Individual Donors," in *Life After Reform: When the Bipartisan Campaign Reform Act Meets Politics,* ed. Michael J. Malbin (Lanham, MD: Rowman and Littlefield, 2003), 65 and table 4.1.

30. For the 2002 income data, see U.S. Census Bureau, *Statistical Abstract of the United States 2004–5: The National Data Book,* 124th ed. (Baton Rouge: Claitor's Law Books and Publishing Division, 2005), table 669; for educational attainment in 2000 see ibid., table 214.

31. Richard Briffault, "Public Funding and Democratic Elections," *University of Pennsylvania Law Review* 148 (1999): 563, 575.

32. These estimates can be found in Thomas Piketty and Emmanuel Saez, "Income Inequality in the United States 1913–1998," *Quarterly Journal of Economics* 118 (February 2003): 5, table 1.

33. The National Election Studies, Center for Political Studies, University of Michigan, *The NES Guide to Public Opinion and Electoral Behavior* (Ann Ar-

bor: University of Michigan, Center for Political Studies, 1972–2002, table 3.1.1.) http://www.umich.edu/~nes/nesguide/nesguide.htm (accessed January 21, 2005). See also the file titled "Ideology by Income." The medians from the years 1990 to 2000 reveal that 26 percent of the rich are liberals, 23 percent are moderates, and 49 percent are conservatives. The data show significant variation during this era. The percentage of the richest identifying as liberals varied by 17 percent (with a high of 32 percent and a low of 15 percent), and conservatives exhibited a range of 11 percent (with a high of 53 percent and a low of 42 percent). The averages for each group (liberals 25 percent, moderates 21 percent, and conservatives 47 percent) do not depart all that much from the medians.

34. Ibid. See also the file titled "Ideology by Income."

35. Ibid., table 2.A.2. The NES offers two different surveys of partisan identification: one three-point scale and one seven-point scale. The latter includes both "independent Democrats" and "independent Republicans." The three-point scale does not. Unfortunately, the NES offers demographic breakdowns only for the three-point scale. As a result, we do not know what proportion of the rich identified themselves as "pure independents" and "partisan independents." That number must be higher than the 10 percent of pure independents among the rich.

36. It is difficult to determine the annual household income for the 68th percentile. I have averaged the lower limits for the top quintile and the second highest quintile to come up with the figure of "about $70,000." U.S. Census Bureau, "Historical Income Tables, Households, (Table) H-1. Income Limits for Each Fifth and Top 5 Percent of Households (All Races): 1967 to 2001," July 8, 2004. http://www .census.gov/hhes/income/histinc/h01.html.

37. National Election Studies, *NES Guide,* tables 2.A.2 and 3.1 and demographic breakdowns of the two tables.

38. From 1972 to 2002, National Election Studies found on average that 13.2 percent of conservatives and 12.8 percent of liberals reported giving money to a campaign. See ibid., table 6B.5.

39. See Center for Responsive Politics, "527 Committee Activity Top 50 Federally Focused Organizations," www.opensecrets.org (accessed February 14 and February 19, 2003).

40. See Center for Responsive Politics, "Top Individual Contributors to 527 Committees 2004 Election Cycle," www.opensecrets.org (accessed January 14, 2005).

41. Thomas B. Edsall and Derek Willis, "Fundraising Records Broken by Both Major Political Parties: Democrats Got More Money Than GOP for 1st Time Since '70s," *Washington Post,* December 3, 2004.

42. If we assume little or no intersection between the contributors who join an environmental group and those who join a pro-gun group, the number of contributors who are affiliated with both groups must be somewhere over 40 percent of the entire contributor pool.

43. The actual total membership must be far lower than the number quoted. I have generously and falsely assumed that none of the members of these groups has

a membership in another one of the Group of Ten organizations. The total membership is no lower than the membership of the largest group. Hence, environmentalists make up slightly less than 2 percent of the adult population of the United States. On the Group of Ten and their role in American politics, see "Group of Ten Environmental Organizations." CQ Electronic Library, CQ Public Affairs Collection, envtaz-0000027736. http://library.cqpress.com/cqpac/envtaz-0000027736 (accessed September 3, 2003). Originally published in David Hosansky, *Environment A to Z* (Washington, DC: CQ Press, 2000).

44. National Election Studies, *NES Guide,* table 3.1.

45. Jamin Raskin and Jon Bonifaz, "Equal Protection and the Wealth Primary," *Yale Law and Policy Review* 11 (1993): 273, 279–80.

46. Ibid., 273.

47. Smith, *Unfree Speech,* 152–65.

48. See Robert J. Franciosi, "Elections in Arizona, Clean and Unclean," in *Welfare for Politicians: Taxpayer Financing of Campaigns,* ed. John Samples (Washington, DC: Cato Institute, 2004), 66.

49. Norman J. Ornstein, Thomas E. Mann, and Michael J. Malbin, *Vital Statistics on Congress, 1999–2000* (Washington, DC: AEI Press, 2000), 21–22, 26–27.

50. For purposes of this figure, *conservative* was defined as encompassing all ADA scores between 0 and 30, *moderate* as scores between 31 and 70, and *liberal* as scores between 71 and 100.

51. See Hibbing and Theiss-Morse, *Stealth Democracy,* 239: "On most issues, the American people do not want to play an active role in the shaping of public policy, but they do want to be assured that if an occasion should arise when they are moved to participate, their participation would be welcome and meaningful."

52. Robert Dahl, *A Preface to Democratic Theory* (Chicago: University of Chicago Press, 1956), 90.

53. Jonathan Weisman, "Late Deals Got Tax Cut Done: With Deadline Looming, Negotiators Kept Cost at $350 Billion," *Washington Post,* May 30, 2003.

54. Richard Bennedetto, "10-Year Tax Cuts Signed into Law," *USA Today,* May 28, 2003.

55. Juliet Eilperin, "House Approves Tax Relief Bill: $82 Billion Measure Aimed at 6.5 Million Poor Families," *Washington Post,* June 13, 2003.

56. Ibid.

57. Amy Goldstein and Helen Dewar, "Senate Panel Approves Medicare Plan with Prescription Coverage; House Version Offers Similar Benefits," *Washington Post,* June 13, 2003.

58. Mary Agnes Carey, "Provisions of the Medicare Bill," *CQ Weekly,* January 24, 2004, 238.

59. I write "suggest" because this case encompasses a single dependent variable and two potential independent variables. We have more independent variables than cases and hence can draw no firm conclusions. Accordingly, this case should be considered heuristic rather than relevant to policy.

60. See Boards of Trustees, Federal Hospital Insurance and Federal Supplementary Medical Insurance Trusts Funds, *The 2004 Annual Report of the Boards of Trustees of the Federal Hospital Insurance and Federal Supplementary Medical Insurance Trusts Funds* (Washington, DC: Centers for Medicare and Medicaid Services), 60.

61. I am indebted to my colleague Jagadeesh Gokhale for information and for analysis of this complex legislation.

62. Perhaps those who object to the policy are really objecting to the distribution of rents from the spending. One might argue that campaign contributions precluded a policy that transfers its benefits from the drug companies to taxpayers or to the recipients of the benefit. For example, Congress could have used the government's power as the single purchaser of prescription drugs for Medicare to drive down the price of the products, thereby depriving the companies of profits that would accrue to taxpayers (in the form of lower taxes) or to recipients (in the form of more medicine). Yet policymakers might rationally have chosen against driving down prices in order to provide money for research and development for future medicines. They might, in other words, have not favored the welfare of the current generation more than that of future generations.

63. U.S. Census Bureau, "Registered Voter Turnout Improved in 2000 Presidential Election, Census Bureau Reports," Press Release, February 27, 2002. http://www.census.gov/Press-Release/www/releases/archives/voting/000505.html (accessed March 6, 2006).

64. The AARP could have a PAC but has chosen not to set one up. See Charles R. Morris, *The AARP: America's Most Powerful Lobby and the Clash of Generations* (New York: Times Books, 1996), 238–39. See also "Still the Biggest Bruiser," *Economist,* February 15, 2005, 26: "Although the AARP does not give a dime to any politician and refuses to endorse them, even if attractively ancient, its imprint is on dozens of other laws affecting entitlement programmes."

65. Stephen Holmes and Cass Sunstein, *The Costs of Rights: Why Liberty Depends on Taxes* (New York: Norton, 1999), chap. 3.

66. Daniel H. Weinberg, "A Brief Look at Postwar U.S. Income Inequality," updated May 13, 2004, http://www.census.gov/hhes/income/incineq/p60asc.html: "The long-run increase in income inequality is related to changes in the Nation's labor market and its household composition. The wage distribution has become considerably more unequal with more highly skilled, trained, and educated workers at the top experiencing real wage gains and those at the bottom real wage losses. One factor is the shift in employment from those goods-producing industries that have disproportionately provided high-wage opportunities for low-skilled workers, towards services that disproportionately employ college graduates, and towards low-wage sectors such as retail trade. . . . At the same time, long-run changes in living arrangements have taken place that tend to exacerbate differences in household incomes. For example, divorces and separations, births out of wedlock, and the increasing age at first marriage have led to a shift away from married-couple

households and toward single-parent and non-family households, which typically have lower incomes. Also, the increasing tendency over the period for men with higher-than-average earnings to marry women with higher-than-average earnings has contributed to widening the gap between high-income and low-income households."

67. National Opinion Research Center at the University of Chicago, *General Social Survey*, Codebook Variable: GOVEINQ, Question 802B, http://webapp.icpsr.umich.edu/GSS/.

68. Ibid., Codebook Variable: EQINC, table 746.

69. Ibid., Codebook Variable: Equalize, Table 767G.

70. See Library of Congress, Congressional Research Service, "Cash and Noncash Benefits for Persons with Limited Income: Eligibility Rules, Recipient and Expenditure Data, FY1998–FY2000," *CRS Report RL 31228,* November 19, 2001 (Washington, DC: Government Printing Office).

71. We have little evidence that these increases have done much to decrease poverty. See the research summarized in Jonathan Rauch, "Forget Haves and Have-Nots: Think Do's and Do-Nots," *National Journal,* September 19, 2003.

72. *Historical Tables, Budget of the U.S. Government,* Fiscal Year 2003 (Washington, DC: U.S. Government Printing Office, 2002), table 2.1, p. 30.

73. Internal Revenue Service, *Individual Income Tax Returns, Tax Year 2000, 1—Selected Income and Tax Items, by Size and Accumulated Size of Adjusted Gross Income—Continued* (Washington, DC: Internal Revenue Service, 2001), table 1.1. See also U.S. Congress, Joint Committee on Taxation, "Distribution of Certain Federal Tax Liabilities by Income Class for Calendar Year 2000 (JCX-45-00)," April 11, 2000.

74. For example, 52 percent of members of the lowest income group reported they did not vote in 2000, compared to 12 percent of those in the highest income group. Indeed, the figure of 52 percent was much larger than that of any other income group surveyed in 2000. See National Election Studies, *NES Guide,* table 6a.2.1. People in the lowest income group are also about three times more likely to not care who won the 2000 presidential election than are people in the highest income group. See ibid., table 6d.7.1.

75. R. Allen Hays, *Who Speaks for the Poor? National Interest Groups and Social Policy* (New York: Routledge, 2001), chap. 4.

76. Chris Edwards and Tad DeHaven, "Corporate Welfare Update," *Tax and Budget Bulletin* no. 7 (Washington, DC: Cato Institute, May 2002).

77. For a good discussion of the electoral origins of pork barrel spending, see Gregory Bovitz, "Electoral Consequences of Porkbusting in the U.S. House of Representatives," *Political Science Quarterly* 117 (2002): 455–57.

78. Steven J. Balla et al., "Partisanship, Blame Avoidance, and the Distribution of Legislative Pork," *American Journal of Political Science* 46 (July 2002): 515–25.

79. McConnell v. Federal Election Commission, 540 U.S. 93, 118, n. 5 (2003).

80. The majority in *McConnell v. FEC* cite the authority of the *Buckley* decision

regarding access as well as a number of witnesses testifying to the appearance of buying access if not actual influence. See McConnell v. FEC, 150.

81. Ibid.

82. Richard Hall and Frank Wayman, "Buying Time: Moneyed Interests and the Mobilization of Bias in Congressional Committees," *American Political Science Review* 84 (1990): 802–3.

83. Ibid., 814.

84. Ibid., 815.

85. Wawro defines legislative entrepreneurship thus: "Members engage in legislative entrepreneurship when they invest time, staff, and other resources to acquire knowledge of particular policy areas, draft legislation addressing issues in those areas, and shepherd their proposals through the legislative process by building and maintaining coalitions." Gregory Wawro, *Legislative Entrepreneurship in the U.S. House of Representatives* (Ann Arbor: University of Michigan Press), 2.

86. Ibid., 92, 96, table 4.4. Wawro utilizes a two-stage least squares regression analysis to deal with the typical problems of simultaneous determination found in most campaign finance topics. He concludes, "The coefficient on the entrepreneurship instrument is not statistically distinguishable from zero for either Democrats or Republicans [members of Congress]. We cannot say with much confidence that entrepreneurship has any effect on investor PAC contributions. From these results, it does not appear that members will engage in legislative entrepreneurship in order to attract contributions from investor PAC's."

87. The same was true in 1988. Sorauf writes: "To be stubbornly skeptical about it, however, we have no systematic evidence that contributions do in fact produce access." Frank Sorauf, *Money in American Elections* (Glendale, IL: Scott, Foresman/Little, Brown College Division, 1988), 314. This evidence leads to the same conclusion if one wishes to think of access as a problem of corruption of representation rather than a problem of political equality.

88. Michelle L. Chin, Jon R. Bond, and Nehemia Geva, "A Foot in the Door: An Experimental Study of PAC and Constituency Influence on Access," *Journal of Politics* 62 (May 2000): 543.

89. Marie Hojackni and David Kimball, "PAC Contributions and Lobbying Contacts in Congressional Committees," *Political Research Quarterly* 54 (March 2001): 176.

90. Scott H. Ainsworth, *Analyzing Interest Groups: Group Influence on People and Policies* (New York: Norton, 2002), 199–200.

Chapter Six

1. "The 107th Congress: The Senate." CQ Electronic Library, CQ Public Affairs Collection. http://library.cqpress.com/cqpac/vsap00-0000711306 (accessed

December 5, 2005). Originally published in Harold Stanley and Richard Niemi, *Vital Statistics on American Politics* (Washington, DC: CQ Press, 2001).

2. Editorial, "Steve Forbes Bows Out," *New York Times,* March 16, 1996.

3. B. Drummond Ayres Jr., "Feinstein Claims Victory in Senate Race," *New York Times,* November 19, 1994.

4. See Bradley A. Smith, *Unfree Speech: The Folly of Campaign Finance Reform* (Princeton: Princeton University Press, 2001), 70, for a list of some wealthy self-financiers who have lost along with a few who won.

5. See the results for the relevant year posted at State of New Jersey, Office of the Attorney General, Division of Elections. http://www.state.nj.us/lps/elections/results_2000_doe.html. Democrats enjoy a 7 percent advantage in registered voters in New Jersey; see http://www.state.nj.us/lps/elections/elec2000/gen_reg_cty_2000.html.

6. Frank Sorauf, *Money in American Politics* (Glenview, IL: Scott, Foresman/Little, Brown College Division, 1988), 300–301.

7. Robert Schlesinger and John Kruger, "Garden State Prepares for June 6 Primaries; Dem Senate: Florio vs. Corzine Pits Experience vs. Money," *The Hill,* May 31, 2000.

8. See "Sen. Jon Corzine," in Michael Barone, Grant Ujifusa, and Douglas Matthews, *Almanac of American Politics 2004* (Washington, DC: National Journal, 2003). http://nationaljournal.com/pubs/almanac/2004/people/nj/njs1.htm.

9. As it happened, Corzine decided to return to New Jersey and was elected governor. See David Kocieniewski, "Corzine's Running for Governor," *New York Times,* December 3, 2004.

10. There were other criticisms of term limits. One response appealed to democratic principles: if the people of a district did not like their member of Congress, they could simply vote him or her out of office. Term limits, on the other hand, denied the electorate the choice of voting for a candidate they preferred.

11. In at least one case—Thomas Mann of the Brookings Institution—a leader of the opposition to term limits also led the fight to enact McCain-Feingold. For his opposition to term limits, see Thomas E. Mann, "Congressional Term Limits: A Bad Idea Whose Time Should Never Come," in *The Politics and Law of Term Limits,* ed. Edward H. Crane and Roger Pilon (Washington, DC: Cato Institute, 1994).

12. James Madison in *The Federalist,* ed. Jacob E. Cooke (Middletown, CT: Wesleyan University Press, 1961), 349: "A dependence on the people is no doubt the primary controul on the government."

13. The authors of the Constitution, however, did not include a provision for rotation in office. Madison supported rotation in office. See Stephen C. Erickson, "A Bulwark Against Faction: James Madison's Case for Term Limits," *Policy Review* 63 (Winter 1993): 76.

14. The period before FECA was from 1950 to 1974; the period after FECA

encompasses 1976 to 2002. I exclude 1946 and 1948 as outliers that raised the pre-FECA average slightly.

15. James E. Campbell and Steve J. Jurek, "The Decline of Competition and Change in Congressional Elections," in *The United States Congress: A Century of Change*, ed. Sunil Ahuja and Robert Dewhirst (Columbus: Ohio State University Press, 2003), 20.

16. Ibid., 10.

17. James G. Gimpel, *Legislating the Revolution* (Boston: Allyn and Bacon, 1996), 8.

18. Lew Irwin, "A 'Permanent' Republican House? Patterns of Voter Performance and the Persistence of House Control," *Forum* 2 (2004): 11. Irwin defines *competitive seats* as seats for which the Republican candidates receive between 45 percent and 55 percent of the vote. The number of such seats declined by more than half from 1992 to 2000.

19. Gary King and Andrew Gelman, "Estimating Incumbency Advantage without Bias," *American Journal of Political Science* 34 (November 1990): 1143.

20. To estimate incumbency advantage, scholars need to know the vote share of both an incumbent and a candidate from the incumbent's party for the same district for the same year. This is impossible to observe directly because the incumbent runs or a candidate of his or her party runs. Scholars can, however, estimate the unobserved vote share in a district in a year.

21. See Gelman and King's empirical analysis for the twentieth century in "Estimating Incumbency Advantage," 1158. Their estimator may be found at 1151.

22. Ibid., 1138.

23. For perhaps the most persuasive version of this argument see Gary W. Cox and Jonathan N. Katz, *Elbridge Gerry's Salamander: The Electoral Consequences of the Reapportionment Revolution* (New York: Cambridge University Press, 2002), 7.

24. This conclusion is evident from examining average spending by incumbents and challengers in cases where the incumbent wins with more than 60 percent of the vote, where the incumbent wins with less than 60 percent of the vote, and where the incumbent loses. The data for congressional elections from 1980 to 1998 may be found in Norman J. Ornstein, Thomas E. Mann, and Michael J. Malbin, *Vital Statistics on Congress, 1999–2000* (Washington, DC: AEI Press, 2000), 82–83.

25. Campbell and Jurek, "Decline of Competition," 16.

26. Ibid., 17.

27. Philip L. Hersch and Gerald S. McDougall, "Campaign War Chests as a Barrier to Entry in Congressional Races," *Economic Inquiry* 32 (1994): 632–33.

28. Jay Goodliffe, "The Effect of War Chests on Challenger Entry in U.S. House Elections," *American Journal of Political Science* 45 (2001): 831.

29. Earlier studies postulated or found some deterrent effect of war chests on challengers. See Robert K. Goidel and Donald A. Gross, "A Systems Approach

to Campaign Finance in U.S. House Elections," *American Politics Quarterly* 22 (1994): 125–53; Janet M. Box-Steffensmeier, "A Dynamic Analysis of the Role of War Chests in Campaign Strategy," *American Journal of Political Science* 40 (1996): 352. Some work has focused on theory and identified a few situations in which war chests might deter challengers. See David Epstein and Peter Zemsky, "Money Talks: Deterring Quality Challengers in Congressional Elections," *American Political Science Review* 89 (1995): 295–308. These studies suffer from two shortcomings. First, a war chest affects and is affected by the election cycle. We can best measure war chests aimed at deterring challengers right after an election. Once the next election cycle begins, the war chest may be created in response to a challenge rather than to deter a contest. Second, and more important, previous studies do not take account of an incumbent's previous vote share. See Goodliffe, "Effect of War Chests," 832. An incumbent who had won by a substantial margin might well have a large war chest; at the same time, potential challengers would know that the incumbent was formidable as evinced by his or her winning margin. If we only look at war chests and the likelihood of a challenge to an incumbent, we might conclude that war chests deter challengers. That result, however, would be due to not considering the deterrent effects of an incumbent's vote share on challengers' decisions to run.

30. Goodliffe, "Effect of War Chests," 838. The effect on high-quality challengers is not statistically significant.

31. Goodliffe reports his statistical results for high-quality and low-quality challengers in the columns labeled "Model 2" columns at ibid., 836–37. None show a strong deterrent effect for war chests.

32. Jeffrey Milyo and Timothy Groseclose, "The Electoral Effects of Incumbent Wealth," *Journal of Law and Economics* 42 (1999): 714.

33. Scholars also trace the rise in incumbency advantage to 1966; see Cox and Katz, *Elbridge Gerry's Salamander,* 5. Gelman and King indicate that incumbency advantage entered a new path around 1970. See Gelman and King, "Estimating," 1158.

34. Contributions from political action committees go overwhelmingly to incumbents. See Stephen Ansolabehere and James M. Snyder Jr., "Money and Office: The Sources of Incumbency Advantage in Congressional Campaign Finance," in *Continuity and Change in House Elections,* ed. David W. Brady, John Cogan, and Morris Fiorina (Stanford: Stanford University Press, 2000), 65ff.

35. Anthony Corrado, "Party Soft Money," in *Campaign Finance Reform: A Sourcebook,* ed. Anthony Corrado, Thomas E. Mann, Daniel R. Ortiz, Trevor Potter, and Frank J. Sorauf (Washington, DC: Brookings Institution Press, 1997), 173

36. See Ornstein et al., *Vital Statistics,* 64, for the 1998 data.

37. Future scholarship may yield more mixed results regarding this point. One economist has advanced a theoretical case that under certain conditions limiting contributions could enhance welfare. See Stephen Coate, "Pareto-Improving

Campaign Finance Policy," *American Economic Review* 3 (June 2004): 628–55. In the final days of preparation of this work, an article appeared that reported on a forthcoming study of state legislative elections that concludes that "stricter limits on individuals, corporations, labor unions, and PACs are associated with narrower margins of victory and a greater number of candidates in elections." See Thomas Stratmann, "Some Talk: Money in Politics; A (Partial) Review of the Literature," *Public Choice* 124 (2005): 150. Whether this finding will bear up over time remains to be seen.

38. One must use the subjunctive because spending limits standing alone are at the time of writing unconstitutional.

39. For a review of this complicated literature, see Stratmann, "Some Talk," 137–40. Stratmann notes that some studies have found that incumbent spending is productive at the margins in U.S. Senate races but not in the House.

40. Gary C. Jacobson, "Enough Is Too Much: Money and Competition in House Elections," in *Elections in America*, ed. Kay Lehman Schlozman (Boston: Allen and Unwin, 1987), 176. Scholars have found that campaign spending is much more productive for challengers than for incumbents in France. Two economists who studied the 1993 legislative elections there determined that challenger spending was about twice as effective as spending by incumbents. They conclude that if spending limits were lowered by 50 percent, incumbents would have gained an extra ten percent of the popular vote over their closest challengers. Filip Palda and Kristian Palda, "The Impact of Campaign Expenditures on Political Competition in the French Legislative Elections of 1993," *Public Choice* 94 (1998): 168.

41. John R. Lott Jr., "Brand Names and Barriers to Entry in Political Markets," *Public Choice* 51 (1986): 88.

42. John R. Lott Jr., "Explaining Challengers' Campaign Expenditures: The Importance of Sunk Nontransferable Brand Name," *Public Finance Quarterly* 17 (January 1989): 109.

43. Ibid., 116.

44. Lott makes the excellent point that brand names are not the basic problem. The information costs (and related benefits) of discriminating between incumbents and challengers lead voters to rely on brand names in politics as in toothpaste. See Lott, "Brand Names," 91.

45. Jacobson, "Enough Is Too Much," 183.

46. Ibid., 192.

47. John J. Coleman and Paul F. Manna, "Congressional Campaign Spending and the Quality of Democracy," *Journal of Politics* 62 (2000), 771.

48. Ibid., 773.

49. Ibid., 775.

50. Ibid., 780; See also John J. Coleman, "Distribution of Campaign Spending," 929.

51. Coleman, "Distribution of Campaign Spending," 923, 931.

52. Markus Prior, "News vs. Entertainment: How Increasing Media Choice

Widens Gaps in Political Knowledge and Turnout," *American Journal of Political Science* 49 (July 2005), 589.

53. One study has challenged this conclusion. Alan Gerber argues that previous studies distorted the effects of incumbent spending by omitting factors in their models that would affect all campaign spending during an election. Once these factors are accounted for, Gerber believes, incumbent spending in Senate elections from 1974 to 1992 had about the same effects as challenger spending. That spells trouble for challengers because incumbents generally spend much more than their opponents. Overall, Gerber concludes, incumbents' spending boosted their returns by more than 6 percent in the period he studied. Alan Gerber, "Estimating the Effect of Campaign Spending on Senate Election Outcomes Using Instrumental Variables," *American Political Science Review* 92 (June 1998): 409. His research implies that incumbent spending strongly affects the competitiveness of Senate elections. Gerber argues that accurate estimates of the effects of incumbent outlays suggest that spending limits might increase the likelihood of winning for challengers. Ibid., 410.

54. Michael J. Malbin and Thomas L. Gais, *The Day After Reform: Sobering Campaign Finance Lessons from the American States* (Albany: Rockefeller Institute Press, 1998), 162, 166.

55. Patrick Basham and Martin Zelder, "Does Cleanliness Lead to Competitiveness? The Failure of Maine's Experiment with Taxpayer Financing of Campaigns," Cato Policy Analysis no. 456 (Washington, DC: Cato Institute, 2002). On the other hand, some as-yet unpublished research by Kenneth Mayer at the University of Wisconsin, Madison suggests public financing may reduce incumbency reelection rates. For a report on this research, see Stratmann, "Some Talk," 150.

56. As Sam Peltzman puts it: "Economic analysis begins by posing a counterfactual: What would the world have been like without regulation? Then the analyst compares the actual world to the counterfactual. Regulation is deemed successful only if its intended effects are realized to a greater degree than could have been reasonably expected according to the counterfactual benchmark." See Sam Peltzman, *Regulation and the Natural Progress of Opulence* (Washington, DC: AEI Press, 2005), 13–14.

57. See Jost, "Campaign Finance Reform."

58. More money has gone to the general elections because the grants seek to cover all costs for the fall campaigns; in contrast, the matching funds for the primaries cover only part of the costs of running. I am grateful to Allison Hayward for this point.

59. See the appendix to Scott Thomas, "The Presidential Election Public Funding Program," available at www.fec.org, for a comprehensive list of the candidates receiving public funding since 1976.

60. Data about presidential primary candidates come from *Congressional Quarterly's Guide to U.S. Elections,* ed. John L. Moore, Jon P. Preimesberger, and David R. Tarr (Washington, DC: Congressional Quarterly, 2001), 1:339–410.

61. This conclusion comes with a caveat. The methods of selecting a president varied during the two periods. Prior to 1972, party leaders dominated the selection of a party's presidential candidate; primaries played a small role. Beginning in 1968, primaries became increasingly important. By 1976, the votes cast in primaries determined the nominee. That difference makes it all the more surprising that there were more entries before 1976 in the primaries than afterward.

62. Peltzman notes that regulation often continues trends already noted prior to the advent of the regulation. See Peltzman, *Regulation and the Natural Progress of Opulence*, 12.

63. Stephen R. Weissman and Ruth A. Hassan, *Public Opinion Polls Concerning Public Financing of Federal Elections, 1972–2000: A Critical Analysis and Proposed Future Directions* (Washington, DC: Campaign Finance Institute, 2005), 2–3. This report is inclined to see the cup as half full regarding public support for public financing. Yet the report and this book agree that the public's response to public financing depends a great deal on the wording of questions.

64. See The Gallup Organization, "Gallup Poll #140, Question qn3a_formb," December 1938, http://institution.gallup.com. Subsequent references to data gathered by the Gallup Organization will refer to this URL.

65. In 1974, Gallup asked a similar question in a different format; see ibid., "Gallup Poll #917, question qn8_14," October. 1974. The response was similar to that for the 1974 question reported in the text. Hence I excluded this similar response from the table in the text.

66. See The Roper Center for Public Opinion Research at the University of Connecticut, Public Opinion Online, accession numbers 0021471, 0021474, and 0021486, http://www.ropercenter.uconn.edu/ipoll.html. Subsequent references to data gathered by the Roper Center will refer to this URL.

67. See ibid., accession number 0021490.

68. In 1979 and 1980, 53 percent and 54 percent of the public, respectively, reported being satisfied with presidential public financing. See ibid., accession numbers 0078552, 0078909.

69. See ibid., accession numbers 0347449, 0337260, 0315431.

70. See The Gallup Organization, "General Election Tracking Poll, 1996, week 9, qn 56_1," October–November 1996.

71. Polls results are generally accurate within an indicated range with a specified probability, often 95 percent. That implies that 5 percent of the time, the true population parameter will be outside the indicated range because of sampling error. This appears to be the case with the result reported in the text given that similar questions about this topic asked at nearly the same time report vastly different results.

72. Roper Center, accession number 0276554.

73. Roper Center, accession number 0276552.

74. The Gallup Organization, Gallup Poll, "March Wave 1, 1997, qn 12c."

75. Ibid, "November Wave 1, question: qn7f."

76. Ibid., "March Wave 1, 1997, qn12a."

77. Roper Center, accession numbers 0007846, 0144043, 0237790, 0237790, 0276551, 0352428, 0352427.

78. Roper Center, accession numbers 0339778, 0274653, 0221203.

79. William G. Mayer, "Public Attitudes on Campaign Finance," in *A User's Guide to Campaign Finance Reform*, ed. Gerald C. Lubenow (Lanham, MD: Rowman and Littlefield, 2001), 59–61.

80. Weissman and Hassan (*Public Opinion Polls*, 13–14) propose including both the benefits and the costs of public funding in survey questions. On the effects of mentioning the costs of the program, see ibid., 3.

81. The problem is inherent to surveys asking about policymaking. See Robert Weissberg, *Polling, Policy, and Public Opinion: The Case against Heeding the "Voice of the People"* (New York: Palgrave Macmillan, 2002), 33–34.

82. Candice J. Nelson, "Spending in the 2000 Election," in *Financing the 2000 Election*, ed. David B. Magleby (Washington, DC: Brookings Institution Press, 2002), 35. Another survey found that 10 percent of Americans contribute to campaigns. See Stephen Ansolabehere, John M. de Figueiredo, and James M. Snyder Jr., "Why Is There So Little Money in U.S. Politics?" *Journal of Economic Perspectives* 17 (Winter 2003): 108.

83. Malbin and Gais, *Day After Reform*, 68, figure 4-1, and 70.

84. "Recommendations of the Senate Watergate Committee." CQ Electronic Library, CQ Voting and Elections Collection, hsdc74-0001211704. http://library.cqpress.com/elections/hsdc74-0001211704 (accessed December 5, 2005). Originally published in *Historic Documents of 1974* (Washington, DC: CQ Press, 1975). In 1992, when Congress was considering public financing of campaigns, a majority killed an amendment to the bill that would have required advertising paid for by tax money to add the tag line "The preceding political advertisement was paid for with taxpayer funds." See "Campaign Finance, 1991–1992 Legislative Chronology." CQ Electronic Library, CQ Public Affairs Collection, catn89-0000013716. http://library.cqpress.com/cqpac/catn89-0000013716 (accessed December 5, 2005). Originally published in *Congress and the Nation, 89–92*, vol. 8 (Washington, DC: CQ Press, 1993).

85. The advantages of rapid fundraising might be offset by the votes lost because a candidate has fewer donors; see Dhammika Dharmapala and Filip Palda, "Are Campaign Contributions a Form of Speech? Evidence from Recent US House Elections," *Public Choice* 112 (July 2002): 81–114.

Chapter Seven

1. Political scientists often take at their word politicians who say they are pursuing the public interest in restricting campaign finance. A study of a congressional effort to restrict spending on political communications uncritically accepts as true

the stated purpose of the Political Broadcast Act of 1970: "to reduce costs of major American election campaigns by setting limits on how much individual candidates could spend on radio and television." Robert L. Peabody, Jeffrey M. Berry, William G. Frasure, and Jerry Goldman, *To Enact a Law: Congress and Campaign Financing* (New York: Praeger, 1972), 5. The same authors then attribute the law to "growing concern among American public officials, interest groups, the mass media, and private citizens over the use and possible abuse of television for political campaign purposes." Ibid., 6. Unfortunately, this naïve acceptance of the stated goals of legislators has marked much academic writing about campaign finance restrictions. For a more recent example, see Diana Dwyre and Victoria A. Farrar-Myers, *Legislative Labyrinth: Congress and Campaign Finance Reform* (Washington, DC: CQ Press, 2001), 244.

2. Brian Roberts, review of *Politics, Markets, and Congressional Policy Choices* by Peter VanDoren, *American Political Science Review* 86 (December 1992): 1074.

3. The public choice school of political economy has emphasized that the study of government and economics should begin with realistic premises about human conduct. For a brief introduction to public choice by one of its founders, see James M. Buchanan, "Politics without Romance: A Sketch of Positive Public Choice Theory and Its Normative Implications," in *The Logical Foundations of Constitutional Liberty*, vol. 1 of *The Collected Works of James M. Buchanan* (Indianapolis: Liberty Fund, 1999), 45–59. At least one historian has mentioned the self-interest of politicians. Writing about the 1970s, Julian E. Zelizer argues that politicians changed the campaign finance proposals "to satisfy their own needs." Julian E. Zelizer, "The Struggle Over Campaign Finance, 1956–1974," in *Money and Politics,* ed. Paula Baker (University Park: Penn State University Press, 2002), 74.

4. David R. Mayhew, *Congress: The Electoral Connection* (New Haven: Yale University Press, 1974).

5. Some political scientists have argued that representatives respond to changes in the public mood with strategic behavior. They modify their votes and policy positions or face defeat at the polls. See James A. Stimson, Michael B. MacKuen, and Robert Erikson, "Dynamic Representation," *American Political Science Review* 89 (September 1995): 543–45. I am suggesting a third option. Representatives can impede the translation of shifts in policy mood by changing the rules of electoral struggle.

6. See Michael Barone, "American Politics in the Networking Era," *National Journal,* February 25, 2005. Note that the relative value of volunteers to the parties may be changing. In the 2004 election, Republicans had four times as many volunteers than the Democrats to use in getting out the vote. See ibid.

7. See Pew Research Center for the People and the Press, *Media Consumption and Believability Study* (Washington, DC: Pew Research Center, 2004), 13.

8. Committee on House Administration, *History of the United States House of Representatives, 1789–1994* (Washington, DC: Government Printing Office, 1994).

9. See U.S. Senate, "Party Division in the Senate, 1789 to the Present." http://www.senate.gov/pagelayout/history/one_item_and_teasers/partydiv.htm (accessed March 3, 2006).

10. National Election Studies, *The NES Guide to Public Opinion and Electoral Behavior* (Ann Arbor: University of Michigan Center for Political Studies, 1995–2000), table 5A.1. http://www.umich.edu/~nes/nesguide/gd-index.htm#3 (accessed August 1, 2003).

11. See the data about public mood at the website for James A. Stimson, a professor of political science at the University of North Carolina, http://www.unc.edu/~jstimson/, and James A. Stimson, *Public Opinion in America,* 2d ed. (Boulder: Westview, 1998).

12. See the idea of anticipation of the public mood in Stimson et al., "Dynamic Representation," 545.

13. The government did not effectively require full disclosure of contributions until 1974. Hence, information about money in politics prior to that date will be an informed estimate at best.

14. Burton A. Abrams and Russell F. Settle, "The Economic Theory of Regulation and the Financing of Presidential Elections," *Journal of Political Economy* 86 (April 1978): 250.

15. The relevant part of the speech is as follows: "As the process of election becomes more complex and more costly, we must make it possible for those without personal wealth to enter public life without being obligated to a few large contributors. Therefore, I will submit legislation to revise the present unrealistic restriction on contributions—to prohibit the endless proliferation of committees, bringing local and State committees under the act—to attach strong teeth and severe penalties to the requirement of full disclosure of contributions—and to broaden the participation of the people, through added tax incentives, to stimulate small contributions to the party and to the candidate of their choice." See *Public Papers of the Presidents of the United States: Lyndon B. Johnson, 1966* (Washington, DC: Government Printing Office, 1967), 1:3–12. http://www.lbjlib.utexas.edu/johnson/archives.hom/speeches.hom/660112.asp.

16. Robert E. Mutch, *Congress, Campaigns, and Courts* (New York: Praeger, 1988), 30–31.

17. Herbert Alexander, *Financing the 1968 Election* (Lexington, MA: Lexington Books, 1971), 44, 50–51. Alexander estimates that about 30 percent of McCarthy's funding in 1968 came from fifty large donors.

18. Lyn Ragsdale, *Vital Statistics on the Presidency: Washington to Clinton* (Washington, DC: CQ Press, 1996), 105.

19. Dan T. Carter, *The Politics of Rage: George Wallace, the Origins of the New Conservatism, and the Transformation of American Politics* (Baton Rouge: Louisiana State University Press, 1996), 11, 14. In fact, Wallace depended largely on "hundreds of thousands of low- and middle-income Americans who mailed ten

and twenty dollar contributions—usually in cash—to the permanent 'Wallace Campaign' headquarters outside Montgomery." Ibid, 14.

20. "The 1968 and 1970 federal election campaigns saw a skyrocketing of political campaign spending by both major parties. There also was a profusion of affluent candidates which made political spending a major campaign issue in itself. By 1971, after Nixon's veto of the first reform bill, members came under considerable pressure to pass a bill that would be applicable to the 1972 presidential and congressional elections." "Inside Congress, 1969–1972 Overview." CQ Electronic Library, CQ Public Affairs Collection, catn69-0000863968. http://library.cqpress .com/cqpac/catn69-0000863968 (accessed December 5, 2005). Originally published in *Congress and the Nation, 69–72*, vol. 3 (Washington, DC: CQ Press, 1973).

21. Peabody et al., *To Enact a Law*, 7.

22. Abrams and Settle, "Economic Theory of Regulation," table 2, p. 249.

23. Peabody et al., *To Enact a Law*, 61.

24. For a history of proposed spending limits in campaign finance regulation, see Mutch, *Congress*, 32–34, 69–70.

25. Committee on House Administration, History, http://clerk.house.gov/ histHigh/Congressional_History/partyDiv.php. See also U.S. Senate, "Party Divisions," http://www.senate.gov/pagelayout/history/one_item_and_teasers/partydiv .htm/.

26. Mutch, *Congress*, 31–32.

27. *Federal Election Campaign Act*, Public Law 92-225, 92nd Cong., 2d sess. (February 7, 1972) (hereafter FECA 1971).

28. Ibid., Title I, § 102.

29. *Bipartisan Campaign Reform Act of 2002*, Public Law 107-155, 107th Cong., 2d sess. (March 27, 2002), § 323(b)(22). Public communication is defined as a "federal election activity" that may not be paid for by soft money. For an authoritative gloss on these restrictions, see Robert F. Bauer, *More Soft Money Hard Law* (Washington, DC: Perkins Coie LLP, 2003), 75–79.

30. FECA 1971, Title I, §§ 102, 104.

31. See the statement of Sen. Charles Percy (R-IL) quoted in Peabody et al., *To Enact a Law*, 17.

32. See *Campaign Contributions and Expenditures, California, 1970* (Princeton: Citizens' Research Foundation, n.d.) and *Campaign Contributions and Expenditures, New York, 1970* (Princeton: Citizens' Research Foundation, n.d.). Both of these documents may be found in the public records room of the Federal Election Commission.

33. "Inside Congress, 1969–1972 Overview," CQ Electronic Library, CQ Congress Collection, catn69-0000863968. http://library.cqpress.com/congress/catn69-0000863968 (accessed December 6, 2005). Originally published in *Congress and the Nation, 69–72*, vol. 3 (Washington, DC: CQ Press, 1973).

34. It is somewhat unclear how much McCarthy spent on media in New Hamp-

shire. His campaign manager, David Hoeh, reported much later that he originally planned to spend about $30,000 on television and radio. David C. Hoeh, *1968 McCarthy New Hampshire: "I Hear America Singing"* (Rochester, MN: Lone Oak, 1994), 390–91. Later the campaign found a "financial angel" who supported high spending on media. Ibid., 416. Hoeh also estimated that he spent at least $225,000 in total; since campaigns of that era spent 57 percent of their total spending on the media (Peabody et al., *To Enact a Law,* 7), Hoeh's number implies about $128,000 in media outlays. Herbert Alexander, the most careful student of campaign financing of the past forty years, estimated that McCarthy spent $75,000 on television and the same again on other media. Alexander, *Financing the 1968 Election,* 39. I have used the Alexander estimates. No estimates about McCarthy's spending in New Hampshire suggest his outlays would come in under the limits set out in FECA 1971.

35. Again there is ambiguity about the Wallace total. Herbert Alexander provides the $9 million estimate. Alexander, *Financing the 1968 Election,* 92. Ragsdale indicates that Wallace spent $7.2 million in 1968. Ragsdale, *Vital Statistics,* 143. I have again used the estimate of Alexander, the leading scholar in the field.

36. "Inside Congress, 1969–1972 Overview," CQ Electronic Library, CQ Congress Collection, catn69-0000863968. http://library.cqpress.com/congress/catn69-0 000863968 (accessed December 6, 2005). Originally published in *Congress and the Nation, 69–72,* vol. 3 (Washington, DC: CQ Press, 1973).

37. Herbert E. Alexander, Eugenia Grohman, Caroline D. Jones, and Clifford W. Brown Jr., *Financing the 1972 Election* (Lexington, MA: Lexington Books, 1976), 273.

38. FECA 1971, Title I, § 104(e).

39. Alexander et al., *Financing the 1972 Election,* 273. Direct mail became especially important: "[I]n some cases direct mailing was not employed merely as a substitute for broadcast communication, but was regarded as a superior means for reaching specially targeted groups with individualized messages." Ibid., 318–19. Over time, direct mail has become a common substitute for broadcast campaign spending; FECA 1971 accidentally pushed the parties toward the discovery of this method. Because it was an important part of Republican electoral success in the early 1980s, the law intended to thwart Republican candidates may have actually hastened their successes by making the virtues of direct mail campaigning evident.

40. Herbert E. Alexander, *Financing Politics: Money, Elections, and Political Reform* (Washington, DC: CQ Press, 1976), 194.

41. Nixon did not sign the bill until late February 1972, and it went into effect sixty days after his signing.

42. Theodore H. White wrote in 1973 that the two candidates represented "the same moralities"; see Theodore H. White, *The Making of the President 1972* (New York: Atheneum, 1973), 108.

43. Ibid.

44. Alexander et al., *Financing the 1972 Election,* 107.

45. White, *Making of the President 1972,* 83. White claims that McGovern cleverly harmed Muskie by demanding disclosure of campaign contributions. Muskie would not agree to such disclosure because much of his money came from "Republicans who despised Nixon and feared reprisal" if it were known they were giving to the Muskie campaign. Ibid.

46. White, *Making of the President 1972,* 105.

47. Ibid., 107.

48. Alexander et al., *Financing the 1972 Election,* 166–69.

49. "Campaign finance reform in the 1970s: The Watergate election." In *Guide to U.S. Elections,* ed. J. L. Moore, J. P. Preimesberger, and D. R. Tarr, vol. 1. (Washington, DC: CQ Press, 2001). CQ Electronic Library, CQ Voting and Elections Collection. http://library.cqpress.com/elections/gusel1-152-7221-392979 (accessed December 6, 2005). Document ID: gusel1-152-7221-392979.

50. Ibid.

51. Alexander, *Financing Politics,* 142.

52. "Watergate: A Constitutional Crisis; 1972–1974 Political Overview." CQ Electronic Library, CQ Congress Collection, catn73-0009170307. http://library .cqpress.com/congress/catn73-0009170307 (accessed December 6, 2005). Originally published in *Congress and the Nation, 73–76,* vol. 4 (Washington, DC: CQ Press, 1977).

53. "Watergate: A Constitutional Crisis; 1972–1974 Political Overview."

54. White House counsel Charles Colson admitted to concocting a plan to depreciate the reputation of Daniel Ellsberg, who leaked the Pentagon Papers. Colson was indicted for attempting to "influence, obstruct and impede the conduct and outcome" of Ellsberg's 1973 trial. "Criminal Information Filed by Watergate Special Prosecutor Against Former White House Special Counsel C. Colson; Colson Guilty Plea." CQ Electronic Library, CQ Public Affairs Collection, hsdc74-0001211692. http://library.cqpress.com/cqpac/hsdc74-0001211692 (accessed December 6, 2005). Originally published in *Historic Documents of 1974* (Washington, DC: CQ Press, 1975).

55. "Other documents showed that Nixon once suggested that Internal Revenue Service audit the tax returns of every member of Congress—and that Cabinet members and top White House aides be audited as well to deflect criticism. Nixon wrote to Haldeman: 'What I have in mind is that the IRS run audits of all top members of the White House staff, all members of the Cabinet and all members of Congress,' Nixon wrote. 'It could be said, if questions are raised, that this is what we are doing because of letters we have received indicating that people in government do not get IRS checks because of their special position.'" Harry F. Rosenthal, "Watergate Scandal May Have Sprung from '71 Nixon Memo to Haldeman," *Washington Post,* May 29, 1987.

56. Testifying before the Senate Watergate Committee, former White House

chief of staff H. R. Haldeman admitted funding "dirty tricks." See "Watergate Crisis, 1972–1976 Political Chronology," CQ Electronic Library, CQ Congress Collection, catn73-0009170361. http://library.cqpress.com/congress/catn73-0009170361 (accessed December 8, 2005). Originally published in *Congress and the Nation, 73–76,* vol. 4 (Washington, DC: CQ Press, 1977).

57. "Watergate: A Constitutional Crisis; 1972–1974 Political Overview."

58. Ibid.

59. Ibid.

60. Ibid.

61. Details of these contributions can be found in Alexander et al., *Financing the 1972 Election,* 708–10.

62. "Watergate Crisis, 1972–1976 Political Chronology." One other contributor became controversial during the Watergate period. In 1969 and 1970, $100,000 in cash was given by the financier Howard Hughes to President Nixon's close friend Charles G. "Bebe" Rebozo. Rebozo said the money was an advance contribution for the president's 1972 campaign and that he held it in a safe deposit box because a finance chairman had not been appointed. He returned the money to Hughes in June 1973. "Watergate: A Constitutional Crisis, 1972–1974 Political Overview."

63. "Watergate Crisis, 1972–1976 Political Chronology."

64. Ibid.

65. Ibid. See also "Final Watergate Report: A Summary Report of the 28-Month Investigation of the Watergate Scandal." CQ Electronic Library, CQ Public Affairs Collection, hsdc75-0001221794. http://library.cqpress.com/cqpac/hsdc75-0001221794 (accessed December 6, 2005). Originally published in *Historic Documents of 1975* (Washington, DC: CQ Press, 1976).

66. Ibid.

67. "Watergate: A Constitutional Crisis; 1972–1974 Political Overview."

68. "Watergate Crisis, 1972–1976 Political Chronology."

69. "Final Watergate Report."

70. Charles C. Euchner, John Anthony Maltese, and Michael Nelson, "Presidential Campaign Finance in the Nineteenth and Twentieth Centuries." CQ Electronic Library, CQ Voting and Elections Collection, g2przi-135-7417-397830. http://library.cqpress.com/elections/g2przi-135-7417-397830 (accessed December 6, 2005). Originally published in *Guide to the Presidency,* vol. 1 (Washington, DC: CQ Press, 2002).

71. "Watergate Crisis, 1972–1976 Political Chronology."

72. For the self-righteousness of Nixon's critics, see Charles. R. Morris, *Time of Passion, 1960–1980* (New York: HarperCollins, 1984), 153–54.

73. "Recommendations of the Senate Watergate Committee." CQ Electronic Library, CQ Public Affairs Collection, hsdc74-0001211704. http://library.cqpress.com/cqpac/hsdc74-0001211704 (accessed December 6, 2005). Originally published in *Historic Documents of 1974* (Washington, DC: CQ Press, 1975).

74. John W. Kingdon, *Agendas, Alternatives, and Public Policies,* 2nd ed. (New York: Longman, 2003), chap. 5.

75. "Recommendations of the Senate Watergate Committee."

76. Ibid.

77. Ibid.

78. Alexander et al., *Financing the 1972 Election,* 632.

79. "Campaign Finance Reform in the 1970s: The Watergate Election." CQ Electronic Library, CQ Voting and Elections Collection, gusel1-152-7221-392979. http://library.cqpress.com/elections/gusel1-152-7221-392979 (accessed December 6, 2005). Originally published in *Guide to U.S. Elections,* ed. John L. Moore, Jon P. Preimesberger, and David R. Tarr, vol. 1 (Washington, DC: CQ Press, 2001).

80. There are more serious arguments about money and the Watergate crisis. Herbert Alexander states that Republican fundraising success in 1972 led to Watergate: "The Republicans had an excessive amount of money available and, as a consequence, had the flexibility to indulge themselves in the ventures. That led to Watergate. . . . In politics, too much money can be as damaging as too little money. A campaign with a lean budget does not indulge in elaborate espionage and sabotage schemes." Alexander, *Financing Politics,* 194. To explain the crisis he offers a variant of the traditional argument that there's too much money in politics. Yet we might ask: What is "an excessive amount of money"? Adjusted for inflation, there was almost as much spending per capita in 1936 as in 1972. Looked at as a proportion of national wealth, almost all presidential elections from 1900 to 1968 cost more than the 1972 contest (the exception was 1948). Abrams and Settle, "Economic Theory of Regulation," table 2, p. 249. None of these elections had campaigns engaged in "elaborate espionage and sabotage schemes."

81. The conference report on the bill was approved by a vote of 60 to 16 in the U.S. Senate and 365 to 24 in the House of Representatives. "Campaign Finance Reform, 1974 Legislative Chronology," CQ Electronic Library, CQ Congress Collection, catn73-0009170395. http://library.cqpress.com/congress/catn73-0009170395 (accessed December 6, 2005). Originally published in *Congress and the Nation,* 73–76, vol. 4 (Washington, DC: CQ Press, 1977).

82. See *Federal Election Campaign Act Amendments of 1974,* Public Law 93-443, 93rd Cong., 2d sess. (October 15, 1974), Title I, § 101(c)(1)(A), (C).

83. Alexander et al., *Financing the 1972 Election,* 272.

84. Ibid., 271.

85. The 1974 law permitted $200,000 total spending in New Hampshire; in 1972, the McGovern campaign spent at least $161,000 in that state. Some large contributors, however, paid some bills directly. McGovern may well have exceeded the 1974 limit. He also would have come close to the spending limit for the Wisconsin primary, the fourth of 1972. Ibid., 112. McGovern spent $440,000 in Wisconsin; the 1974 limit would have been $474,400. Ibid.

86. McGovern spent $3,190,000 in 1972 in California. See ibid., 118. The limit under the 1974 law would have been $2,429,920 (the state's voting-age population multiplied by sixteen cents).

87. Ibid., 165.

88. *Federal Election Campaign Act Amendments of 1974,* Title I, § 101(c)(1)(C).

89. Ibid., Title I, § 101(c)(1)(D). Small states with one representative were limited to twelve cents per adult in the state or $150,000, whichever was larger.

90. "The Political Year, 1972." CQ Electronic Library, CQ Voting and Elections Collection, catn69-0008167132. http://library.cqpress.com/elections/catn69-0008167132 (accessed December 6, 2005). Originally published in *Congress and the Nation, 69–72,* vol. 3 (Washington, DC: CQ Press, 1973).

91. If we extend the zone of electoral vulnerability in 1972 to those who received 60 percent of the vote or less, we find that twenty-one winners in the Senate, or two-thirds of the whole group, might have reason to believe they would face tough races for reelection. Data calculated by the author from returns found at "Senate General Elections, All States, 1972 Summary," CQ Electronic Library, CQ Voting and Elections Collection, avg1972-2us1. http://library.cqpress.com/elections/avg1972-2us1 (accessed December 6, 2005). Originally published in *CQ Voting and Elections Collection (Web site)* (Washington, DC: CQ Press, 2003).

92. Lance Tarrance Jr. suggested the importance of this example in a private conversation.

93. Norman J. Ornstein, Thomas E. Mann, and Michael J. Malbin, *Vital Statistics on Congress, 1999–2000* (Washington, DC: AEI Press, 2000), 57.

94. Ibid., 64.

95. "House General Elections, All States, 1972 Summary," CQ Electronic Library, CQ Voting and Elections Collection, avg1972-3us1. http://library.cqpress.com/elections/avg1972-3us1 (accessed December 6, 2005). Originally published in *CQ Voting and Elections Collection (Web site)* (Washington, DC: CQ Press, 2003).

96. "Senate General Elections, All States, 1972 Summary." CQ Electronic Library, CQ Voting and Elections Collection, avg1972-2us1. http://library.cqpress.com/elections/avg1972-2us1 (accessed December 6, 2005). Originally published in *CQ Voting and Elections Collection (Web site)* (Washington, DC: CQ Press, 2003).

97. Common Cause, *Campaign Finance Monitoring Project,* 10 vols. (Washington, DC: Common Cause, 1974). These documents are available in the public records room of the Federal Election Commission.

98. "Had it not been for Watergate, there would have been no contribution limits to debate." Mutch, *Congress,* 66.

99. Thomas Gais, *Improper Influence: Campaign Finance Law, Political Interest Groups, and the Problem of Equality* (Ann Arbor: University of Michigan Press, 1996), 2.

100. Ibid., 38–39, 69.

101. Ibid., 32–33, 38–39.

102. See Thomas B. Edsall, "Liberals Form Fund to Defeat President," *Washington Post,* August 8, 2003.

103. Gais, *Improper Influence,* 3.

104. Steven M. Gillon, *"That's Not What We Meant to Do": Reform and Its Unintended Consequences in Twentieth-Century America* (New York: Norton, 2000), 212–14. The union leaders reasoned that because businesses had not utilized PACs in the past, they would not do so in the future.

105. Gais (*Improper Influence,* 166) argues that over time this bias benefited business groups the most; Gillon (*"That's Not What We Meant to Do,"* 214–15) agrees.

106. Thomas Gais, email correspondence with the author.

107. "Political Contributions and Campaign Spending, 1965–1968 Overview," CQ Electronic Library, CQ Public Affairs Collection, catn65-0000762884. http://library.cqpress.com/cqpac/catn65-0000762884 (accessed December 13, 2005). Originally published in *Congress and the Nation, 65–68,* vol. 2 (Washington, DC: CQ Press, 1969).

108. See Federal Election Commission, *Public Funding of Presidential Elections* (Washington, DC: Federal Election Commission, 2005).

109. "Election Laws and Procedures, 1973–1976 Legislative Chronology," CQ Electronic Library, CQ Voting and Elections Collection, catn73-0009170386. http://library.cqpress.com/elections/catn73-0009170386 (accessed December 6, 2005). Originally published in *Congress and the Nation, 73–76,* vol. 4 (Washington, DC: CQ Press, 1977).

110. Ibid. The 1973 bill proposed giving each House candidate fifteen cents multiplied by the voting-age population of his or her particular district or $90,000, whichever sum was greater. I have assumed the sum would always have been $90,000. By 1971, House districts were constitutionally required to be roughly equal in population. If we take the voting-age population of the United States in 1971, divide by the number of seats in the House (435) and multiply by fifteen cents, we discover that each House candidate would have received about $48,500. Hence, $90,000 would have always been the larger sum.

111. For a history of proposed spending limits in campaign finance regulation, see Mutch, *Congress,* 32–34, 69–70.

112. Abrams and Settle, "Economic Theory of Regulation," table 2, p. 249.

113. 26 U.S.C. § 9004(a)(1) (2003): "The eligible candidates of each major party in a presidential election shall be entitled to equal payments under section 9006 in an amount which, in the aggregate, shall not exceed the expenditure limitations applicable to such candidates under section 320(b)(1)(B) of the Federal Election Campaign Act of 1971."

114. Abrams and Settle, "Economic Theory of Regulation," 251.

115. Ibid., 256.

116. See Terry M. Moe, "The Politics of Bureaucratic Structure," in *Can the*

Government Govern? ed. John E. Chubb and Paul E. Peterson (Washington, DC: Brookings Institution, 1989), 267–68.

117. For a summary of the theory and evidence for capture by regulated interests, see Sam Peltzman, "The Economic Theory of Regulation after a Decade of Deregulation," Brookings Papers in Economic Activity 1989 (Washington, DC: Brookings Institution, 1989), 5–9.

118. Mutch, *Congress,* 84–86.

119. Ibid., 86.

120. "Recommendations of the Senate Watergate Committee."

121. Mutch, *Congress,* 87–88.

122. Buckley v. Valeo, 424 U.S. 1, 126 (1976).

123. "Election Laws and Procedures, 1973–1976 Legislative Chronology."

124. Wertheimer is quoted in Helen Dewar, "Campaign Reformers Eye Elimination of the FEC; Proposal Is Readied to Create an Agency, Stripped of Politics, to Promptly Enforce New Finance Law," *Washington Post,* April 2, 2002.

Chapter Eight

1. David C. King, "The Polarization of American Parties and Mistrust of Government," in *Why People Don't Trust Government,* ed. Joseph Nye Jr., Philip D. Zelikow, and David C. King (Cambridge: Harvard University Press, 1997), 161–62.

2. See the partisan divisions reported in U.S. Congress, *Congressional Directory* (Washington, DC: Joint Committee on Printing, 1977 and biennial thereafter).

3. The bill is an anomaly for my hypothesis. Given that, I must show that the bill is not a *significant* anomaly that calls into question the hypothesis. The idea of a significant anomaly and its role in science is explored in Stephen Toulmin, Richard Rieke, and Allan Janik, *An Introduction to Reasoning* (New York: Macmillan, 1984), 319.

4. Bob Williams and CQ Staff, "Pledge Flap Ruffles Hill: Are Amendments Ahead?" *CQ Weekly,* June 29, 2002, 1708.

5. "Campaign Finance, 1991–1992 Legislative Chronology," CQ Electronic Library, CQ Congress Collection, catn89-0000013716. http://library.cqpress.com/congress/catn89-0000013716 (accessed December 6, 2005). Originally published in *Congress and the Nation, 89–92,* vol. 8 (Washington, DC: CQ Press, 1993).

6. Ibid.

7. "Campaign Finance, 1993–1994 Legislative Chronology," CQ Electronic Library, CQ Public Affairs Collection, catn93-12-3817-209303. http://library.cqpress.com/cqpac/catn93-12-3817-209303 (accessed December 6, 2005). Originally published in *Congress and the Nation, 93–96,* vol. 9 (Washington, DC: CQ Press, 1997).

8. James G. Gimpel, *Legislating the Revolution* (Boston: Allyn and Bacon, 1996), 1.

9. The evidence for this claim may be found in chapter 7 of this book and the work of Gary Jacobson cited therein.

10. In 1993 and 1994, the FEC also worked on regulations meant to stop members of Congress from spending campaign money on personal needs. See "Campaign Finance Spending Regulations, 1993–1994 Legislative Chronology," CQ Electronic Library, CQ Congress Collection, catn93-0000141395. http://library .cqpress.com/congress/catn93-0000141395 (accessed December 6, 2005). Originally published in *Congress and the Nation, 93–96,* vol. 9 (Washington, DC: CQ Press, 1997).

11. I emphasize that I am using the name *McCain* to refer to all the sponsors of McCain-Feingold and their advisors on legislative strategy. The collective name for the bill refers to a number of members of Congress including John McCain, Russell Feingold, Christopher Shays, Martin Meehan, Olympia Snowe, James Jeffords, and others. Since I have discovered no evidence of disagreements among the sponsors, this stylization seems defensible.

12. "Campaign Finance, 1999–2000 Legislative Chronology," CQ Electronic Library, CQ Congress Collection, catn97-97-6356-326176. http://library.cqpress .com/congress/catn97-97-6356-326176 (accessed December 6, 2005). Originally published in *Congress and the Nation, 97–01,* vol. 10 (Washington, DC: CQ Press, 2002).

13. Stephen Ansolabehere, John M. de Figueiredo, and James M. Snyder Jr., "Why Is There So Little Money in U.S. Politics?" *Journal of Economic Perspectives* 17 (Winter 2003): 117.

14. Lacking direct measures of constituency preferences, political scientists often use the two-party presidential vote in a district to indicate ideological preferences. See Stephen Ansolabehere, James M. Snyder Jr., and Charles Stewart III, "Candidate Positioning in House Elections," *American Journal of Political Science* 45 (January 2001): 140, and the seven studies cited therein using presidential votes in this fashion.

15. Shweta Govindarajan, "Dems Target Shays in Race for House," *The Hill,* June 16, 2004, 19.

16. In the House and the Senate, these differences in the average Bush vote constitute one standard deviation from the mean.

17. They may be found for each district in Michael Barone, Richard E. Cohen, and Grant Ujifusa, *The Almanac of American Politics 2002* (Washington, DC: National Journal, 2001).

18. Unfortunately, a comparable set of Cook ratings does not exist for the Republican senators who voted for McCain-Feingold.

19. I used the ADA scores for 1999–2000 for members elected prior to 2000. I used the ADA scores for 2001, the first session of the 107th Congress, for members elected in 2000.

20. It is thus somewhat misleading to accept the conventional view that moder-

ate Republicans were essential to the success of McCain-Feingold. The Republican supporters of the bill were not all that moderate and, in any case, their vulnerability at the polls mattered more than their ideology. For the view that moderate Republicans were vital to passing campaign finance regulation, see Diana Dwyre and Victoria A. Farrar-Myers, *Legislative Labyrinth: Congress and Campaign Finance Reform* (Washington, DC: CQ Press, 2001), 237.

21. In fact, the average Republican who supported McCain-Feingold (ADA score: 20) was closer ideologically to the average Republican who was against the bill (ADA score: 5.6) than he or she was to the bill's sponsor, Christopher Shays (ADA score: 40). McCain would have found a similar story in the Senate. The average Republican who supported his bill (ADA mean score: 18.6) was to the left of the average Republican who voted against it (ADA score 3.2), but both were conservatives by any measure. For McCain, appeals to liberalism would not work with Republican members of Congress. That said, the ideological differences noted here do provide a clue to why the law passed.

22. Congressional Quarterly's party unity score is a percentage of votes in which a representative supported his or her party when a majority of voting Democrats opposed a majority of voting Republicans. See "The 107th Congress: The House of Representatives," CQ Electronic Library, CQ Public Affairs Collection, vsap00-0000711322. http://library.cqpress.com/cqpac/vsap00-0000711322 (accessed December 6, 2005). Originally published in Harold Stanley and Richard Niemi, *Vital Statistics on American Politics* (Washington, DC: CQ Press, 2001).

23. The term *branding exercise* was suggested by Robert F. Bauer when reviewing this manuscript. Based on his experiences with the writing of McCain-Feingold, Bauer believes the branding motive was more important in attracting votes by congressional Republicans than was their vulnerability. I suggest that both mattered and that members need not have chosen between them.

24. Voters generally know little about campaign finance laws; see William G. Mayer, "Public Attitudes on Campaign Finance," in *A User's Guide to Campaign Finance Reform,* ed. Gerald C. Lubenow (Lanham, MD: Rowman and Littlefield, 2001), 513.

25. "Campaign Finance, 1995–1996 Legislative Chronology," CQ Electronic Library, CQ Congress Collection, catn93-0000141394. http://library.cqpress.com/congress/catn93-0000141394 (accessed December 6, 2005). Originally published in *Congress and the Nation, 93–96,* vol. 9 (Washington, DC: CQ Press, 1997).

26. Stephen Ansolabehere and James M. Snyder Jr., "Money and Office: The Sources of Incumbency Advantage in Congressional Campaign Finance," in *Continuity and Change in House Elections,* ed. David W. Brady, John Cogan, and Morris Fiorina (Stanford: Stanford University Press, 2000), 40–64.

27. "Campaign Finance Reform, 1997–1998 Legislative Chronology," CQ Electronic Library, CQ Congress Collection, catn97-97-6356-326161. http://library.cqpress.com/congress/catn97-97-6356-326161 (accessed December 6, 2005). Origi-

nally published in *Congress and the Nation, 97–01,* vol. 10 (Washington, DC: CQ Press, 2002).

28. Dwyre and Farrar-Myers (*Legislative Labyrinth,* 242) mention the exclusion of the PACs from the bill in 1997 but provide no analysis of why McCain dropped the PAC sections.

29. "McCain-Feingold Campaign Financing Bill, 1998 Legislative Chronology." CQ Electronic Library, CQ Public Affairs Collection, cqal98-0000191100. http://library.cqpress.com/cqpac/cqal98-0000191100 (accessed December 6, 2005). Originally published in *CQ Almanac 1998* (Washington, DC: CQ Press, 1999). That number overstates initial Republican support for the bill. The revised McCain-Feingold bill fell victim to a filibuster in the Senate, coming up eight votes short of invoking cloture. That defeat all put precluded the danger that campaign finance legislation would pass in 1998. Knowing that, some Republican House members were free to vote for Shays-Meehan to prove they were against corruption.

30. David Nather, "Campaign Finance Bill Evokes Opportunity and Trepidation," *CQ Weekly,* March 2, 2002, 569.

31. Marianne Holt, "The Surge in Party Money in Competitive 1998 Congressional Elections," in *Outside Money: Soft Money and Issue Advocacy in the 1998 Congressional Elections,* ed. David B. Magleby (Lanham, MD: Rowman and Littlefield, 2000), 32.

32. Wilcox's work is discussed in Nather, "Campaign Finance Bill," 569.

33. The sponsors of the increase in hard money limits were Fred Thompson (R-TN) and Dianne Feinstein (D-CA). For some Democrats, the increase in hard money limits might have been appealing because their interests as incumbents trumped their commitment to their party. This interpretation draws on comments by Robert Bauer in private conversation.

34. Matthew Tully, "Riders to Tell If Campaign Finance Bill Flies or Dies," *CQ Weekly,* March 10, 2002, 522. Thus Fred Thompson (R-TN), a supporter of McCain-Feingold, noted: "I've always said it's just a matter of time before Democrats express in public what they've always expressed in private. That the soft money ban would hurt them more than it would hurt us" (ibid.).

35. Breaux and the unidentified lobbyist are quoted in Andrew Taylor and Derek Willis, "As Campaign Finance Debate Nears, Maneuvers and Worries Intensify," *CQ Weekly,* March 17, 2001, 591.

36. Seth Gitell, "The Democratic Party Suicide Bill," *Atlantic Monthly,* July–August 2003, 106.

37. My analysis assumes that Democratic leaders focused on their relative position in fundraising. Some Democratic leaders—for example, Tony Coelho—argued that Democrats should not worry about their relative position and simply raise any money they could, a position that assumed Republicans would always raise more money than Democrats. I owe this point to Robert Bauer.

38. Nather, "Campaign Finance Bill," 569.

39. Joseph Lieberman (D-CT) remarked in 2001, "We've taken so strong a position as a party in favor of this bill and against soft money that we've got to stay the course." See Taylor and Willis, "As Campaign Finance Debate Nears," 591.

40. The 527 option existed for several years prior to the enactment of McCain-Feingold and was used in the 2000 election. See Frances R. Hill, "Softer Money: Exempt Organizations and Campaign Finance," *Tax Notes* 91 (April 16, 2001): 388–89.

41. Derek Willis, "Campaign Finance Kickoff," *CQ Weekly,* January 27, 2001, 215.

42. See the comment by Boxer quoted in the introduction at n. 18.

43. Shaw is quoted in Juliet Eilperin, "Feeling the Sting of 'Soft Money': Some in House GOP Rethink Position on Campaign Reform," *Washington Post,* October 14, 2000.

44. Robert F. Bauer, *More Soft Money Hard Law* (Washington, DC: Perkins Coie LLP, 2003), 76.

45. Derek Willis, "Debating McCain-Feingold," *CQ Weekly,* March 10, 2001, 524.

46. Anthony Corrado, "Financing the 2000 Election," in *The Election of 2000,* ed. Gerald M. Pomper (New York: Chatham House, 2001), 108–9.

47. Bayh is quoted in Tully, "Riders to Tell If Campaign Finance Bill Flies or Dies," 522.

48. Michael Pfau, R. Lance Holbert, Erin Alison Szabo, and Kelly Kaminski, "Issue Advocacy v. Candidate Advertising: Effects on Candidate Preference and Democratic Process," *Journal of Communication* 52 (June 2002): 312. This article reports a study of the effects of actual issue ads and other advertising on first-time voters. As the authors note, it is uncertain how far we can generalize from this study to the population as a whole; ibid., 313.

49. In an earlier version of this manuscript I assumed that the Enron scandal that broke at the beginning of 2002 helped the legislation pass. Robert Bauer, who followed the development of the bill closely, has convinced me that the Enron episode did not matter that much: "[T]he floor debates, especially in the House, did make use of Enron's collapse—but this always struck me as a talking point, not really a factor moving the initiative toward a successful conclusion. No one I knew at any time thought that this was a meaningful scandal with a bearing on passage of the bill." Robert F. Bauer, email correspondence to the author, August 29, 2005.

50. *Bipartisan Campaign Reform Act of 2002,* Public Law 107-55, 107th Cong., 2d sess., March 27, 2002, §§ 307, 319. The limits are increased sixfold for Senate races and threefold for House races. The provisions also covered self-financiers. The Senate also saw some failed efforts at opportunism by members. Robert Torricelli (D-NJ) added a provision requiring broadcasters to sell advertising time to candidates and parties at the lowest rate offered. (The broadcasters succeeded in removing this provision in the House.)

51. Democrats did understand the consequences of the most self-serving aspects of the law. Both the minority leader and the ranking Democratic member of the Rules Committee noted that the plain effect of the "millionaire amendment" would be "incumbent protection." See Robert F. Bauer, "When 'The Pols Make the Calls': *McConnell's* Theory of Judicial Deference in the Twilight of *Buckley*," *University of Pennsylvania Law Review* 153 (November 2004): 27.

52. Brian Roberts, review of *Politics, Markets, and Congressional Policy Choices* by Peter Van Doren, *American Political Science Review* 86 (December 1992): 1094.

53. Recently two scholars have fashioned a formal model that indicates the parties might have agreed to end soft money fundraising because the costs (in terms of the appearance of corruption) outweighed the benefits to both. See David Gill and Christine S. Lipsmeyer, "Soft Money and Hard Choices: Why Political Parties Might Legislate Against Soft Money Donations," *Public Choice* 123 (2005): 411–38. The formal model depends on donors' splitting contributions between the parties. As noted above, soft money donors in fact rarely engaged in such dual funding.

Chapter Nine

1. See McConnell v. Federal Election Commission, 540 U.S. 93 (2003).

2. See Stephen Breyer, "Madison Lecture: Our Democratic Government," *New York University Law Review* 77 (2002): 245–72. See also Robert F. Bauer, "When 'The Pols Make the Calls': *McConnell's* Theory of Judicial Deference in the Twilight of *Buckley*," *University of Pennsylvania Law Review* 153 (2004): 13.

3. McConnell v. Federal Election Commission, 137.

4. James Madison in *The Federalist*, ed. Jacob E. Cooke (Middletown, CT: Wesleyan University Press, 1961), 59.

5. Representative Clay Shaw as quoted in Juliet Eilperin, "Feeling the Sting of 'Soft Money': Some in House GOP Rethink Position on Campaign Reform," *Washington Post*, October 14, 2000.

6. McConnell v. Federal Election Commission, 171.

7. As Richard Hasen notes, "In an era of faxes, web pages, and e-mails, it is hard to imagine any contribution limit that would fail the test of constitutionality." Richard L. Hasen, "*Buckley* Is Dead, Long Live *Buckley*: The New Campaign Finance Incoherence of *McConnell v. Federal Election Commission*," *University of Pennsylvania Law Review* 153 (2004): 44.

8. McConnell v. Federal Election Commission, 129.

9. See Bruce E. Cain, "Reasoning to Desired Outcomes: Making Sense of *McConnell v. FEC*," *Election Law Journal* 3 (2004): 217, 218–19.

10. McConnell v. Federal Election Commission, 150.

11. Hasen, "*Buckley* Is Dead," 44–45.

12. *Bipartisan Campaign Reform Act of 2002,* Public Law 107-55, 107th Cong., 2d sess., March 27, 2002, § 323a.

13. Ibid., § 323b.

14. See Hasen, "*Buckley* Is Dead," 50.

15. *Bipartisan Campaign Reform Act of 2002,* § 323d.

16. See Hasen, "*Buckley* Is Dead," 50–51.

17. McConnell v. Federal Election Commission, 356.

18. The term comes from Hasen, "*Buckley* Is Dead," 57.

19. I borrow this term from J. M. Balkin, "Populism and Progressivism as Constitutional Categories," *Yale Law Journal* 104 (1995): 1942.

20. See Michael Barone, "American Politics in the Networking Era," *National Journal,* February 25, 2005: "The parties went about raising their turnout in different ways. The Democrats depended on labor unions, as they had in the past, and on the turnout efforts of billionaire-funded '527' organizations. (These are named after a section of the Internal Revenue Code, and a number of these groups were funded by rich men like George Soros, who spent $27 million trying to defeat George W. Bush). . . . Over two years, the Bush campaign built an organization of 1.4 million active volunteers. This was unprecedented. By way of comparison, the Democratic National Committee has said it enlisted 233,000 volunteers during the 2004 campaign" (22).

21. I owe this point to Cleta Mitchell.

22. McCain has said, "Theodore Roosevelt was the great reformer. He took on the robber barons. He was a great conservationist. He . . . you know, we've got to return to his kinds of principles in my view." See "Bill Moyers Interviews Sen. John McCain," *NOW with Bill Moyers,* PBS transcript, December 13, 2002, http://www.pbs.org/now/transcript/transcript_mccain.html.

23. Republican members have not consistently supported liberalization. Many voted for the 1974 law, and the GOP tried to ban PACs as late as 1992 because labor unions used such committees to support the Democratic Party. See "Campaign Finance, 1991–1992 Legislative Chronology." CQ Electronic Library, CQ Congress Collection, catn89-0000013716. http://library.cqpress.com/congress/catn89-0000013716 (accessed December 7, 2005). Originally published in *Congress and the Nation, 89–92,* vol. 8 (Washington, DC: CQ Press, 1993).

24. About half of the money used by the Club for Growth was raised and spent by its 527 group. See Glenn Justice, "F.E.C. Sues Republican Group over Political Contributions," *New York Times,* September 20, 2005.

25. See the group's mission statement at http://www.clubforgrowth.org/aboutclub.php.

26. See the comments of Commissioner Michael Toner, reported in Sharon Theimer, "FEC Sues Pro-Republican Political Group," *Washington Post,* September 21, 2005.

27. Robert F. Bauer, *More Soft Money Hard Law* (Washington, DC: Perkins Coie LLP, 2003), 87.

28. Derek Willis and CQ Staff, "Critics Say Political Groups Formed to Evade New Fundraising Rules," *CQ Weekly,* November 30, 2002, 3112.

29. Campaign Finance Institute, Press Release, "Democrats Harvested Ten Times as Much in under-$200 Donations as in 2000; Bush's Small Donors Quadrupled," July 23, 2004, http://www.cfinst.org/pr/index.html.

30. Dan Belz and Thomas B. Edsall, "Democrats Forming Parallel Campaign: Interest Groups Draw GOP Fire," *Washington Post,* March 10, 2004.

31. This "achievement" of the law seems rather accidental. The Bush campaign discouraged the Republican Party from using the 527 vehicle largely because the president wished to retain control over his campaign. As a result, the Republicans started late and raised far less than did the Democratic 527s. Had the Republicans raised the same amount—a likely prospect given the history of campaign finance— the total sum of soft money in the 2004 campaign would have been close to the expected value of $650 million.

32. McCain argued that the 527 fundraising reflected poorly on the FEC, not on his law. See John McCain, "Plugging the Loophole," *Newsweek,* September 12, 2004. This is not persuasive. The 527 option was known to members of Congress in 2002; such groups had played a prominent role in the 2000 election. Congress could have banned the 527 groups in 2002. Moreover, Congress could have overridden the FEC's decision to permit 527 fundraising and spending at any time during the 2004 election. A majority of Congress clearly did not think McCain-Feingold covered 527 groups. Insofar as one believes 527 soft money corrupts politics—and McCain apparently does—the McCain-Feingold was a failure from the start.

33. It was possible, but perhaps not likely. House Democrats might well have supported Pence-Wynn but for their reasonable fear that the bill that came out of the conference committee would eliminate 527 groups (their stake in the bill) while liberalizing party donations (the Republican stake). This analysis is based on conversations with individuals familiar with the evolution of the legislation.

34. Suzanne Nelson, "Groups Opposing Bill on 527s Prepare for Hearing," *Roll Call,* March 7, 2005. See the opinion piece by two leaders of nonprofits on the Left and the Right: Nan Aron and David Keating, "Avoid the Rush to Judgment: Don't Abolish 527s," *Roll Call,* July 20, 2005.

35. See the comments of the campaign professionals in "Consultant Q&A: Campaigning on the Internet," *Campaigns and Elections,* September 2002, 51.

36. Danielle Endres and Barbara Warnick, "Text-Based Interactivity in Candidate Campaign Web Sites: A Case Study from the 2002 Elections," *Western Journal of Communication* 68 (Summer 2004): 322–43.

37. Carl M. Cannon, "Flexing Internet Muscles," *National Journal,* October 9, 2004, 3047–51.

38. See *Bipartisan Campaign Reform Act of 2002,* outline, §§ 306 (two mentions), 501 (two mentions), 502, 510.

39. For the final regulations, see Federal Election Commission, "Prohibited and Excessive Contributions: Non-federal Funds or Soft Money," *Federal Register,* vol. 67, no. 145, July 29, 2002, 49064. The FEC summarized the reasons for the exclusion of the Internet: "A national political party, an association of State party officials, an LLC that provides technical services to campaigns, a State political party, a public interest group, and a labor union urged the Commission not to include the Internet in the definition of 'public communication.' Four comments pointed to the lack of inclusion of the Internet in the list of modes of public communications, noting that Congress had had an opportunity to include the Internet in this definition, but declined to do so." Ibid., 49071.

40. See Shays and Meehan v. Federal Election Commission, 337 F. Supp. 2d 28 (D.C. Cir. 2004).

41. For the breadth of the resistance, see Brian Faler, "FEC Hears Bloggers' Bid to Share Media Exemption," *Washington Post,* July 12, 2005.

42. Suzanne Nelson, "Court Could Revisit 'Buckley': Spending Cap in Vermont at Issue," *Roll Call,* May 16, 2005.

43. For a similar warning, see Hasen, "*Buckley* Is Dead," 71.

44. Federal Election Commission, *Federal Election Campaign Laws* (Washington, DC: Federal Election Commission, 2005) runs to 221 pages.

45. See 2 U.S.C. §§ 441a–f, 441k (2005).

46. See 2 U.S.C. § 441e(a) (2005).

47. The allegations of contributions from the Chinese and the resulting influence during the Clinton era indicate the political incentives that favor prohibiting foreign contributions. However, it is possible that foreign nationals may contribute to 527 groups that are not affiliated with the political parties or campaigns. See Alexander Bolton, "Overseas Campaign Cash Ok," *The Hill,* June 1, 2004.

48. See the *Foreign Agents Registration Act,* 22 U.S.C. §§ 611, 612 (2005). Along with name and status, an agent must disclose "a comprehensive statement of the nature of registrant's business; a complete list of registrant's employees and a statement of the nature of the work of each; the name and address of every foreign principal for whom the registrant is acting, assuming or purporting to act or has agreed to act; the character of the business or other activities of every such foreign principal, and, if any such foreign principal be other than a natural person, a statement of the ownership and control of each; and the extent, if any, to which each such foreign principal is supervised, directed, owned, controlled, financed, or subsidized, in whole or in part, by any government of a foreign country or foreign political party, or by any other foreign principal."

49. A leading contemporary theorist of natural rights notes that "background rights are highly abstract, and many different sets of rules or laws may be consistent with them." Randy Barnett, "A Law Professor's Guide to Natural Law and Natural Rights," *Harvard Journal of Law and Public Policy* 20 (Summer 1997): 655, 678.

50. 2 U.S.C. §§ 441b–c (2005).

51. Robert E. Mutch, *Congress, Campaigns, and Courts* (New York: Praeger, 1988), chap. 1.

52. 2 U.S.C. §§ 441b(b)(2)(C), 441b(b)(4)(A) (2005).

53. See Fred S. McChesney, *Money for Nothing: Politicians, Rent Extraction, and Political Extortion* (Cambridge: Harvard University Press, 1997); Robert H. Sitkoff, "Politics and the Business Corporation," *Regulation* 27 (Winter 2003–4): 30–36. Sittkoff sees some restrictions on corporate giving as protection for business from government: "To the extent that legislators actively raise funds through threats and other means, acquiescing in a ban on direct corporate contributions would be a rational corporate response. Not surprisingly, corporate leaders embraced the Tillman Act for precisely that reason." Sitkoff, "Politics and the Business Corporation," 34.

54. I have not located any evidence that politicians extort campaign contributions from labor unions.

55. See Committee for Economic Development, "Corporate Executives Polled on Campaign Finance System." http://www.ced.org/docs/cfr_poll_factsheet.pdf (accessed December 12, 2005). The Council for Economic Development notes that this "survey of corporate America about campaign finance was conducted by The Tarrance Group, who surveyed 300 randomly chosen senior executives (vice president or above) from firms that had annual revenues of approximately $500 million or more." They do not report the level of significance or confidence intervals for the poll. See also Research and Policy Committee of the Committee for Economic Development, *Investing in the People's Business: A Business Proposal for Campaign Finance Reform* (Washington, DC: Committee for Economic Development, 1999).

56. See Research and Policy Committee of the Committee for Economic Development, *Investing in the People's Business,* 32ff. Some also argue that corporations sought the original ban on corporate contributions to protect their businesses from extortion.

57. Jeffrey Milyo, David Primo, and Timothy Groseclose, "Corporate PAC Campaign Contributions in Perspective," *Business and Politics* 2 (2000): 75–88.

58. Thomas B. Edsall, "Republican 'Soft Money' Groups Find Business Reluctant to Give," *Washington Post,* June 8, 2004.

59. For example, Bruce Cain recommends "legislative reforms weakening the power of individuals to carry out unilateral threats against interest groups—for instance, restrictions on the powers of committees, subcommittees, and oversight responsibility. The advantage of this approach is that it focuses upon the institutional conditions that make extortion possible without infringing upon the constituents' First Amendment rights." Bruce E. Cain, "Moralism and Realism in Campaign Finance Reform," *University of Chicago Legal Forum* (1995): 126.

60. For example, in 2005, a majority of Americans thought business corporations make too much profit, and three of four respondents believed that "too much

power is concentrated in the hands of a few large companies." See Pew Research Center, *Mapping the Political Landscape 2005* (Washington, DC: Pew Research Center 2005), 82, items m and n. See also Mark A. Smith, *American Business and Political Power: Public Opinion, Elections, and Democracy* (Chicago: University of Chicago Press, 2000), 101, which documents the public's growing distaste for business. Public sentiment about labor unions suggests a somewhat different situation. Since 1985 Pew has not found a majority with an unfavorable overall opinion of labor unions; since 1997, its polls have found that a majority have a favorable view of unions. See Pew Research Center, *Mapping the Political Landscape,* 105.

61. The tax form checkoff accomplishes much the same end as a direct mail appeal by a candidate. Such appeals are quite expensive and often lose money in the short run. See Daniel M. Shea, *Campaign Craft: The Strategies, Tactics, and Art of Political Campaign Management* (Westport, CT: Praeger, 1996), 192–93.

62. The disclosure requirements of federal election law may found in 2 U.S.C. § 434 (2005). Many states are at least as demanding: "Most states impose even stricter disclosure provisions for nonfederal elections. Almost all require campaigns to itemize contributions below the federal threshold of $200. Eight states set thresholds as low as $20 or $25, and several others require reporting of all contributions, no matter what their size." William McGeveran, "Mrs. McIntyre's Checkbook: Privacy Costs of Political Contribution Disclosure," *University of Pennsylvania Journal of Constitutional Law* 6 (September 2003): 1, 10.

63. A concise review of the additional disclosure requirements introduced by BCRA may be found in Bauer, *More Soft Money,* 123–30.

64. It has become a "motherhood issue," something that everyone favors. See McGeveran, "Mrs. McIntyre's Checkbook," 1. Representative John Doolittle (D-NY) proposed a deregulated alternative to McCain-Feingold that depended on disclosure. The appellants in *Buckley* argued that "narrowly drawn disclosure requirements are the proper solution to virtually all of the evils Congress sought to remedy." Buckley v. Valeo, 424 U.S. 1, 49 (1976), 60.

65. Buckley v. Valeo, 66–67. Disclosure also reinforces contribution limits, a fourth putative benefit. I do not deal with this claim. The benefit in question depends on the benefit of contribution limits. If by the value of its three main benefits does not outweigh its costs and thus justify disclosure, it is unlikely that reinforcing contribution limits would save the policy.

66. See Gary King, Robert O. Keohane, and Sidney Verba, *Designing Social Inquiry: Scientific Inference in Qualitative Research* (Princeton: Princeton University Press, 1994), chap. 3.

67. See Mayer, "In Defense of Negative Campaigning," 51–52, 61–66.

68. McGeveran raises several doubts about the corruption justification for disclosure in "Mrs. McIntyre's Checkbook," 29–31.

69. Newspapers may include information about contributions and politics simply because their customers enjoy reading such information apart from its effects

on voting and corruption. Such private consumption, however, cannot justify the public subsidy inherent in mandated disclosure of contributions.

70. I use a distinction between risk and uncertainty introduced by Frank H. Knight, *Risk, Uncertainty, and Profit* (Boston: Hart, Schaffner & Marx, 1921), chap. 7.

71. Ibid., 47.

72. See National Election Studies, Center for Political Studies, University of Michigan, *The NES Guide to Public Opinion and Electoral Behavior* (Ann Arbor: University of Michigan, Center for Political Studies, 1995–2000), table 5A.5. http://www.umich.edu/~nes/nesguide/nesguide.htm (accessed August 21, 2003). I have excluded the response for 2002 on the assumption that the events of September 11, 2001, were exogenous shocks that would distort the analysis.

73. Ibid., table 5A.2 and author's calculations. The correlation coefficient between disclosure and believing that government is run for the benefit of all is −.58.

74. Ibid., table 5A.4. The coefficient correlation between disclosure and the "quite a few" response is .64

75. That curious conclusion invites a closer look at the data. It is possible that what is disclosed (and not disclosure itself) is the cause of the observed relation. That is, disclosure might reveal contributions that undermine public confidence. Disclosure would thus be highly correlated with a third factor—the revealed contributions—that are themselves the cause of the declining confidence. For example, disclosure is highly correlated with the belief that "the government is pretty much run by a few big interests looking out for themselves." Ibid., table 5A.2. The correlation is .7. Perhaps disclosure prompted people to conclude that a few big interests run the government, thereby undermining faith in the state. If so, campaign finance law would have provided its own rationale for restricting speech. We can say, at a minimum, that the case for disclosure has not been made by its effects on public opinion.

76. The student of campaign finance might object at this point that I have ignored an important variation in federal disclosure during the past thirty years. The law did not mandate the disclosure of party soft money from the late 1970s until 1992. It also did not require revelation of donations to 527 groups from 1994 to 2000. Perhaps these undisclosed contributions undermined the effect of disclosure. Undisclosed soft money spending by the parties is compatible with both a rapid and steep rise in the trust index and a rapid and steep fall in the trust index. The era of undisclosed 527 contributions saw a rapid rise in the trust index. The existence of undisclosed contributions does not appear to have had a consistent effect on public confidence in government. Such donations certainly did not prevent rapid rises in public trust at various times.

77. Nathaniel Persily and Kelli Lammie, "Perceptions of Corruption and Campaign Finance: When Public Opinion Constitutes Constitutional Law," *University of Pennsylvania Law Review* 153 (December 2004), passim.

78. Jeffrey Milyo and David Primo, "Campaign Finance Laws and Political Efficacy: Evidence from the States," *Election Law Journal* 5 (2006): table 2, p. 33.

79. Buckley v. Valeo, 66–67.

80. See Elizabeth Garrett, "The William J. Brennan Lecture in Constitutional Law: The Future of Campaign Finance Laws in the Courts and in Congress," *Oklahoma City University Law Review* 27 (2002): 665.

81. Arthur Lupia, "Shortcuts versus Encyclopedias: Information and Voting Behavior in California Insurance Reform Elections," *American Political Science Review* 88 (1994): 63–76.

82. See Garrett, "William J. Brennan Lecture," passim.

83. Stephen Ansolabehere, John M. de Figueiredo, and James M. Snyder Jr., "Why Is There So Little Money in U.S. Politics?" *Journal of Economic Perspectives* 17 (Winter 2003): 5.

84. Ibid., 9.

85. Ibid., 11–14.

86. Ibid.

87. Ibid.

88. "If unthinking support for disclosure is widespread, silence about its privacy costs is nearly universal." McGeveran, "Mrs. McIntyre's Checkbook," 7.

89. Alan F. Westin, *Privacy and Freedom* (New York: Atheneum, 1967), 7.

90. McGeveran, "Mrs. McIntyre's, Checkbook," 16.

91. Ibid., 19. See also James Rachels, "Why Privacy Is Important," *Philosophy and Public Affairs* 4 (Summer 1975): 92: "[T]here is a close connection between our ability to control who has access to us and to information about us, and our ability to create and maintain different sorts of social relationships with different people."

92. Putting a person in a false light was identified early on as a tort related to disclosure of information. See William L. Prosser, "Privacy," *California Law Review* 48 (1960): 338, 407. In addition, "Distortion is the manipulation of the way a person is perceived and judged by others. It consists of being exposed to the public inaccurately." See Daniel J. Solove, "A Taxonomy of Privacy," *University of Pennsylvania Law Review* forthcoming.

93. Buckley v. Valeo, 64.

94. NAACP v. Alabama, 357 U.S. 449 (1958).

95. Buckley v. Valeo, 74.

96. Brown v. Socialist Workers '74 Campaign Committee (Ohio), 459 U.S. 87 (1982); Federal Election Commission v. Hall-Tyner Election Campaign Committee, 678 F.2d 416 (2d Cir. 1982), cert. denied, 459 U.S. 1145 (1983). For a history of the Socialist Workers exemption, see Federal Election Commission, Advisory Opinion Number 2003-2, April 4, 2003. http://ao.nictusa.com/ao/no/030002.html (accessed March 13, 2006).

97. Federal Election Commission v. Hall-Tyner Election Campaign Committee, 427.

98. See the example cited in Daniel J. Solove, "The Virtues of Knowing Less: Justifying Privacy Protections against Disclosure," *Duke Law Journal* 53 (2003): 967, 995.

99. See James V. Grimaldi and Thomas B. Edsall, "Super Rich Step into Political Vacuum: McCain-Feingold Paved Way for 527s," *Washington Post,* October 17, 2004. Soros pledged $10 million to the Democratic groups in 2003. Republicans responded by claiming that Soros had bought the Democratic Party. "'Several people were frightened away,' Soros said. The attacks were 'very effective. I can't quote names. Several people said they do not want to get involved because they can't afford to expose themselves the way I can, particularly people in responsible positions in publicly quoted companies.'" Chief Justice Warren Burger expressed a similar concern about disclosure in Buckley v. Valeo, 237.

100. Senator John McCain, 107th Cong., 1st sess., *Congressional Record* (2001), 147:S3116.

101. McGeveran, "Mrs. McIntyre's Checkbook," 22.

102. The first state to adopt the secret ballot did so in 1888. All states now require it. See "Ballot Types," CQ Electronic Library, CQ Encyclopedia of American Government, elaz2d-156-7497-402987. http://library.cqpress.com/eag/elaz2d-156-7497-402987 (accessed December 7, 2005). Originally published in John L. Moore, *Elections A to Z* (Washington, DC: CQ Press, 2003).

103. Bruce Ackerman and Ian Ayres, *Voting with Dollars: A New Paradigm for Campaign Finance* (New Haven: Yale University Press, 2002), 93ff. The authors initially do not set out a specific contribution limit beyond noting that it should be "at a stratospheric height that will be practically insignificant to all but the very richest Americans." Ibid., 48. Later we learn that the limits are $5,000, $15,000, or $100,000 depending on the office, with a $100,000 annual cap on private donations (100–101).

104. Ibid., 101.

105. Kenneth Mayer points out that the secret ballot is an individual right that may be waived by a citizen. See Kenneth R. Mayer, "Political Realities and Unintended Consequences: Why Campaign Finance Reform Is Too Important to Be Left to the Lawyers," *University of Richmond Law Review* 37 (May 2003): 1069, 1086.

106. Ibid., 1096. Mayer continues, "How hard will it be for a candidate to assess the credibility of a claim, either public or private, that a donor gave $10,000? Not hard at all, as it turns out. Consider that after ten years, or however long a period before records are revealed for auditing purposes, everyone knows that a false statement is certain to be exposed. When a false claim becomes known, the people who made it will see their credibility drop to zero in all future interactions, as well as face retribution from politicians who will be unhappy about being duped. Even those donors who indeed want to send confusing signals would benefit by a long-standing pattern of honesty, because that reputation would enhance the credibility of a false claim if it is ever made, and even a single false claim would raise doubts

about a donor's true activities. Nobody with long term stakes in the political process will be willing to risk this" (1097).

107. The Publicity Act of 1910 (as well as the later Federal Corrupt Practices Act) required disclosure in theory. In fact, few donations were disclosed, and the nation certainly did not have the system of mandatory disclosure that arrived in the early 1970s. See Bradley A. Smith, *Unfree Speech: The Folly of Campaign Finance Reform* (Princeton: Princeton University Press, 2001), 24–26.

108. As noted above, voters apparently do not care all that much about disclosure in casting their votes. However, that conclusion cannot be carried over into a system without contribution limits. Soft money contributions were both unlimited and disclosed but went to the political parties. Such donations were controversial from time to time, but they did not appear to have significant effects on the outcomes of elections.

109. Mandatory disclosure provides a subsidy for the news media, which are relieved of the costs of finding the contribution data.

110. Donors who have an expensive taste for privacy might well fall into this category.

111. "[B]efore Bentham and Kant, classical natural rights 'liberals' employed a mixture of moral rights and consequentialist arguments in defense of the political protection of certain natural rights." Randy Barnett, "The Moral Foundations of Modern Libertarianism," in *Varieties of Conservatism*, ed. Peter Berkowitz (Stanford: Hoover, 2004), 55.

112. 2 U.S.C. § 434(b)(3)(A) (2005). Disclosure thresholds in the states are almost always much lower than the federal thresholds. See McGeveran, "Mrs. McIntyre's Checkbook," 10.

113. 2 U.S.C. § 434(f)(1) (2005).

114. McGeveran, "Mrs. McIntyre's Checkbook," 30. He points out that "[i]n fact, extrapolating from FEC data, it appears that the number of contributions to candidates of under $200 is over twice the number of those over $750. In the 1999–2000 election cycle, individual contributions of less than $200 to congressional candidates totaled $169,289,822. . . . Using an unrealistically conservative assumption that all contributions in this category were $199 each, that still would mean that there were at least 850,703 contributions of this size. In contrast, individual contributions of $750 or more totaled $250,825,446. . . . Using an equally unrealistic assumption that all these contributions were at the very bottom of the range, $750, then no more than 334,433 contributions were at this level. This somewhat crude extrapolation is necessary because contributions under $200 are not reported to the FEC individually." See ibid., n. 35.

115. Since the evidence of the impotence of donations comes from an era in which individual contributions were limited to $1,000, some might argue that the floor for disclosure should start there. That would be an improvement over the current regime provided that the floor increased in line with inflation.

116. 2 U.S.C. § 434(f)(3) (2005).

117. The law regulates interest groups largely to prevent circumvention of other aspects of the law. That is, current law assumes that if interest group ads were not restricted, political actors would move some fundraising and spending from the regulated sphere of candidates and parties to an unregulated sphere of interest groups. It is an indirect way to prevent corruption, at least in theory. Yet interest groups spend money on ads to advance their political views. They use the ads to support candidates and causes that reflect those views. That is called political struggle, not corruption.

118. Norman J. Ornstein, Thomas E. Mann, and Michael J. Malbin, *Vital Statistics on Congress, 1999–2000* (Washington, DC: AEI Press, 2000), 111.

119. 2 U.S.C. § 437c–g (2005).

120. See Democracy 21, Project FEC Task Force, *No Bark, No Bite: The Case for Closing the Federal Election Commission and Establishing a New System for Enforcing the Nation's Campaign Finance Laws* (Washington, DC: Democracy 21, 2002). The first page of this report complains that the FEC has not acted as a "real law enforcement agency."

121. For critical accounts of the FBI and civil liberties, see Richard Gid Powers, *Secrecy and Power: The Life of J. Edgar Hoover* (New York: Free Press, 1987); David B. Kopel and Paul H. Blackman, *No More Wacos: What's Wrong with Federal Law Enforcement and How to Fix It* (Amherst, NY: Prometheus Books, 1997).

122. See the organizational chart of the Library of Congress at http://www.loc.gov/about/org/index.html.

123. B. Holly Schadler to the Federal Election Commission, offering comments on Draft Advisory Opinion 2003-37, February 4, 2004. http://www.fec.gov/aos/2003/aor2003-37com4.pdf (accessed).

124. For example, as of 2004, Lawrence Noble was executive director of the Center for Responsive Politics. Noble is a former general counsel of the Federal Election Commission.

125. For an inside view of the conflict between party and ideals at the FEC, see Bradley Smith, "CLE Presentation," Meeting of the Republican National Lawyers Association, March 19, 2004, http://www.fec.gov/members/smith/smithspeech05.pdf. In my experience, several Republicans have been dissatisfied with the party's decision about the 527 groups. In part, they believe that the decision did not serve the long-term interests of the GOP. They also believed that the decision contravened ideals they had long espoused.

126. It is not true, however, that *only* ideals matter, as asserted in Seth Gittell, "The Democratic Party Suicide Bill," *Atlantic Monthly,* July–August 2003, 106.

Index

Page numbers in italics refer to figures and tables